Moderators and Mediators of Youth Treatment Outcomes

Moderators and Mediators of Youth Treatment Outcomes

EDITED BY MARIJA MARIC

PIER J. M. PRINS

THOMAS H. OLLENDICK

OXFORD
UNIVERSITY PRESS

Oxford University Press is a department of the University of
Oxford. It furthers the University's objective of excellence in research,
scholarship, and education by publishing worldwide.

Oxford   New York
Auckland   Cape Town   Dar es Salaam   Hong Kong   Karachi
Kuala Lumpur   Madrid   Melbourne   Mexico City   Nairobi
New Delhi   Shanghai   Taipei   Toronto

With offices in
Argentina   Austria   Brazil   Chile   Czech Republic   France   Greece
Guatemala   Hungary   Italy   Japan   Poland   Portugal   Singapore
South Korea   Switzerland   Thailand   Turkey   Ukraine   Vietnam

Oxford is a registered trademark of Oxford University Press
in the UK and certain other countries.

Published in the United States of America by
Oxford University Press
198 Madison Avenue, New York, NY 10016

Library of Congress Cataloging-in-Publication Data
Moderators and mediators of youth treatment outcomes / edited by Marija Maric,
Pier J. M. Prins, and Thomas H. Ollendick.
p. ; cm.
Includes bibliographical references and index.
ISBN 978-0-19-936034-5 (hb : alk. paper)
I. Maric, Marija, editor.   II. Prins, Pier J. M., editor.   III. Ollendick, Thomas H., editor.
[DNLM: 1. Adolescent.   2. Child.   3. Mental Disorders—therapy.   4. Risk Factors.
5. Treatment Outcome. WS 350.2]
RJ503
616.8900835—dc23
2014050019

9 8 7 6 5 6 4 3 2 1
Printed in the United States of America
on acid-free paper

To my daughter Lana Stella.
—Marija Maric

To Noëlle, and our children Jonne and Kyra.
—Pier J. M. Prins

To my wife, Mary, daughters Laurie and Katie, sons-in-law David and Billy,
and grandchildren, Braden, Ethan, Calvin, Addison, Victoria, and William.
Without them, life would be so much less fun, rewarding, and meaningful.
—Thomas H. Ollendick

CONTENTS

PREFACE

Despite impressive progress and achievements in child psychotherapy research over the past six decades, which have yielded many exciting findings and effective treatments for a large variety of child problems, there is an increasing recognition of the need to change perspectives. A shift is needed from questions related to efficacy and effectiveness of interventions ("Did it work?") to questions related to mediation and moderation of intervention outcomes ("How and why did it work, and for whom?").

Almost one-third of children and adolescents who are treated with evidence-based psychosocial interventions for a variety of problems do not improve, indicating the need to increase the therapeutic impact of existing treatments, to develop new treatments, or to better match treatments to the specific needs of youth and their families.

An important way to guide these efforts is the study of moderators and mediators of treatment outcome. Moderation research may determine conditions under which treatments are most effective and for whom, and mediation research may result in the improvement of interventions by showing which processes may be considered important mechanisms of action, and which components of these interventions are critical in influencing these important processes. The need to study mechanisms of therapeutic action was stressed early on, from the early years of psychotherapy research, but mostly remained unexplored until the 1990s, when mediators began to be empirically tested. Still, very little progress has been made.

This book aims to give an up-to-date overview of the extant research on moderation and mediation in treatment outcome research for major child and adolescent problems. The authors of the chapters, all experts in their various domains, provide theoretical conceptualizations of important moderation and mediation models underlying various youth interventions, summarize existing evidence from empirical research, and highlight current challenges and solutions related to the conduct of moderation and mediation research in youth populations.

The book is primarily written for clinical child and adolescent researchers who will hopefully produce the next generation of research to advance our knowledge base. However, the book will also be of interest to all child and adolescent mental health clinicians in training and practicing professionals, including psychotherapists, psychiatrists, and pediatricians. Thus, it is suitable for those being educated in the field, as well as for those with a more advanced knowledge of the subject.

ACKNOWLEDGMENTS

The editors are grateful to many individuals at Oxford University Press for their excellent support and guidance in the process of the development of this volume as well as its production. They are also grateful to their respective Departments of Developmental Psychology at the University of Amsterdam, and the Department of Psychology at Virginia Polytechnic Institute and State University. Finally, Dr. Ollendick is grateful to the National Institute of Mental Health for its support of his research over the past many years.

Marija Maric, Ph.D., is Assistant Professor of Clinical Developmental Psychology in the Department of Developmental Psychology at the University of Amsterdam (The Netherlands). Dr. Maric is conducting studies on moderation and mediation in the area of youth anxiety disorders, and youth with comorbid anxiety disorders and ADHD. She has published scientific articles on mediators of cognitive behavioral treatment for anxiety-based school refusal, and on ways to improve the use of mediation analyses in youth treatment outcome research. She teaches courses in developmental psychopathology and psychological interventions for youth. Dr. Maric also works as a cognitive behavior therapist at UvA Minds, an Academic Treatment Center for Children and Parents.

Pier J. M. Prins, Ph.D., is Professor Emeritus of Clinical Child Psychology at the Department of Developmental Psychology at the University of Amsterdam (The Netherlands). He has published extensively in the area of clinical child psychology and has been involved in several large-scale, multi-site treatment-outcome projects dealing with various childhood problems. His current research focuses on training executive functions and the use of gamification for children with cognitive control problems such as ADHD. Dr. Prins is a licensed child cognitive behavior therapist.

Thomas H. Ollendick, Ph.D., is University Distinguished Professor in Clinical Psychology and Director of the Child Study Center at Virginia Polytechnic Institute and State University, Blacksburg, Virginia. He is the author or co-author of several research publications, book chapters, and books. He is the immediate past editor of *Behavior Therapy* (2009–2013) and founding and current co-editor of *Clinical Child and Family Psychology Review*. His clinical and research interests range from the study of diverse forms of child psychopathology to the assessment, treatment, and prevention of these child disorders from a social learning/social cognitive theory perspective. He was awarded the Career/Lifetime Achievement Award from the Association for Behavioral and Cognitive Therapies in 2013.

CONTRIBUTORS

Carl Bolano, B.A.
Child and Adolescent Anxiety and
    Mood Program (ChAAMP)
San Diego State University
California, USA

Colleen M. Cummings, Ph.D.
Department of Psychology
Temple University
Pennsylvania, USA

David Daley, Ph.D.
Faculty of Medicine & Health Sciences
The University of Nottingham
Nottingham, UK

Maja Deković, Ph.D.
Department of Clinical Child &
    Family Studies
Utrecht University
The Netherlands

Rebecca A. Graham, M.S.
Child and Family Stress, Anxiety and
    Phobia Lab
University of New Orleans
Louisiana, USA

Lynn Hernandez, Ph.D.
Department of Psychology
The University of Rhode Island
Rhode Island, USA

Joanna Herres, Ph.D.
Department of Psychology
Temple University
Pennsylvania, USA

David A. Heyne, Ph.D.
Institute of Psychology
Leiden University
The Netherlands

Philip C. Kendall, Ph.D.
Department of Psychology
Temple University
Pennsylvania, USA

Andrea Lavigne, Ph.D.
Department of Psychology
The University of Rhode Island
Rhode Island, USA

Daniel Le Grange, Ph.D.
Department of Psychiatry
University of California,
    San Francisco
California, USA

Matthew D. Lerner, Ph.D.
Department of Psychology
Stony Brook University
New York, USA

Katharine L. Loeb, Ph.D.
School of Psychology
Fairleigh Dickinson University
New Jersey, USA

David P. MacKinnon, Ph.D.
Department of Psychology
Arizona State University
Arizona, USA

Nicole E. Mahrer, M.A.
Department of Psychology
Arizona State University
Arizona, USA

Heather Makover, M.A.
Department of Psychology
Temple University
Pennsylvania, USA

Marija Maric, Ph.D.
Department of Developmental
    Psychology
University of Amsterdam
The Netherlands

Brandy R. Maynard, M.S.W., Ph.D.
School of Social Work
Saint Louis University
Missouri, USA

Stuart B. Murray, Ph.D.
Department of Psychiatry
University of California, San Diego
California, USA

Thomas H. Ollendick, Ph.D.
Department of Psychology
Virginia Polytechnic Institute and
    State University
Virginia, USA

Pier J. M. Prins, Ph.D.
Department of Developmental
    Psychology
University of Amsterdam
The Netherlands

Irwin N. Sandler, Ph.D.
Department of Psychology
Arizona State University
Arizona, USA

Floor M. Sauter, Ph.D.
Institute of Psychology
Leiden University
The Netherlands

Karen T. G. Schwartz, B.S.
Joint Doctoral Program in Clinical
    Psychology
San Diego State Univesity
California, USA

Sabine Stoltz, Ph.D.
Department of Developmental
    Psychology
Radboud University
The Netherlands

Anna Swan, M.A.
Department of Psychology
Temple University
Pennsylvania, USA

Joanne E. Taylor, Ph.D.
School of Psychology
Massey University
New Zealand

Jenn-Yun Tein, Ph.D.
Department of Psychology
Arizona State University
Arizona, USA

Saskia van der Oord, Ph.D.
Department of Psychology and
    Educational Sciences
KU Leuven
Belgium
Department of Psychology
University of Amsterdam
The Netherlands

Carl F. Weems, Ph.D.
Department of Psychology
Iowa State University
Iowa, USA

V. Robin Weersing, Ph.D.
Joint Doctoral Program in Clinical
   Psychology
San Diego State University
California, USA

Susan W. White, Ph.D.
Department of Psychology
Virginia Polytechnic Institute and
   State University
Virginia, USA

Reinout W. Wiers, Ph.D.
Department of Psychology
University of Amsterdam
The Netherlands

Sharlene A. Wolchik, Ph.D.
Department of Psychology
Arizona State University
Arizona, USA

Mark Wood, Ph.D.
Department of Psychology
University of Rhode Island
Rhode Island, USA

Moderators and Mediators of Youth Treatment Outcomes

Moderators and Mediators in Treatment Outcome Studies of Childhood Disorders

The What, Why, and How

PIER J. M. PRINS, THOMAS H. OLLENDICK,
MARIJA MARIC, AND DAVID P. MACKINNON ■

INTRODUCTION

Since the critical reviews of Eysenck (1952) and Levitt (1957, 1963), which questioned the efficacy of psychotherapy, we have witnessed an explosion of treatment outcome research over the past six decades which has shown that treating children for various emotional and behavioral problems is more effective than doing nothing. The number of empirically supported treatments has been steadily increasing (Weisz & Kazdin, 2010). However, close to one-third of the children who are being treated for various problems do not improve, illustrating the need to improve existing treatments, develop new treatments, and match these to the needs of specific children and their families (Ollendick & King, 2012). In order to understand for whom the treatments work, and why the treatments work for some children but not for others (non-responder issue), we need to identify moderators and mediators of treatment outcome.

There are two important ways to improve the efficacy of our treatments and eventually their effectiveness in real-world clinical settings: the first is to find predictors and moderators of treatment outcome so that specific treatments can be given to specific subgroups of children under select treatment contexts, so that any one form of treatment will have its maximum impact. Second, knowledge about the specific mechanisms, so-called mediators, through which treatments work can be used to focus and improve treatment outcomes (Kraemer, Wilson, Fairburn, & Agras, 2002).

Moderators are variables for which treatment has a differential effect at different values of the moderating variable. Mediating variables are variables that describe the process through which treatment achieves its effects. Figure 1.1 displays the underlying idea of moderation and mediation. For moderation, there is no causal relation between treatment (X) and outcome (Y); the relation between treatment and outcome differs only across levels of the moderating variable (Z). For mediation, the treatment (X) causes the mediator (M), which then causes the outcome (Y).

Diagrams for moderating and mediating variables (Figure 1.1) demonstrate the difference between these two constructs; the causal sequence is shown with directed arrows in the mediation model to demonstrate a mediation relation. For moderation, an interaction XZ corresponds to a potentially different X-to-Y relation at values of Z.

Moderating and mediating variables should not be confused with predictors of treatment outcomes. Predictors are pre-treatment variables that have a main effect on treatment outcomes, but no interactive effect (such as moderators).

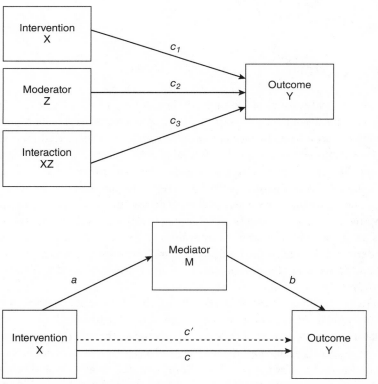

Figure 1.1. A graphical representation of single moderator and single mediator models.

Such a measure can predict response in different treatment groups, but the effect size of the treatment is the same regardless of the value of the target measure.

Although the majority of treatment outcome studies focuses on treatment efficacy (i.e., Did my intervention work?) and although considerable progress has been made toward developing effective treatments for various child problems (Ollendick & King, 2012; Weisz & Kazdin, 2010), only a minority of studies seeks to understand for whom or how treatments actually work. Over 10 years ago, there was a surprising lack of research regarding the mechanisms involved in empirically supported treatments for youth anxiety and depression (Prins & Ollendick, 2003; Weersing & Weisz, 2002)—a situation that today has hardly been altered, not only for the internalizing disorders and problems but also for the externalizing disorders of childhood, including conduct and attentional problems (Maric, Wiers, & Prins, 2012).

In this chapter, we first discuss predictors and moderators of treatment outcome and how these variables may be used to improve treatment efficacy. Then, in the next section, we focus on issues of treatment mediation. In the final section of this chapter, we discuss design and statistical issues in moderation and, more particularly, in mediation research. We conclude with a perspective on future moderation and mediation research.

PREDICTORS AND MODERATORS OF TREATMENT OUTCOMES

Early on, Baron and Kenny (1986), Holmbeck (1997), and Kraemer et al. (2002) indicated that treatment moderators specify for whom or under what conditions treatments work best. As noted above, several types of psychotherapy have been found to be effective for approximately two-thirds of children and adolescents with a variety of psychiatric disorders (Ollendick & King, 2012); however, such findings tell us very little about for whom or under what conditions these treatments work best. Knowledge of such variables will inform us not only for whom and under what conditions our treatments work, but also for which types of youth and under what conditions they do *not* work. Such knowledge will be extremely useful if we are to improve treatment outcomes for the approximate one-third of youth who do not currently respond to our efficacious treatments. In turn, such knowledge may help us make informed decisions about specific inclusion and exclusion criteria to use in selecting which types of individuals to include in future randomized clinical trials (RCTs) and for which individuals we need to design new and more effective interventions for our clinical practices, as well as in determining potentially new and different contexts under which those treatments will need to be delivered. In the final analysis, treatment decision-making will be potentially enhanced by such knowledge, as we can begin to prescribe certain treatments for certain individuals and in certain contexts.

In their seminal paper, Kraemer and colleagues (2002) specified that candidate moderator variables must exist and must be measured *before* the random assignment to two or more intervention conditions in an RCT. In effect, we look for an interaction effect between the moderator variables and different treatment conditions to establish a moderation effect. Since the moderator variables are measured prior to random assignment, they are uncorrelated with treatment assignment, and we can be assured that a systematic bias is not present in interpreting the observed interaction effect. These pre-treatment moderator variables are sometimes referred to as "prescriptive indicators" (MacKinnon, Lockhart, Baraldi, & Gelfand, 2013) because the differential response represented by the interaction between the moderator and the treatment suggests that differential effects might be optimized by prescribing different treatments for different subgroups. In a sense, a "personalized" approach to treatment might be achieved as a result of such findings.

In their paper, Kraemer and colleagues also distinguish between predictors of treatment outcome and moderators of treatment outcomes. Basically, predictors of outcome are nonspecific inasmuch such variables predict outcomes irrespective of treatment assignment. Generally, predictor variables are associated with the main effects of the candidate variables. They are associated with treatment outcomes, but not differentially or "prescriptively" so. MacKinnon et al. (2013) refer to these variables as "prognostic indicators"—they predict change across treatment conditions. In contrast, as noted, moderator effects are associated with an interaction between the candidate variable and the treatment conditions, predicting and specifying differential treatment outcomes, dependent on levels of the candidate variable and the contexts under which the treatment is delivered.

A host of variables can serve as predictors or moderators of treatment outcomes. Among the most common variables are socio-demographic, parent, and family characteristics, child characteristics, school-related factors, and aspects of the disorder itself. Such variables frequently include sex of the child, age of the child, ethnicity/race of the child, culture, socioeconomic status, family structure, family climate, parenting practices, parent psychopathology, school climate, severity of the targeted disorder, duration of the targeted disorder, and comorbid conditions associated with the targeted disorder. Importantly, all of these variables are present before treatment assignment and can either predict or moderate treatment outcomes. As but one example, assume that we were interested in determining the effectiveness of two different interventions—cognitive behavioral therapy (CBT) and interpersonal psychotherapy (IPT)—in the treatment of major depressive disorder in youth between 7 and 14 years of age. We would enlist an RCT to address this question, and all participants would be randomly assigned to one of the two treatment conditions. In this example, the treatments would be delivered on an individual basis and in an outpatient clinical setting for 16 sessions. We might anticipate that parental depression, family conflict, family structure, and low socioeconomic status would be nonspecific predictors of poor treatment outcomes across both treatments, but that age of the participant and comorbid anxiety disorders would be differentially related to treatment outcome such that IPT would be more effective than CBT with the older children and with youth with co-occurring anxiety disorders. In contrast, we might hypothesize that CBT would be more effective than IPT for the younger children and youth with co-occurring disruptive behavior disorders. We might also speculate that some variables, such as sex of the child, ethnicity, and severity and duration of the disorder, would not predict or moderate treatment outcomes. Such hypotheses would be based on both theory and empirical evidence (Hinshaw, 2007; Kraemer et al., 2002) associated with the the treatments (CBT vs. IPT), the etiology of depression, and the developmental psychopathology of the disorder in children and adolescents (Ollendick & Shirk, 2011). Assuming such findings were obtained, and were replicated in a second RCT, we would be able to advance our evidence-based practice armamentarium by using IPT and CBT *selectively* or *prescriptively* to match client characteristics for which these treatments were found to be differentially effective. Of course, such a study would not address other potential moderator variables, such as culture or family structure of the participants, that were not systematically examined in the hypothetical study. Additional research would be needed to determine the "reach" of these findings and their generalizability to such samples.

Similarly, we might wish to explore the same treatments under different formats or contexts, which would constitute another example of moderating variables. For example, we might wish to explore these treatments in a family format or a group format, both in clinical settings, and compare them to our individually administered treatment in the clinical setting. Further, we might wish to contrast these findings with those obtained in a school setting or an inpatient setting or on the Internet. Perhaps, we would want to explore the differential effectiveness of these treatments in a brief intervention format (i.e., 6–8 sessions) compared to the more traditional 12–16-session format, or perhaps two sessions per week rather than the standard one session per week. In the final analysis, we would hope to determine the best treatments for certain types of youth with varying characteristics in varying types of delivery formats and settings.

The possible predictors and moderators of treatment outcomes are truly numerous and, of course, not all possibilities can be systematically examined in any one study. Rather, the pursuit should be guided by theory, clinical experience, and previous empirical work (Arean & Kraemer, 2013; Kraemer, Frank, & Kupfer, 2006). Knowledge of both risk and protective factors associated with various disorders may be useful in this regard and will likely guide the selection of candidate variables (e.g., child age, over-protective parenting, dismissive parenting, active coping strategies, peer social support, etc.). Similarly, clinical experience might guide us in the identification of candidate predictor or moderator variables. For example, unsuccessful attempts to implement Parent Management Training programs without taking into consideration family dysfunction and marital discord will likely signal possible predictors or moderators of treatment outcomes.

As indicated by MacKinnnon and colleagues (2013), there are many reasons to pursue predictor/moderation analyses in treatment outcome research. First, attention to predictors and moderators recognizes the complexity of the problems that we study and treat. Such an approach acknowledges both individual differences in children, adolescents, and families, as well as parameters of treatment that might differentially affect outcomes. Second, and relatedly, outcomes of moderation research can help determine the specificity of our treatments and provide us a more personalized therapeutic approach. Such analyses can help us identify not only for whom the treatments work but also for whom they do not work, and possibly even those for whom iatrogenic effects are observed. As noted above, our efficacious treatments do not work for about one-third of the children and families we treat. As but one example, comorbidity is a frequently examined variable that is thought to predict or moderate treatment outcomes. Yet, mixed findings have been obtained. In a systematic review of the effects of comorbidity on treatment outcomes of youth treated for anxiety, depression, conduct problems, and attention-deficit hyperactivity disorder, Ollendick, Jarrett, Grills-Taquechel, Hovey, and Wolff (2008) reported that comorbidity did *not* predict or moderate *immediate* treatment outcomes; however, Farrell, Waters, Milliner, and Ollendick (2012) recently reported that although these comorbid problems did not predict immediate treatment outcomes for youth with obsessive-compulsive disorder (OCD) who were treated with a group CBT program, comorbid problems—and in particular the presence of attention deficit hyperactivity disorder (ADHD)—did predict poorer *long-term* outcomes. Similar long-term effects, but not short-term effects, of comorbid anxiety/depression have been shown for children treated for early onset conduct problems by Beauchaine, Webster-Stratton, and Reid (2005). Thus, the effects of predictor or moderator variables need to be examined over time to determine their short-term as well as long-term effects. The findings of Farrell et al. (2012) suggest that the treatment may need to be modified for youth with OCD who are comorbid with ADHD, while the findings of Beauchaine and colleagues (2005) indicate that family treatment for conduct problems may need to be modified in the treatment of conduct problems in youth who are comorbid with anxiety/depression. An understanding of the characteristics of the sample (presence of ADHD or anxiety/depression in these studies) and the format of treatment (group CBT treatment for OCD or family treatment for conduct problems) that affect the effectiveness of treatments across groups and time can hopefully lead to better treatment outcomes.

Finally, moderation analyses can also be useful in determining the generalizability of our findings and whether or not iatrogenic effects occur from our various treatments (MacKinnon et al., 2013). A test of moderation can not only provide information about whether two treatments differ from one another due to characteristics of the sample or the contexts under which the treatments are delivered, but also reveal whether the treatments have similar effects across these dimensions. For example, if a significant moderation effect is not levels of comorbidity, different ethnicities, and contexts (e.g., individual, group), we then have evidence that the treatments can be applied to both subgroups and both contexts. The consistency of the treatments across subgroups and contexts provides important information about the generalizability of the effectiveness of our treatments. So, too, moderation tests can provide us important information about subgroups or factors for which the treatments are counterproductive and produce unintended, negative effects. It is certainly possible that our treatments can produce unintended, negative effects under certain contexts or with certain subgroup characteristics. As but one brief example, use of graduated exposures in the treatment of children with specific phobias may produce negative outcomes for children who are not only phobic but also depressed, especially so if implemented too early in treatment (Davis, Ollendick, & Ost, 2012). Such negative effects are extremely important to discover and to address in the delivery of our generally "effective" treatments.

Importantly, the results of mediation research may also assist us in determining ways to modify our treatments to achieve better treatment outcomes. This is a topic to which we now turn our attention.

MEDIATORS OF TREATMENT OUTCOMES

The case for studying mediators of change in child and adolescent treatment outcome research has also been made repeatedly over the past several decades (e.g., Kazdin & Kendall, 1998; MacKinnon et al., 2013; Weersing & Weisz, 2002). Mediators of treatment outcome indicate the processes and mechanisms through which a treatment might produce its effects and may help us identify the most effective treatment ingredients (Arean & Kraemer, 2013; Kraemer, Kierman, Essex, & Kupfer, 2008).

Since the early days of psychotherapy research, attention has been given to the principles of psychotherapeutic change. However, discussions of therapeutic mechanisms (e.g. Goldfried, 1980) were not based—as Kendall (2009) has noted—on the solid ground of RCT research and were lacking knowledge of evidence of treatment efficacy. Historically, only after significant treatment effects were established have researchers started to examine mediators of change.

A host of variables may serve as potential mediators of treatment outcomes. There are many potential mediators for any given therapeutic approach or treatment modality for any one psychological problem or disorder. In the field of youth treatment, candidate mediators may be related to child (e.g., information processing, emotion regulation, coping), parental (e.g., parenting practices, parent's own anxiety or depression), familial (e.g., cohesion, conflict), and/or school (e.g., relationship with teacher) functioning. The first task is to narrow down the large number of candidate mediators (Kraemer et al., 2002). This can be done in a number of ways. In most cases, *treatment theory* provides the basis for the mediators to be investigated. As the treatment is designed to produce changes in certain disorder-related symptoms, the researchers should carefully consider which variables to target. For example, CBT for youth with depression should be associated with increased skill sets (e.g., social skills, social problem-solving skills) and cognitive dysfunctions (e.g., overgeneralization, cognitive distortions) associated with behavioral activation and cognitive restructuring. Improved skills are expected to increase the child's sense of mastery and the likelihood that he or she will engage in social and pleasant activities.

In addition to treatment theory, findings from research on specific therapeutic interventions may inform the choice of potential mediators (MacKinnon, 2008). For example, De Boo and Prins (2007) analyzed the components of four social skills training (SST) programs and suggested three candidate mediators of their effects for children with ADHD. As such, social cognitive skills, parenting style, and medication-induced reduction of ADHD key symptoms were examined as potential mediators of SST outcome for children with ADHD.

Another way to choose potential mediators is to conceptualize potential mediators as risk factors for psychopathology. Developmental psychopathology research helps inform the study of mediators in youth psychotherapy by defining such risk factors (Dekovic, Asscher, Manders, Prins, & van der Laan, 2012). In the internalizing domain, the child's cognitive distortions and misinterpretation of threat and danger have been found to be risk factors for the development of anxiety problems and as such are candidate mediators in anxiety treatment (Field, Hadwin, & Lester, 2011). In the externalizing domain, deficits in social cognition and emotion recognition have been found to be related to the development of disruptive behavior problems, and thus may be candidate mediators (Hawes, Price, & Dadds, 2014).

Clinical researchers should also consider testing both specific and nonspecific factors as mediators of treatment outcomes. Specific factors refer to the processes aimed to be changed by an active treatment (e.g., avoidance behavior and dysfunctional thoughts in CBT). A behavioral technique such as exposure therapy aims to reduce avoidance behaviors, physiological processes, and cognitive/subjective fear responses. The specific mechanisms through which exposure results in approach behaviors are still the subject of debate (Craske & Mystowski, 2006), but collectively successful CBT would be expected to be associated with significant change across behavioral, cognitive, and physiological processes (Ollendick & Shirk, 2011). So, too, might nonspecific factors. Nonspecific processes refer to characteristics that are shared by most treatments and include the therapeutic alliance, the therapist's competence, and adherence to the treatment protocol (Chatoor & Krupnick, 2001; Ollendick & Shirk, 2011).

We should note that, based on theory and empirical work, some variables may be candidates for both mediational and moderational analyses, such as negative cognitions. Cole and Turner (1993), for example, in a cross-sectional study, examined the mediating and moderating role of cognitive symptoms in child depression. The authors found that attributional style mediated, but did not moderate, the relationship between child competence and depressive symptoms. Curry et al. (2006) studied pre-treatment severity of depression as a moderator of treatment outcome. Changes in depressive symptoms over time were also studied as mediators of treatment outcomes in this study, using behavioral activation as an outcome variable.

Finally, treatments can be counterproductive, producing unintended, negative effects. These iatrogenic effects (i.e., mechanisms leading to worse treatment outcomes) may be found under certain contexts or with certain subgroup characteristics (moderator effects, see above). Dishion, Spracklen, Andrews, and Patterson (1996), for example, found that group deviancy training predicted future deviant behavior in adolescence. Group therapy processes were suggested to account for these iatrogenic effects, but formal mediation tests of these processes were not undertaken in this study. As the debate on the potential benefits of youth group therapy continues (e.g., Weiss et al., 2005), focus on mediators of therapy outcomes can provide a fine-grained analysis of group processes that may lead to iatrogenic effects and to positive treatment outcomes. It may also clarify whether these effects are being moderated by other factors, such as personality of group members.

The study of mediators not only may suggest mechanisms of psychotherapeutic action and thereby improve clinical practice, but also may be a means of testing models of psychopathology. Wilson and Rapee (2005), for example, in a study with socially phobic adults, found that changes in certain types of cognition following treatment were associated with positive changes in symptoms of social phobia at 3-month follow-up, while changes in other types of cognition were not. Social phobic symptoms were independently predicted only by within-treatment reductions in the degree to which individuals personally believed that negative social events were indicative of unfavorable self-characteristics, while social phobic symptoms were not predicted by the belief that negative social events would result in negative evaluations by other people. Thus, in this study, it was possible to test cognitive models of social phobia, with regard to the specificity of cognitive biases in social phobia. Studies such as these provide information on the potential causal or maintaining role that specific types of cognitive biases may play in the symptoms of social anxiety. But results also may inform the adjustment of treatment protocols. The authors conclude that the "modification of negative beliefs regarding what unfavorable social events mean about one's personal attributes may be an important aim for treatment programmes for social phobia" (p. 387).

Treatment models may also be tested through an analysis of potential mediators. Stice, Presnell, Gau, and Shaw (2007), for example, tested two preventive intervention models underlying bulimia nervosa in adolescent girls, "the dissonance model" versus "the healthy weight model." The authors hypothesized that if the intervention(s) would decrease bulimic symptoms in the absence of changes in the hypothesized mediators or would decrease the mediators in the absence of effects on bulimic symptoms, this would suggest a limitation or problem with the underlying intervention theory. Results showed that the dissonance intervention (critiquing the thin ideal) produced significant treatment outcomes that were mediated by changes in the thin ideal internalization. The hypothesis that change in healthy eating and exercise—the healthy weight model—would mediate the healthy weight intervention effects was not supported.

Changing the focus in treatment outcome research toward identifying mediators of therapeutic change will advance the clinical child research area by providing answers to questions that cannot be answered by efficacy and effectiveness studies alone. Questions such as what the effective change principles are for specific conditions, which treatment components have the most therapeutic impact, or whether new approaches really are unique or work through common change principles, are essential for improving the content and impact of effective interventions (Kendall, 2009).

DESIGN AND STATISTICAL ISSUES IN THE STUDY OF TREATMENT MODERATORS AND MEDIATORS

Despite the valuable insight that studying moderators and mediators can improve youth treatment outcome research and practice, there may be issues that keep clinical researchers away from testing these important variables. Issues such as the design of the study and statistical considerations are outlined next, in order to describe at least two of these issues.

Studying treatment mediators may be conceptually and methodologically more challenging than studying treatment moderators. Most researchers are familiar with the analysis of interaction effects used to investigate moderators. In contrast, methodology for the detailed analysis of mediated effects is of relatively recent origin (Compton, Rosenfield, Hofmann, & Smits, 2014; MacKinnon, 2008). This section therefore focuses on discussions related to the issues of treatment mediation. Where necessary, we also turn to issues of treatment moderation and the important situation where both moderation and mediation may be present in treatment research.

Mediational pathways in treatment research will in most cases be multiple and complex (e.g., multi-causality, reciprocal causality [Kazdin & Nock, 2003]). Behavioral interventions may work through behavioral processes, physiological dimensions, cognitive mediators, or all three, which may involve complex pathways in which the sequence of change will be difficult to disentangle (Chu & Harrison, 2007).

In addition to potentially complex pathways for individual mediators, it is likely that more than one candidate mediator should be examined in a mediation study. Most mediation studies conducted thus far have attempted to demonstrate the mediating role of a single mediator. Given that so few mediational research studies exist, designing a study with a single candidate mediator—and performing a strong mediational test on that mediator—is realistic. However, clinical reality is complex, and examining at least two mediators more accurately reflects the complexity of treatment mediation. Additionally, combining moderators and mediators in one and the same analysis may lead to more informative decisions regarding potent treatment processes. It may also be possible to obtain greater insight into mediating processes by investigating how processes differ across mediators or moderators. More complex designs and measurements will therefore be necessary.

When multiple candidate mediators are included in the design of a mediational study, it is possible to evaluate the *specificity of mediational effects*

(MacKinnon, 2008). Kazdin and Nock (2003) have emphasized the importance of testing whether interventions affect mediators specific to that intervention, but not mediators specific to other interventions. Stice, Rohde, Seeley, and Gau (2010), for example, compared several preventive intervention programs for adolescents at risk for depression and tested whether each preventive intervention program affected the theoretically specific mediators, but not mediators specific to the other program (e.g., reductions in negative cognition and increase in pleasant activities would mediate effects of group CBT; while increases in emotional expression and reductions in loneliness would mediate effects of a supportive expressive program). The results of this study on mediators (negative cognition, pleasant activities, loneliness, emotional expression) of preventive interventions for depression in adolescents yielded limited support for the hypothesized mediators, suggesting that nonspecific factors may play an important mediational role, though perhaps other factors may also exist. There was mixed support for the specificity of the mediators. Group CBT participants showed significant reductions in loneliness and improvements in emotional expression, in addition to the expected effects for negative cognitions and pleasant activities, which suggests that this program affects both specific and nonspecific factors.

In a recent study on the mediational effects of multi-systemic therapy (MST) outcome, Dekovic et al. (2012) investigated specificity effects of three dimensions of parenting: positive discipline, inept discipline, and relationship quality (see Chapter 5). Similarly, Hinshaw, Owens, Wells, Kraemer, Abikoff, Arnold, et al. (2000) noted that the specificity of mediation effects can be related to types of outcome: symptom level, functional impairment (e.g., social skills deficits), or comorbidities. Moreover, specificity may also be related to type of informants; a lack of concordance may be found among parent-rated findings, self-reports of the child, behavioral observations, and clinician reports.

An important aspect of any treatment mediation is the evaluation of the theoretical basis of the link from treatment to mediator and the link from mediator to outcome (Lipsey, 1993; MacKinnon, 2008). Action theory refers to the extent to which treatment actions lead to changes in mediators. Testing the X-to-M link in mediation analysis (path a, Figure 1.1) provides evidence about whether treatment actions changed the mediators as expected. Etiological theory or conceptual theory focuses on the extent to which the mediators are related to the outcome variable of interest. Mediators are typically selected because they are causally related to the outcome variable based on theory and prior empirical research. If there is not a significant relation of M to Y (path b, Figure 1.1), the theoretical basis of the program can be questioned. If there is not a significant effect of X on M, then the treatment may need to be altered to change the mediator. The challenge for the treatment developer is to pick mediators that can be changed by treatment resources at hand and to pick mediating variables that cause the outcome variable.

Do interventions work through the same process in different subgroups? This is a question of *moderated mediation*. Lochman (2000) suggested testing whether the mediating processes that account for intervention effects are comparable or different across developmental periods (earlier stages of development versus adolescent phase), for instance in parenting programs for externalizing problems. Different factors may mediate treatment outcome in subgroups defined by the moderators. CBT, for example, may affect a sense of self-efficacy for both children and adolescents, but increase in self-efficacy leads to a decrease in anxiety symptoms in adolescents only (Maric et al., 2012). Another example of moderated mediation is the study by Chronis-Tuscano, O'Brien, Johnston, Jones, Clarke, Raggi, et al. (2011) that focused on whether the relation between maternal ADHD and improvement in child behavior following parent training was mediated by change in negative parenting. In other words, the relationship between maternal ADHD symptoms and attenuated response to parent training might be explained by the failure of mothers with elevated ADHD symptoms to reduce their use of negative parenting behaviors (e.g., giving repeated commands without providing opportunity to comply; inconsistent discipline). These parental behaviors seem to characterize the adult with ADHD, who tends to be emotionally reactive and to have difficulty inhibiting her responses.

Finally, an interesting example of hypothesized moderated mediation was given recently by Hawes, Price, and Dadds (2014). Research on callous unemotional (CU) traits in children suggests that key components of effective family-based interventions that focus on the reduction of negative parenting will be less relevant and will result in less behavioral change for high CU children compared to low CU children. For the high CU children, increases in parental warmth and positive reinforcements may be needed and may be more effective for managing misbehavior than reducing harsh/inconsistent discipline.

In *reciprocal mediation models*, one is assuming a different order of causal relations, that is, there is a reciprocal causation between the mediator and the treatment condition, so that both treatment → mediator → outcome and treatment → outcome → mediator can be true. In the externalizing domain, for example, Beauchaine et al. (2005) tried to model reciprocal effects of parenting on child behavior, and of child behavior on parenting. These mutual dyadic influences cannot be modeled with traditional mediational tests that use a static post-treatment mediator but require longitudinal modeling to capture change over time. Beauchaine et al. (2005) used growth curve modeling techniques to examine the reciprocal effects of parenting and child behavior on one another across pre-treatment, post-treatment, and 1-year follow-up assessments.

In a recent intervention study, Hogendoorn et al. (2014) tested whether an increase in perceived control during CBT for youth anxiety preceded or followed a change in anxious feelings. A reciprocal effect was found in which an increase in perceived control and decrease in (parent-reported) anxiety symptoms influenced each other over time.

In *sequential mediation models*, two or more mediators intervene in a series between treatment condition and outcomes (treatment → mediator 1 → mediator 2 → outcomes). Dekovic et al. (2012) illustrate "sequential mediation" with a strong mediational design: five monthly within-intervention assessments between pre- and post-test in a large MST treatment outcome RCT ($N = 256$).

Three mediators of interest were pursued: parental sense of competence, changes in a parenting dimension, and changes in parent-child relation quality.

MST led to increases in parental sense of competence (first mediational link); this in turn led to changes in parenting dimensions (second mediational link). However, change in quality of relation was not related to a reduction in externalizing behaviors (third mediational link). In other words, this study intended to test several "mediational models," and the results supported a sequential pattern of change. Given the complexity of childhood disorders, it is likely that therapeutic change is sequential, requiring change in a cascading process of mediation.

Most researchers are familiar with the Baron and Kenny (1986) paper that presented an important approach for the investigation of mediation: (1) treatment needs to affect the treatment outcome (path c, Figure 1.1); (2) treatment condition should predict changes in the mediator (path a, Figure 1.1); (3) while controlling for the treatment, change in the mediator should be significantly associated with change in the treatment outcome (path b, Figure 1.1); when change in the mediator is statistically controlled for, the effect of treatment on change in treatment outcome is attenuated (path c', Figure 1.1).

Although the Baron and Kenny (1986) approach is often used and cited for mediation in the social sciences, recent approaches have improved methodology for mediation analysis, which may be of particular interest for the area of youth treatment outcome research. For example, MacKinnon, Lockwood, Hoffman, West, and Sheets (2002) found that the Baron and Kenny method has low Type I error rates and low statistical power in studies with relatively small sample sizes (e.g., $N = 50$), even requiring exorbitant sample sizes when effects are small (Fritz & MacKinnon, 2007). Hence, chances are that no mediation relation will be found, unless the effect or sample size is large. MacKinnon et al. (2002) further found that the most important conditions for mediation are that the a coefficient is statistically significant (condition 2, Baron and Kenny approach) and that the b coefficient (condition 3, Baron and Kenny approach) is statistically significant, based on Type 1 error rates and statistical power. As a result, only conditions 2 and 3 of the Baron and Kenny approach are required to establish mediation. Although this joint significant test for mediation is accurate, it does not provide an estimate of the mediated effect. An estimate of the mediated effect, called a product of coefficient test, equals the product of coefficients from the independent variable to the mediator (a path in Figure 1.1) and the coefficient from the mediator to the dependent variable adjusted for the independent variable (b path in Figure 1.1). Confidence intervals for the mediated effect provide an additional way to investigate treatment effects because they provide a range of possible values of the mediated effect. The most accurate confidence intervals are obtained using the distribution of the product or resampling methods (MacKinnon, Lockwood, & Williams, 2004) and there is now software available to conduct these analyses (Muthén & Muthén, 2010; Preacher & Hayes, 2008) including online calculators (e.g., Rmediation by Tofighi & MacKinnon, 2011). Confidence intervals for more complicated mediation models, such as multiple mediation models, can be obtained using these methods, so they provide a general way to assess mediated effects in treatment research, even in complex models.

That the test of mediation can have more power than the test of the total effect (MacKinnon et al., 2002) is important, especially in light of several studies (i.e., Kazdin & Wassell, 1999; Kolko et al., 2000) that did not continue with further mediation analyses because of the nonsignificance of the first step (path c) of the Baron and Kenny analyses. In the product of coefficient approach, the use of conditions 1 and 4 of the Baron and Kenny method may still be of help with regard to the interpretation of the mediating effect, whether the mediation is partial (i.e., if some of the change in the treatment outcome caused by the treatment happens via the mediator) or total (i.e., if all the change in the treatment outcome caused by the treatment happens via the mediator). In youth treatment outcome studies, "total mediation" will less often be the case because of the potential multiple mediators occurring during the treatment.

The mediation model is a longitudinal model in which treatment changes a mediator, which then changes an outcome. The importance of temporal precedence is a primary assumption of mediation analysis (Cole & Maxwell, 2003; MacKinnon, 2008). The MacArthur approach (Kraemer et al., 2002; Kraemer et al., 2008) for the investigation of moderators and mediators of treatment outcome provides a clear way to organize analyses of moderator and mediator variables in randomized clinical trials, including information on the direction of effects, and differences with other third variables in the "treatment-outcome model" (e.g., predictors). This approach promotes strict rules regarding the temporal precedence requirement for mediation (i.e., mediator occurs during the treatment and as a consequence of treatment, and prior to treatment outcome; Kraemer et al., 2002), which may pose challenges to researchers investigating statistical mediation in half-longitudinal models (i.e., pre- and post-assessments of mediators and outcomes) or in studies without at least three waves of data collection. There are now many alternative longitudinal mediation models, including autoregressive models (Cole & Maxwell, 2003) and models that focus on different types of change over time (Cheong, MacKinnon, & Khoo, 2003; Fritz, 2014; MacKinnon, 2008; Selig & Preacher, 2009).

Often, when choosing the statistical method to study moderation and mediation in youth treatment outcome studies, concerns are raised regarding the required sample size. As mentioned above, the simulation study by MacKinnon et al. (2002) showed that the Baron and Kenny approach has low power and therefore requires a large sample size to have sufficient power to detect effects. From a simulation study by Fritz and MacKinnon (2007), the joint significance test and tests based on the bootstrap or product of coefficients test have the most power to detect mediated effects (MacKinnon, 2008), but the sample size requirements can be large. For small effect size (corresponding to a correlation of .1) for both the a and b paths, a sample of approximately 558 is needed to have .8 power to detect effects for the percentile bootstrap method. If both effects are large (corresponding to a correlation of .5) for the a and b paths, a minimum sample size of approximately 35 is required (Fritz & MacKinnon, 2007). Thus, in general, sample size requirements are substantial for mediation analysis, but these sample size requirement numbers do not include the increased power of a longitudinal design and other methods to increase power to detect mediation besides raising sample size (Fritz, Cox, & MacKinnon, 2013; O'Rourke & MacKinnon, 2014). The required sample size findings are especially relevant for youth psychotherapy research since small samples are common. The importance of statistical power and interpretation of temporal sequence makes a longitudinal design critical for youth psychotherapy research.

The most recent developments in mediation analysis have focused on the assumptions necessary for causal interpretation of mediation effects, especially the influence of confounding variables on mediation conclusions. In particular, when treatment is randomized, the effect of treatment on the mediator and the effect of treatment on the outcome can be considered a causal effect. However, randomization of the treatment does not ensure randomization of the mediator to persons in each group. As a result, the relation of the mediator to the outcome can be confounded because the mediator has not been randomly assigned. Much recent work on mediation has addressed the challenges to assessing causal mediation (Imai, Keele, & Tingley, 2010; Valeri & VanderWeele, 2013) and approaches to assessing sensitivity to violations of assumptions, such as determining how big a confounder effect would have to be to make a mediated effect zero (Cox, Kisbu-Sakarya, Miočević, & MacKinnon 2014; MacKinnon & Pirlott, 2014). It is worth noting that including confounding variables in analysis may increase the likelihood of detecting mediation. A clear conclusion from this research is that treatment researchers are encouraged to measure variables that could affect the mediating and outcome variables even in randomized designs.

CONCLUDING COMMENTS

The two most important questions raised in youth mental health research today are *how* treatments for emotional and behavioral disorders in children and adolescents work, and *for whom* they work best. As outlined in this chapter, in any youth intervention study, some type of moderation and mediation analysis will be both desired and feasible. Studying specific and nonspecific mediators, combining moderators and mediators into one and the same study, and testing temporal changes in the most important mechanisms, using innovative methodology, are all ways in which we can make progress in youth intervention research, both theoretically and clinically. In the chapters that follow, some of these developments are articulated for a host of disorders and treatments.

REFERENCES

Arean, P. A., & Kraemer, H. C. (2013). *High-quality psychotherapy research: From conception to piloting to national trials.* New York: Oxford University Press.

Baron, R. M., & Kenny, D. A. (1986). The moderator-mediator variable distinction in social psychological research: Conceptual, strategic, and statistical considerations. *Journal of Personality and Social Psychology, 51*, 1173–1182.

Beauchaine, T. P., Webster-Stratton, C., & Reid, M. J. (2005). Mediators, moderators, and predictors of 1-year outcomes among children treated for early-onset conduct problems: A latent growth curve analysis. *Journal of Consulting and Clinical Psychology, 73*, 371–388.

Chatoor, L., & Krupnick, J. (2001). The role of non-specific factors in treatment outcome of psychotherapy studies. *European Child and Adolescent Psychiatry, 10*(Suppl. 1), 119–125.

Cheong, J., MacKinnon, D. P., & Khoo, S. T. (2003). Investigation of mediational processes using parallel process latent growth curve modeling. *Structural Equation Modeling, 10*, 238–262.

Chu, B., & Harrison, T. L. (2007). Disorder-specific effects of CBT for anxious and depressed youth: A meta-analysis of candidate mediators of change. *Clinical Child and Family Psychology Review, 10*, 352–372.

Chronis-Tuscano, A., O'Brien, K. A., Johnston, C., Jones, H. A., Clarke, T. L., Raggi, V. L., et al. (2011). The relation between maternal ADHD symptoms & Improvement in child behavior following brief behavioral parent training is mediated by change in negative parenting. *Journal of Abnormal Child Psychology, 39*, 1047–1057.

Cole, D. A., & Maxwell, S. E. (2003). Testing mediational models with longitudinal data: Questions and tips in the use of structural equation modeling. *Journal of Abnormal Psychology, 112*, 558–577.

Cole, D. A., & Turner, J. E. (1993). Models of cognitive mediation and moderation in child depression. *Journal of Abnormal Psychology, 102*, 271–281.

Compton, S. N., Rosenfield, D., Hofmann, S. G., & Smits, J. A. J. (2014). Advances in data analytic methods for evaluating treatment outcome and mechanisms of change: Introduction to the special issue. *Journal of Consulting and Clinical Psychology, 82*(5), 743–745.

Cox, M. G., Kisbu-Sakarya, Y., Miočević, M., & MacKinnon, D. P. (2014). Sensitivity plots for confounder bias in the single mediator model. *Evaluation Review, 37*(5), 405–431. PMCID: PMC Journal—In Process. doi: 10.1177/0193841X14524576

Craske, M. G., & Mystowski, J. (2006). Exposure therapy and extinction: Clinical studies. In M. G. Craske, D. Hermans, & D. VanSteenwegen (Eds.), *Fear and learning: Basic science to clinical application* (pp. 23–41). Washington, DC.: APA Books.

Curry, J., Rohde, P., Simons, A., Silva, S., Vitiello, B., Kratochvil, C., ... March, J. (2006). Predictors and moderators of acute outcome in the Treatment for Adolescents with Depression Study (TADS). *Journal of the American Academy of Child and Adolescent Psychiatry, 45*(12), 1427–1439.

Davis, T. E., III, Ollendick, T. H., & Ost, L. G. (Eds.) (2012). *Intensive one-session treatment of specific phobias.* New York: Springer Publications.

de Boo, G. M., & Prins, P. J. M. (2007). Social incompetence in children with ADHD: Possible moderators and mediators in social skills training. *Clinical Psychology Review, 27*, 78–97.

Dekovic, M., Asscher, J. J., Manders, W. A., Prins, P. J. M., & van der Laan, P. (2012). Within intervention change: Mediators of intervention effects during multisystemic therapy. *Journal of Consulting and Clinical Psychology, 80*(4), 574–587.

Dishion, T. J., Spracklen, K. M., Andrews, D. W., & Patterson, G. R. (1996). Deviancy training in male adolescent friendships. *Behavior Therapy, 27,* 373–390.

Eysenck, H. (1952). The effects of psychotherapy: An evaluation. *Journal of Consulting Psychology, 16,* 319–324.

Farrell, L., Waters, A., Milliner, E., & Ollendick, T. H. (2012). Comorbidity and treatment response in paediatric obsessive-compulsive disorder: A pilot study of group cognitive-behavioural therapy. *Psychiatry Research, 199,* 115–123.

Field, A. P., Hadwin, J. A., & Lester, K. J. (2011). Information processing biases in child and adolescent anxiety: A developmental perspective. In W. K. Silverman & A. P. Field (Eds.), *Anxiety disorders in children and adolescents* (2nd ed., pp. 103–129). New York: Cambridge University Press.

Fritz, M. S. (2014). An exponential decay model for mediation. *Prevention Science, 15*(5), 611–622. PMCID: PMC3778070. doi: 10.1007/s11121-013-0390-x

Fritz, M. S., Cox, M. G., & MacKinnon, D. P. (2013). Increasing statistical power in mediation models without increasing sample size. *Evaluation & the Health Professions.* Advance online publication. PMCID: PMC Journal. doi: 10.1177/0163278713514250

Fritz, M. S., & MacKinnon, D. P. (2007). Required sample size to detect the mediated effect. *Psychological Science, 18*(3), 233–239.

Goldfried, M. R. (1980). Toward the delineation of therapeutic change principles. *American Psychologist, 35,* 991–999.

Hawes, D. J., Price M. J., & Dadds, M. R. (2014). Callous-unemotional traits and the treatment of conduct problems in childhood and adolescents: A comprehensive review. *Clinical Child and Family Psychology Review, 17*(3), 248–267.

Hinshaw, S. P., Owens, E. B., Wells, K. C., Kraemer, H. C., Abikoff, H. B., Arnold, L. E., et al. (2000). Family processes and treatment outcome in the MTA: Negative/ineffective parenting practice in relation to multimodal treatment. *Journal of Abnormal Child Psychology, 28*(6), 555–568.

Hinshaw, S. P. (2007). Moderators and mediators of treatment outcome for youth with ADHD: Understanding for whom and how interventions work. *Journal of Paediatric Psychology, 32,* 664–675.

Hogendoorn, S., Prins, P. J. M., Boer, F., Vervoort, L., Wolters, L., Moorlag, H., Nauta, M., Garst, H., Hartman, C., & de Haan, E. (2014). Mediators of cognitive-behavioral therapy for anxiety-disordered children and adolescents: Cognition, perceived control, and coping. *Journal of Clinical Child and Adolescent Psychology, 43*(2), 486–500.

Holmbeck, G. N. (1997). Toward terminological, conceptual, and statistical clarity in the study of mediators and moderators: Examples from the clinical-child and paediatric psychology literatures. *Journal of Consulting and Clinical Psychology, 65,* 599–610.

Imai, K., Keele, L., & Tingley, D. (2010). A general approach to causal mediation analysis. *Psychological Methods, 15,* 309–334.

Kazdin, A. E., & Kendall, P. C. (1998). Current progress and future plans for developing treatments: Comments and perspectives. *Journal of Clinical Child Psychology, 27,* 217–226.

Kazdin, A. E., & Nock, M. K. (2003). Delineating mechanisms of change in child and adolescent therapy: Methodological issues and research recommendations. *Journal of Child Psychology and Psychiatry, 44,* 1116–1129.

Kazdin, A. E., & Wassell, G. (1999). Barriers to treatment participation and therapeutic change among children referred for conduct disorder. *Journal of Clinical Child Psychology, 28*, 160–172.

Kendall, P. C. (2009). Commentary. Principles of therapeutic change circa 2010. *Applied & Preventive Psychology, 13*, 19–21.

Kolko, D. J., Brent, D. A., Baugher, M., Bridge, J., & Birmaher, B. (2000). Cognitive and family therapies for adolescent depression: Treatment specificity, mediation, and moderation. *Journal of Consulting and Clinical Psychology, 68*, 603–614.

Kraemer, H. C., Frank, E., Kupfer, D. J. (2006). Moderators of treatment outcomes. *Journal of the American Medical Association, 296*, 1286–1289.

Kraemer, H. C., Wilson, G. T., Fairburn, C. G., & Agras, W. S. (2002). Mediators and moderators of treatment effects in randomized clinical trials. *Archives of General Psychiatry, 59*, 877–883.

Kraemer, H. C., Kierman, M., Essex, M., & Kupfer, D. J. (2008). How and why criteria defining moderators and mediators differ between the Baron & Kenny and MacArthur approaches. *Health Psychology, 27*(2), S101–S108.

Levitt, E. E. (1957). The results of psychotherapy with children: An evaluation. *Journal of Consulting and Clinical Psychology, 21*, 189–196.

Levitt, E. E. (1963). Psychotherapy with children: A further evaluation. *Behaviour Research and Therapy, 60*, 326–329.

Lipsey, M. W. (1993). Theory as method: Small theories of treatments. In L. B. Sechrest & H. G. Scott (Eds.), *Understanding causes and generalizing about them* (pp. 5–38). San Francisco, CA: Jossey-Bass.

Lochman, J. E. (2000). Parent and family skills training in targeted prevention programs for at risk youth. *The Journal of Primary Prevention, 21*, 253–265.

MacKinnon, D. P. (2008). *Introduction to statistical mediation analysis.* Mahwah, NJ: Erlbaum.

MacKinnon, D. P., Lockhart, G., Baraldi, A. N., & Gelfand, L. A. (2013). Evaluating treatment mediators and moderators. In J. S. Cromer & P. C. Kendall (Eds.), *The Oxford handbook of research strategies for clinical psychology* (pp. 262–286). New York: Oxford University Press.

MacKinnon, D. P., Lockwood, C. M., Hoffman, J. M., West, S. G., & Sheets, V. (2002). Comparison of methods to test mediation and other intervening variable effects. *Psychological Methods, 7*, 83–104.

MacKinnon, D. P., Lockwood C. M., & Williams, J. (2004). Confidence limits for the indirect effect: Distribution of the product and resampling methods. *Multivariate Behavioral Research, 39*, 99–128.

MacKinnon, D. P., & Pirlott, A. G. (2015). Statistical approaches for enhancing causal interpretation of the M to Y relation in mediation analysis. *Personality and Social Psychology Review, 19*, 30–43. doi: 10.1177/1088868314542878

Maric, M., Wiers, R. W. H., & Prins, P. J. M. (2012). Ten ways to improve the use of statistical mediation analysis in the practice of child and adolescent treatment research. *Clinical Child and Family Psychology Review, 15*(3), 177–191.

Muthén, L. K., & Muthén, B. O. (1998–2010). *Mplus user's guide* (6th ed.). Los Angeles, CA: Muthén & Muthén.

Ollendick, T. H., Jarrett, M. A., Grills-Taquechel, A. E., Hovey, L. D., & Wolff, J. C. (2008). Comorbidity as a predictor and moderator of treatment outcome in youth

with anxiety, affective, attention deficit/hyperactivity disorder, and oppositional/
conduct disorders. *Clinical Psychology Review, 28,* 1447–1471.

Ollendick, T. H., & King, N. J. (2012). Evidence-based treatments for children and
adolescents: Issues and controversies. In P. C. Kendall (Ed.), *Child and adolescent therapy: Cognitive-behavioral procedures* (pp. 499–519). New York: Guilford
Publications.

Ollendick, T. H., & Shirk, S. R. (2011). Clinical interventions with children and adolescents: Current status, future directions. In D. H. Barlow (Ed.), *Oxford handbook of
clinical psychology* (pp. 762–788). Oxford: Oxford University Press.

O'Rourke, H. P., & MacKinnon, D. P. (2014). When the test of mediation is more powerful than the test of the total effect. *Behavior Research Methods.* Advance online
publication. PMCID: PMC Journal. doi: 10.3758/s13428-014-0481-z

Preacher, K. J., & Hayes, A. F. (2008). Asymptotic and resampling strategies for assessing and comparing indirect effects in multiple mediator models. *Behavior Research
Methods, 40,* 879–891.

Prins, P. J. M., & Ollendick, T. H. (2003). Cognitive change and enhanced coping: Missing mediational links in cognitive behavior therapy with anxiety disordered children. *Clinical Child and Family Psychology Review, 6*(2), 87–105.

Selig, J. P., & Preacher, K. J. (2009). Mediation models for longitudinal data in developmental research. *Research in Human Development, 6*(2–3), 144–164.

Stice, E., Presnell, K., Gau, J., & Shaw, H. (2007). Testing mediators of intervention
effects in randomized controlled trials: An evaluation of two eating disorder prevention programs. *Journal of Consulting and Clinical Psychology, 75*(1), 20–32.

Stice, E., Rohde, P., Seeley, J. R., & Gau, J. M. (2010). Testing mediators of intervention effects in randomized controlled trials: an evaluation of three depression prevention programs. *Journal of Consulting and Clinical Psychology, 78*(2),
273–280.

Tofighi, D., & MacKinnon, D. P. (2011). Rmediation: An R package for mediation analysis confidence limits. *Behavior Research Methods, 43,* 692–700.

Valeri, L., & VanderWeele, T. J. (2013). Mediation analysis allowing for
exposure–mediator interactions and causal interpretation: Theoretical assumptions and implementation with SAS and SPSS macros. *Psychological Methods,
18*(2), 137.

Weersing, R. V., & Weisz, J. R. (2002). Mechanisms of action in youth psychotherapy.
Journal Child Psychology and Psychiatry, 43, 3–29.

Weiss, B., Caron, A., Ball, S., Tapp, J., Johnson, M., & Weisz, J. R. (2005). Iatrogenic
effects of group treatment for antisocial youth. *Journal of Consulting and Clinical
Psychology, 73,* 1036–1044.

Weisz, J. R., & Kazdin, A. E. (2010). *Evidence-based psychotherapies for children and
adolescents* (2nd ed.). New York: Guilford Press.

Wilson, J. K., & Rapee, R. M. (2005). The interpretation of negative social events in
social phobia: Changes during treatment and relationship to outcome. *Behaviour
Research and Therapy, 43,* 373–389.

2

Moderators and Mediators of Treatments for Youth With Anxiety

JOANNA HERRES, COLLEEN M. CUMMINGS, ANNA SWAN, HEATHER MAKOVER, AND PHILIP C. KENDALL ■

INTRODUCTION

Given the high prevalence and associated impairment of anxiety in youth (Costello, Mustillo, Erkanli, Keeler, & Angold, 2003; Mychailyszyn, Mendez, & Kendall, 2010; Settipani & Kendall, 2013), it is essential to understand how and for whom anxiety treatments work. Anxiety is characterized by distressing physiological responses to perceived danger, increased negative self-talk, attention to threat cues, and behavioral avoidance of anxiety-provoking situations. Cognitive behavioral therapy (CBT) addresses these areas through (1) skill building: psychoeducation about anxiety, somatic management strategies, and cognitive restructuring techniques; and (2) practice: gradual exposure to feared situations (Albano & Kendall, 2002). Most treatment outcome research has examined the efficacy of CBT.

CBT is considered a well-established treatment for youth anxiety disorders (Hollon & Beck, 2013). Despite research supporting the efficacy of CBT, there remains approximately 30%–40% of youth for whom CBT is less than fully efficacious (e.g., Walkup et al., 2008). Identifying moderators and mediators of treatment outcome is paramount in determining how to best treat youth with anxiety. This chapter first examines non-specific predictors (i.e., baseline measures that have a main effect) and moderators of treatment outcome (i.e., baseline measures that have an interactive effect; Kraemer, Wilson,

Table 2.1. VARIABLES EXAMINED AS POTENTIAL PREDICTORS AND/OR MODERATORS
OF TREATMENT OUTCOMES FOR YOUTH ANXIETY AND FINDINGS FROM PREVIOUSLY
PUBLISHED PREDICTOR AND MODERATOR ANALYSES

Variable	Previous Predictor	Previous Moderator
PRE-TREATMENT VARIABLES		
Symptom severity	1, 2	
Comorbid anxiety disorders		
Comorbid externalizing problems	3	
Comorbid depressive symptoms	4–6	
Comorbid autism spectrum disorder		7
Social phobia	8	6, 9, 10
DEMOGRAPHICS		
Gender		
Age	11	
Race/Ethnicity		
FAMILY VARIABLES		
Parent involvement in therapy	12, 11	
Parental psychopathology	11, 4, 14	11, 13
Other family factors	15, 16	6
THERAPY VARIABLES		
Number of sessions	17	
Therapist variables	18	

NOTE: Previous studies are listed by order of appearance in table. A full citation
can be found in the reference section: 1 = Kley et al. (2012); 2 = Liber et al. (2010);
3 = Halldorsdottir et al. (2014); 4 = Berman et al. (2000); 5 = O'Neil & Kendall
(2012); 6 = Compton et al. (2014); 7 = Puleo & Kendall (2011); 8 = Crawley et al.
(2008); 9 = Liber et al. (2008); 10 = Manassis et al. (2002); 11 = Bodden et al. (2008);
12 = Wood et al. (2006); 13 = Cobham et al. (1998); 14 = Legerstee et al. (2008);
15 = Crawford & Manassis (2001); 16 = Victor et al. (2007); 17 = Crawley et al. (2013);
18 = Chu & Kendall (2009).

Fairburn, & Agras, 2002), including baseline diagnoses, symptom severity,
and characteristics of the youth, caregiver, and therapist (previous findings
are summarized in Table 2.1). Then, we review candidate mediators of CBT
for youth anxiety, including cognitive, behavioral, and affective change. This
chapter provides clinicians with a guide for matching patients to treatments
that provide the most benefit and for targeting key mechanisms of therapeutic change.

PREDICTORS AND MODERATORS OF TREATMENT OUTCOME FOR YOUTH ANXIETY SYMPTOM SEVERITY

Youth with more severe anxiety symptoms exhibit higher levels of anxiety post-treatment (e.g., Garcia et al., 2010). However, in terms of response to treatment, research shows that youth with more severe diagnostician-rated anxiety demonstrate similar treatment gains to youth with less severe presentations (Walkup et al., 2008). Stated differently, youth with higher principal anxiety disorder severity ratings at pre-treatment are no more likely than youth with lower severity to continue to meet diagnostic criteria for their primary anxiety diagnosis at post-treatment (Berman, Weems, Silverman, & Kurtines, 2000; Compton et al., 2014). Studies that examined anxiety symptom severity as a predictor of global post-treatment symptomatology (as opposed to dichotomous, post-treatment responder status) reported significant relationships between initial symptom severity and treatment outcome. For example, in a study of predictors of CBT outcome, Kley, Heinrichs, Bender, and Tuschen-Caffier (2012) found that participants who reported higher levels of social anxiety at pre-treatment reported greater reductions in symptoms post-treatment. Similarly, Liber, van Widenfelt, and colleagues (2010) found that youth with higher pre-treatment anxiety symptoms demonstrated greater pre- to post-treatment change in parent-reported internalizing symptoms.

Comorbidity

Numerous studies have found similar treatment gains for youth with and without comorbid diagnoses (e.g., Berman et al., 2000; Rapee, 2003). However, although the presence of comorbid disorders *in general* does not appear to affect child anxiety treatment outcomes, the presence of *specific types* of comorbidities may differentially predict treatment outcome. Liber, van Widenfelt, and colleagues (2010) found that youth with comorbid anxiety and non-anxiety disorders reported higher post-treatment anxiety levels than youth with comorbid anxiety disorders. Testing moderating effects of autism spectrum disorder (ASD) symptoms, Puleo and Kendall (2011) found that youth with anxiety who also were rated by parents to exhibit moderate levels of ASD were less engaged and completed fewer homework tasks in individual CBT (ICBT) compared to family CBT (FCBT).

Although one might expect that comorbid externalizing symptoms would have an adverse effect on youths' ability to attend to and engage in therapy sessions, several studies comparing anxious youth with and without comorbid externalizing disorders have found comparable treatment gains (e.g., Manassis et al., 2002; Rapee, 2003). However, in one report, anxious youth with comorbid attention deficit hyperactivity disorder (ADHD) had a poorer immediate treatment response and were less likely to maintain anxiety gains at 6-month follow-up (Halldorsdottir et al., 2014). The potential interference of more severe externalizing symptoms in treatment should not be discounted.

The findings regarding the role of comorbid depression on CBT for youth anxiety are mixed. Some studies report similar treatment outcomes for youth with and without comorbid depressive disorders (e.g., Alfano et al., 2009), and others report that youth with comorbid depression show poorer treatment response (e.g., Berman et al., 2000). O'Neil and Kendall (2012) found that youth with comorbid depression *diagnoses* demonstrated similar treatment outcomes to those without such a diagnosis; however, when a continuous measure of depressive symptoms was examined, comorbid self-reported depressive *symptoms* predicted less favorable treatment response. Although youth with a depressive disorder were intentionally not included in the child/adolescent anxiety multimodal study (CAMS), participants with depressive symptoms demonstrated higher levels of anxiety symptomatology throughout treatment and were more likely to continue to meet diagnostic criteria for their primary anxiety disorder at post-treatment (Compton et al., 2014). Given the overlap of anxiety and depression (Cummings, Caporino, & Kendall, 2014), research should evaluate interventions that intentionally address both types of symptoms (e.g., Ehrenreich, Goldstein, Wright, & Barlow, 2009).

Social Anxiety Disorder

A primary diagnosis of social phobia (SP; now "Social Anxiety Disorder" in the *Diagnostic and Statistical Manual of Mental Disorders*, 5th edition [*DSM-5*], 2013) has emerged as a predictor and moderator of treatment response (e.g., Crawley, Beidas, Benjamin, Martin, & Kendall, 2008). Compton and colleagues (2014) examined the moderating effects of principal anxiety diagnosis on reductions in anxiety symptoms across four treatment conditions: the medication sertraline (SRT), CBT, combined SRT and CBT, and pill placebo. They found that youth with primary SP demonstrated slightly better treatment outcomes when treated with SRT than CBT, whereas youth with primary generalized anxiety demonstrated more favorable outcomes with CBT compared to SRT.

Though SP youth may initially have difficulty engaging in group therapy because they find it overwhelming, SP youth could benefit from group CBT (GCBT) because it offers enhanced exposure to feared social situations. However, Manassis and colleagues (2002) found that more socially anxious youth reported greater treatment gains in ICBT compared to GCBT. Liber and colleagues (2008) examined the interactive effect of SP and treatment condition found that SP youth who received GCBT demonstrated greater treatment gains (based on fathers' report of internalizing symptoms) than those who received ICBT, though this effect was not significant for mother and child reports and was only present in the subsample of participants who completed treatment. More research is needed to identify ideal conditions for addressing the needs of socially anxious youth. Of note, Social Effectiveness Therapy for Children (SET-C) is a group treatment specifically designed for youth with social phobia that has demonstrated favorable results (Beidel et al., 2007).

Gender

Studies consistently indicate that gender does not moderate CBT outcomes for anxious youth (Nilsen, Eisemann, & Kvernmo, 2013). Although two early studies found that females but not males responded significantly better to FCBT than to ICBT (Barrett, Dadds, & Rapee, 1996; Cobham, Dadds, & Spence, 1998), a more recent study designed and powered to specifically test for moderators found no significant gender differences between ICBT, FCBT, and a control condition (Kendall et al., 2008).

Race/Ethnicity

Minority youth are underrepresented in the existing literature on youth anxiety treatment (Ginsburg, Becker, Kingery, & Nichols, 2008). One study that examined the effects of race and ethnicity on treatment outcome did not find significant differences across groups (Nilsen et al., 2013). Another study found that Hispanic/Latino youth showed similar levels of treatment gains to European-American youth (Silverman et al., 1999). Similarly, Treadwell, Flannery-Schroeder, and Kendall (1995) found no significant difference in treatment response for Caucasian and African-American youth. These studies point to the utility of CBT for both minority and non-minority youth.

Age

Findings from studies examining age as a potential predictor of treatment outcome are inconclusive, possibly because of inconsistent grouping of participants by age. For instance, Kendall et al. (2008) compared 7–10-year-olds to 11–14-year-olds and found that the groups did not significantly differ in treatment response, whereas Bodden et al. (2008) compared 8–12-year-olds to 13–17-year-olds and found that the younger group had better outcomes. These age variations make it difficult to meaningfully compare findings across studies. Further, age can only be used as a proxy of developmental level. Future studies should examine developmental level, rather than general age, as a potential predictor/moderator of treatment response.

Bennett et al. (2013) conducted a meta-analysis using data from 16 randomized controlled trials (RCTs) comparing CBT for youth anxiety to a wait-list or attention-control group for youth anywhere between the ages of 6 and 19. Tests for interactions between age and the effect of CBT revealed that age did not moderate treatment outcome. This may be because the CBT protocol used in these studies allowed therapists to tailor the content of treatment for effective use with both children and adolescents.

Parental Involvement

Barmish and Kendall (2005) examined the effect of parental involvement in treatment and found that effect sizes were comparable across nine CBT outcome studies regardless of parental involvement. To account for variations in the nature of parental involvement, studies have continued to compare the efficacy of ICBT and FCBT. One study found greater improvement in symptoms in a family-focused treatment compared to treatment with minimal family involvement (Wood et al., 2006). However, Bodden et al. (2008) found that more children responded to treatment in ICBT (53%) compared to FCBT (28%), though differences abated by 3-month follow-up. The results of a meta-analysis by Spielmans, Pasek, and McFall (2006) showed that CBT with an added parent component did not outperform ICBT for depressed or anxious youth. Further, Silverman, Kurtines, Jaccard, and Pina (2009) found that CBT with minimal parent involvement and CBT with active parent involvement were both effective in reducing anxiety. Taken together, findings do not suggest that parent involvement in CBT differentiates outcomes for anxious youth. This could be because FCBT does not target specific parental factors that contribute to or maintain the child's anxiety (Breinholst, Esbjørn, Reinholdt-Dunne, & Stallard, 2012; Wei & Kendall, 2014).

Parent Psychopathology

Parents' level of anxiety might impact the effectiveness of FCBT (Bodden et al., 2008). Anxious parents may model and reinforce avoidance because they are more likely to accommodate their child's anxiety and communicate an attitude that their child cannot handle anxiety-provoking situations. That said, recent findings suggest that parental psychopathology does not always affect treatment outcome for anxious youth (Podell & Kendall, 2011). Bodden and colleagues (2008) found a significant interaction between treatment condition and parental anxiety: FCBT was more likely to be beneficial for children with non-anxious parents, whereas ICBT had significantly better response only for children of anxious parents. In an effort to understand this finding, the authors speculated that parental psychopathology may have hindered the transfer of control of CBT skills from the parent to the child.

Moderating effects of parental psychopathology may differ across development. Cobham et al. (1998) found a significant interaction between age and parental psychopathology: Children in the 7–10 age range were more likely to respond favorably to treatment if they had non-anxious parents, whereas older participants in the 11–14 age range did not. Several other studies showed similar results, though they did not test interactive effects of child age and parental anxiety. Bodden et al. (2008) found that 8–12-year-old participants whose parents had an anxiety disorder had a lower rate of CBT response than participants whose parents did not have an anxiety disorder. This finding did not hold for 13–17-year-olds. Similarly, Berman et al.'s (2000) finding that relations between parent symptoms and treatment outcome were significant for children aged 6–11 but not for adolescents aged 12–17. Conversely, Legerstee and colleagues (2008) found that maternal anxiety predicted poorer response to CBT with a parent-training component for adolescents (aged 12–16), though the moderating effect of age was not tested with an interaction.

Family Factors

Few studies have examined family factors as predictors or moderators of treatment outcomes. In one study, Crawford and Manassis (2001) reported that lower family dysfunction, parental frustration, and parenting stress at baseline predicted better treatment response. However, there was no interaction between family factors and treatment condition, and thus these family factors were not moderators of treatment outcome. Victor, Bernat, Bernstein, and Layne (2007) found that children who report more family cohesion experienced significantly greater decreases in anxiety severity and impairment compared to children from families with low cohesion. This difference in treatment response was significant only for an ICBT plus parent training condition and not in an ICBT-only condition. Analyses of the CAMS data did not find a moderating effect of change in family dysfunction (Compton et al., 2014). Although parent-reported family dysfunction improved significantly from pre- to post-treatment only for CAMS treatment responders, this did not differ by treatment condition.

Therapy Dose

Another potential predictor of treatment response is the dose of therapy, or number of sessions. Does implementing CBT in fewer sessions than the typical course of CBT (approximately 16 sessions) impact treatment efficacy? Initial work has been conducted to evaluate the efficacy of an 8-session version of CBT (Beidas, Mychailyszyn, Podell, & Kendall, 2013). Brief CBT (BCBT) is an adaptation of a traditional 16-session program that retains the core components and strategies. Preliminary research suggests that BCBT is effective in reducing youth anxiety, but that it is not as effective as the full course (Crawley et al., 2013). With an intended focus on exposure, one-session treatment (up to 3 hours in length) has been found to be effective in reducing symptoms in youth with specific phobias (Ollendick et al., 2009). Future research should compare the relative efficacy of treatments that vary by number of sessions.

Therapist Variables

Treatment outcomes may be associated with variations in therapist characteristics. Many efficacy trials include therapists who are comparable in training and experience. However, therapist characteristics vary more in community settings. Therefore flexibility in the administration of the treatment protocol may contribute to an effective outcome (Kendall & Chu, 2000; Kendall, Chu, Gifford, Hayes, & Nauta, 1998). Chu and Kendall (2009) found that flexibility significantly predicted increases in child engagement, which in turn predicted post-treatment diagnosis and impairment. Several studies have identified specific therapist behaviors that contribute to youths' perception of a positive therapeutic alliance (e.g., collaboration; a non-"teachy" style), which impacts treatment outcome (Creed & Kendall, 2005; Podell et al., 2013).

Summary of Predictors and Moderators of Treatment Outcome

Although many youth with anxiety experience meaningful benefits from CBT, not all youth respond similarly. Understanding for whom and under what circumstances treatment works best guides the refinement and tailoring of treatments for youth anxiety. Based on our review regarding pre-treatment variables as potential predictors/moderators of change, youth with more severe pre-treatment symptomatology do not demonstrate worse treatment response than youth with fewer pre-treatment symptoms, though they continue to exhibit higher levels of anxiety. Given that some older socially anxious youth with comorbid depressive symptoms show a less favorable treatment response, the development and evaluation of transdiagnostic interventions that simultaneously address mood and anxiety symptoms may enhance outcomes. Research should clarify which treatment modalities (e.g., group vs. individual) are most beneficial for SP youth who show poorer treatment gains than youth without SP (e.g., Kerns et al., 2013).

The age of youth receiving services does not impact treatment outcome, but this finding is perhaps due to the fact that therapy is adapted (flexible application) for youth across varying developmental levels (e.g., childhood vs. adolescence). Future research should focus on the effectiveness of manual-based interventions in real-world settings. Most studies comparing treatment outcome across diverse groups are conducted in settings designed to enhance treatment delivery, with special attention to overcoming barriers to care and targeting barriers to obtaining a diverse sample of participants (Schraufnagel, Wagner, Miranda, & Roy-Byrne, 2006). Access to care and adherence to treatment programs are hurdles that have not yet been addressed.

Few studies have explicitly examined the impact of the number of sessions on outcome. BCBT for youth anxiety is a promising alternative, though the relative efficacy of BCBT to CBT has not yet been evaluated. Youth with specific phobias have shown significant improvements with only one-session exposure treatments. Briefer treatment alternatives, such as BCBT or one-session exposure, could aid in dissemination and implementation efforts by improving the feasibility of conducting CBT in community and school settings (Beidas et al., 2012).

Though further research on predictors and moderators of treatment outcome is needed, previous studies have identified several indicators of "for whom" and "under what conditions" treatments for youth anxiety disorders are most effective. Clinicians can use this information to individualize treatment by matching patients to treatment conditions that will provide them with the most benefit. Taken together, previous findings highlight comorbid non-anxiety symptoms and a primary diagnosis of social phobia as important factors to consider in treatment planning.

MEDIATORS OF TREATMENT OUTCOMES FOR YOUTH ANXIETY

Identifying treatment mediators, defined as variables that change during treatment and account for changes in outcome, can help streamline therapeutic techniques, increase treatment effect sizes, and inform training efforts (Barrett, Farrell, Pina, Peris, & Piacentini, 2008; Chu & Harrison, 2007; Kendall, Comer, Chow, 2013). The examination of treatment mediators in the child anxiety literature is just now emerging in the field, with some promising findings.

Candidate Mediators

The first step in identifying candidate mediators is to identify changes that occur as a result of treatment. Davis and Ollendick (2005) reviewed empirically supported treatments for pediatric specific phobias and identified treatments that were effective in reducing subjective fear and cognitive and behavioral symptoms. Chu and Harrison (2007) conducted a broader review of child and adolescent RCTs that examined at least one theory-based candidate mediator. They found that behavioral and cognitive changes were reported relatively frequently, with fewer studies reporting physiological changes or changes in coping. A review by Prins and Ollendick (2003) identified cognition and coping as potential mediators of change in CBT. Once candidate mediators have been identified, a next step is to conduct formal tests of mediation (Prins & Ollendick, 2003). Below, we review the youth anxiety treatment literature regarding theoretically relevant candidate mediators examined in the CBT literature: cognition, behavior, coping efficacy, physiological/ affective change, parenting, homework compliance, and the therapeutic alliance.

Cognition

Negative self-talk differentiates anxiety-disordered from non-anxiety-disordered children (Sood & Kendall, 2007). The content of the negative self-statements of anxious youth tends to include future-oriented thinking associated with danger, harm, and threat (Schniering & Rapee, 2004). Anxious youth often overestimate the chance of a negative outcome and the consequences of such an outcome, evaluate themselves negatively, and can be preoccupied with their thoughts (Szabó & Loviband, 2004). However, the causal nature of negative self-statements and anxiety in children requires further clarification (Sood & Kendall, 2007). Anxiety cognitions are a frequent treatment target in CBT. Through cognitive restructuring, children learn to recognize patterns of anxious thinking, to challenge their thoughts, and to respond with more adaptive coping thoughts through examining evidence and reframing (Kearney, 2005).

In a study of predictors of treatment response, Muris, Mayer, den Adel, Roos, and van Wamelen (2009) found that changes in anxiety symptoms were associated with changes in negative automatic thoughts and perceived control over anxiety-related events. In CAMS, the introduction of cognitive restructuring techniques was noted to accelerate improvements in CBT among anxious youth, with specific impact on anxious self-talk (Peris et al., 2014). Although neither Muris et al. (2009) nor Peris et al. (2014) conducted formal tests of mediation, their findings suggest that cognitive variables may serve as potential mediators of CBT outcomes.

Five studies have evaluated cognitive factors as potential treatment mediators for anxious youth. Treadwell and Kendall (1996) examined several cognitive variables as mediators of CBT among 151 children with an anxiety disorder randomized to treatment or wait list. Negative self-talk and the ratio of negative to positive self-statements were found to mediate change in anxiety, but positive and depressive self-talk was not. A second study by Kendall and Treadwell (2007), with a different sample, further supported the mediating role of anxious and negative self-statements, but not positive and depressive self-statements. In a third study, Lau, Chan, Li, and Au (2010) examined the effectiveness of the same CBT program with Chinese children ($N = 45$) in community clinics. Anxious thoughts appeared to mediate the association between treatment status and child-reported outcome. Temporal precedence of the mediators was not established in these three studies; so it cannot be concluded with confidence that anxious negative self-talk is a causal agent rather than simply a covariate of change (see MacKinnon, Fairchild, & Fritz, 2007). Nonetheless, these findings provide promising evidence for cognitive change as an important mechanism in treatment.

In a study that did assess temporality, Hogendoorn and colleagues (2013) found that an increase in positive thoughts mediated CBT outcome. Contrary to Kendall and Treadwell's (2007) findings, changes in negative thoughts did not precede change in anxiety symptoms. Perceived control demonstrated a bidirectional relationship with anxiety symptoms and was only partially supported as a mediator. Hogendoorn and colleagues (2013) note strengths of their study, including the use of four assessment points to establish temporal precedence, as well as statistical analyses that allow for the examination of reciprocal relationships among variables. Of note, they did not include a control condition. In the CAMS, anxious self-talk did not mediate changes in anxiety symptoms for any of the treatment conditions (SRT, CBT, and combination treatment) when compared to placebo (Kendall et al., 2014). The authors suggest possible reasons for the inconsistency of this finding with previous findings. For instance, in order to establish temporal precedence of the mediator, Kendall and colleagues (2014) examined outcome at 3-month follow-up, rather than post-treatment.

The mediational relationship may not hold when outcome is assessed at follow-up. Also, the authors suggest that reductions in anxious self-talk may have been associated with reductions in anxiety in previous studies (which did not establish temporal precedence) because anxious self-talk is a *symptom* of anxiety, but not necessarily a mediator of treatment. Overall, the above findings lend support to cognitive change as an important component of CBT for anxiety. Further delineation is needed regarding the timing of assessment and the types of cognitive change examined.

Behavior

Behavioral change is a viable candidate mediator of treatment for anxiety disorders. Avoidance is a trademark behavior associated with anxiety (Mineka & Zinbarg, 2006). Given that avoidance is considered a core feature in the pathology of anxiety, exposure tasks have been regarded as one of the most important therapeutic ingredients in CBT for youth anxiety (Bouchard, Mendlowitz, Coles, & Franklin, 2004), and some evidence suggests that treatment gains do not occur until the exposure part of treatment (Kendall et al., 1997). In the CAMS, the introduction of exposure tasks accelerated progress in CBT and lessened avoidance behaviors (although not formally tested as mediators; Peris et al., 2014).

Coping and social skills have also been tested as behavioral mediators. Lau and colleagues (2010) found that changes in coping mediated the association between treatment status and child report of outcome. Although Lau et al. (2010) did not establish temporal precedence, these findings suggest that coping is a potential treatment mediator. In the study by Hogendoorn et al. (2014), increases in coping skills (i.e., direct problem-solving strategies, positive cognitive restructuring, and distraction) preceded decreases in parent-reported anxiety symptoms and were therefore possible mediators of CBT. In the CAMS, changes in perceived coping efficacy were found to mediate improvement in anxiety symptoms in the combined, CBT, and SRT conditions when compared with placebo (Kendall et al., 2014).

Youth with social phobia may avoid opportunities to develop appropriate social skills. Alfano and colleagues (2009) hypothesized that improved social skills would mediate treatment outcome for youth with social phobia. They utilized data from two clinical trials: one (Beidel, Turner, & Morris, 2000) in which 67 socially anxious youth were randomized to either Social Effectiveness Therapy for Children (SET-C) or an active, nonspecific intervention; and a second (Beidel et al., 2007) that included 122 children randomized to receive SET-C, fluoxetine, or pill placebo. Of note, the authors did not use the control group when testing mediation, so it cannot be concluded with certainty that changes in the mediator were due solely to treatment. Contrary to hypotheses, improved social skill (measured by observer ratings of social effectiveness on behavioral tasks) did not help explain treatment outcomes. Alfano and colleagues (2009) noted that the complex interplay of social interactions, behaviors, anxiety, and appraisals warrants further study. For instance, the authors suggested that peer reactions, social opportunities, and self-perceptions of social effectiveness may be other important areas of study, rather than simply objective ratings of social skill.

Affect/Physiology

Affective and physiological processes play a role in both the conceptualization of anxiety, as well as its successful treatment. The subjective experience of negative emotions (e.g., fear) is hypothesized to decrease following treatment, as the youth learns skills to cope with anxiety and increasingly engages in anxiety-provoking experiences through behavioral exposure. Physiological processes are part of anxiety, as the youth often experiences bodily reactions to anxiety-provoking stimuli in the form of the "fight or flight" response. Remaining in the presence of an anxiety-provoking stimulus until it no longer causes distressing levels of arousal results in habituation (Kendall et al., 2005). Within this model, changes in subjective experience of negative emotions and physiological indicators of fear may mediate treatment. Currently, no studies have formally tested physiological processes as mediators of treatment for anxious youth. Alfano et al. (2009) examined an affective variable, a child-rated measure of perceived loneliness, as a potential mediator for youth with social anxiety. As hypothesized, changes in loneliness partially accounted for improvements in social anxiety after participating in SET-C. Because loneliness was assessed conjointly with outcome measures, temporal precedence of the mediator was not established, nor was a control condition included in the model.

Other Candidate Mediators

PARENTING BEHAVIOR

Research has shown that parenting factors, such as overprotection/overcontrol, are associated with youth anxiety (e.g., Bögels & Brechman-Toussaint, 2006; Rapee, 2012). Parental modeling of anxiety is also important (Burnstein & Ginsburg, 2010). Many treatments for youth anxiety include some form of parental involvement that aims to reduce maladaptive parenting behavior. Theoretically, treatments that include parents may increase generalizability and maintenance of gains (Barmish & Kendall, 2005). However, prior research does not demonstrate increased treatment gains with parental involvement in treatment (e.g., Breinholst, Esbjorn, Reinholdt-Dunne, & Stallard, 2012), and no studies have examined improvement in parenting as a mediator of change in treatment of anxious youth. More work in this area is clearly warranted, and future studies should examine parenting as a mediator of change in the treatment of anxious youth (Jansen et al., 2012). Additional work should explore specific types of parental involvement as important components of treatment, particularly those that directly target problematic parenting in each family, rather than a more general "one-size-fits all" approach (Breinholst et al., 2010).

HOMEWORK COMPLIANCE

CBT consists of weekly out-of-session homework assignments in which the client reviews and practices topics covered in the previous session. Homework is considered integral to the success of CBT (Hudson & Kendall, 2002). Evidence supports the role of homework compliance in CBT outcomes (Kazantzis, Whittington, & Datillio, 2010) with an overall small to medium effect size in the treatment of anxiety disorders (Kazantzis, Deane, & Ronan, 2000). Homework assignments may consist of recording thoughts and feelings, practicing relaxation exercises, and reviewing steps of effective problem solving. Further, between-session exposure exercises give youth the opportunity to practice facing their fears in natural settings. There is variability in the amount of regular homework compliance.

Evidence for the importance of homework in CBT for anxiety mostly comes from studies with adults (Edelman & Chambless, 1993, 1995). Research on the role of homework in CBT for children and adolescents has yielded mixed results. Tiwari et al. (2013) found that treatment responders were significantly more likely to have been assigned a homework task than non-responders. However, Hughes and Kendall (2007) found that homework completion did not predict CBT outcome when controlling for the therapeutic relationship. Clients who have a positive relationship with their therapists may be more likely to comply with the homework assignments. The specific contribution of homework compliance in CBT for youth anxiety disorders is unclear, and no studies have examined homework as a mediator of treatment response.

THE THERAPEUTIC ALLIANCE

Often regarded as relevant to the general change process, the alliance/relationship (i.e., perceptions of therapist warmth, agreement on goals and tasks, and client/therapist collaboration) is considered by some to be an important contributor to the success of psychotherapy (Norcross, 2011). Although studies offer support for the association between the therapeutic alliance and outcome in child psychotherapy (Cummings et al., 2013), with an average correlation of .22 (Shirk, Karver, & Brown, 2011), few studies have examined the specific impact of the therapeutic alliance on treatment outcomes in samples of anxious youth. The few studies that have examined the role of the therapeutic alliance in treatment for youth anxiety have not conducted formal tests of mediation.

Summary of Mediators of Youth Anxiety Treatment

Identifying treatment mediators remains an important step in furthering the effective treatment of anxious youth. Knowledge about mediation can streamline therapeutic methods, aid in training future therapists, and inform dissemination efforts. Studies propose cognitive, behavioral, physiological/affective, parenting, and therapeutic processes as candidate mediators for the treatment of anxious youth. Future investigations should include measures of treatment process (Prins & Ollendick, 2003). Among the studies that tested for mediation, temporal precedence of the mediator was typically not established, limiting the ability to draw firm conclusions and make causal inferences (MacKinnon et al., 2007). Mediational pathways can be bidirectional, multi-causal, reciprocal, and complex (Kazdin & Nock, 2003). Once a mediator is established, the next step may be to test a treatment enhanced with the mediator against the original treatment (Chu & Harrison, 2007). Further, there is a need to consider treatment mediators among minority populations, across varying modes of treatment delivery and formats, and when therapy is combined with medication.

CLINICAL IMPLICATIONS

Research on moderators and mediators of treatment outcomes provides important information that may be used by clinicians to maximize treatment efficacy for youth with anxiety disorders. Clinicians treating youth with more severe pre-treatment symptomatology can expect that this group will show comparable treatment gains to those with more moderate pre-treatment symptoms, despite continuing to show more severe symptomatology after treatment. However, adolescents with social anxiety and co-occurring depressive symptoms may show less favorable treatment response. Future treatment development is needed to better address these co-occurring symptoms with a transdiagnostic approach. Importantly, CBT appears to be effective for youth of all ages and genders. The outcome of these treatments for youth from diverse backgrounds is less clear, and further research should clarify whether CBT is effective in real-world settings for youth of all racial/ethnic backgrounds. Clinicians may encounter barriers to treating youth in community settings, though youth from diverse backgrounds have shown good treatment response in settings designed to enhance treatment delivery. Clinicians should consider factors related to the parenting styles and parent psychopathology before making decisions about whether to use a family-based or individual CBT approach, as these factors may impact treatment outcomes for youth.

Identifying mediators of treatment outcome can help inform clinical training and streamline therapeutic techniques. Research provides partial support for cognitive and behavioral changes as mediators of treatment outcome. Cognitive changes, such as decreasing negative self-talk and increasing the ratio of positive to negative self-statements (Kendall & Treadwell, 2007), as well as increasing positive thoughts (Hogendoorn et al., 2013), have been demonstrated to mediate improvements in anxiety symptoms. Moreover, the introduction of cognitive restructuring strategies may help to accelerate change in anxiety (Peris et al., 2014). Behavioral change, such as decreasing avoidance of anxiety-provoking situations through the use of exposure tasks, is also supported as a mediator of treatment outcome. Using exposures during cognitive-behavioral therapy may accelerate treatment gains and decrease avoidant behavior contributing to anxiety symptoms (Peris et al., 2014). More research is needed to study therapeutic processes like the therapeutic alliance, homework compliance, and parenting behaviors (e.g., accommodation) as candidate mediators of therapeutic change. Clinicians should address therapy-interfering behaviors like failure to complete therapy homework and parental accommodation of avoidant behaviors, as these factors may impede therapeutic progress.

REFERENCES

Albano, A. M., & Kendall, P. C. (2002). Cognitive behavioral therapy for children and adolescents with anxiety disorders: Clinical research advances. *International Review of Psychiatry, 14*, 129–134.

Alfano, C. A., Pina, A. A., Villalta, I. K., Beidel, D. C., Ammerman, R. T., & Crosby, L. E. (2009). Mediators and moderators of outcome in the behavioral treatment of childhood social phobia. *Journal of the American Academy of Child & Adolescent Psychiatry, 48*, 945–953. doi: 10.1097/CHI.0b013e3181af8216

Barmish, A. J., & Kendall, P. C. (2005). Should parents be co-clients in cognitive-behavioral therapy for anxious youth? *Journal of Clinical Child and Adolescent Psychology, 34*, 569–581. doi: http://dx.doi.org/10.1207/s15374424jccp3403_12

Barrett, P. M., Dadds, M. R., & Rapee, R. M. (1996). Family treatment of childhood anxiety: A controlled trial. *Journal of Consulting and Clinical Psychology, 64*, 333–342. doi: 10.1037/0022-006X.64.2.333

Barrett, P. M., Farrell, L., Pina, A. A., Peris, T. S., & Piacentini, J. (2008). Evidence-based psychosocial treatments for child and adolescent obsessive-compulsive disorder. *Journal of Clinical Child and Adolescent Psychology, 37*, 131–155. doi: 10.1080/15374410701817956.

Beidas, R. S., Mychailsyzn, M., Podell, J., & Kendall, P. C. (2013). Brief Cognitive Behavioral Therapy (BCBT) for anxious youth: The inner workings, *Cognitive and Behavioral Practice, 20*, 134–146.

Beidas, R. S., Mychailyszyn, M. P., Edmunds, J. M., Khanna, M. S., Downey, M. M., & Kendall, P. C. (2012). Training school mental health providers to deliver cognitive-behavioral therapy. *School Mental Health, 4*(4), 197–206. doi: 10.1007/s12310-012-9074-0

Beidel, D. C., Turner, S. M., & Morris, T. L. (2000). Behavioral treatment of childhood social phobia. *Journal of Consulting and Clinical Psychology, 68*, 1072–1080. doi: 10.1037/0022-006X.68.6.1072

Beidel, D. C., Turner, S. M., Sallee, F. R., Ammerman, R. T., Crosby, L. A., & Pathak, S. (2007). SET-C versus fluoxetine in the treatment of childhood social phobia. *Journal of the American Academy of Child & Adolescent Psychiatry, 46*, 1622–1632. doi: 10.1097/chi.0b013e318154bb57

Bennett, K., Manassis, K., Walter, S., Cheung, A., Wilansky-Traynor, P., Diaz-Granados, N., . . . Wood, J. (2013). Cognitive behavioral therapy age effects in child and adolescent anxiety: An individual patient data meta-analysis. *Depression and Anxiety, 30*, 829–841.

Berman, S. L., Weems, C. F., Silverman, W. K., & Kurtines, W. M. (2000). Predictors of outcome in exposure-based cognitive and behavioral treatments for phobic and anxiety disorders in children. *Behavior Therapy, 31,* 713–731. doi: 10.1016/S0005-7894(00)80040-4

Bodden, D. H., Bogels, S. H., Nauta, M. H., DeHaan, E., Ringarose, J., Applebloom, C., . . . Applebloom-Greets, K. C. (2008). Child versus family cognitive-behavioral therapy in clinically anxious youth: An efficacy and partial effectiveness study, *Journal of American Academy of Child and Adolescent Psychiatry, 47,* 1384–1394. doi: 10.1097/CHI.0b013e318189148e

Bögels, S. M., & Brechman-Toussaint, M. L. (2006). Family issues in child anxiety: Attachment, family functioning, parental rearing and beliefs. *Clinical Psychology Review, 26*(7), 834–856. doi: 10.1016/j.cpr.2005.08.001

Bouchard, S., Mendlowitz, S. L., Coles, M. E., & Franklin, M. (2004). Considerations in the use of exposure with children. *Cognitive and Behavioral Practice, 11,* 56–65. doi: 10.1016=S1077-7229(04)80007-5

Breinholst, S., Esbjørn, B. H., Reinholdt-Dunne, M., & Stallard, P. (2012). CBT for the treatment of child anxiety disorders: A review of why parental involvement has not enhanced outcomes. *Journal of Anxiety Disorders, 26,* 416–424. doi: 10.1016/j.janxdis.2011.12.014

Burnstein, M., & Ginsburg, G. S. (2010). The effect of parental modeling of anxious behaviors and cognitions in school-aged children: An experimental pilot study. *Behavior Research and Therapy, 48,* 506–515. doi: 10.1016/j.brat.2010.02.006

Chu, B. C., & Kendall, P. C. (2009). Therapist responsiveness to child engagement: flexibility within manual-based CBT for anxious youth. *Journal of Clinical Psychology, 65,* 736–754. doi: 10.1002/jclp.20582

Chu, B. C., & Harrison, T. L. (2007). Disorder-specific effects of CBT for anxious and depressed youth: A meta-analysis of candidate mediators of change. *Clinical Child and Family Psychological Review, 10,* 352–372. doi: 10.1007/s10567-007-0028-2

Cobham, V. E., Dadds, M. R., & Spence, S. H. (1998). The role of parental anxiety in the treatment of childhood anxiety. *Journal of Consulting and Clinical Psychology, 66,* 893–905. doi: 10.1037/0022-006X.66.6.893

Compton, S., Peris, T., Almirall, D., Birmaher, B., Sherrill, J., Kendall, P. C., . . . Albano, A. M. (2014). Predictors and moderators of treatment response in childhood anxiety disorders: Results from the CAMS trial. *Journal of Consulting and Clinical Psychology, 82,* 212–224.

Costello, E. J., Mustillo, S., Erkanli, A., Keeler, G., & Angold, A. (2003). Prevalence and development of psychiatric disorders in childhood and adolescence. *Archives of General Psychiatry, 60,* 837–844. doi: 10.1001/archpsyc.60.8.837

Crawford, A., & Manassis, K. (2001). Familial predictors of treatment outcome in childhood anxiety disorders. *Journal of the American Academy of Child & Adolescent Psychiatry, 40,* 1182–1189. doi: 10.1097/00004583-200110000-00012

Crawley, S., Beidas, R., Benjamin, C., Martin, E., & Kendall, P. (2008). Treating socially phobic youth with CBT: Differential outcomes and treatment considerations. *Behavioural and Cognitive Psychotherapy, 36,* 379–389.

Crawley, S. A., Kendall, P. C., Benjamin, C. L., Brodman, D. M., Wei, C., Beidas, R. S., . . . Mauro, C. (2013). Brief cognitive-behavioral therapy for anxious youth: Feasibility and initial outcomes. *Cognitive and Behavioral Practice, 20,* 123–133.

Creed, T. A., & Kendall, P. C. (2005). Therapist alliance-building behavior within a cognitive-behavioral treatment for anxiety in youth. *Journal of Consulting and Clinical Psychology, 73,* 498–505. doi: 10.1037/0022-006X.73.3.498

Cummings, C., Caporino, N., & Kendal, P. C. (2014) Comorbidity of anxiety and depression in children and adolescents. *Psychological Bulletin, 111,* 244–255.

Cummings, C. M., Caporino, N. E., Settipani, C. A., Read, K. L., Compton, S. N., March, J., & . . . Kendall, P. C. (2013). The therapeutic relationship in cognitive-behavioral therapy and pharmacotherapy for anxious youth. *Journal of Consulting and Clinical Psychology, 81*(5), 859. doi: 10.1037/a0033294

Davis, T. R., & Ollendick, T. H. (2005). Empirically supported treatments for specific phobia in children: Do efficacious treatments address the components of a phobic response? *Clinical Psychology: Science and Practice, 12,* 144–160. doi: 10.1093/dipsy/bpi018

Edelman, R. E., & Chambless, D. L. (1993). Compliance during sessions and homework in exposure-based treatment of agoraphobia. *Behaviour Research and Therapy, 31,* 767–773.

Edelman, R. E., & Chambless, D. L. (1995). Adherence during session and homework in cognitive-behavioral group treatment of social phobia. *Behaviour Research and Therapy, 33,* 575–577.

Ehrenreich, J. T., Goldstein, C. R., Wright, L. R., & Barlow, D. H. (2009). Development of a unified protocol for the treatment of emotional disorders in youth. *Child and Family Behavior Therapy, 31,* 20–37.

Garcia, A., Sapyta, J., Moore, P., Freeman, J., Franklin, M., March, J., & Foa, E. (2010). Predictors and moderators of treatment outcome in the Pediatric Obsessive Compulsive Treatment Study (POTS I). *Journal of the American Academy of Child and Adolescent Psychiatry, 49,* 1024–1033.

Ginsburg, G. S., Becker, K. D., Kingery, J., & Nichols, T. (2008). Transporting CBT for childhood anxiety disorders into inner-city school-based mental health clinics. *Cognitive And Behavioral Practice, 15,* 148–158. doi: 10.1016/j.cbpra.2007.07.001

Halldorsdottir, T., Ollendick, T. H., Ginsburg, G., Sherrill, J., Kendall, P. C., Walkup, J., . . . & Piacentini, J. (2014). Treatment Outcomes in Anxious Youth with and without Comorbid ADHD in the CAMS. *Journal of Clinical Child and Adolescent Psychology,* (ahead-of-print), 1–7.

Hogendoorn, S. M., Prins, P. J., Boer, F., Vervoort, L., Wolters, L. H., Moorlag, H., . . . De Haan, E. (2014). Mediators of Cognitive Behavioral Therapy for anxiety-disordered children and adolescents: Cognition, perceived control, and coping. *Journal of Clinical Child and Adolescent Psychology, 43*(3), 486–500. doi: 10.1080/15374416.2013.807736

Hollon, S., & Beck, A. (2013). Cognitive and cognitive-behavioral therapies. In M. J. Lambert (Ed.), *Handbook of psychotherapy and behavior change* (pp. 393–443). Hoboken, NJ: John Wiley & Sons.

Hudson, J. L., & Kendall, P. C. (2002). Showing you can do it: The use of homework assignments in cognitive behavioral treatment for child and adolescent anxiety disorders. *Journal of Clinical Psychology, 58,* 525–534.

Hughes, A. A., & Kendall, P. C. (2007). Prediction of cognitive behavior treatment outcome for children with anxiety disorders: Therapeutic relationship and homework compliance. *Behavioural and Cognitive Psychotherapy, 35,* 487–494. doi: 10.1017/S1352465807003761

Jansen, M., van Doorn, M. M., Lichtwarck-Aschoff, A., Kuijpers, R., C., Theunissen, H., Korte, M., . . . Granic, I. (2012). Effectiveness of a cognitive-behavioral therapy (CBT) manualized program for clinically anxious children: Study protocol of a randomized controlled trial. *BMC Psychiatry, 12,* 16. doi: 10.1186/1471-244X-12-16

Kazantzis, N., Deane, F. P., & Ronan, K. R. (2000). Homework assignments in cognitive and behavioral therapy: A meta-analysis. *Clinical Psychology: Science and Practice, 7,* 189–202.

Kazantzis, N., Whittington, C., & Datillio, F. M. (2010). Meta-analysis of homework effects in cognitive and behavioral therapy: A replication and extension. *Clinical Psychology: Science and Practice, 17,* 144–156.

Kazdin, A. E., & Nock, M. K. (2003). Delineating mechanisms of change in child and adolescent therapy: Methodological issues and research recommendations. *Journal of Child Psychology and Psychiatry, 44,* 1116–1129. doi: 10.1111/1469-7610.00195

Kearney, C. A. (2005). *Social anxiety and social phobia in youth: Characteristics, assessment, and psychological treatment.* New York: Springer.

Kendall, P. C., Comer, J. S., & Chow, C. (2013). The randomized controlled trial: Basics and beyond. *The Oxford Handbook of Research Strategies for Clinical Psychology,* 40–61.

Kendall, P. C., & Chu, B. C. (2000). Retrospective self-reports of therapist flexibility in a manual-based treatment for youths with anxiety disorders. *Journal of Clinical Child and Adolescent Psychology, 29,* 209–220.

Kendall, P. C., Chu, B. C., Gifford, A., Hayes, C., & Nauta, M. (1998). Breathing life into a manual: Flexibility and creativity with manual-based treatments. *Cognitive and Behavioral Practice, 5,* 177–198.

Kendall, P. C., Cummings, C. M., Villabø, M., Narayanan, M., Treadwell, K., Kenny, D., . . . Albano, A. M. (2014). Mediators of change in the Child/Adolescent Anxiety Multimodal Treatment Study (CAMS).

Kendall, P. C., Flannery-Schroeder, E., Panichelli-Mindel, S. M., Southam-Gerow, M., Henin, A., & Warman, M. (1997). Therapy for children with anxiety disorders: A second randomized clinical trial. *Journal of Consulting and Clinical Psychology, 65,* 366–380. doi: 10.1037/0022-006X.65.3.366

Kendall, P. C., Robin, J. A., Hedtke, K. A., Suveg, C., Flannery-Schroeder, E., & Gosch, E. (2005). Considering CBT with anxious youth? Think exposures. *Cognitive and Behavioral Practice, 12,* 136–150. doi: 10.1016/S1077-7229(05)80048-3

Kendall, P. C., & Treadwell, K. R. (2007). The role of self-statements as a mediator in treatment for youth with anxiety disorders. *Journal of Consulting and Clinical Psychology, 75,* 380–389. doi: 10.1037/0022-006X.75.3.380

Kerns, C., Read, K., Klugman, J., & Kendall, P. C. (2013). Cognitive behavioral therapy for youth with social anxiety: Differential short- and long-term treatment outcomes. *Journal of Anxiety Disorders, 27,* 210–215.

Kley, H., Heinrichs, N., Bender, C., & Tuschen-Caffier, B. (2012). Predictors of outcome in a cognitive-behavioral group program for children and adolescents with social anxiety disorder. *Journal of Anxiety Disorders, 26,* 79–87.

Kraemer, H., Wilson, G., Fairburn, C. G., & Agras, W. (2002). Mediators and moderators of treatment effects in randomized clinical trials. *Archives of General Psychiatry, 59,* 877–883. doi: 10.1001/archpsyc.59.10.877.

Lau, W., Chan, C. K., Li, J. C., & Au, T. K. (2010). Effectiveness of group cognitive-behavioral treatment for childhood anxiety in community clinics. *Behaviour Research and Therapy, 48*, 1067–1077.

Legerstee, J. S., Huizink, A. C., van Gastel, W. W., Liber, J. M., Treffers, P. A., Verhulst, F. C., & Utens, E. J. (2008). Maternal anxiety predicts favourable treatment outcomes in anxiety-disordered adolescents. *Acta Psychiatrica Scandinavica, 117*, 289–298. doi: 10.1111/j.1600-0447.2008.01161.x

Liber, J., McLeod, B., Van Widenfelt, B. M., Goedhart, A. W., van der Leeden, A. J., Utens, E. M. W. J., & Treffers, P. D. (2010). Examining the relation between the therapeutic alliance, treatment adherence, and outcome of cognitive behavioral therapy for children with anxiety disorders. *Behavior Therapy, 41*, 172–186. doi: 10.1016/j.beth.2009.02.003

Liber, J., van Widenfelt, B., Utens, E., Ferdinand, R., Van der Leeden, A., Van Gastel, W., & Treffers, P. (2008). No differences between group versus individual treatment of childhood anxiety disorders in a randomized clinical trial. *Journal of Child Psychology and Psychiatry, 49*, 886–893.

Liber, J., van Widenfelt, B., van der Leeden, A., Goedhart, A., Utens, E., & Treffers, P. (2010). The relation of severity and comorbidity to treatment outcome with cognitive behavioral therapy for childhood anxiety disorders. *Journal of Abnormal Child Psychology, 38*, 683–694.

Liber, J. M., McLeod, B. D., Van Widenfelt, B. M., Goedhart, A. W., van der Leeden, A. J., Utens, E. M., & Treffers, P. D. (2010). Examining the relation between the therapeutic alliance, treatment adherence, and outcome of cognitive behavioral therapy for children with anxiety disorders. *Behavior Therapy, 41*, 172–186. doi: 10.1016/j.beth.2009.02.003

MacKinnon, D. P., Fairchild, A. J., & Fritz, M. S. (2007). Mediation analysis. *Annual Review of Psychology, 58*, 593–614. doi: 10.1146/annurev.psych.58.110405.085542

Manassis, K., Mendlowitz, S., Scapillato, D., Avery, D., Fiksenbaum, L., Freire, M., . . . Owens, M. (2002). Group and individual cognitive-behavioral therapy for childhood anxiety disorders: A randomized trial. *Journal of the American Academy of Child and Adolescent Psychiatry, 41*, 1423–1430.

Mineka, S., & Zinbarg, R. (2006). A contemporary learning theory perspective on the etiology of anxiety disorders: It's not what you thought it was. *American Psychologist, 61*, 10–26. doi: 10.1037/0003-066X.61.1.10

Muris, P., Mayer, B., den Adel, M., Roos, T., & van Wamelen, J. (2009). Predictors of change following cognitive-behavioral treatment of children with anxiety problems: A preliminary investigation on negative automatic thoughts and anxiety control. *Child Psychiatry and Human Development, 40*, 139–151. doi: 10.1007/s10578-008-0116-7

Mychailyszyn, M. C., Mendez, J. L., & Kendall, P. C. (2010). School functioning in youth with and without anxiety disorders: Comparisons by diagnosis and comorbidity. *School Psychology Review, 39*, 106–121.

Nilsen, T., Eisemann, M., & Kvernmo, S. (2013). Predictors and moderators of outcome in child and adolescent anxiety and depression: A systematic review of psychological treatment studies. *European Child & Adolescent Psychiatry, 22*(2), 69–87. doi: 10.1007/s00787-012-0316-3

Norcross, J. C. (Ed.). (2011). *Psychotherapy relationships that work* (2nd ed.). New York: Oxford University Press.

Ollendick, T. H., Ost, L-G., Reuterskiold, L., Costa, N., Cederlund, R., Sirbu, C., . . . Jarrett, M. A. (2009). One-session treatment of specific phobias in youth: A randomized clinical trial in the United States and Sweden, *Journal of Consulting and Clinical Psychology*, *77*, 504–516.

O'Neil, K., & Kendall, P. (2012). Role of comorbid depression and co-occurring depressive symptoms in outcomes for anxiety-disordered youth treated with Cognitive-Behavioral Therapy. *Child and Family Behavior Therapy*, *34*, 197–209.

Peris, T. S., Compton, S. N., Kendall, P. C., Birmaher, B., Sherrill, J., March, J., . . . & Piacentini, J. (2014). Trajectories of change in youth anxiety during cognitive behavior therapy. *Journal of Consulting and Clinical Psychology.*

Podell, J. L., & Kendall, P. C. (2011). Mothers and fathers in family cognitive-behavioral therapy for anxious youth. *Journal of Child and Family Studies*, *20*, 182–195. doi: http://dx.doi.org/10.1007/s10826-010-9420-5

Podell, J. L., Kendall, P. C., Gosch, E. A., Compton, S. N., March, J. S., Albano, A. M., . . . & Piacentini, J. C. (2013). Therapist factors and outcomes in CBT for anxiety in youth. *Professional Psychology: Research and Practice*, *44*, 89.

Prins, P. J. M., & Ollendick, T. H. (2003). Cognitive change and enhanced coping: Missing mediational links in cognitive behavior therapy with anxiety-disordered child. *Clinical Child and Family Psychology Review*, *6*, 87–105.

Puleo, C. M., & Kendall, P. C. (2011) Anxiety disorders in typically developing youth: Autism spectrum symptoms as a predictor of cognitive–behavioral treatment. *Journal of Autism and Developmental Disorders*, *41*, 275–286.

Rapee, R. M. (2012). Family factors in the development and management of anxiety disorders. *Clinical Child and Family Psychological Review*, *15*, 69–80. doi: 10.1007/s10567-011-0106-3

Rapee, R. M. (2003). The influence of comorbidity on treatment outcome for children and adolescents with anxiety disorders. *Behaviour Research and Therapy*, *41*, 105–112.

Schniering, C. A., & Rapee, R. M. (2004). The relationship between automatic thoughts and negative emotions in children and adolescents: A test of the cognitive content-specificity hypothesis. *Journal of Abnormal Psychology*, *113*, 464–470. doi: 1 0.1037/0021-843X.113.3.464

Settipani, C., & Kendall, P. (2013). Social functioning in youth with anxiety disorders: Association with anxiety severity and outcomes from cognitive-behavioral therapy. *Child Psychiatry and Human Development*, *44*, 1–18.

Schraufnagel, T. J., Wagner, A. W., Miranda, J., & Roy-Byrne, P. P. (2006). Treating minority patients with depression and anxiety: What does the evidence tell us?. *General Hospital Psychiatry*, *28*(1), 27–36.

Shirk, S. R., Karver, M. S., & Brown, R. (2011). The alliance in child and adolescent psychotherapy. *Psychotherapy*, *48*, 17–24. doi: 10.1037/a0022181

Silverman, W. K., Kurtines, W. M., Ginsburg, G. S., Weems, C. F., Lumpkin, P. W., & Carmichael, D. H. (1999). Treating anxiety disorders in children with group cognitive behavioral therapy: A randomized clinical trial. *Journal of Consulting and Clinical Psychology*, *67*, 995–1003.

Silverman, W. K., Kurtines, W. M., Jaccard, J., & Pina, A. A. (2009). Directionality of change in youth anxiety treatment involving parents: An initial examination. *Journal of Consulting and Clinical Psychology*, *77*(3), 474–485. doi: 10.1037/a0015761

Sood, E. D., & Kendall, P. C. (2007). Assessing anxious self-talk in youth: The Negative Affectivity Self-Statement Questionnaire-Anxiety Scale. *Cognitive Therapy and Research, 31*, 603–618. doi: 10.1007/s10608-006-90043-8

Spence, S. H. (1998). A measure of anxiety symptoms among children. *Behaviour Research and Therapy, 36*(5), 545–566. doi: 10.1016/S0005-7967(98)00034-5

Spielmans, G. I., Pasek, L. F., & McFall, J. P. (2006). What are the active ingredients in cognitive and behavioral psychotherapy for anxious and depressed children? A meta-analytic review. *Clinical Psychology Review, 27*, 642–654. doi: 0.1016/j.cpr.2006.06.001

Szabó, M., & Lovibond, P. F. (2004). The cognitive content of thought-listed worry episodes in clinic-referred anxious and nonreferred children. *Journal of Clinical Child and Adolescent Psychology, 33*, 613–622. doi: 10.1207/s15374424jccp3303_18

Tiwari, S., Kendall, P. C., Hoff, A. L., Harrison, J. P., & Fizur, P. (2013). Characteristics of exposure sessions as predictors of treatment response in anxious youth. *Journal of Clinical Child & Adolescent Psychology, 42*, 34–43, doi: 10.1080/15374416.2012.738454

Treadwell, K. H., Flannery-Schroeder, E. C., & Kendall, P. C. (1995). Ethnicity and gender in relation to adaptive functioning, diagnostic status, and treatment outcome in children from an anxiety clinic. *Journal of Anxiety Disorders, 9*, 373–384. doi: 10.1016/0887-6185(95)00018-J

Treadwell, K. H., & Kendall, P. C. (1996). Self-talk in youth with anxiety disorders: States of mind, content specificity, and treatment outcome. *Journal of Consulting and Clinical Psychology, 64*, 941–950.

Victor, A. M., Bernat, D. H., Bernstein, G. A., & Layne, A. E. (2007). Effects of parent and family characteristics on treatment outcome of anxious children. *Journal of Anxiety Disorders, 21*, 835–848. doi: 10.1016/j.janxdis.2006.11.005

Walkup, J. T., Albano, A., Piacentini, J., Birmaher, B., Compton, S. N., Sherrill, J. T., . . . Kendall, P. C. (2008). Cognitive behavioral therapy, sertraline, or a combination in childhood anxiety. *The New England Journal of Medicine, 359*, 2753–2766.

Wei, C., & Kendall, P. C. (2014). Parental involvement: Contribution to childhood anxiety and its treatment. *Clinical Child and Family Psychology Review, 17*(4), 319–339.

Wood, J. J., Piacentini, J. C., Southam-Gerow, M., Chu, B. C., & Sigman, M. (2006). Family cognitive behavioral therapy for child anxiety disorders. *Journal of the American Academy of Child & Adolescent Psychiatry, 45*(3), 314–321. doi: 10.1097/01.chi.0000196425.88341.b0

3

Moderators and Mediators of Treatments for Youth With Traumatic Stress

JOANNE E. TAYLOR, REBECCA A. GRAHAM,
AND CARL F. WEEMS ■

INTRODUCTION

In their seminal review of treatments for sexually abused children, Finkelhor and Berliner (1995) consider sexual abuse to be "a special treatment and evaluation challenge" (p. 1415) because it is an experience, not a disorder, which can lead to a variety of psychological manifestations. In many respects, these comments apply not only to sexual abuse, but also to other types of trauma experienced by youth. There are several aspects of trauma and the trauma experience that present special challenges not only to treatment outcome evaluation, but also to identifying the circumstances under which (and the mechanisms through which) a treatment might achieve its effects. This chapter aims to provide an appreciation of these challenges, alongside the research to date in understanding treatment moderators and mediators for youth who have experienced trauma.

DESCRIPTION OF THE PROBLEM

Prevalence

Research suggests that traumatic events are prevalent in youth, with some estimates indicating that more than 25% of children and young people in the United States are exposed to a traumatic event by the age of 16 (Costello, Erkanli, Fairbank, & Angold, 2002). Other community surveys have reported exposure to major stressful events such as abuse or natural disaster to be around 47%–72% of youth aged 11–19 (Bal, Crombez, Van Oost, & De Boudeaudhuji, 2003; Bal, Van Oost, De Boudeaudhuji, & Crombez, 2003). Adolescents are particularly vulnerable to experiencing traumatic events, as their negotiation of developmental tasks such as increasing independence and autonomy can expose them to a range of situations that have trauma potential, such as sexual assault, peer-related violence, and other high-risk situations (Wolfe, Rawana, & Chiodo, 2006). Some of the most commonly investigated events include natural disasters, sexual abuse, physical abuse/maltreatment, exposure to violence, war, bombing, kidnapping, traffic accidents, and loss (e.g., death of a loved one). Youth may also be in situations where they are secondary victims of or witnesses to trauma, such as witnessing domestic violence or seeing someone killed through community or school violence.

Definitions

The events described above are often referred to as *traumatic*, although the term *trauma* is also used to describe psychological reactions to the event. This is an important distinction in light of Finkelhor and Berliner's (1995) admonition that traumatic events are experiences, not disorders or syndromes. This distinction has major implications for understanding treatment outcomes for several reasons. First, while a range of psychological reactions are common in youth, not all young people develop serious psychological problems following trauma (e.g., Bonnano, Brewin, Kaniasty, & La Greca, 2010; Kendall-Tackett, Williams, & Finkelhor, 1993). Some demonstrate relatively positive adjustment and proficient functioning despite their experiences (including the experience of post-traumatic growth; see Calhoun & Tedeschi, 2006; Prati & Pietrantoni, 2009), although this may not persist for the long term and may be limited to certain areas of functioning (Haskett, Nears, Sabourin Ward, & McPherson, 2006).

Second, the psychological effects of trauma in youth are diverse and vast (Cohen, Berliner, & Mannarino, 2000; Martin, Campbell, & Hansen, 2010; Silverman et al., 2008). Treatment outcome research has tended to focus on targeting specific symptoms, but this approach ignores the complexity of the trauma reaction, which is influenced by factors such as developmental processes, comorbidity, and trauma history (Cohen et al., 2000). There are important differences in terms of whether the trauma is a single event or a more chronic, repeated set of events. Poly-victimization has been increasingly recognized as a key consideration in ongoing research, given that maltreated children often experience several types of maltreatment, simultaneously, across time, or both (Finkelhor, Ormrod, & Turner, 2007; Herrenkohl & Herrenkohl, 2009; Leeson & Nixon, 2010; Saunders, 2012). Finally, the effects of traumatic events can change across development and the life cycle (Ehlert, 2013; Woolley, Dickson, Evans, Harvey, & Taylor, 2008). For example, acute or chronic exposure to abuse "disrupts normal developmental progress in an unpredictable fashion" (Wolfe et al., 2006, p. 643). The effects of abuse and other traumas can be delayed and can change over time.

All of these factors impact attempts to research treatment outcomes for trauma because trauma is an inherently complex phenomenon, and individuals respond to traumatic events very differently. Research suggests that exposure to traumatic experiences can trigger a number of negative outcomes in children and adolescents, including diagnosable and sub-threshold depression, anxiety, and fear, childhood traumatic grief, aggressive behavior, and other externalizing and internalizing behavior problems (Carrión, Weems, Ray, & Reiss, 2002; Carrión, Weems, & Reiss, 2007; Scheeringa, Zeanah, Myers, & Putnam, 2003). Some treatment outcome research aims to address the trauma experience as a whole (e.g., abuse or neglect), whereas other research treats specific effects of the experience, most often post-traumatic stress disorder (PTSD), which is the major focus of this chapter.

The extant research has tended to define PTSD using the diagnostic criteria from the *Diagnostic and Statistical Manual of Mental Disorders* (currently in its 5th edition [*DSM-5*]; American Psychiatric Association, 2013), which specifies symptoms of re-experiencing, avoidance, and hyperarousal following a traumatic event. The fourth text-revised edition of the *DSM* (*DSM-IV-TR*; American Psychiatric Association, 2000) defined a traumatic event as an experience that involves threatened death or severe injury to an individual, or witnessing an individual experience threatened death or severe injury, and further specified that an individual must respond to that event with intense fear, helplessness, or horror. The recent revision in the *DSM-5* relocates PTSD in a new chapter on trauma- and stressor-related disorders, and trauma is now defined as exposure to actual or threatened death, serious injury, or sexual violence in one (or more) of the following ways: (1) directly experiencing the traumatic event(s); (2) witnessing, in person, the event(s) as it occurred to others; (3) learning that the traumatic event(s) occurred to a close family member or close friend, and in the case of actual or threatened death of a family member or friend, the event(s) must have been violent or accidental; (4) experiencing repeated or extreme exposure to aversive details of the traumatic event(s) (e.g., first responders collecting human remains; police officers repeatedly exposed to details of child abuse) (APA, 2013). These changes reflect a desire to move away from subjective intensity toward objective criteria in defining trauma; however, research is needed to further develop and create an empirical taxonomy of traumatic stressors (see Taylor & Weems, 2009).

Post-traumatic stress reactions and PTSD have been associated with a wide range of traumatic events, including sexual or physical abuse (Ackerman, Newton, McPherson, Jones, & Dykman, 1998; Cohen, Berliner, & Mannarino, 2003; Davis & Siegel, 2000; Shaw, 2000), natural disasters (e.g., hurricanes or earthquakes; Goenjian et al., 2005; La Greca, Silverman, Vernberg, & Prinstein, 1996; Lonigan, Shannon, Taylor, Finch, & Sallee, 1994), exposure to violence (either in the context of neighborhood violence or youth surviving war; Ajudukovic, 1998; Berton & Stabb, 1996; Seedat, Njeng, Vythilingum, & Stein,

2004; Stein et al., 2003), motor vehicle accidents (Keppel-Benson, Ollendick, & Benson, 2002; McDermott & Cvitanovich, 2000), separation (e.g., parental incarceration), loss (e.g., death of a loved one; Taylor, Weems, Costa, & Carrión, 2009), physical neglect (e.g., denying the child shelter or proper medical care), physical trauma (e.g., being burned, breaking a limb, sprains), and emotional abuse (e.g., belittling the child or denying affection; Blakeney, Robert, & Meyer, 1998; Richmond, Thompson, Deatrick, & Kauder, 2000; Rodriguez-Srednicki & Twaite, 2004a, 2004b).

The treatment research studies on traumatic stressors have tended to select participants on the basis of exposure to one or more of the above-mentioned events who also have elevated symptoms of post-traumatic stress or meet full diagnostic criteria for PTSD. While this approach has advanced our understanding of treatment responses for particular types of trauma, it has also meant that the research has often not been able to capture the nuances and complexities identified above. For example, there is a tendency to examine outcomes for sexual abuse separately from other types of abuse and maltreatment, which ignores the fact that different types of maltreatment tend to co-occur (although some treatments have good outcomes across a variety of different trauma types; Chaffin, 2006; Cohen, Mannarino, Murray, & Igelman, 2006). Furthermore, participants in such studies are often selected to ensure that the sample reflects a "pure" trauma experience, yet we know that victims of abuse can experience sexual, physical, and emotional abuse simultaneously (Finkelhor et al., 2007; Goodyear-Brown, Fath, & Myers, 2012), and that there is a high level of comorbidity in the effects of trauma, wherein serious psychological problems often do not occur in isolation (Cohen et al., 2000; Goodyear-Brown et al., 2012; Stallard, 2006). These issues raise questions about the external validity of attempts to understand what affects treatment outcome, which we will keep in mind as we discuss the current state of the treatment outcome research.

DESCRIPTION OF TREATMENT OUTCOME LITERATURE FOR PTSD IN YOUTH

Intervention modalities for treating PTSD in youth include trauma-focused cognitive behavioral therapy (TF-CBT), eye movement desensitization and reprocessing (EMDR), pharmacological interventions, and several specific psychosocial interventions (see, e.g., Carrión, Kletter, Weems, Berry, & Rettger, 2013; Scheeringa & Weems, 2014; Scheeringa, Weems, Cohen, Amaya-Jackson, & Guthrie, 2011; Taylor & Weems, 2011; Weems et al., 2009). TF-CBT is a well-established treatment and is the most common treatment for childhood PTSD (Kowalik, Weller, Venter, & Drachman, 2011; Silverman et al., 2008). The criteria for a well-established treatment include at least two studies using experimental between-group design that are conducted by different researchers/groups and demonstrate the superiority of the manualized treatment to a placebo or existing treatment, or its equivalence in outcome to another established empirically supported treatment (Chambless & Ollendick, 2001). TF-CBT was originally developed for sexually abused children but has since been adapted for children exposed to different types of trauma (Cohen et al., 2006). There are multiple TF-CBT treatments that have been shown to be efficacious in treating youth in the extant literature (i.e., Cohen, Deblinger, Mannarino, & Steer, 2004; Cohen, Mannarino, Berliner, & Deblinger, 2000; Deblinger, Lippman, & Steer, 1996; Jaberghaderi, Greenwald, Rubin, Zand, & Dolatabadi, 2004; King et al., 2000).

A recent randomized trial comparing the efficacy of TF-CBT with trauma-focused cognitive therapy (without exposure; CT) in 33 children and youth aged 7–17 who had experienced a single-incident trauma such as a motor vehicle accident, assault, or house fire (Nixon, Sterk, & Pearce, 2012) is illustrative of TF-CBT. Nixon et al. (2012) found that at post-treatment, 65% of participants who received TF-CBT and 56% of those who received CT no longer met criteria for PTSD, and gains were maintained at a 6-month follow-up. In this study, a detailed treatment manual was developed from previous cognitive behavioral therapy (CBT) resources (i.e., Deblinger & Heflin, 1996; Rapee, Wignall, Hudson, & Schniering, 2000; Stallard, 2002) in which initial treatment sessions focused on psychoeducation, relaxation training, and learning other strategies useful for anxiety management. Subsequent sessions involved identification of cognitive errors and learning how to restructure one's thoughts (e.g., challenging irrational cognitions). The latter sessions focused on exposure therapy, both imaginal and in vivo. The final session focused on relapse prevention techniques and rewarding the children with a completion certificate for their progress. The intervention also included a parenting component, which focused on teaching parents how to implement anxiety management techniques with their children and included behavioral training if needed.

TF-CBT is consistently found to be superior to other approaches in treating PTSD following maltreatment, including sexual and physical abuse (www.musc.edu/tfcbt). This abuse-specific approach targets trauma-related symptoms and includes a non-offending parenting component to increase parental support of the child and reduce the parent's own emotional distress related to the trauma (Cohen et al., 2006; Fitzgerald & Cohen, 2012).

TF-CBT has also been evaluated against other active treatments in several randomized control trials (RCTs) with children and youth with a range of sexual abuse experiences and has been found to produce superior outcomes for PTSD, as well as other symptoms such as depression, social functioning, dissociation, sexual problems, externalizing behavior problems, and parenting skills, up to 2 years following treatment (Cohen et al., 2004; Cohen & Mannarino, 1998; Cohen, Mannarino, & Knudsen, 2005; Deblinger et al., 1996; King et al., 2000). TF-CBT has also been effective in treating physically abused children (Kolko, 1996). In either individual or group format, TF-CBT is considered the treatment of choice for maltreatment victims aged 3–15 (Becker & Kirsch, 2008; Chaffin & Friedrich, 2004; Corcoran, 2004; Saunders, 2012) and has been identified in several guideline and best-practice documents as the most efficacious and well-supported treatment for child physical and sexual abuse (Chadwick Center for Children and Families, 2004; National Institute for Clinical Excellence, 2005; Saunders, Berliner, & Hanson, 2004; Silverman et al., 2008).

TF-CBT is also supported in several meta-analytic reviews regarding abuse and maltreatment in children and youth (Macdonald, Higgins, & Ramchandani, 2006; Silverman et al., 2008; Trask, Walsh, & DiLillo, 2011). The trauma narrative component of TF-CBT has recently been found to be particularly important in reducing abuse-related fear and improving parental abuse-specific distress, while TF-CBT without this component produced the most improvement in parenting practices and externalizing child behavior problems (and results were different for PTSD outcomes, as noted below; Deblinger, Mannarino, Cohen, Runyon, & Steer, 2011). It may be that these differential results are at least partly due to the fact that the absence of one component meant that more time could be spent on the remaining therapy components for which the various outcomes were found. For example, omitting the trauma narrative component meant that parents and therapists dedicated more time to the parent training component of the therapy, which could result in better self-reported parenting practices and child's externalizing behavior (Deblinger et al., 2011). In contrast, including a trauma narrative component meant that parents spent more time involved in this process than working on parenting skills, hence the differential improvements on abuse-related outcomes.

School-based group cognitive behavioral therapy is a probably efficacious treatment for youth with PTSD (Kataoka et al., 2003; Stein et al., 2003), which means that (a) at least two experiments demonstrate superior outcomes compared to untreated control groups, (b) two studies completed by the same researchers meet the criteria for a well-established treatment, or (c) a small series of single-case design experiments meet well-established-treatment criteria (see Table 1 in Chambless & Ollendick, 2001, p. 689). Stein et al. (2003) evaluated Group Cognitive-Behavioral Intervention for Trauma in Schools (CBITS) in 126 sixth-grade children exposed to community violence who were experiencing trauma reactions. CBITS consisted of 10 weekly group sessions, which focused on psychoeducation, graded exposure, cognitive and coping skills training (e.g., thought stopping), and social skills training. In comparison to the wait-list group, children in the CBITS group showed significant reductions in self-ratings of PTSD symptoms and depressive symptoms and in parents' ratings of their child's psychosocial dysfunction, which were maintained at 6-month follow-up.

Cognitive behavioral therapy for PTSD is a possibly efficacious treatment for youth with PTSD (Silverman et al., 2008), which means that there is at least one study demonstrating the efficacy of the treatment compared to an alternative treatment or no-treatment control group, as well as the absence of conflicting evidence (Chambless & Ollendick, 2001). A randomized controlled trial of CBT by Smith et al. (2007) studied the efficacy of CBT with 24 youth aged 8–18 who experienced a single-incident trauma such as a motor vehicle accident, interpersonal violence, or witnessing violence. This treatment model was based on the PTSD model of Ehlers and Clark (2000) with adaptations for youth (Yule, Smith, & Perrin, 2005). Unique components of this treatment (CBT versus TF-CBT) included the close integration of cognitive restructuring with reliving (e.g., revisiting the site of the trauma, writing and drawing techniques regarding reliving of the trauma) and the use of stimulus discrimination techniques (i.e., with respect to traumatic reminders). Additionally, parents were seen after the individual session with their child, as well as in joint parent-child sessions if necessary.

Another possibly efficacious treatment for PTSD in youth is eye movement desensitization and reprocessing (EMDR; Adrúiz, Bluthgen, & Knopfler, 2011; Chemtob, Nakashima, & Carlson, 2002; Jaberghaderi et al., 2004). First introduced in 1989 (Shapiro, 1989, 1995, 2001), EMDR is an eight-phase treatment for reprocessing traumatic memories, focused on the belief that intense emotions characteristic of a traumatic event can prevent the brain from accurately processing these memories, which then become dysfunctionally stored and lead to the development of psychopathology (e.g., flashbacks and other traumatic responses to non-traumatic stimuli; reviewed in Adrúiz et al., 2011). A study by Chemtob et al. (2002) compared EMDR to a wait-list condition in 32 Pacific Island children (aged 6–12 years) exposed to Hurricane Iniki. The four sessions/weeks of EMDR consisted of imaginal exposures, which occurred while the child tracked therapist hand movements with their eyes. There were significant improvements in PTSD symptoms as well as depressive and anxious symptomology in the EMDR group (targeting PTSD and fear via graduated imaginal exposures). Jaberghaderi et al. (2004) provided further support for the use of EMDR when comparing CBT and EMDR in sexually abused Iranian girls aged 12–13, although there were only seven girls in each group. EMDR was more efficient than CBT for this small group, and youth in the EMDR group reached termination criteria sooner than those in the CBT group. However, statistical power was limited because of the small sample size, and thus these results should be interpreted cautiously.

Other possibly efficacious treatments include but are not limited to resilient peer treatment (Fantuzzo et al., 1996), cognitive processing therapy (Ahrens & Rexford, 2002), family therapy (Kolko, 1996), and child-parent psychotherapy (Lieberman, Van Horn, & Ippen, 2005). Experimental psychosocial treatments include support group therapy (Deblinger, Stauffer, & Steer, 2001), psychological debriefing (Stallard et al., 2006), standard group therapy (Berliner & Saunders, 1996), and individual or group plus career support (Trowell et al., 2002; see Silverman et al., 2008, for a more thorough review of evidence for PTSD treatment efficacy).

Given the relatively large amount of support for TF-CBT and CBT intervention techniques and clear possible mechanisms of effect in relation to other techniques (e.g., EMDR), the rest of this chapter focuses primarily on moderators and mediators of CBT-informed intervention outcomes.

THEORETICAL MODELS AND EMPIRICAL RESULTS OF MODERATION STUDIES FOR TREATMENT OUTCOMES FOR YOUTH EXPOSED TO TRAUMATIC STRESS

Overview

Examination of moderation and mediation in treatment for traumatic stress and PTSD in youth is in its infancy. Much of the work to date is exploratory, as opposed to research on mediators of symptom formation (e.g., see Haskett et al., 2006; Trickey, Siddaway, Meiser-Stedman, Serpell, & Field, 2012). There is generally a greater focus on moderation than mediation, but no theoretical models for moderation or mediation exist, despite calls for a directed regression approach where decisions about which variables to regress onto which other variables are guided by a theoretical or conceptual model (e.g., Jaccard, Guilamo-Ramos, Johansson, & Bouris, 2006).

Possible reasons for this are likely related to the issues of complexity discussed above, including heterogeneity in the effects of abuse. Given this inherent complexity, it is also likely that moderation and mediation studies need to be conceptually and statistically complex in terms of accounting for multiple mediators, longitudinal mediation, moderated mediation, and mediated moderation (MacKinnon, Fairchild, & Fritz, 2007). For example, mediators may vary as a function of moderators where the mediator differs for subgroups of participants, across variables such as age, gender, or type of maltreatment. Furthermore, the effects of moderation can also be mediated, such as the case where a treatment effect is greater for high-risk youth, and the interaction between risk-taking and exposure to the treatment then affects a mediating variable such as type of maltreatment or changes in cognitions (MacKinnon et al., 2007). Given the lack of extant theoretical models, Figure 3.1 depicts a relatively simple schematic model of moderators and mediators focusing on the CBT conceptualization of treatment for PTSD.

Theoretical Model of Moderators

In Panel A, the relatively simple process of change in PTSD symptoms is depicted wherein putative moderators influence the extent of change from pre-treatment to post-treatment or to a follow-up point. A few of the potential moderators reviewed below (e.g., maternal depression) are listed in Panel A as examples of the factors that may influence change. In this model, there is theoretically a moderator-by-time interaction such that change is less for one level of the moderator. Most of the empirical studies reviewed below use this simple model to examine moderation. For example, there might be less change in levels of PTSD from pre- to post-treatment for those children whose parents have high levels of depression (Weems & Scheeringa, 2013). However, it is important to note that moderation may also be evident in a treatment condition/treatment type-by-time

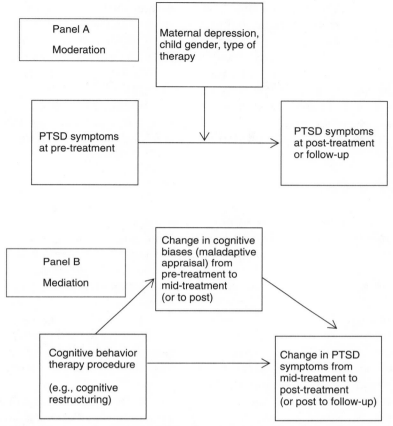

Figure 3.1. Schematic theoretical models of moderation and mediation for youth PTSD treatment outcomes.

interaction, such as CBT producing larger effect sizes than a non-CBT condition. The meta-analyses reviewed below take this approach to identifying moderators. Finally, there may also be treatment condition/treatment type-by-putative moderator-by-time interactions such that a certain treatment modality may work better (produce larger effects) for different conditions of a moderator. For example, CBT with extended exposure sessions may work better for youth with severe or recalcitrant PTSD symptoms, with CBT and no exposure working just as well for those with less severe symptoms. To date, however, these types of studies have not been conducted.

The type of intervention techniques used, parental characteristics, and child characteristics have a theoretical basis for potentially moderating the effects of change in symptoms. For example, the Silverman et al. (2008) review highlights the importance of examining the role of parental characteristics in differential outcomes (see also Cohen & Mannarino, 1996, 2000). Moreover, the extant anxiety disorders treatment research suggests that maternal depression may impede treatment and/or treatment maintenance in child internalizing interventions (Berman, Weems, Silverman, & Kurtines, 2000; Southam-Gerow, Kendall, & Weersing, 2001). Theoretically, depressed mothers may have difficulty maintaining treatment gains. Scheeringa and Zeanah (2001) have proposed theoretical models of the parent-child relationship to guide future research. In their moderating effect model, the caregivers' relationships with their children affect the strength of the relations between the traumatic events and the children's symptomatic responses. Maternal depression may therefore affect this relationship and create a context of prolonged treatment-resistant PTSD in offspring.

Empirical Results on Moderators

Most of the research investigating possible moderators of treatment for trauma-exposed youth has been done in the context of meta-analyses. However, all but three of these meta-analyses have not investigated moderators for PTSD outcome measures specifically, but have instead reported moderators for broader outcomes, including behavior problems (e.g., acting out, externalizing symptoms), sexualized behavior, anxiety and stress, depression, psychological distress, social functioning, self-concept, and "other" problems (Hetzel-Riggin, Brausch, & Montgomery, 2007; Sánchez-Meca, Alcázar, & López-Soler, 2011; Skowron & Reinemann, 2005; Trask et al., 2011). Sánchez-Meca et al. (2011) did include PTSD outcomes but grouped them in an "other outcomes" category along with affective disorders and loneliness symptoms.

Harvey and Taylor (2010a), Corcoran and Pillai (2008), and Silverman et al. (2008) have examined treatment moderators in relation to PTSD outcomes, the former two in terms of sexual abuse only and the latter regarding traumatic events in general. Silverman et al.'s (2008) meta-analysis revealed several moderating influences on effect sizes for post-traumatic stress symptoms, in terms of type of treatment and type of trauma. CBT produced a much higher effect size ($d = .50$) than non-CBT conditions ($d = .19$). The average effect size was higher for sexual abuse treatments ($d = .46$) than treatments for other types of trauma ($d = .38$). Parent involvement in treatment compared with control conditions (wait-list and active controls combined) had little moderating influence on post-traumatic stress outcomes (but did moderate other outcomes such as anxiety and depression). Effects for child-only and child-plus-parent treatments were .44 and .42, respectively. These effects changed slightly when the comparison was active controls only (.54 and .46, respectively; Silverman et al., 2008).

Harvey and Taylor's (2010a, 2010b) meta-analysis focused exclusively on treatments for sexually abused children and adolescents. Again, CBT approaches produced the largest PTSD/trauma treatment effect ($g = 1.37$) compared with eclectic ($g = .40$) and other approaches ($g = .74$) (Hedges's g is a variation of Cohen's d that corrects for bias due to small sample sizes; Hedges & Olkin, 1985; Hedges, 1991). Family ($g = 2.11$) and individual ($g = 1.31$) treatments had better effects than group-based therapies ($g = .89$), and treatments that incorporated some family involvement produced better outcomes (g = 1.44) than those in which family was not involved (g = .67). This would suggest that some family or non-offending parental involvement in therapy is beneficial, at least in the context of sexual abuse trauma. Still, some studies have found no improved outcomes with parental involvement in CBT (e.g., King et al., 2000), although these findings are thought to be explained by small sample sizes and the focus on the child in therapy (King et al., 2003).

Others have reported minimal benefits of parent-involved treatment (Corcoran & Pillai, 2008). Other moderators in Harvey and Taylor's (2010a, 2010b) meta-analysis included study design, source of information, and therapy structure. Larger effect sizes were associated with experimental design (g = 1.41; compared with quasi-experimental, g = .81), manualized therapy (g = 1.41; compared with semi-structured, g = .65, and unstructured, g = .64), and child or youth self-report (g = 1.25; versus parent-report, g = .64). Trends emerged for better outcomes with shorter length of sexual abuse, a greater number of sessions, and shorter session length, but there was insufficient data to consider these to be robust (although a subsequent outcome study has found better outcomes for avoidance and re-experiencing symptoms with longer length of treatment; Deblinger, Mannarino, Cohen, Runyon, & Steer, 2011). However, the meta-analysis as a whole indicated that therapy has different effects, depending on the outcome being measured, and that few studies provide sufficient information about participant and abuse characteristics to permit examination of these as possible moderating variables (Harvey & Taylor, 2010a). Since then, Deblinger et al. (2011) have reported that a trauma focus in therapy may not necessarily require a written narrative for improvement in PTSD symptoms.

A few studies on child physical abuse and neglect have investigated possible moderators of treatment outcome, although none is specific to PTSD symptoms. Severity of physical neglect did not moderate the effects of a mentoring and skills group intervention for preadolescent youth in foster care (Taussig, Culhane, Garrido, Knudtson, & Petrenko, 2012). Chaffin et al. (2009) found that a motivational intervention improved retention in parent-child interaction therapy (PCIT) for parents who had a low to moderate baseline level of motivation.

As noted, few empirical studies have investigated moderators of treatment outcomes for youth with PTSD. Research thus far has examined gender (Quota, Palosaari, Diab, & Punamai, 2012; Tol et al., 2010), social support (Tol et al., 2010), peri-traumatic dissociation (Quota et al., 2012), maternal depressive symptoms (Nixon et al., 2012; Weems & Scheeringa, 2013), unhelpful traumatic beliefs (Nixon et al., 2012), and maternal PTSD symptoms (Nixon et al., 2012; Weems & Scheeringa, 2013) as potential moderators of treatment success.

Tol and colleagues (Tol et al., 2010) conducted a school-based psychosocial randomized treatment intervention for 403 children (n = 221 control wait list; n = 182 treatment; aged 8–13 years) affected by political violence in Indonesia. Children participated in 15 treatment sessions combining CBT with creative-expressive techniques in a structured classroom format. The treatment intervention was based on the ecological resilience theoretical framework

(Tol, Jordans, Reis, & De Jong, 2009), which posits that negative, maladaptive psychological symptoms may be decreased through the introduction of protective factors in children and their social-ecological environment (e.g., family, peer, neighborhood variables, such as hope and social support). Tol et al. (2010) aimed to improve coping strategies and strengthen peer-level social support in the participating children through cooperative play (i.e., working together to overcome a challenge). Congruent with their hypothesis that treatment would decrease the children's symptoms via augmentation of the protective resources in their environment, results showed that children receiving social support from adults outside the household showed larger treatment benefits on functional impairment. Girls in general showed larger treatment benefits in PTSD symptoms, as did children in smaller households. Thus, gender, size of the household, and level of social support all moderated the treatment effects. The authors concluded that less family connectedness (i.e., bigger families) as well as being female made children in this sample more vulnerable to developing PTSD symptoms and thus more likely to show improvement with treatment. Social support served as a moderator such that children with higher levels of social support from adults outside the household showed larger treatment benefits.

Quota et al. (2012) tested the moderating role of risk and protective factors on intervention effectiveness in 442 youth aged 10–13 with PTSD due to war conditions. These Palestinian children were recruited from schools in areas exposed to the 2008–2009 war in Gaza. Randomly selected youth were assigned to a wait-list control group or participated in a psychosocial intervention (based on Teaching Recovery Techniques Intervention, TRT; Smith, Dyregrov, & Yule, 2000), which has been found to effectively reduce post-traumatic stress and depressive symptoms in children traumatized by war (Ehntholt, Smith, & Yule, 2005) and natural disasters (Giannopoulo, Dikaiakou, & Yule, 2006). TRT is similar to TF-CBT methods, incorporating psychoeducation, coping skills training, and creative expressive elements of treatment. Groups of 15 children each received the intervention during school hours for approximately 4 weeks. Quota et al. (2012) found overall modest effectiveness of the intervention in reducing mental health symptoms and found that gender moderated treatment outcomes such that the intervention reduced clinically significant levels of post-traumatic stress symptoms in boys but not girls. This finding both supports (Wolmer, Hamiel, Barchas, Slone, & Laor, 2011; effectiveness only in boys) and contrasts (Bolton et al., 2007; effectiveness only in girls) previous research findings documenting gender-specific benefits from a psychosocial intervention after a war.

Quota et al. (2012) also found peri-traumatic dissociation, defined as "losing the sense of time and space and experiencing depersonalization, disorientation, and derealization at the time of the traumatic event" (p. 289) moderated treatment effectiveness such that girls with lower levels of peri-traumatic dissociation showed greater reductions in clinically significant post-traumatic stress symptoms post-treatment. Peri-traumatic dissociation has been found to be a risk factor for the development of PTSD in children (Schäfer, Barkmann, Riedesser, & Schulte-Markwort, 2006) and has been found to interfere with successful therapy outcomes in adults with anxiety disorders (Michelson, June, Vives, Testa, & Marchione, 1998).

In a study described above, Nixon and colleagues (Nixon et al., 2012) found that pre-treatment levels of maternal depressive symptoms and unhelpful traumatic beliefs moderated children's PTSD treatment outcomes. Pre-treatment levels of maternal post-traumatic stress did not show the same effect. Similarly, Weems and Scheeringa (2013) also found that maternal depression moderated child PTSD symptom change; however, differences in outcome were observed only at follow-up, not at post-treatment assessment (i.e., children of mothers with high depression had similar pre- to post-treatment improvement as mothers with low depression, but were more likely to show increases [relapse] at follow-up). Findings indicated that maternal PTSD symptoms did not moderate child PTSD symptom change in a sample of 25 preschool children (aged 3–6 years). Nixon et al. (2012) speculated that mothers' depression might limit their levels of engagement and support in their child's therapy. For example, because of their negative or restricted affect, depressed mothers may not encourage their children to practice their coping skills outside therapy, therefore decreasing the likelihood that the techniques learned during therapy sessions are generalized into the child's everyday life. To date, maternal depression has emerged as a potentially important moderator of treatment outcomes for youth exposed to traumatic stress.

THEORETICAL MODELS AND EMPIRICAL RESULTS OF MEDIATION STUDIES FOR TREATMENT OUTCOMES FOR YOUTH EXPOSED TO TRAUMATIC STRESS

Theoretical Model of Mediators

Panel B in Figure 3.1 presents a schematic of mediators of outcome for CBT for youth with PTSD. Here the putative mediator is influenced or changed by a certain technique, and this change in the putative mediator is responsible for the change in PTSD symptoms (or related outcome) effected by the technique. In CBT interventions, there are theoretically a large number of broad classes of potential mediators (including cognitive factors, behavioral factors, physiological factors, and social contextual factors). Changes in cognitions, cognitive processing, or cognitive biases are salient examples. For example, a certain CBT technique, such as identifying and challenging irrational or negative cognitions, may effect changes in negative cognitive errors, and these changes in negative cognitive errors might mediate the effect that the technique of identifying and challenging cognitions has on the change seen in PTSD symptoms across treatment. Similarly, exposure techniques, changes in behavior (e.g., facing feared stimuli), or techniques used to control arousal (e.g., relaxation training) may effect change in one or more intermediary variables, such as physiological arousal in the context of a trauma cue, and the changes in the intermediary variable may be responsible for the change seen on the outcome variable. As reviewed below, there is very little empirical data on the mechanisms (mediators) that effect change in outcomes for youth exposed to trauma; thus it is important to realize that, because of the lack of mediation research, we do not exactly know whether these theories are true. For example, it is also possible that exposure mediates changes in negative cognitions, which leads to positive changes in PTSD outcome variables.

Empirical Results

Relatively few studies have explored potential mediators of PTSD-related therapy outcomes for maltreated youth. Cohen and Mannarino (2000) tested the impact of children's abuse-related attributions and perceptions, family cohesion and adaptability, parental support of the child, and parental emotional reaction to the child's abuse as potential mediators of treatment outcome for 49 children aged 7–14 years in abuse-focused CBT or non-directive supportive therapy (the two treatment groups were combined for these analyses). Abuse-related attributions and perceptions, as well as family adaptability, significantly mediated PTSD outcomes (although only accounted for 21% of the variance; Cohen & Mannarino, 2000). In other words, changes in abuse-specific issues contributed to PTSD symptoms, as did the extent of family flexibility in response to situational and developmental stress, although the latter may be more related to familial structure and predictability (Cohen & Mannarino, 2000). Children's attributions and perceptions had a consistent impact on other outcome measures as well, suggesting that therapy for sexually abused children and youth may be beneficial if it addresses these issues. Related to this, there have also been calls to examine the possible mediating role of addressing feelings of shame in treatment for not only sexual abuse but physical abuse as well (Deblinger & Runyon, 2005). Compared to their earlier findings with preschool children (Cohen & Mannarino, 1996, 1998), there was no impact of parental emotional reaction on treatment outcomes, suggesting that older children's symptoms are influenced less by their parents than younger children's psychological symptoms (Cohen & Mannarino, 2000).

Studies of PCIT to treat physical abuse, while not directly examining mediators of PTSD outcomes, have indicated that change occurs because of reduced negative parent-child interactions (Chaffin et al., 2004; Hakman, Chaffin, Funderburk, & Silovsky, 2009). For example, Chaffin et al.'s (2004) RCT with 110 physically abusive parents of children aged 4–12 years compared PCIT with PCIT plus individualized enhanced services and a standard community-based support group. At follow-up, 19% of parents in the PCIT group were re-reported for physical abuse, compared to 49% of parents in the community condition, and the beneficial effect of PCIT was partially mediated by a greater reduction in parental negative interactions in that group, as measured by behavioral observation methods (Chaffin et al., 2004).

In terms of other types of trauma, research exploring potential mediators of the treatment of youth with PTSD is also very scarce. Only two studies have examined potential mediators of PTSD treatment in youth. In the study previously mentioned by Tol et al. (2010), play social support was found to mediate treatment effects but in an unexpected direction. Results showed that more social support was associated with smaller reductions in PTSD symptoms. Additionally, none of the other variables tested in the study (i.e., hope, positive coping, peer social support) was found to be a significant mediator. However, the mediating variables were assessed at the same time point as the dependent variable, limiting conclusions about the temporal relationships between changes in social support and changes in PTSD symptoms.

Smith and colleagues (Smith et al., 2007) tested changes in maladaptive cognitions as a mediator between individual TF-CBT and PTSD symptoms in 24 youth aged 8–18 years who were exposed to single-incident traumatic events (e.g., motor vehicle accidents, interpersonal violence, witnessing violence). After 10 weekly individual sessions, 92% of participants no longer met criteria for PTSD, compared to 42% of the wait-list participants, and treatment effects were maintained at 6-month follow-up. Furthermore, the effects of CBT were partially mediated by changes in maladaptive appraisals about the trauma and its aftermath. However, misappraisals and changes in post-traumatic stress symptoms were measured simultaneously, again limiting the ability to make temporal conclusions. It is also unknown if changes in maladaptive cognitions would mediate symptoms in youth exposed to multiple traumatic experiences.

CHALLENGES AND RECOMMENDATIONS FOR FUTURE MEDIATOR/MODERATOR RESEARCH

Future research designed specifically to evaluate potential moderators and mediators of treatment outcome for youth with PTSD is vital. Dismantling treatment frameworks that have been shown to be efficacious in treating PTSD in youth would allow future researchers and clinicians to identify which symptoms of PTSD respond best to which aspects of treatment (Kowalik et al., 2011), improving the ability to tailor treatment to specific groups of children and youth. Furthermore, additional research should assess moderators and mediators of treatment effects at multiple time points, instead of concurrently with the dependent variable, to allow conclusions to be made about temporal relationships based on study findings (Kazdin, 2007). For example, Tol et al. (2010) found that play social support mediated treatment outcomes for youth with PTSD, but they were unable to conclude temporal precedence of the mediator because the mediator and dependent variable in the study were measured concurrently.

Future research should also seek to conduct multilevel longitudinal studies looking at moderators and mediators of treatment effects of PTSD in youth suffering from a single traumatic event, multiple traumatic events, or traumas experienced by a large number of youth (e.g., natural disasters). Thus, future research should reflect the broad range of traumatic experiences in terms of frequency and type of trauma in order to provide comparison between studies.

Finally, as emphasized by Tol et al. (2010), further research on protective factors as moderators of treatment outcome (e.g., resilience) would greatly assist in developing future interventions aimed to improve positive outcomes and reduce negative outcomes for youth. These suggestions are consistent with the US National Institute of Mental Health's (NIMH) strategic plan to develop a new generation of clinical trials designed to gather data that can be used for personalized decision-making in medicine and to focus funding on clinical research, while not only assessing group differences, but also clarifying individual patterns of intervention response (see http://www.nimh.nih.gov/about/strategic-planning-reports/index.shtml#strategic-objective3). The identification of moderators helps identify the individual characteristics of those who respond well or poorly to a given intervention, and the study of mediators helps to identify the essential processes involved in change. Such data on treatments for youth exposed to traumatic stress could thereby eventually serve to help personalize intervention recommendations for individuals.

IMPLICATIONS FOR CLINICAL PRACTICE

While the extant research has not advanced to recommend specific advice on tailoring interventions, identifying moderators and mediators of treatment outcomes for youth with PTSD holds promise for clinical practice. As reviewed by Silverman et al. (2008), establishing moderators and mediators of intervention outcomes will show what treatments work, for whom, and how. The transfer of this knowledge to clinicians worldwide will allow clinicians to provide the most efficient, tailored treatment for youth with PTSD to meet individuals' specific needs. Such an approach is, again, consistent with NIMH's strategic plan to develop personalized medicine in mental health (see http://www.nimh.nih.gov/about/strategic-planning-reports/index.shtml#strategic-objective3).

On the other hand, testing moderators and mediators may also help in identifying the critical or core ingredients in unified treatment approaches for emotional disorders (including trauma-exposed youth). For example, the realization that core features of anxious emotion may transcend specific anxiety problems has led researchers to conclude that there are basic key ingredients in treatment across anxiety problems (Barlow, 2004; Moses & Barlow, 2006). Given the diverse outcomes following exposure to traumatic stress, unified approaches may be just as important in clinical practice as tailored intervention manuals. Such possibilities await future research.

AUTHOR NOTE

The first author would like to sincerely thank Dr. Gillian Craven for her invaluable assistance in sourcing literature for this chapter.

REFERENCES

Ackerman, P. T., Newton, J. E. O., McPherson, W. B., Jones, J. G., & Dykman, R. A. (1998). Prevalence of post-traumatic stress disorder and other psychiatric diagnoses in three groups of abused children (sexual, physical, and both). *Child Abuse and Neglect, 22*(8), 759–774.

Adrúiz, M. E., Bluthgen, C., & Knopfler, C. (2011). Helping child flood victims using group EMDR intervention in Argentina: Treatment outcome and gender differences. *International Perspectives in Psychology: Research, Practice, Consultation, 1*(S), 58–67.

Ahrens, J., & Rexford, L. (2002). Cognitive processing therapy for incarcerated adolescents with PTSD. *Journal of Aggression, Maltreatment & Trauma, 6*, 201–216.

Ajudukovic, M. (1998). Displaced adolescents in Croatia: Sources of stress and post-traumatic stress reaction. *Adolescence, 33*, 209–218.

American Psychiatric Association. (2000). *Diagnostic and statistical manual of mental disorders* (4th ed., text rev.). Washington, DC: Author.

American Psychiatric Association. (2013). *Diagnostic and statistical manual of mental disorders* (5th ed.). Arlington, VA: American Psychiatric Publishing.

Bal, S., Crombez, G., Van Oost, P., & De Boudeaudhuji, I. (2003). The role of social support in well-being and coping with self-reported stressful events in adolescents. *Child Abuse and Neglect, 27*, 1377–1395.

Bal, S., Van Oost, P., De Boudeaudhuji, I., & Crombez, G. (2003). Avoidant coping as a mediator between self-reported sexual abuse and stress-related symptoms in adolescents. *Child Abuse and Neglect, 27*, 883–897.

Barlow, D. H. (2004). Psychological treatments. *American Psychologist, 59*, 869–878.

Becker, J. V., & Kirsch, L. G. (2008). Sexual and other abuse of children. In R. J. Morris & T. R. Kratochwill (Eds.), *The practice of child therapy* (4th ed., pp. 411–432). Mahwah, NJ: Lawrence Erlbaum Associates.

Berliner, L., & Saunders, B. (1996). Treating fear and anxiety in sexually abused children: Results of a controlled two-year follow-up study. *Child Maltreatment, 1*, 294–309.

Berman, S. L., Weems, C. F., Silverman, W. K., & Kurtines, W. K. (2000). Predictors of outcome in exposure-based cognitive and behavioral treatments for phobic and anxiety disorders in children. *Behavior Therapy, 31*, 713–731.

Berton, M. W., & Stabb, S. D. (1996). Exposure to violence and posttraumatic stress disorder in urban adolescents. *Adolescence, 31*(122), 489–498.

Blakeney, P., Robert, R., & Meyer, W. (1998). Psychological and social trauma recovery of children disfigured by physical trauma: Elements of treatment supported by empirical data. *International Review of Psychiatry, 10*(3), 196–200.

Bolton, P., Bass, J., Betancourt, T., Speelman, L., Onyango, G., Clougherty, K. F. . . . Verdeli, H. (2007). Interventions for depression symptoms among adolescent survivors of war and displacement in northern Uganda: A randomized controlled trial. *Journal of the American Medical Association, 298*(5), 519–527.

Bonnano, G. A., Brewin, C. R., Kaniasty, K., & La Greca, A. M. (2010). Weighing the costs of disaster: Consequences, risks, and resilience in individuals, families, and communities. *Psychological Science in the Public Interest, 11*(1), 1–49.

Calhoun, L. G., & Tedeschi, R. G. (2006). The foundations of posttraumatic growth: An expanded framework. In L. G. Calhoun & R. G. Tedeschi (Eds.), *Handbook of posttraumatic growth: Research and practice* (pp. 3–23). Mahwah, NJ: Lawrence Erlbaum Associates.

Carrión, V. G., Kletter, H., Weems, C. F., Berry. R. R., & Rettger, J. P. (2013). Cue-centered treatment for youth exposed to interpersonal violence: A randomized controlled trial. *Journal of Traumatic Stress, 26*(6), 654–662.

Carrión, V. G., Weems, C. F., Ray, R., & Reiss, A. L. (2002). Toward an empirical definition of PTSD: The phenomenology of PTSD symptoms in youth. *Journal of the American Academy of Child and Adolescent Psychiatry, 41*(2), 166–173.

Carrión, V. G., Weems, C. F., & Reiss, A. L. (2007). Stress predicts brain changes in the children: A pilot longitudinal study on youth stress, posttraumatic stress disorder, and the hippocampus. *Pediatrics, 119*(3), 509–516.

Chadwick Center for Children and Families (2004). *Closing the quality chasm in child abuse treatment: Identifying and disseminating best practices.* San Diego, CA: Author.

Chaffin, M. (2006). The changing focus of child maltreatment research and practice within psychology. *Journal of Social Issues, 62*(4), 663–684.

Chaffin, M., & Friedrich, B. (2004). Evidence-based treatments in child abuse and neglect. *Children and Youth Services Review, 26*(11), 1097–1113.

Chaffin, M., Silovsky, J. F., Funderburk, B., Valle, L. A., Brestan, E. V., Balachova, T., . . . Bonner, B. L. (2004). Parent-child interaction therapy with physically abusive parents: Efficacy for reducing future abuse reports. *Journal of Consulting and Clinical Psychology, 72*(3), 500–510.

Chaffin, M., Valle, L. A., Funderburk, B., Gurwitch, R., Silovsky, J., Bard, D., . . . Kees, M. (2009). A motivational intervention can improve retention in PCIT for low-motivation child welfare clients. *Child Maltreatment, 14*(4), 356–368.

Chambless, D. L., & Ollendick, T. H. (2001). Empirically supported psychological interventions: Controversies and evidence. *Annual Review of Psychology, 52*(1), 685–716.

Chemtob, C. M., Nakashima, J., & Carlson, J. G. (2002). Brief treatment for elementary school children with disaster-related posttraumatic stress disorder: A field study. *Journal of Clinical Psychology, 58*(1), 99–112.

Cohen, J. A., Berliner, L., & Mannarino, A. P. (2000). Treating traumatized children: A research review and synthesis. *Trauma, Violence, and Abuse, 1*(1), 29–46.

Cohen, J. A., Berliner, L., & Mannarino, A. P. (2003). Psychosocial and pharmacological interventions for child crime victims. *Journal of Traumatic Stress, 16*(2), 175–186.

Cohen, J. A., Deblinger, E., Mannarino, A. P., & Steer, R. A. (2004). A multisite, randomized controlled trial for children with sexual abuse-related PTSD symptoms. *Journal of the American Academy of Child and Adolescent Psychiatry, 43*(4), 393–402.

Cohen, J. A., & Mannarino, A. P. (1996). Factors that mediate treatment outcome of sexually abused preschool children. *Journal of the American Academy of Child and Adolescent Psychiatry, 35*(10), 1402–1410.

Cohen, J. A., & Mannarino, A. P. (1998). Factors that mediate treatment outcome of sexually abused preschool children: Six- and 12-month follow-up. *Journal of the American Academy of Child and Adolescent Psychiatry, 37*, 44–51.

Cohen, J. A., & Mannarino, A. P. (2000). Predictors of treatment outcome in sexually abused children. *Child Abuse and Neglect, 24*(7), 983–994.

Cohen, J. A., Mannarino, A. P., Berliner, L., & Deblinger, E. (2000). Trauma-focused cognitive behavioral therapy for children and adolescents: An empirical update. *Journal of Interpersonal Violence, 15*(11), 1202–1223.

Cohen, J. A., Mannarino, A. P., & Knudsen, K. (2005). Treating sexually abused children: 1 year follow-up of a randomized controlled trial. *Child Abuse and Neglect, 29*(2), 135–145.

Cohen, J. A., Mannarino, A. P., Murray, L. K., & Igelman, R. (2006). Psychosocial interventions for maltreated and violence-exposed children. *Journal of Social Issues, 62*(4), 737–766.

Corcoran, J. (2004). Treatment outcome research with the non-offending parents of sexually abused children: A critical review. *Journal of Child Sexual Abuse, 13*(2), 59–84.

Corcoran, J., & Pillai, V. (2008). A meta-analysis of parent-involved treatment for child sexual abuse. *Research on Social Work Practice, 18*(5), 453–464.

Costello, J. E., Erkanli, A., Fairbank, J. A., & Angold, A. (2002). The prevalence of potentially traumatic events in childhood and adolescence. *Journal of Traumatic Stress, 15*(2), 99–112.

Davis, L., & Siegel, L. J. (2000). Posttraumatic stress disorder in children and adolescents: A review and analysis. *Clinical Child and Family Psychology Review, 3*(3), 135–154.

Deblinger, E. H., & Heflin, A. H. (1996). *Treating sexually abused children and their nonoffending parents: A cognitive behavioral approach.* Thousand Oaks, CA: Sage.

Deblinger, E., Lippmann, J., & Steer, R. (1996). Sexually abused children suffering posttraumatic stress symptoms: Initial treatment outcome findings. *Journal of the American Professional Society on the Abuse of Children, 1*(4), 310–321.

Deblinger, E., Mannarino, A. P., Cohen, J. A., Runyon, M. K., & Steer, R. A. (2011). Trauma-focused cognitive behavioral therapy for children: Impact of the trauma narrative and treatment length. *Depression and Anxiety, 28*(1), 67–75.

Deblinger, E., & Runyon, M. K. (2005). Understanding and treating feelings of shame in children who have experienced maltreatment. *Child Maltreatment, 10*(4), 364–375.

Deblinger, E., Stauffer, L. B., & Steer, R. A. (2001). Comparative efficacies of supportive and cognitive behavioral group therapies for young children who have been sexually abused and their nonoffending mothers. *Child Maltreatment, 6*(4), 332–343.

Ehlers A., & Clark, D. M. (2000). A cognitive model of posttraumatic stress disorder. *Behaviour Research and Therapy, 38*(4), 319–345.

Ehlert, U. (2013). Enduring psychobiological effects of childhood adversity. *Psychoneuroendocrinology, 38*(9), 1850–1857.

Ehntholt, K. A., Smith, P. A., & Yule, W. (2005). School-based cognitive-behavioural therapy group intervention for refugee children who have experienced war-related trauma. *Clinical Child Psychology and Psychiatry, 10*(2), 235–250.

Fantuzzo, J., Sutton-Smith, B., Atkins, M., Meyers, R., Stevenson, H., Coolahan, K., . . . Manz, P. (1996). Community-based resilient peer treatment of withdrawn maltreated preschool children. *Journal of Consulting and Clinical Psychology, 64*(6), 1377.

Finkelhor, D., & Berliner, L. (1995). Research on the treatment of sexually abused children: Review and recommendations. *Journal of the American Academy of Child and Adolescent Psychiatry, 34*(11), 1408–1423.

Finkelhor, D., Ormrod, R. K., & Turner, H. A. (2007). Poly-victimization: A neglected component in child victimization. *Child Abuse and Neglect, 31*(1), 7–26.

Fitzgerald, M. M., & Cohen, J. (2012). Trauma-focused cognitive-behavioral therapy. In P. Goodyear-Brown (Ed.), *Handbook of child sexual abuse: Identification, assessment, and treatment* (pp. 199–228). Hoboken, NJ: John Wiley & Sons.

Giannopoulo, J., Dikaiakou, A., & Yule, W. (2006). Cognitive–behavioural group intervention for PTSD symptoms in children following the Athens 1999 earthquake: A pilot study. *Clinical Child Psychology and Psychiatry, 11*, 543–553.

Goenjian, A. K., Walling, D., Steinberg, A. M., Karayan, I., Najarian, L. M., & Pynoos, R. (2005). A prospective study of posttraumatic stress and depressive reactions among treated and untreated adolescents 5 years after a catastrophic disaster. *American Journal of Psychiatry, 162*(12), 2302–2308.

Goodyear-Brown, P., Fath, A., & Myers, L. (2012). Child sexual abuse: The scope of the problem. In P. Goodyear-Brown (Ed.), *Handbook of child sexual abuse: Identification, assessment, and treatment* (pp. 3–28). Hoboken, NJ: John Wiley & Sons.

Hakman, M., Chaffin, M., Funderburk, B., & Silovsky, J. (2009). Change trajectories for parent-child interaction sequences during parent-child interaction therapy for child physical abuse. *Child Abuse and Neglect, 33*(7), 461–470.

Harvey, S. T., & Taylor, J. E. (2010a). A meta-analysis of the effects of psychotherapy with sexually abused children and adolescents. *Clinical Psychology Review, 30*(5), 517–535.

Harvey, S. T., & Taylor, J. E. (2010b). Erratum to "A meta-analysis of the effects of psychotherapy with sexually abused children and adolescents" [Clinical Psychology Review 30 (2010) 517–535]. *Clinical Psychology Review, 30*(8), 1049–1050.

Haskett, M. E., Nears, K., Sabourin Ward, C., & McPherson, A. V. (2006). Diversity in adjustment of maltreated children: Factors associated with resilient functioning. *Clinical Psychology Review, 26*(6), 796–812.

Hedges, L. V. (1991). Statistical considerations. In H. Cooper & L. V. Hedges (Eds.), *The handbook of research synthesis* (pp. 29–40). New York: Russell Sage Foundation.

Hedges, L. V., & Olkin, I. (1985). *Statistical methods for meta-analysis*. San Diego: Academic Press.

Herrenkohl, R. C., & Herrenkohl, T. I. (2009). Assessing a child's experience of multiple maltreatment types: Some unfinished business. *Journal of Family Violence, 24*, 485–496.

Hetzel-Riggin, M. D., Brausch, A. M., & Montgomery, B. S. (2007). A meta-analytic investigation of therapy modality outcomes for sexually abused children and adolescents: An exploratory study. *Child Abuse and Neglect, 31*(2), 125–141.

Jaberghaderi, N., Greenwald, R., Rubin, A., Zand, S. O., & Dolatabadi, S. (2004). A comparison of CBT and EMDR for sexually-abused Iranian girls. *Clinical Psychology and Psychotherapy, 11*, 358–368.

Jaccard, J., Guilamo-Ramos, V., Johansson, M., & Bouris, A. (2006). Multiple regression analyses in clinical child and adolescent psychology. *Journal of Clinical Child and Adolescent Psychology, 35*(3), 456–479.

Kataoka, S. H., Stein, B. D., Jaycox, L. H., Wong, M., Escudero, P., Tu, W., Zaragoza, C., & Fink, A. (2003). A school-based mental health program for traumatized Latino immigrant children. *Journal of the American Academy of Child and Adolescent Psychiatry, 42*(3), 311–318.

Kazdin, A. E. (2007). Mediators and mechanisms of change in psychotherapy research. *Annual Review of Clinical Psychology, 3*, 1–27.

Kendall-Tackett, K. A., Williams, L. M., & Finkelhor, D. (1993). Impact of sexual abuse on children: A review and synthesis of recent empirical studies. *Psychological Bulletin, 113*, 164–180.

Keppel-Benson, J. M., Ollendick, T. H., & Benson, M. J. (2002). Post-traumatic stress in children following motor vehicle accidents. *Journal of Child Psychology and Psychiatry, 43*(2), 203–212.

King, N. J., Heyne, D., Tonge, B. J., Mullen, P., Myerson, N., Rollings, S., & Ollendick, T. H. (2003). Sexually abused children suffering from post-traumatic stress disorder: Assessment and treatment strategies. *Cognitive Behaviour Therapy, 32*(1), 2–12.

King, N. J., Tonge, B. J., Mullen, P., Myerson, N., Heyne, D., Rollings, S., . . . Ollendick, T. H. (2000). Treating sexually abused children with posttraumatic stress symptoms: A randomized clinical trial. *Journal of the American Academy of Child and Adolescent Psychiatry, 39*(11), 1347–1355.

Kolko, D. J. (1996). Individual cognitive behavioral treatment and family treatment and family therapy for physically abused children and their offending parents: A comparison of clinical outcomes. *Child Maltreatment, 1*, 322–342.

Kowalik, J., Weller, J., Venter, J., & Drachman, D. (2011). Cognitive behavioral therapy for the treatment of pediatric posttraumatic stress disorder: A review and meta-analysis. *Journal of Behavior Therapy and Experimental Psychiatry, 42*(3), 405–413.

La Greca, A. M., Silverman, W. S., Vernberg, E. M., & Prinstein, M. J. (1996). Posttraumatic stress symptoms in children after Hurricane Andrew: A prospective study. *Journal of Consulting and Clinical Psychology, 64*, 712–723.

Leeson, F., & Nixon, R. D. V. (2010). Therapy for child psychological maltreatment. *Clinical Psychologist, 14*(2), 30–38.

Lieberman, A. F., Van Horn, P., & Ippen, C. G. (2005). Toward evidence-based treatment: Child-parent psychotherapy with preschoolers exposed to marital violence. *Journal of the American Academy of Child & Adolescent Psychiatry, 44*, 1241–1248.

Lonigan, C. J., Shannon, M. P., Taylor, C. M., Finch, A. J, Jr., & Sallee, F. R. (1994). Children exposed to disaster: II. Risk factors for the development of posttraumatic symptomatology. *Journal of the American Academy of Child and Adolescent Psychiatry, 33*, 94–105.

Macdonald, G. M., Higgins, J. P. T., & Ramchandani, P. (2006). Cognitive-behavioural interventions for children who have been sexually abused. *Cochrane Database of Systematic Reviews*, Issue 4. Art. No. CD001930.

MacKinnon, D. P., Fairchild, A. J., & Fritz, M. S. (2007). Mediation analysis. *Annual Review of Psychology, 58*, 593–614.

Martin, E. K., Campbell, C., & Hansen, D. J. (2010). Child sexual abuse. In J. C. Thomas & M. Hersen (Eds.), *Handbook of clinical psychology competencies* (pp. 1481–1514). New York: Springer.

McDermott, B. M., & Cvitanovich, A. (2000). Posttraumatic stress disorder and emotional problems in children following motor vehicle accidents: An extended case series. *Australian and New Zealand Journal of Psychiatry, 34*, 446–452.

Michelson, L., June, K., Vives, A., Testa, S., & Marchione, N. (1998). The role of trauma and dissociation in cognitive-behavioral psychotherapy outcome and maintenance for panic disorder with agoraphobia. *Behaviour Research and Therapy, 36*(11), 1011–1050.

Moses, E. B., & Barlow, D. H. (2006). A new unified treatment approach for emotional disorders based on emotion science. *Current Directions in Psychological Science, 15*, 146–150.

National Institute of Clinical Excellence (2005). *Post-traumatic stress disorder (PTSD): The management of PTSD in adults and children in primary and secondary care.* www.nice.org.uk

Nixon, R. D. V., Sterk, J., & Pearce, A. (2012). A randomized trial of cognitive behavior therapy and cognitive therapy for children with posttraumatic stress disorder following single-incident trauma. *Journal of Abnormal Child Psychology, 40*, 327–337.

Prati, G., & Pietrantoni, L. (2009). Optimism, social support, and coping strategies as factors contributing to posttraumatic growth: A meta-analysis. *Journal of Loss and Trauma, 14*, 364–388.

Quota, S. R., Palosaari, E., Diab, M., & Punamaki, R. (2012). Intervention effectiveness among war-affected children: A cluster randomized controlled trial on improving mental health. *Journal of Traumatic Stress, 25*, 288–298.

Rapee, R. M., Wignall, A., Hudson, J. L., & Schniering, C. A. (2000). *Treating anxious children and adolescents: An evidence-based approach*. Oakland, CA: New Harbinger Press.

Richmond, T. S., Thompson, H. J., Deatrick, J. A., & Kauder, D. R. (2000). Journey towards recovery following physical trauma. *Journal of Advanced Nursing, 32*, 1340–1348.

Rodriguez-Srednicki, O., & Twaite, J. A. (2004a). Understanding and reporting child abuse: Legal and psychological perspectives: Part one: Physical abuse, sexual abuse, and neglect. *Journal of Psychiatry and the Law, 32*, 315–359.

Rodriguez-Srednicki, O., & Twaite, J. A. (2004b). Understanding and reporting child abuse: Legal and psychological perspectives: Part two: Emotional and secondary abuse. *Journal of Psychiatry and the Law, 32*, 443–481.

Sánchez-Meca, J., Alcázar, A. I., & López-Soler, C. (2011). The psychological treatment of sexual abuse in children and adolescents: A meta-analysis. *International Journal of Clinical and Health Psychology, 11*(1), 67–93.

Saunders, B. E. (2012). Determining best practice for treating sexually victimized children. In P. Goodyear-Brown (Ed.), *Handbook of child sexual abuse: Identification, assessment, and treatment* (pp. 173–197). Hoboken, NJ: John Wiley & Sons.

Saunders, B. E., Berliner, L., & Hanson, R. F. (Eds.) (2004). *Child physical and sexual abuse: Guidelines for treatment* (Revised report: April 26, 2004). Charleston, SC: National Crime Victims Research and Treatment Center.

Schäfer, I., Barkmann, C., Riedesser, P., & Schulte-Markwort, M. (2006). Posttraumatic syndromes in children and adolescents after road traffic accidents: A prospective cohort study. *Psychopathology, 39*(4), 159–164.

Scheeringa, M. S., & Weems, C. F (2014). Randomized placebo-controlled D-Cycloserine with cognitive behavior therapy for pediatric posttraumatic stress. *Journal of Child and Adolescent Psychopharmacology, 24*, 69–77.

Scheeringa, M. S., Weems, C. F., Cohen, J., Amaya-Jackson, L., & Guthrie, D. (2011). Trauma-focused cognitive-behavioral therapy for posttraumatic stress disorder in three through six year-old children: A randomized clinical trial. *Journal of Child Psychology and Psychiatry, 52*, 853–860.

Scheeringa, M. S., & Zeanah, C. H. (2001). A relational perspective on PTSD in early childhood. *Journal of Traumatic Stress, 14*, 799–815.

Scheeringa, M. S., Zeanah, C. H., Myers, L., Putnam, F. W. (2003). New findings on alternative criteria for PTSD in preschool children. *Journal of the American Academy of Child and Adolescent Psychiatry, 42*(5), 561–570.

Seedat, S., Njeng, N. F., Vythilingum, B., & Stein, D. J. (2004). Trauma exposure and posttraumatic stress symptoms in urban African school. *The British Journal of Psychiatry, 184*, 169–175.

Shapiro, F. (1989). Efficacy of the eye movement desensitization procedure in the treatment of traumatic memories. *Journal of Traumatic Stress Studies, 2*, 199–223.

Shapiro, F. (1995). *Eye movement desensitization and reprocessing: Basic principles, protocols and procedures.* New York: Guilford.

Shapiro, F. (2001). *Eye movement desensitization and reprocessing: Basic principles, protocols, and procedures* (2nd ed.). New York: Guilford.

Shaw, J. A. (2000). Children, adolescents, and trauma. *Psychiatric Quarterly, 71*, 227–243.

Silverman, W. K., Ortiz, C. D., Viswesvaran, C., Burns, B. J., Kolko, D. J., Putnam, F. W., & Amaya-Jackson, L. (2008). Evidence-based psychosocial treatments for children and adolescents exposed to traumatic experiences. *Journal of Clinical Child and Adolescent Psychology, 37*(1), 156–183.

Skowron, E., & Reinemann, D. H. S. (2005). Effectiveness of psychological interventions for child maltreatment: A meta-analysis. *Psychotherapy: Theory, Research, Practice, Training, 42*, 52–71.

Smith, P., Dyregrov, A., & Yule, W. (2000). *Children and war: Teaching recovery techniques.* Bergen, Norway: Foundation for Children and War.

Smith, P., Yule, W., Perrin, S., Tranah, T., Dalgleish, T., & Clark, D. M. (2007). Cognitive-behavioral therapy for PTSD in children and adolescents: A preliminary randomized controlled trial. *Journal of the American Academy of Child and Adolescent Psychiatry, 46*(8), 1051–1061.

Southam-Gerow, M. A., Kendall, P. C., & Weersing, V. R. (2001). Examining outcome variability: Correlates of treatment response in a child and adolescent anxiety clinic. *Journal of Clinical Child Psychology, 30*, 422–436.

Stallard, P. (2002). *Think good—feel good: A cognitive behavior therapy workbook for children and young people.* Chichester, UK: John Wiley & Sons.

Stallard, P. (2006). Psychological interventions for post-traumatic reactions in children and young people: A review of randomized controlled trials. *Clinical Psychology Review, 26*, 895–911.

Stallard, P., Velleman, R., Salter, E., Howse, I., Yule, W., & Taylor, G. (2006). A randomized controlled trial to determine the effectiveness of an early psychological intervention with children involved in road traffic accidents. *Journal of Child Psychology and Psychiatry, 47*, 127–134.

Stein, B. D., Jaycox, L. H., Kataoka, S. H., Wong, M., Tu, W., Elliot, M. N., & Fink, A. (2003). A mental health intervention for schoolchildren exposed to violence. *Journal of the American Medical Association, 290*, 603–611.

Taussig, H. N., Culhane, S. E., Garrido, E., Knudtson, M. D., & Petrenko, C. L. M. (2012). Does severity of physical neglect moderate the impact of an efficacious preventive intervention for maltreated children in foster care? *Child Maltreatment, 18*(1), 56–64.

Taylor, L. K., & Weems, C. F. (2009). What do youth report as a traumatic event? Toward a developmentally informed classification of traumatic stressors. *Psychological Trauma, 1*, 91–106.

Taylor, L. K., & Weems, C. F. (2011). Cognitive-behavior therapy for disaster exposed youth with posttraumatic stress: Results from a multiple-baseline examination. *Behavior Therapy, 42*, 349–363.

Taylor, L. K., Weems, C. F., Costa, N. M., & Carrión, V. G. (2009). Loss and the experience of emotional distress in childhood. *Journal of Loss and Trauma, 14*, 1–16.

Tol, W. A., Komproe, I. H., Jordans M. J. D., Gross, A. L., Susanty, D., Macy, R. D., & de Jong, J. T. V. M. (2010). Mediators and moderators of a psychosocial intervention for children affected by political violence. *Journal of Consulting and Clinical Psychology*, *78*(6), 818–828.

Trask, E. V., Walsh, K., & DiLillo, D. (2011). Treatment effects for common outcomes of child sexual abuse: A current meta-analysis. *Aggression and Violent Behavior*, *16*, 6–19.

Trickey, D., Siddaway, A. P., Meiser-Stedman, R., Serpell, L., & Field, A. P. (2012). A meta-analysis of risk factors for post-traumatic stress disorder in children and adolescents. *Clinical Psychology Review*, *32*, 122–138.

Trowell, J., Kolvin, I., Weeramanthri, T., Sadowski, H., Berelowitz, M., Glaser, D., & Leitch, I. (2002). Psychotherapy for sexually abused girls: Psychopathological outcome findings and patterns of change. *British Journal of Psychiatry*, *180*(3), 234–247.

Weems, C. F., & Scheeringa, M. S. (2013). Maternal depression and treatment gains following a cognitive behavioral intervention for posttraumatic stress in preschool children. *Journal of Anxiety Disorders*, *27*, 140–146.

Weems, C. F., Taylor, L. K., Costa, N. M., Marks, A. B., Romano, D. M., Verrett, S. L., & Brown, D. M. (2009). Effect of a school-based test anxiety intervention in ethnic minority youth exposed to Hurricane Katrina. *Journal of Applied Developmental Psychology*, *30*, 218–226.

Wolfe, D. A., Rawana, J. S., & Chiodo, D. (2006). Abuse and trauma. In D. A. Wolfe & E. J. Mash (Eds.), *Behavioral and emotional disorders in adolescents: Nature, assessment, and treatment* (pp. 642–671). New York: Guilford.

Wolmer, L., Hamiel, D., Barchas, J. D., Slone, M., & Laor, N. (2011). Teacher delivered resilience-focused intervention in schools with traumatized children following the second Lebanon War. *Journal of Traumatic Stress*, *24*, 309–316.

Woolley, C. C., Dickson, J., Evans, I. M., Harvey, S., & Taylor, J. E. (2008, March). *Sexual Abuse and Mental Injury: Practice Guidelines for Aotearoa New Zealand*. Wellington, New Zealand: Accident Compensation Corporation. Retrieved from http://www.acc.co.nz/

Yule, W., Smith, P., & Perrin, S. (2005). Posttraumatic stress disorders. In P. Graham (Ed.), *Cognitive behaviour therapy for children and families* (pp. 342–358). Cambridge: Cambridge University Press.

4

Moderators and Mediators of Treatments for Youth With Depression

V. ROBIN WEERSING, KAREN T. G. SCHWARTZ, AND CARL BOLANO ■

INTRODUCTION

Depression in Youth

Depression in youth is prevalent, disabling, and recurrent. Nearly 5% of children experience clinically significant mood disorder at any given time; this prevalence rate surges to 10%–20% in the teen years, with the result that nearly 1 in 5 youth will have experienced an episode of depression by the end of puberty (Avenevoli, Knight, Kessler, & Merikangas, 2008). Depressive disorder interferes markedly with peer and family relationships and school achievement (Jaycox et al., 2009; Kessler, Foster, Saunders, & Stang, 1995; Lewinsohn et al., 1994) and is associated with suicide attempt and completion (Barbe, Bridge, Birmaher, Kolko, & Brent, 2004a; Rao, Weissman, Martin, & Hammond, 1993), the third leading cause of death for adolescents and young adults (Centers for Disease Control and Prevention [CDC], 2010). Depression is linked to risky behavior and poorer physical health, including higher rates of obesity (Goodman & Whitaker, 2002; Jaycox et al., 2009; Lewinsohn et al., 1994). Depression also is highly comorbid with other mental health problems. Anxiety disorders may precede and follow depression, and they are the most closely associated form of psychopathology in terms of shared risk and etiological underpinnings (for discussion, see Garber & Weersing, 2010). Depression also may serve as a risk factor for the development of substance use and abuse (Gotlib, Lewinsohn, & Seeley, 1995; Rice, Lifford, Thomas, & Thapar, 2007). Perhaps most prominently, depression in youth is a potent risk factor for the recurrence of depressive disorder in adulthood and across the lifespan. Of adolescents who experience an episode, 25% will have a recurrence within 1 year, 40% within 2 years, and 70% within 5 years (Mash & Wolfe, 2016).

Efficacy of Treatment

Given the major public health impact of youth depression, efforts have been made to develop efficacious treatments. The effect sizes in psychosocial clinical trials for youth depression have been quite variable, ranging from zero to over 1 (a very large effect), a pattern driven both by high variability in response within treatment groups and very substantial differences in control condition response rates. In addition to issues with variability, the youth depression treatment literature as a whole has experienced a notable contraction in the estimated *mean* effect of intervention over the past two decades, with mean effect sizes moving from some of the largest in the mental health literature to some of the smallest (see Weisz, McCarty, & Valeri, 2006).

This pattern of results has presented a challenge for crafting best practice recommendations for the treatment of youth depression, a task made even more difficult by uneven sampling of population characteristics in the literature. For example, as described earlier, the prevalence of depression rises dramatically in the teen years and, understandably, the majority of clinical trials have focused on depressed adolescents. For the most part, depressed children have been included only in (a) early-stage studies with small samples and less rigorous assessment (e.g., selecting youth screening high on self-reported of depression questionnaires, rather than conducting diagnostic assessment; Butler et al., 1980), or (b) studies with a very broad age range, but minimal power to examine age or developmental level as a moderator of response (e.g., Wood, Harrington, & Moore, 1996). In a similar fashion, cultural and ethnic groups have been unevenly represented across trials. Investigations of interpersonal psychotherapy (IPT) for adolescent depression have been largely conducted in samples of Latino youth, with two published randomized IPT trials conducted in Puerto Rico and the remaining trials including substantial representation of Latino youth living in the mainland United States. In contrast, the cognitive behavioral therapy (CBT) literature has historically included predominantly non-Hispanic Caucasian families (Huey & Polo, 2008).

However, despite these challenges, the literature does support some general conclusions about treatment efficacy (see Weersing & Gonzalez, 2009). For depressed adolescents with mild to moderate depression, treatment with CBT or IPT should be considered efficacious and likely superior to watchful waiting, simple attention from a caring adult, or non-directive therapy (see Brent et al., 1997; Mufson et al., 2004; Rohde et al., 2004). The definition of the terms *mild* and *moderate* vary across studies, but studies that characterized their samples in this fashion still tend to include teens that meet at least minimal diagnostic criteria for a depressive disorder (usually Major Depression). In contrast, youth with moderate to severe levels of depression meet diagnostic criteria, with scores on normed symptom measures in the clinically significant range and also demonstrate impairment across several areas of their life (e.g., Children's Global Assessment Scale [CGAS; Shaffer et al., 1983] functioning score less than 50; TADS, 2004), have longer term histories of depressive illness (e.g., history of failed antidepressant treatment; Brent et al., 2008), or high levels of suicidality (e.g., Brent et al., 1997). For these moderately to severely depressed adolescents, the results of CBT alone are more mixed (cf. Brent et al., 1997; TADS, 2004) and combination treatment with CBT and medication may be a wise choice (Brent et al., 2008; March et al., 2004). The benefits of IPT and medication combination treatment remain untested. For depressed children, CBT appears to hold promise, although the evidence base is thinner than with depressed teens. The value of IPT remains largely unexplored in pre-pubertal depressed youth (although current trials are in progress; National Institute of Mental Health, 2014).

To move the field beyond these very general conclusions will require (a) better understanding of why the youth depression literature has produced such inconsistent findings, and (b) systematic, theoretically driven attempts to fill critical gaps in the literature. In an effort to aid this process, in the following critical review, we focus on the two efficacious interventions for youth depression—CBT and IPT—and attempt to answer two key questions. First, what is the underlying theory driving the treatment, and do the available data in the clinical trial literature support this theory of intervention? Second, what are the boundaries of these theories? Are these interventions universally applicable to the treatment of depressed youth, or should these treatments be expected to work more or less well with different types of depression, in the presence of comorbid disorders, and across demographic groups? This first question is a search for evidence of treatment mechanism and mediators of intervention effects, while the second is one of moderation. By examining the available evidence on mediators and moderators of CBT and IPT for youth depression, we aim to illuminate the current state of the field and provide useful guidance on developing an agenda for future research.

MEDIATION AND THEORIES OF INTERVENTION

Depression is often viewed as a prime example of a diathesis-stress model of psychopathology. Broadly, depression is thought to arise from (a) the experience of stressful life events (e.g., Kendler, Thornton, & Gardner, 2001); in combination with (b) genetic vulnerability toward mood dysregulation in response to stress (e.g., Caspi et al., 2003); (c) maladaptive behavioral responses to stress (avoidance, poor interpersonal problem-solving skills; e.g., Gazelle & Rudolph, 2004); and (d) inaccurate, overly negative cognitive interpretations of stressful events (e.g., Gladstone & Kaslow, 1995). This general theory of depressive psychopathology has spawned a range of intervention theories, each crafted to interrupt various processes of disorder. Below, we describe the intervention theories underlying the two evidence-based psychosocial treatments for youth depression, CBT and IPT, and detail the extent to which the empirical literature has (or more often has not) tested the mediators targeted by these theories.

Mediators of CBT Effects

THEORY OF INTERVENTION

Two major cognitive theories have been proposed to explain the etiology and maintenance of depression: classic Beckian cognitive theory (Beck, Rush, Shaw, & Emery, 1979) and learned helplessness theory (Abramson, Metalsky, & Alloy, 1989). Both of these approaches are cognitive vulnerability models. In each, biased, overly negative cognitive processing is thought to arise from stressful early life experience. Individuals "learn" that the world is an unsafe and unpredictable place, that they are not adept at handling stress, and that the future is likely to be dark and filled with insurmountable challenges. When faced with stressful circumstances in the present, these beliefs (cf. schemas, explanatory styles) are activated, interfere with effective coping, and are associated with dysphoric mood, behavioral avoidance, and, eventually, clinical depression. Furthermore, depressogenic thinking is resistant to disconfirmation, in part, because of enduring styles of information processing that promote belief maintenance (e.g., selective abstraction of negative information). In addition to these cognitive vulnerability models, purely behavioral accounts of depression have been proposed. Lewinsohn and colleagues (1974; Lewinsohn, 1975) suggested that depression may result directly from low levels of positive reinforcement and high levels of punishment and aversive control. As a result, individuals withdraw from negative interactions and avoid situations that may produce low mood; this exacerbates the problem of low positive reinforcement, as withdrawal also diminishes opportunities for reinforcing feelings of pleasure and experiences of mastery. The resulting cycle of avoidance and negative mood induction leads to clinically impairing depression. The depressive cycle may be brought about through environmental change (e.g., a friend moving away) or a mismatch between environmental demands and behavioral skills (e.g., insufficient social skills to cope with onset of dating).

These cognitive and behavioral theories of depression were developed to explain the etiology and maintenance of adult depression. However, there is evidence that depressed youth exhibit patterns of information processing similar to depressed adults (e.g., Gladstone & Kaslow, 1995). Certainly, experiencing negative, uncontrollable events has been linked to helpless behavior and apathy in adults and in youth (and cross-species). In adolescents, first onset and recurrence of depression are often preceded by family conflict, physical illness, breakup of romantic relationships, and loss of friendships (Lewinsohn, Allen, Seeley, & Gotlib, 1999). Of these, familial stress may play a particularly important role; parental depression, parent-child conflict, parental divorce, low family

cohesion, and high levels of "expressed emotion" have all been found to significantly increase the risk of depression in adolescents (e.g., Goodman & Gotlib,
2002; Lewinsohn et al., 1994, 1996; Tompson et al., 2010).

Moving from intervention theory to implementation, CBT programs for
youth depression typically begin with psychoeducation about depression
and the theory of intervention, include an early application of behavioral
techniques (such as pleasant activity scheduling) in order to bolster current
mood, and then move into cognitive restructuring. Beyond this core structure,
CBT manuals differ in (a) supplemental cognitive and behavioral techniques
employed (e.g., problem-solving, social skills, relaxation), (b) relative focus on
cognitive change versus behavioral skill building, (c) overall number of sessions and dosing of each technique, (d) format (from structured skills group
to principle-based individual sessions), and (e) level of parental involvement.
Across this diversity in manuals, improvement in negative cognitive style and
behavioral mood regulation skills are hypothesized to be the mechanisms of
action of CBT effects.

Empirical Evidence Supporting Mediation Model

To date, only four investigations have tested whether change in cognitive or behavioral processes mediated the impact of CBT on depression at
post-treatment: (a) the Kolko and colleagues (2000) reanalysis of the Brent et al.
(1997) comparative trial of cognitive, family, and supportive therapy; (b) the
Ackerson et al. (1998) trial of cognitive bibliotherapy for teens with mild depression seen in primary care; (c) a secondary paper by Kaufman et al. (2005) examining the process and outcome of CBT adapted for youth with depression and
comorbid conduct disorder; and (d) a secondary analysis by Jacobs et al. (2009)
of the Treatment of Adolescents with Depression Study (TADS), a multi-site
randomized trial of CBT and medication management, singly and in combination. All of these investigations focused on treatment of adolescent (versus child)
depression and relied on youth self-report of cognitive (four studies) and behavioral processes (one study). Given the small size of this literature, we review each
of these in some detail.

In the original Brent comparative efficacy trial (1997), CBT was tested against
family and supportive therapies in a sample of moderately to seriously depressed
adolescents with high levels of suicidality. Across multiple measures of depression, CBT was found to be more efficacious than these alternate interventions
at post-treatment assessment. To probe mechanisms of intervention effects,
Kolko et al. (2000) investigated the mediating role of several cognitive and family process variables, hypothesizing that CBT and family therapy should show
specific effects on their theoretical mechanisms of action, and that change in
these theoretically specific mechanisms should statistically mediate the impact
of intervention on depression outcome. As hypothesized, CBT did have a significantly greater effect on cognitive distortions, but was not superior to family

or supportive therapy in changing hopelessness. Change in cognitive distortion did not mediate the effect of CBT on depression symptoms, although low power may have limited ability to find significant effects (e.g., the subsample youth with complete mediator data did not show a significant effect of the CBT on depression, unlike in the full sample). Interestingly, and contrary to hypotheses, CBT also had superior effects than alternate interventions on family functioning and marital satisfaction at post-treatment, suggesting that the most efficacious intervention overall (CBT) may have produced broad, general change rather than theoretically specific effects on mediators.

Stronger support comes from an investigation of a CBT bibliotherapy program for depressed teens. Ackerson et al. (1998) found that youth who were given a CBT self-help book demonstrated a reduction in depression symptoms 4 weeks later. Teens also had a significant reduction in depressogenic thinking as assessed by the Dysfunctional Attitudes Scale (DAS), but they did not show significant change in negative automatic thoughts, as assessed with the Automatic Thoughts Questionnaire (ATQ), despite a positive effect size for the measure. Change in dysfunctional attitudes did mediate the effects of the intervention on youth-reported depression symptoms, but the conditions for mediation were not met for other measures of depression (i.e., interviewer ratings). Again, power may have been a limiting factor in this investigation, as cell sizes were below 15 and only the largest effects demonstrated statistical significance.

In the Kaufman reanalysis of the Rohde et al. (2004) trial of CBT for youth with comorbid major depression and conduct disorder, CBT was found to significantly impact one cognitive process measure. Change in cognitions did statistically mediate program effects on depression symptoms (all constructs were measured post-treatment); however, effects were inconsistent across measures of cognition, and the specific pattern of findings was opposite to that of Ackerson—small but significant effects on the ATQ but non-significant results for the DAS, with an effect size near zero. Furthermore, Kaufman failed to find evidence of mediation for three additional measures tapping problem-solving, social skills, and involvement in pleasant activities—all of which were targeted by the CBT program under investigation.

The most recent analysis of mediators of adolescent depression treatment was based on the multi-site TADS study (2003) comparing CBT plus medication (combination treatment) to CBT alone, medication (fluoxetine) alone, and pill placebo. In the original TADS trial, CBT failed to outperform pill placebo, contrary to the authors' a priori hypotheses. Combination therapy was the most broadly efficacious intervention, although medication alone equaled combination on some depression metrics and did separate from placebo better than CBT. The TADS trial stirred no small level of controversy at the time of its publication, with questions raised about the sample (more ill, male, and comorbid than many trials) and quality and content of the specific CBT protocol (which was previously untested; see Weersing, Rozenman, Gonzalez, 2009, for discussion). In this context, Jacobs et al. (2009) sought to explore mediators of the TADS effects, focusing on the DAS perfectionism subscale (measured pre- and post-treatment). In this analysis, DAS perfectionism did partially mediate the superior effects of combination treatment (compared to alternate arms) on interviewer-rated depression symptoms. Statistically, when DAS perfectionism change scores were included in models of depression outcome, combination therapy and medication alone had very similar rates of improvement, and these two conditions remained superior to CBT and placebo. DAS perfectionism also served as a mediator of the superior effect of combination (versus medication only) on suicidality. These results are consistent with a mediating role for cognitive change in CBT effects, although this conclusion is weakened by (a) the overall poor effects of CBT alone in TADS on both the outcomes and mediator, and (b) the lack of fine-grained data on the timing of change in cognitive process and outcomes. It is also possible that DAS perfectionism changes followed symptomatic improvement, and improvement in perfectionistic thinking was reflective of improved mood.

Mediators of IPT Effects

THEORY OF INTERVENTION

Interpersonal psychotherapy (IPT) is a well-established, efficacious treatment for adult unipolar depression (Klerman, Weissman, Rounsaville, & Chevron, 1984). Two research teams have adapted the adult IPT model to match the developmental presentation of adolescent depression. Mufson and colleagues (1999) produced the first adaptation of the model, while Rosello and colleagues (2008) independently developed a culturally adapted version of IPT for Puerto Rican adolescents. Both share a core theoretical framework; the Mufson model has been more elaborated in the literature (e.g., Mufson, Dorta, Moreau, & Weissman, 2011), and we thus use it as our base example of IPT intervention theory and techniques.

IPT models conceptualize depression as occurring within an interpersonal matrix and target the resolution of psychosocial stresses that coincide with the onset of teen patients' index depressive episode. As discussed previously, depressed youth experience a high level of severe psychosocial stress, are exposed to family and parental conflict, and are dependent for their needs on parents with high rates of psychopathology (see Hammen et al., 1999). In addition, specific, aversive family communication styles have been identified as significant predictors of depression in youth (e.g., Asarnow et al., 1993). Furthermore, in adolescents, depression is often preceded by negative interpersonal events separate from the family, such as the breakup of romantic relationships and loss of friendships (Lewinsohn et al., 1999). Unlike CBT, IPT does not claim a causal role for these environmental stresses in creating depression (e.g., by specifically triggering depressogenic thinking, or by directly reducing opportunities for positive reinforcement). Instead, patients are taught that depression and life stress frequently co-occur and that, regardless of the cause of depression (adversity, biology), the alleviation of interpersonal problems will likely result in an attenuation of depressive symptoms.

In the first phase of IPT, the difficult environmental context of teen patients' lives is categorized into one of five common problem areas: grief, role disputes, role transitions, interpersonal deficits, or issues with single-parent families (an adaptation from adult IPT; see Mufson et al., 2011). In the remainder of treatment, specific strategies are specified for working through each of the problem areas over the course of 12 sessions, with an overall emphasis on restoring (or creating) meaningful, low-conflict social relationships. For example, in working with a stressful role transition (such as changing from elementary to middle school), an IPT therapist may help a teen (a) mourn the loss of his or her old, comfortable role; (b) discuss the challenges involved in the transition; (c) attempt to discover the benefits of the new role or, at least, form reasonable expectations about the new role; and (d) help the teen's interpersonal system adjust to the role transition. This final task—interacting directly with the adolescent's family—is a modification of the adult IPT model, similar to the increased involvement of parents in developmental adaptations of CBT. IPT formulation and techniques are not fundamentally incompatible with the cognitive view of depression. In fact, there are several similarities, including problem-solving and skill-building activities, albeit infused with specific, recent social experiences.

EMPIRICAL EVIDENCE SUPPORTING THE MEDIATION MODEL

There has yet to be a randomized controlled trial of IPT that has tested the mediating processes thought to underlie the effects of the intervention. Some indirect evidence on the mechanisms of IPT action comes from a review by Weersing, Rozenman, and Gonzalez (2009). In this review, the authors coded secondary outcomes of randomized trials for adolescent depression along cognitive, behavioral, and interpersonal dimensions. Effect sizes for treatment versus control were calculated, and IPT, CBT, and family therapy were compared in terms of their relative impact on these theoretically relevant outcomes. At post-treatment assessment, IPT did produce changes in self-reported social functioning by the adolescents, although the specific interpersonal domains that demonstrated improvement varied across studies. IPT appeared to show the most consistently positive effects on dating relationships and the most variable effects on family functioning (ES ranging from -0.29 to 0.60). Interestingly, IPT also significantly impacted purportedly "cognitive" measures, at a level similar to CBT; however, the cognitive outcomes assessed in IPT studies did tend to have a social component (e.g., measures of social problem-solving). Taken together, these results suggest that IPT does impact the interpersonal targets underlying intervention theory, although it is unclear whether these interpersonal outcomes are functioning as mediators. It is possible, of course, that change in depression symptoms improves social relations, rather than change in social relationships serving as a mechanism of depression recovery. Additional data on the timing of change in interpersonal process and depression symptom reduction are clearly needed.

MODERATION AND BOUNDARIES OF EFFECTS

As discussed in detail in Chapter 1 of this volume, the study of moderators is a search for the boundaries of theory. In understanding the effects of youth depression treatments, we have found it useful to define three classes of moderators. First, we consider *match-to-intervention moderators,* namely baseline characteristics of youth who are a theoretical "match" to one of the existing evidence-based interventions for depression. In CBT for youth depression, cognitive distortions and behavioral mood regulation skills are the core targets of intervention, and change in these process are presumed to mediate intervention effects. Accordingly, it might be hypothesized that youth demonstrating deficits in these domains would be particularly good candidates for CBT treatment versus alternate interventions, such as IPT. CBT would provide a "match" to the hypothesized diatheses that formed the basis of the youth's depression, and, thus, baseline levels of cognitive and behavioral deficits should moderate treatment response *in favor* of CBT (a compensation model of treatment response, see Rude & Rehm, 1991). In contrast, interpersonal relationships and functioning are the central targets of intervention in IPT. Deficits and disruptions in this domain are hypothesized to co-occur with depression and may be linked to the onset and maintenance of episodes. Interpersonal functioning and relationship quality at the beginning of treatment, therefore, serve as theoretically interesting moderators of IPT effects. It could be hypothesized that IPT would be a particularly good match to youth with deficits in these domains or experiencing high levels of interpersonal conflict.

Second, we focus on *contextual moderators* of intervention effects. As discussed earlier, depression is viewed as a stress-sensitive disorder. Both CBT and IPT focus on improving the ability of youth to cope with current stressors by applying the skills learned in treatment (e.g., problem-solving in CBT, social role play and rehearsal in IPT). This structured focus on current stressors and assistance in applying skills should stand in sharp contrast to non-directive, attention only, or placebo control comparison conditions. Youth may especially benefit from CBT or IPT (versus these control conditions) when they are actively experiencing stressful life circumstances. Furthermore, some of the more cognitively focused CBT manuals (e.g., Brent et al., 1997) also may address the lingering impact of past stressors by targeting youths' core beliefs about themselves and the world around them. We thus explore the potential moderating impact of stressful life events and trauma history on response.

Third, we review *generalizability moderators* of CBT and IPT effects to assess whether these interventions are robust to clinical complexity and perform well across diverse family demographic characteristics. In terms of clinical complexity, we probe the effect of these evidence-based interventions versus control in the face of high levels of depressive symptom severity, presence of suicidality, low functioning, comorbidity with other mental health symptoms, and familial comorbidity (e.g., current depression in the parent). We further examine intervention response by youth age, gender, ethnicity and family income.

To aid in interpretation of effects across this complex literature, we provide a summary of moderator findings in Table 4.1, organized under these three categories (match to intervention, context, and generalizability). Investigators have seldom used precisely the same measure of cognitive distortions or family processes across studies. As these different operationalizations of moderators may influence findings (and help to explain divergent results across studies), we have retained this level of complexity by grouping, rather than collapsing, similar variables. For each variable, we indicate whether the potential moderator was significantly associated with superior or inferior effects of active treatment compared to control or whether the test of the *treatment x moderator* interaction was not statistically significant. The majority of trials tested CBT as the active intervention, and CBT effects are presented in the table in standard font. When IPT was tested as the active intervention, results are coded in the table in *italics*. In the following section, we provide a critical review of these findings.

Moderators of CBT Effects

MATCH TO INTERVENTION
Below, we review the empirical literature on cognitive, behavioral, and interpersonal moderators of CBT effects in randomized controlled trials for youth depression. We highlight evidence (or lack of evidence) for treatment specificity and matching effects. As discussed in the overview, matching hypotheses would suggest that CBT should outperform control conditions and alternate treatment models for youth with "matching" deficits in cognitive and behavioral processes at baseline. In contrast, significant moderation in favor of CBT would not be expected for youth with interpersonal deficits, when CBT is compared to models that focus explicitly on interpersonal processes as their mechanism of action (e.g., active IPT, family therapy control conditions).

COGNITIVE MODERATORS
Clinical trials of CBT frequently include measures of cognitive processes as outcomes, and five papers have tested whether baseline levels of these processes served as moderators of intervention effects. As can be seen in Table 4.1, studies employed a diversity of measures of cognitive processes, complicating interpretation of results across the literature. To aid in our review, we group these measures as primarily focusing on (a) cognitive distortions/negative bias, (b) problem-solving skills, or (c) coping style, when coping is defined by cognitive processes (e.g., cognitive reappraisal of stressors) or when coping style involves appropriately choosing and applying strategies (e.g., reflecting executive functioning).

In the examination of cognitive distortions, evidence for the matching hypothesis was mixed. In the TADS study (2004, described earlier), the combination of CBT

Table 4.1. Moderators of Treatment Effects in Youth Depression Clinical Trials

	Intervention Superior	Intervention Inferior	Not Statistically Significant
MATCH TO INTERVENTION			
Cognitive factors			
Cognitive distortions	7		
Negative thoughts			17
Hopelessness	2		6, 7, 17, 20
Self-esteem			21
Dysfunctional Attitudes Scale (DAS)			17
DAS: Perfectionism			12
Coping style	17		
SPSI-R Positive Problem Orientation	5		
SPSI-R Negative Problem Orientation		5	
SPSI-R Rational Problem-Solving			5
SPSI-R Impulsivity-Carelessness Style			5
SPSI-R Avoidant Style			5
Behavioral factors			
Pleasant events schedule			17
Social adjustment	*10*		10, 17
Perceived social support			9
Interpersonal and family factors			
Sociotropy vs. achievement orientation	*11*		11
Family conflict (more)	*10*		7, 17
Marital discord			1
Marital discord x gender	1		
Marital discord x oppositionality	1		
Tx x marital discord x gender			1
FAM task accomplishment			8
FAM role performance (good functioning)	8		

(*continued*)

Table 4.1. CONTINUED

	Intervention Superior	Intervention Inferior	Not Statistically Significant
FAM communication (more clear)	8		
FAM affective expression			8
FAM involvement	8		
FAM control	8		
FAM values and norms	8		
CONTEXTUAL FACTORS			
Stressful life events		9	
No trauma history (youth)	2, 3, 15, 18		
Exposure to traumas, non-abusive (youth)			15
History of abuse (youth)		2, 20	
Exposure to physical abuse (youth)		18	15
Exposure to sexual abuse (youth)		3	15, 18
GENERALIZABILITY			
Features of depression			
Severity of symptoms (high)	2, 7, 11, *11*		9, 17, 20
Global functioning (poor)			7, 17, 20
Age of onset of first MDE (younger)			17
Total number of past MDE	17		
Duration of MDE (shorter)			7, 20
Melancholic features (less)			7
Suicidality (current or lifetime)			4, 7, 17, 20
Non-suicidal self-harm	2		20
Comorbidity			
No. of comorbid disorders (fewer)		2	7
CBCL total problem score			17
Comorbid anxiety (any)	2, 6		7, 17, 20, *22*
Comorbid probable GAD			*22*
Comorbid probable social phobia			*22*
Comorbid probable panic disorder	*22*		
Comorbid disruptive behavior (CD, ODD)			2, 7, 20
Comorbid ADHD	2, 13		17
Comorbid substance abuse		9	17, 20

(continued)

Table 4.1. CONTINUED

	Intervention Superior	Intervention Inferior	Not Statistically Significant
Demographic factors			
Sex (female)			1, 7, 11, 17, 19, 20
Developmental level (younger/ lower)	2, 7		7, 17, 19, 20
Ethnicity (minority status)	2, 17		7, 20
SES (income)	7		2

NOTE: In cases where authors indicated that they planned to test a variable as a moderator but did not report the results, it was presumed that the variable was tested but was not statistically significant. Studies are numbered by first author in alphabetical order: 1. Amaya et al. (2011); 2. Asarnow et al. (2009); 3. Barbe et al. (2004a); 4. Barbe et al. (2004b); 5. Becker-Weidman et al. (2010); 6. Brent et al. (1998); 7. Curry et al. (2006); 8. Feeny et al. (2009); 9. Gau et al. (2012)*; 10. Gunlicks-Stoessel et al. (2011); 11. Horowitz et al. (2007)*; 12. Jacobs et al. (2009); 13. Kratochvil et al. (2009); 14. Lewis et al. (2009); 15. Lewis et al. (2010); 16. Rohde et al. (2001); 17. Rohde et al. (2006); 18. Shamseddeen et al. (2011); 19. Stice et al. (2010); 20. Vitiello et al. (2011); 21. Vostanis et al. (1996); 22. Young, Mufson, & Davies (2006). In the body of the table, moderation results in favor of CBT are presented in plain text; moderation results in favor of IPT are indicated by ***bold italic*** formatting. Also note CBCL = Child Behavior Checklist (Achenbach, 1991); DAS = Dysfunctional Attitude Scale (Spanier, 1976); FAM = Family Assessment Measure (Skinner et al., 1983); SPSI-R = Social Problem Solving Inventory-Revised (D'Zurilla et al., 1996).

and medication was, on average, the most efficacious intervention for depressed adolescents. The superiority of combination treatment on clinician-rated depression symptoms was maintained in the subset of depressed teens with high levels of cognitive distortions, as assessed by the Children's Negative Cognitive Error Questionnaire (CNCEQ). In contrast, participants with lower baseline CNCEQ scores (< 63) responded equally well to combination treatment or to fluoxetine alone, both of which were significantly more effective than CBT or pill placebo (Curry et al., 2006). This ordering of conditions suggests that high levels of cognitive distortion may be an indication for adding on CBT to medication; however, high cognitive distortion did not substantially improve the efficacy of CBT alone in this sample, undercutting a more generalized application of the matching hypothesis. Furthermore, additional analyses in the TADS sample by Jacobs et al. (2009) failed to find evidence of moderation for an alternate measure of cognitive distortion, the DAS perfectionism subscale (also see discussion of this study in the section on mediation in this chapter). High DAS perfectionism scores at baseline predicted poorer outcomes across all treatment groups and pill placebo, but did not moderate the effects of combination or CBT. Rohde and colleagues (2006) also probed the moderating effect of the DAS in a trial testing the efficacy of CBT (a version of the well-known Coping with Depression for Adolescents [CWD-A] program) versus a life skills/tutoring control condition. This sample is unique in the youth depression treatment literature, in that the depressed teen sample was recruited from a juvenile justice center and in addition to meeting diagnostic criteria for Major Depressive Disorder (MDD), all youth met diagnostic criteria for Conduct Disorder as well. As in the TADS sample, in this trial, DAS scores at baseline did not moderate outcome, operationalized in this study as weeks to MDD recovery. Vostanis et al. (1996) also failed to find evidence of moderation in a comparison of a brief CBT model to non-directive therapy; both treatment modalities improved participant self-esteem.

Four additional studies probed for moderating effects of hopelessness. Hopelessness is a core cognitive component of learned helplessness models of depression and conveys a generally negative or empty outlook on the future, due to the abandonment of expectation of potential contentment or success. In a reanalysis of the Brent et al. (1997) trial, hopelessness was associated with poor outcomes across CBT, family therapy, and non-directive treatment (Brent et al., 1998), and larger changes in hopelessness in CBT helped to explain the superiority of CBT over supportive therapy on the outcome of suicidality (Barbe et al., 2004a). However, baseline levels of hopelessness did not change the magnitude of the CBT effect on depression outcomes, relative to comparison treatments. The same team of investigators later examined hopelessness as a predictor and moderator in a major, multi-site clinical trial of Treatment-Resistant Depression in Adolescents (TORDIA; Brent et al., 2008). In this trial, seriously depressed teens who had failed to respond to an initial course of antidepressants were randomly assigned to medication switch, with or without add-on CBT. Hopelessness was tested as a potential moderator of treatment response, which was defined by ≥ 50% improvement on clinician-rated depression symptoms and global ratings of functional improvement (Clinical Global Impressions [CGI]; Guy, 1976). Contrary to the matching hypothesis, *lower* levels of hopelessness at baseline were associated with better response to CBT add-on at the 12-week assessment (Asarnow et al., 2009). However, the moderating effect of hopelessness was not maintained over long-term follow-up in TORDIA (Vitiello et al., 2011), nor was it replicated in the TADS sample (Curry et al., 2006) or CWD-A application to teens with depression and conduct problems (Rohde et al., 2006). As with the original Brent et al. (1997), these investigations found that hopelessness predicted poor response across conditions, leaving the TORDIA trial as the sole investigation finding a moderating relationship.

We turn next from cognitive distortions to problem-solving. Becker-Weidman and colleagues (2010) utilized the Social Problem Solving Inventory-Revised (SPSI-R; D'Zurilla, Nezu, & Maydeu-Olivares, 1996) to identify how different problem-solving styles impacted treatment outcome in the TADS sample of depressed teens. The scale assessed five approaches or orientations toward the process of problem-solving: a generally positive orientation to the process of solving problems (e.g., belief that problems can be solved), a negative problem orientation (e.g., frustration in the face of difficulty implementing solutions), a rational approach to solving problems (e.g., a desire to break problems into small, logical steps), an avoidant style, and an impulsive/careless style. None of these subscales significantly moderated group differences when clinician-rated depression symptoms were the outcome. However, when using the Suicidal Ideation Questionnaire as the outcome measure (SIQ-Jr; Reynolds, 1987), both positive and negative problem orientations were significant moderators. Depressed youth with high levels of positive problem orientation at baseline had lower levels of suicidality in CBT in comparison to alternative treatments (SSRI alone or combination treatment). Treatment groups did not significantly differ from each other for teens with low positive problem orientation. In a similar pattern, treatment groups did not differ in efficacy for individuals with high baseline negative problem orientation, but teens with lower levels of negative problem orientation showed significantly greater improvement in suicidality when treated with CBT. The other treatment groups did not differ from one another. Notably, although this measure was designed to assess many styles of problem-solving, the results collapsed into a positive-negative contrast, with teens who indicated greater affiliation with problem-solving as a skill making better use of CBT as a tool for reducing suicidality.

Finally, coping style was assessed as a predictor and moderator in the CDW-A trial testing the efficacy of CBT for teens with depression and conduct problems. In contrast to the null findings for hopelessness and the DAS, coping style was a significant moderator of effects (Rohde et al., 2006). Youth with positive coping skills at baseline performed dramatically better than youth in control (a life skills/tutoring condition), recovering from MDD in 6 weeks versus 16 weeks. In contrast, no treatment effect was identified in the subsample of teens who reported poor coping skills. This finding points in the opposite direction from that hypothesized by a match-to-diathesis model, suggesting instead that CBT was most effective with youth who already had strengths in coping to build upon (a capitalization versus compensation model; Rude & Rehm, 1991). The coping measure included in this report serves as a useful bridge to our next section on behavioral skill moderators; "coping" included both cognitive and behavioral elements, such as escapism/avoidance in the face of stress.

BEHAVIORAL MODERATORS

Despite the importance of behavioral techniques to the CBT model, very few studies include measures of behavioral mood regulation skills at baseline, and even fewer test whether deficits in these skills moderate treatment. In the Rohde sample of depressed and disruptive teens (Rohde et al., 2006), baseline frequency of pleasant activities was investigated as a potential moderator of the CBT versus life skills/tutoring comparison. Teens' baseline use of pleasant activities to regulate mood was not related to differential response to CBT.

INTERPERSONAL FUNCTIONING AND RELATIONSHIPS
We next turn to an examination of interpersonal moderators. Two investigations have focused on adolescents social networks. In the Rohde trial of CBT for youth with depression and disruptive behavior, baseline social adjustment did not moderate CBT outcome, relative to the life skills control condition (Rohde et al., 2006). Gau et al. (2012) also failed to find a moderating relationship between adolescents' perceived social support from friends and family and the relative benefit of CBT versus an educational control condition.

Three published reports have explored the moderating effects of family conflict. In an analysis of the TADS data, Curry and colleagues (2006) examined whether the relation between treatment assignment and outcome (severity of depression) would vary as a function of parent-child conflict. Parent-child conflict was measured using a combination of scores from both parent and youth baseline reports on Conflict Behavior Questionnaire (CBQ; Prinz, 1977) and did not moderate response to treatment. Family conflict in the TADS sample was further explored by Feeny et al. (2009), using a slightly different operationalization focusing on both the CBQ and specific ratings of contentious issues. Again, conflict did not moderate response to intervention in this sample, although, in this analysis, conflict predicted poor response across all treatments. In a reanalysis of the Rohde trial, family cohesion (defined as low parent-child conflict) did not moderate response to CWD-A (Rohde et al., 2006).

In contrast to these null moderator findings for family conflict, marital discord did appear to be linked to intervention response in the TADS sample through complex interactions between conflict, gender, and youth externalizing behavior. Contrary to their expectations, Amaya and colleagues (2011) found that marital discord alone did not significantly impact differential response to combination of fluoxetine and CBT (COMB), fluoxetine (FLX) alone, CBT alone, or placebo. However, when gender and externalizing problems were added to this model, two distinct, significant three-way interactions were found, moderating acute treatment response. Examining *treatment x discord x gender*, COMB outperformed placebo across all levels of the moderating variables. In high-discord households, FLX also was superior to placebo, regardless of gender. These findings mirror the overall results of TADS, where interventions involving medication outperformed placebo across metrics. Results involving CBT and females were more complex. In high-conflict households, COMB outperformed CBT alone for males but not for female adolescents; indeed, female adolescents in high-conflict homes showed a uniform and undifferentiated response to all active treatments (versus PBO). In contrast, females in low-conflict homes showed a significantly worse response to CBT alone compared to COMB and FLX, with CBT failing to separate from placebo. Unpacking the *treatment x discord x externalizing* symptoms interaction yielded similar effects for combination treatment. Across all levels of moderators, COMB separated from placebo. However, within the subset of highly oppositional adolescents, marital conflict moderated response to intervention. Under conditions of high discord, both treatments involving medication—COMB and FLX—produced superior effects for oppositional youth relative to CBT and placebo. Under conditions of low discord, depressed and oppositional youth benefited significantly more from COMB than all other treatments, with FLX failing to separate from placebo and CBT alone also showing a very poor response rate. Across these many analyses, combination treatment emerged as a robust intervention, and, interestingly, CBT alone appeared to fare particularly poorly under conditions of low marital discord.

Feeney et al. (2009) also explored the moderating role of seven indices of family functioning, drawn from the Family Assessment Measure (FAM-II; Skinner, Steinhauer, & Santa-Barbara, 1983). Notably, parent report of family functioning was not statistically related to outcome for any of the FAM subscales, and all moderator findings are based on adolescent report. Moderator results varied by definition of outcome, with the strongest pattern of moderation for clinician-reported depression severity (CDRS-R). Across analyses, adolescents who reported good family functioning (e.g., stronger agreements and more clarity on values and norms and control/rules, better communication and involvement) were more likely to benefit from combination therapy than FLX alone, CBT alone, or placebo. Conversely, among adolescents who reported worse family functioning, combination and FLX generally showed similar effects, with these conditions separating from CBT alone and placebo. As discussed previously with marital discord, combination therapy emerged as relatively robust to negative interpersonal moderators.

Contextual Moderators

STRESSFUL LIFE EVENTS

Only one CBT trial has investigated the moderating role of stressful life events, an indicated prevention study by Gau et al. (2012) targeting high school students with elevated depression symptoms. In this sample, a significant interaction was observed between treatment type, stress, and substance abuse. The CBT prevention program separated well from the education control for teens with low or moderate levels of stressful life events and substance use. However, for teens with either high levels of stress or significant substance use, the CBT program was not statistically superior to control.

TRAUMA

Three different CBT trials have probed the moderating impact of trauma history on treatment outcomes among depressed adolescents. In a reanalysis of the Brent et al. (1997) comparative efficacy trial of CBT, Barbe et al. (2004b) found a significant interaction between treatment and history of sexual abuse. Too few participants in the family therapy arm had experienced sexual abuse to allow for analysis. When examining the remaining sample, CBT was reliably superior to supportive therapy for youth without a history of sexual abuse; however, for youth with an abuse history, CBT did not outperform the supportive therapy control. In the TADS sample, Lewis et al. (2010) identified four subgroups of youth: those with no trauma history (n = 201); those with trauma history but with no abuse (n = 148); those with experience of physical abuse (n = 40); and those with experience of sexual abuse (n = 38). Reports of trauma were assessed using the PTSD section from the KSADS-PL interview. A significant *trauma x treatment x time* interaction revealed that adolescents with no trauma history had equally positive outcomes in COMB and FLX with worse outcomes observed in CBT and PBO, replicating the findings in the TADS sample as whole. Youth with a trauma history (but not abuse) and youth with a history of physical abuse had similar outcomes, with all four arms failing to statistically separate from each other (combination, FLX, CBT, and placebo). In contrast, youth with a history of sexual abuse had particularly poor outcomes in CBT alone, with all other arms outperforming this condition. Trauma history also was found to moderate short-term (Asarnow et al., 2009; Shamseddeen et al., 2011) and long-term (Vitiello et al., 2011) outcomes of the TORDIA trial. In the main effects findings of the TORDIA study, adjunctive CBT was found to be superior to medication switch alone in a sample of seriously depressed adolescents who had already failed a trial of antidepressant medication. The PTSD portion of the KSADS-PL was used to assess abuse history in this sample, with 13.15% (n = 43) of youth reporting a history of physical abuse (PA) and 15.9% (n = 55) a history of sexual abuse (SA). As in the rest of the CBT literature, youth without a trauma history had superior outcomes in combination (medication switch + adjunctive CBT) therapy in comparison to medication monotherapy (switch to a new antidepressant; Asarnow et al., 2009). However, trauma history significantly moderated response to (a) flatten out the superior effects of combination therapy for youth with sexual abuse and (b) reverse the relative benefits of combination and monotherapy for youth with physical abuse. Indeed, at both post-treatment (Shamsedden et al., 2011) and 18-month follow-up (Vitiello et al., 2011), youth with a history of physical abuse had a statistically superior response to medication monotherapy over combination, even after controlling for differences between PA and non-PA groups on negative clinical indicators such as depression severity, suicidality, and post-traumatic stress symptoms.

Generalizability Moderators

We next turn to an examination of clinical and demographic moderators of CBT response. These results speak to the potential generalizability of CBT effects across the population of depressed youth and limits to the effectiveness of CBT as an intervention when applied to diverse samples.

FEATURES OF DEPRESSION

Five clinical trials examined whether baseline severity moderated youth outcome; of these, three found a significant relationship. In the TADS trial, combination treatment was most efficacious in the mild/moderate depression subgroup; however, combination did not significantly differ from medication

monotherapy in the severe depression subgroup, although both were still superior to CBT alone and placebo (Curry et al., 2006). In the TORDIA trial, combination therapy (adjunctive CBT plus medication switch) was consistently more
efficacious than medication monotherapy, but depression symptom severity
moderated treatment effects in a quadratic pattern (Asarnow et al., 2009). The
participants with low and high symptoms (CDRS-R < 52 or CDRS-R > 66) had
the largest magnitude of CBT effects at post-treatment, although this effect was
not present at 18-month follow-up (Vitiello et al., 2011). In a prevention study,
Horowitz and colleagues (2007) tested baseline scores on two youth-reported
depression scales (CDI and CES-D) as moderators of response to CBT, IPT,
and control. For youth with initially high CDI scores (operationalized a variety of ways), CBT was significantly more efficacious than control condition
and IPT showed a mixed pattern of generally positive effects; however, the
two active treatments did not separate from control for youth with low symptoms. This moderating relationship was not found when analyzing the interactions using the CES-D as the severity measure, nor was it maintained at the
6-month follow-up (Horowitz et al., 2007). In addition, two trials that utilized
youth-report on the Beck Depression Inventory (BDI; Beck, Steer, & Garbin,
1988) did not find significant moderation effects, post-treatment (Gau et al.,
2011; Rohde et al., 2006). Finally, three of these investigations (TADS, Curry
et al., 2006; CWD-A, Rohde et al., 2006; TORDIA, Vitiello et al., 2011) broad-
ened their definition of severity to include global functioning, rated by trained
clinicians using the C-GAS. Level of functioning at intake did not significantly
moderate outcome in any of the three trials.

In addition to severity, various features of depressive illness also have been
tested as potential moderators. In the Rohde et al. (2006) trial of CDW-A, age
of onset of first major depressive episode (MDE) did not significantly moderate
effects; however, those reporting multiple MDEs prior to study enrollment (i.e.,
recurrent depression) saw recovery in 6 weeks when receiving CWD-A, which is
over 6 times faster than the recovery time of participants with recurrent depression who were randomized to the life skills control group (recovery = 38 weeks).
CDW-A did not separate from life skills control in participants who reported a
single depressive experience at intake. Both TADS and TORDIA trials investigated the impact of duration of depressive illness, but neither trial obtained
significant results (Curry et al., 2006; Vitiello et al., 2011). The TADS team (2004)
further used the CDRS-R to create a five-item summative measure of melancholic features (anhedonia, insomnia, appetite disturbance, guilt, psychomotor
retardation). This summed score predicted treatment outcome, where participants with fewer/less severe melancholic features improved more overall, but
the scale did not moderate treatment outcome (Curry et al., 2006). Four studies
investigated the moderating effects of suicidality on treatment outcome: none of
the trials found statistically significant effects (Barbe et al., 2004b; Curry et al.,
2006, Rohde et al., 2006; Vitiello et al., 2011). In the TORDIA sample, youth with
a history of non-suicidal self-injury had poorer outcomes across arms, and youth
without a history of self-harm experienced greater response in combination

treatment than teens with such a history (Asarnow et al., 2009). However, these moderation results were not maintained at follow-up (Vitiello et al., 2011).

COMORBIDITY

As discussed earlier, comorbidity is the rule in depression, with 90% of youth diagnosed with major depression meeting diagnostic criteria for at least one additional disorder and 50% for two or more (Simonoff et al., 1997). The most common comorbidity with depression is anxiety, and four trials have explored the effects of comorbid anxiety on treatment outcome (Asarnow et al., 2009; Brent et al., 1998; Curry et al., 2006; Rohde et al., 2006, Vitiello et al., 2011). In general, the presence of anxiety disorder predicts worse outcomes over time across treatment and control conditions. However, two of the four trials found that outcome for anxious youth were *relatively* better in arms including CBT compared to other treatments (Asarnow et al., 2009; Brent et al., 1998), although superior effects of adjunctive CBT in TORDIA were not maintained at follow-up (Vitiello et al., 2011).

Clinical trials of depression in youth frequently exclude participants who meet diagnostic criteria for serious externalizing comorbidity, such as Conduct Disorder. In this context, trials generally have not found moderating effects of comorbid externalizing symptomatology on depression outcome (Asarnow et al., 2009; Curry et al., 2006; Vitiello et al., 2011). The Rohde et al. trial (2006) recruited depressed and disruptive teens from the juvenile justice system and assessed the impact of comorbid substance use on depression treatment outcome. Though substance use and abuse was more likely to occur in this sample than a general treatment-seeking sample, the study did not identify any moderating effects as a result of comorbid substance use disorder, with CBT separating from life skills control across levels of substance use. In the TORDIA trial, substance use predicted poor treatment outcome overall, but there was no significant interaction with treatment group to indicate a moderating effect. As discussed earlier, Gau and colleagues (2012) did find moderating effects of substance use in their indicated prevention study of CBT for high school students with elevated symptoms of depression. In this investigation, CBT was more efficacious than control for youth scoring in the low to medium range of substance use. However, group differences disappeared when youth exhibited high levels of substance use at baseline. In order to tease apart the "disruptive behavior" category with the TADS sample, Kratochvil and colleagues (2009) extracted and analyzed the subset of externalizing youth meeting criteria for comorbid ADHD (14% of the enrolled sample). Results suggested that depressed youth with ADHD experienced similar improvements in all active intervention arms (COMB = FLX = CBT) compared to placebo. However, youth without ADHD who received combination therapy had greater improvement in their depression symptoms at post-treatment (COMB > (FLX > CBT) = PBO), although by week 36, outcomes across arms were similar (Kratochvil et al., 2009). In contrast, TORDIA participants *with* comorbid ADHD (16% of the sample) had a superior response to combination therapy compared to medication monotherapy, while those without comorbid ADHD did not show significant group differences in outcome (Asarnow et al., 2009).

DEMOGRAPHIC CHARACTERISTICS

Age, gender, ethnicity, and socioeconomic status have all been investigated as potential moderators of CBT response. With regard to age and development, investigators have hypothesized that (a) younger youth may show a superior response to CBT, given that they are earlier in the trajectory of disorder and may have less ingrained depressogenic cognitive and behavioral habits, or (b) older youth may benefit more from CBT, given their more developed abstract reasoning and general cognitive skills. More often than not, age has not been found to moderate response in either direction (Curry et al, 2006; Rohde et al., 2006; Stice et al., 2010), with the TORDIA trial being the sole study to find a greater benefit of adjunctive CBT (versus medication monotherapy) for older youth (Asarnow et al., 2009). In a different operationalization of development, Curry and colleagues (2006) did not find that verbal intelligence moderated outcomes of the TADS trial. Notably, all investigators testing development as a moderator have been conducted in adolescent-only samples, with significant restriction of range on this variable.

Gender also has been suggested as a moderator of CBT effects, with male participants hypothesized to benefit more than female participants given the structure and activity level found in most CBT models. However, three different trials using various CBT manuals reported that gender did not moderate treatment outcome (Amaya et al., 2011; Curry et al., 2006; Rohde et al., 2006, Stice et al., 2010). As discussed in a later section, gender also has been explored as a potential matching variable for choosing between IPT and CBT for depressed youth; results of these analyses have been inconclusive and not statistically significant.

The results for race/ethnicity and socioeconomic status have been more mixed. The TADS trial did not find significant moderating effects of race/ethnicity on the relative ordering of treatments (i.e., combination therapy remained the most efficacious intervention across groups; Curry et al., 2006); however, within TADS, income significantly moderated response. Results suggested that adolescents of families that earned less than \$75,000 per year found combination and medication alone to be equally effective in reducing CDRS-R scores and both more effective than CBT alone or placebo (COMB = FLX > CBT = PBO). In the high-income subgroup (> \$75,000), the three active treatment groups did not significantly differ from one another, but only combination and CBT alone were more efficacious than placebo (Curry et al., 2006). In contrast, the TORDIA trial (Asarnow et al., 2009; Vitiello et al., 2011) did not find moderating effects of socioeconomic status but did so for ethnicity. In TORDIA, stronger effects for combined treatment (CBT + medication switch) were found for Caucasian adolescents relative to adolescents from other racial and ethnic groups. Similarly, the Rodhe et al. (2006) investigation of CBT for youth with depression and disruptive behavior found that CBT was substantially superior than control for Caucasian teens (recovery in 11 versus 27 weeks, respectively; Rohde et al., 2006) but that

CBT and control did not statistically separate for minority participants. Notably, across all these studies, absolute representation of minority group participants was low (less than 30%), and all youth were again adolescents.

Moderators of IPT Effects

As discussed previously, the IPT clinical trial literature for youth depression is substantially smaller than the literature on CBT effects. As available, we next review moderators of IPT effects, following the same structure as our CBT review.

MATCH TO INTERVENTION

Matching hypotheses would suggest that IPT should outperform control conditions and alternate treatment models for youth with "matching" deficits in interpersonal skills, relationship quality, and family functioning at baseline. In contrast, significant moderation in favor of IPT would not be expected for youth with cognitive distortions or behavioral mood regulation deficits.

COGNITIVE AND BEHAVIORAL MODERATORS

While some investigations of IPT have included measures of social problem-solving (see Weersing, Rozenman, & Gonzalez, 2009), baseline levels of cognitive process variables have yet to be assessed as potential moderators of outcome. Furthermore, none of the published investigations of IPT in youth has included measures of behavioral mood regulation skills.

INTERPERSONAL MODERATORS

Data are available that are directly relevant to the interpersonal matching hypothesis. Gunlicks-Stoessel, Mufson, Jekal, and Turner (2010) performed a secondary analysis of an IPT-A effectiveness trial to understand the role of social functioning in IPT treatment outcome. In the primary investigation (Mufson et al., 2004), school counselors were randomized to provide IPT-A or supportive therapy (usual care in this setting) to depressed adolescents; teens receiving IPT-A had superior outcomes for both depression and global functioning. As would be predicted by a match-to-intervention model, IPT-A was especially effective when teens had significant interpersonal problems, with a medium effect size found for mother-child conflict and a large effect size for problems with peer relationships. Quality of dating relationships was not a significant moderator of outcome in this sample, although authors reported problems with reliability of this scale. Global quality of family functioning predicted poor outcomes in both IPT-A and supportive therapy but did not moderate response, suggesting some specificity to the family conflict finding (note that role disputes are a core content area of IPT intervention).

In addition, one IPT prevention study (Horowitz et al., 2009) tested whether the personality characteristics of orientation to social relationships or achievement orientation moderated response to IPT versus CBT in a sample of high school students. Moderation analyses were not performed in the high symptom subsample, and the results thus are not directly comparable to outcomes of treatment trials. Consistent with a match-to-intervention compensation model, higher levels of baseline sociotropy predicted lower levels of depression symptoms in IPT, but this relationship was not present for CBT or control. However, contrary to expectations, achievement orientation also moderated response to IPT and control (but not to CBT), such that individuals with higher levels of achievement orientation evidenced lower levels of depressive symptoms over time.

CONTEXTUAL MODERATORS

To date, no study has examined the moderating effects of stressful life events or trauma history on the efficacy of IPT for depression in children or adolescents.

GENERALIZABILITY MODERATORS

Features of Depression

Depression severity and functioning were tested as moderators in the IPT-A effectiveness trial discussed earlier (Mufson et al., 2004). For both of these variables, IPT was statistically superior to usual school counseling services for the youth who were most severe. In the less severe/higher functioning group, IPT-A and usual care did not separate from each other. The Horowitz et al. (2007) prevention study also tested whether baselines levels of self-reported depression symptoms moderated response to IPT versus CBT or control. As discussed previously in this chapter in the section on CBT, the pattern of results across measures suggested that active interventions were superior to control in youth with elevated symptoms (more analogous to a treatment sample), with CBT effects perhaps being marginally stronger than IPT effects.

Comorbidity

Young, Mufson, and Davies (2006) also reanalyzed data from the IPT-A school effectiveness trial (Mufson et al., 2004) to probe the effects of comorbid anxiety in IPT treatment outcome. Comorbid anxiety disorders (generalized anxiety disorder, social phobia, panic disorder) were present in 68% of teens, and anxiety generally predicted more severe depression at baseline and worse post-treatment outcomes. At a global level, the presence of anxiety did not significantly moderate outcome, although descriptive statistics were in the direction of superior effects of IPT for anxious youth. Among teens with probable panic disorder, moderating effects were statistically significant for both depression symptoms and functioning. IPT-A was significantly superior to supportive therapy control for teens with panic, and the two treatments did not statistically separate for youth without comorbid panic. These results were in line with investigator hypotheses and parallel findings in CBT on the superior efficacy of active interventions (versus control) in the presence of clinically complicating comorbid anxiety.

Demographic Characteristics

Significant moderation by age, gender, ethnicity, or socioeconomic status has not been formally assessed in the IPT youth depression treatment literature. The IPT prevention study discussed earlier (Horowitz et al., 2009) also assessed whether gender moderated the comparative efficacy of IPT, CBT, and control, hypothesizing that female participants would particularly benefit from the interpersonal focus of IPT (and boys from CBT). Gender analyses were not performed in the subsample of youth with high symptoms, a sample analogous to the treated group in many other depression clinical trials; however, in the unselected sample as a whole, gender was not a significant moderator.

CHALLENGES AND FUTURE DIRECTIONS

In this chapter, we have sought to answer two key questions about CBT for depression in youth and IPT for depression in adolescents—the evidence-based psychosocial interventions for this population. The first question is one of mediation. What are the underlying theories driving our efficacious treatments, and to what extent do data on mediators of treatment effects support these theories of intervention? Data on this question are sparse at best. Despite nearly 30 years of CBT clinical trial research in this area, we were able to find only four studies that formally tested whether the cognitive and behavioral processes hypothesized to drive intervention effects statistically mediated the impact of intervention on depression outcomes. All four of these studies focused on depressed adolescents (to the exclusion of children) and self-report of key constructs, and, more often than not, the design of the mediation tests left directionality of effects unclear (i.e., failure to establish temporal precedence of changes). Furthermore, all four studies utilized different CBT treatment manuals that varied in their relative focus on cognitive versus behavioral techniques and number of sessions, and the trials had very different inclusion criteria in terms of level of severity and comorbidity. It is perhaps not surprising that this weak foundation has not yielded a definitive set of results. Cognitive change may be related to change in depression symptoms, depending on the study and the measure, and the field still awaits a positive mediational finding for a behavioral process in CBT for depressed youth. Furthermore, no data are yet available on mediators of IPT effects. Meta-analytic data suggest that CBT and IPT both *may* have theory-specific impacts on potential mediators of intervention effects when these candidate mediators are measured as simple, post-treatment outcomes (Weersing, Gonzalez, & Rozenman, 2009), but there is clearly a need for additional, programmatic research, with a focus on the replication of effects across manuals and investigations (as in multi-site trials) designed to clarify mechanisms of action for our efficacious interventions for youth depression.

The second question examined in this review is that of moderation. Are CBT and IPT broadly applicable to depressed youth, or should these interventions be expected to work more or less well with different types of depression, in the presence of comorbid disorders, and across demographic groups? We began by examining evidence for *match-to-intervention* factors—cognitive, behavioral, or interpersonal characteristics of youth that map onto the theoretical diatheses targeted by CBT and IPT protocols. In the case of CBT, the modal moderator result was a non-significant finding (see Table 4.1); youth with high levels of cognitive distortions or behavioral deficits were generally no more likely to benefit from CBT than youth with lower scores on these measures. When significant results were found, the data were less consistent with a compensation model of CBT effects (match to diathesis) than a capitalization model, in which youth benefited the most when CBT protocols built on their strengths (e.g., good coping skills, positive problem orientation, less hopelessness). Data on match-to-intervention moderators for IPT were more sparse but more consistently supportive of the importance of interpersonal factors in IPT success. One randomized treatment trial indicated that baseline difficulties in social relationships were related to a more positive response to IPT (a compensation model), while an indicated prevention study suggested that heightened importance of interpersonal relationships (sociotrophic personality orientation) also moderated response in favor of IPT (a capitalization model). Although three studies in the literature include both CBT and IPT conditions (Horowitz et al., 2007; Rossello & Bernal, 1999; Rossello, Bernal, & Rivera-Medina, 2008), only the Horowitz prevention trial tackled the interesting question of differential response to these evidence-based treatments. A priori the authors hypothesized significant moderation such that girls and youth with high orientation to relationships would have superior outcomes in IPT, while boys and youth with high achievement orientation would perform better in CBT. Of these, only sociotrophy was significantly related to intervention effects in the hypothesized direction (predicted outcome within IPT).

Indeed, demographic factors as a whole were not strong moderators of intervention effects, despite theoretical reasons to suspect that gender (as above) and developmental level might predict differential response to intervention. With regard to developmental level, and to a lesser extent ethnicity and socioeconomic status, the field suffers from serious problems with restriction of range. As discussed in the introduction to this chapter, the clinical trial literature is dominated by studies of depression in adolescents, and a major direction for future research is the extension of mediator and moderator research into early adolescence and childhood.

CBT and IPT also were largely robust to negative clinical indicators that might be expected to reduce the effects of intervention relative to control. IPT may perform particularly well (compared to supportive therapy) with more severe youth, and the combination of CBT and medication appears to be robust to a wide range of severity indicators (results for CBT monotherapy follow this trend but are more mixed). With regard to comorbidity, there is evidence to suggest that the positive effects of CBT and IPT may be amplified compared to control when youth suffer from comorbid anxiety, and CBT effects have generally remained statistically significant and have been undiminished when youth suffer from significant externalizing comorbidity (with the possible exception of substance abuse). Data are not available on the moderating impact of PTSD, but evidence on the effects of negative family context and trauma history suggest that these factors may diminish the efficacy of CBT. Trauma history has not been investigated as a moderator of IPT efficacy, although this is a theoretically interesting question. IPT has performed well under conditions of current family conflict; IPT could prove to be a particularly relevant intervention and positive match to youth suffering from the effects of past trauma or, equally plausibly, youth with trauma may be better matched to interventions such as CBT that build on strengths in other domains, rather than focusing primarily on interpersonal relationships.

IMPLICATIONS FOR PRACTICE

As discussed in the introduction, developing best-practice recommendations for youth depression has been limited by substantial gaps in the research literature. Data on depressed pre-pubertal children are sorely lacking, and all of the mediator and moderator results reviewed are based on studies of depressed adolescents. Within this essential limitation, there are areas of good news for the effective treatment of depression in youth. First, both CBT and IPT appeared to have reasonable generalizability in their effects—moderation of efficacy by demographic characteristics was rarely significant; intervention effects were robust to comorbidity and many indices of severity; and the combination of CBT and antidepressant treatment, in particular, was consistently superior to control and superior or equivalent to other active interventions, even when significant moderators were present. Second, while the literature is quite small, available data suggest that IPT may be a theoretically coherent intervention. Meta-analytic data indicate that IPT impacts interpersonal relationships (see the section on mediation in this chapter), and moderation findings for interpersonal factors are supportive of the intervention model theory. Compared to many multi-skill CBT protocols, IPT also may be a simpler intervention with a clearer single focus, both for delivering to youth and for training providers under conditions of low resources (cf. Bolton et al., 2003). In contrast, while CBT protocols have clearly demonstrated positive effects for youth depression, clinical trial data have not provided clear support for the CBT theories underlying these manuals. Mediation data are quite mixed, and moderator findings suggest that CBT may perform best as a capitalization intervention rather than as implied by the diathesis models central to CBT theory. As a result, practitioners are left with an efficacious set of CBT tools, but the rationale for why, when, and how to apply these tools in the care of individual youth becomes less clear. Research probing the question of strengths-based versus deficit-based models of CBT may better inform practice recommendations and aid in the development of future interventions for depressed children and adolescents.

AUTHOR NOTE

This work was made possible by support from the National Institutes of Health to V. Robin Weersing (MH084935, MH100260-01, MH064735) and to Carl Bolano (NIH SDSU MARC 5T34GM08303-24).

REFERENCES

Achenbach, T. M. (1991). *Manual for the Child Behavior Checklist/4–18 and 1991 Profile.* VT: University of Vermont Department of Psychiatry.

Ackerson, J., Scogin, F., McKendree-Smith, N., & Lyman, R. (1998). Cognitive bibliotherapy for mild and moderate adolescent depressive symptomatology. *Journal of Consulting and Clinical Psychology, 66*(4), 685–690. doi: 10.1037/0022-006X.66.4.685

Amaya, M., Reinecke, M., Silva, S., & March, J. (2011). Parental marital discord and treatment response in depressed adolescents. *Journal of Abnormal Child Psychology, 39*(3), 401–411.

Abramson, L. Y., Metalsky, G. I., & Alloy, L. B. (1989). Hopelessness depression: A theory-based subtype of depression. *Psychological Review, 96*(2), 358–372. doi: 10.1037/0033-295X.96.2.358

Asarnow, J., Jaycox, L., Tang, L., Duan, N., LaBorde, A., Zeledon, L. R., . . . Wells, K. B. (2009). Long-term benefits of short-term quality improvement interventions for depressed youths in primary care. *The American Journal of Psychiatry, 166*(9), 1002–1010. doi: 10.1097/CHI.0b013e3181977476

Asarnow, J. R., Goldstein, M. J., Tompson, M., & Guthrie, D. (1993). One-year outcomes of depressive disorders in child psychiatric in-patients: Evaluation of the prognostic power of a brief measure of expressed emotion. *Journal of Child Psychology and Psychiatry, 34*(2), 129–137.

Avenevoli, S., Knight, E., Kessler, R. C., & Merikangas, K. R. (2008). Epidemiology of depression in children and adolescents. In J. R. Z. Abela & B. L. Hankin (Eds.), *Handbook of depression in children and adolescents* (pp. 6–32). New York: Guilford Press.

Barbe, R., Bridge, J., Birmaher, B., Kolko, D., & Brent, D. (2004b). Lifetime history of sexual abuse, clinical presentation, and outcome in a clinical trial for adolescent depression. *The Journal of Clinical Psychiatry, 65*, 77–83.

Barbe, R., Bridge, J., Birmaher, B., Kolko, D., & Brent, D. (2004a). Suicidality and its relationship to treatment outcome in depressed adolescents. *Suicide & Life-threatening Behavior, 34*, 44–55.

Beck, A. T., Rush, A. J., Shaw, B. F., & Emery, G. (1979). *Cognitive therapy of depression.* New York: Guilford Press.

Beck, A. T., Steer, R. M., & Garbin, M. (1988). Psychometric properties of the Beck Depression Inventory: Twenty-five years of evaluation. *Clinical Psychology Review, 8*, 77–100.

Becker-Weidman, E., Jacobs, R., Reinecke, M., Silva, S., & March, J. (2010). Social problem-solving among adolescents treated for depression. *Behaviour Research and Therapy, 48*, 11–18.

Brent, D. A., Emslie, G. J., Clarke, G. N., Wagner, K. D., Asarnow, J. R., Keller, M., . . . Zelanzy, J. (2008). Switching to another SSRI or to Venlafaxine with or without cognitive behavioral therapy for adolescents with SSRI-resistant depression: The TORDIA randomized controlled trial. *Journal of the American Medical Association*, *299*(8), 901–913.

Brent, D. A., Holder, D., Kolko, D. J., Birmaher, B., Baugher, M., Roth, C., . . . Johnson, B. A. (1997). A clinical psychotherapy trial for adolescent depression comparing cognitive, family, and supportive therapy. *Archives of General Psychiatry*, *54*(9), 877–885.

Brent, D. A., Kolko, D. J., Birmaher, B., Baugher, M., Bridge, J., Roth, C., & Holder, D. (1998). Predictors of treatment efficacy in a clinical trial of three psychosocial treatments for adolescent depression. *Journal of the American Academy of Child and Adolescent Psychiatry*, *37*(9), 906–914.

Butler, L., Miezitis S., Friedman, R., Cole, E. (1980). The effect of two school-based intervention programs on depressive symptoms in preadolescents. *American Educational Research Journal*, *17*, 111–119.

Caspi, A., Sugden, K., Moffitt, T., Taylor, A., Craig, I. W., Harrington, H., . . . & Poulton, R. (2003). Influence of life stress on depression: Moderation by a polymorphism in the 5-HTT gene. *Science*, *301*(5631), 386–389.

Centers for Disease Control and Prevention. (2010). *10 Leading Causes of Death, United States*. Retrieved from http://www.cdc.gov/injury/wisqars/pdf/10LCID_All_Deaths_By_Age_Group_2010-a.pdf

Curry, J., Rohde, P., Simons, A., Silva, S., Vitiello, B., Kratochvil, C., . . . March, J. (2006). Predictors and moderators of acute outcome in the Treatment for Adolescents with Depression Study (TADS). *Journal of the American Academy of Child and Adolescent Psychiatry*, *45*(12), 1427–1439.

D'Zurilla, T., Nezu, A., & Maydeu-Olivares, A. (1996). *Manual for the Social Problem-Solving Inventory-Revised*. New York: Multi-Health Systems.

Feeny, N., Silva, S., Reinecke, M., McNulty, S., Findling, R., Rohde, P., . . . March, J. S. (2009). An exploratory analysis of the impact of family functioning on treatment for depression in adolescents. *Journal of Clinical Child & Adolescent Psychology*, *38*(6), 814–825.

Garber, J., & Weersing, V. (2010). Comorbidity of anxiety and depression in youth: Implications for treatment and prevention. *Clinical Psychology: Science and Practice*, *17*(4), 293–306.

Gau, J., Stice, E., Rohde, P., & Seeley, J. (2012). Negative life events and substance use moderate cognitive behavioral adolescent depression prevention intervention. *Cognitive Behaviour Therapy*, *41*(3), 241–250. doi: org/10.1080/16506073.2011.649781

Gazelle, H., & Rudolph, K. (2004). Moving toward and away from the world: Social approach and avoidance trajectories in anxious solitary youth. *Child Development*, *75*(3), 829–849.

Gladstone, T., & Kaslow, N. (1995). Depression and attributions in children and adolescents: A meta-analytic review. *Journal of Abnormal Child Psychology*, *23*(5), 597–606.

Goodman, S. H., & Gotlib, I. H. (2002). Transmission of risk to children of depressed parents: Integration and conclusions. In S. H. Goodman & I. H. Gotlib (Eds.),

Children of depressed parents: Mechanisms of risk and implications for treatment (pp. 278–307). Washington, DC: American Psychological Association.

Goodman, E., & Whitaker, R. C. (2002). A prospective study of the role of depression in the development and persistence of adolescent obesity. *Pediatrics, 110*(3), 497–504.

Gotlib, I., Lewinsohn, P., & Seeley, J. (1995). Symptoms versus a diagnosis of depression: Differences in psychosocial functioning. *Journal of Consulting and Clinical Psychology, 63*, 90–100.

Gunlicks-Stoessel, M., Mufson, L., Jekal, A., & Turner, J. (2010). The impact of perceived interpersonal functioning on treatment for adolescent depression: PT-A versus treatment as usual in school-based health clinics. *Journal of Consulting and Clinical Psychology, 78*(2), 260–267.

Guy, W. (1976). *ECDEU assessment manual for psychopharmacology* (2nd ed.). Washington, DC: Government Printing Office.

Hammen, C., Rudolph, K., Weisz, J., Rao, U., & Burge, D. (1999). The context of depression in clinic-referred youth: Neglected areas in treatment. *Journal of the American Academy of Child and Adolescent Psychiatry, 38*, 64–71.

Horowitz, J., Garber, J., Ciesla, J., Young, J., & Mufson, L. (2007). Prevention of depressive symptoms in adolescents: A randomized trial of cognitive-behavioral and interpersonal prevention programs. *Journal of Consulting and Clinical Psychology, 75*(5), 693–706. doi: 10.1037/0022-006X.75.5.693

Huey, S. J., & Polo, A. J. (2008). Evidence-based psychosocial treatments for ethnic minority youth. *Journal of Clinical Child & Adolescent Psychology, 37*, 262–301.

Jacobs, R., Silva, S., Reinecke, M., Curry, J., Ginsburg, G., Kratochvil, C. J., & March, J. S. (2009). Dysfunctional attitudes scale perfectionism: A predictor and partial mediator of acute treatment outcome among clinically depressed adolescents. *Journal of Clinical Child & Adolescent Psychology, 38*(6), 803–813.

Jaycox, L., Stein, B., Paddock, S., Miles, J., Chandra, A., et al. (2009). Impact of teen depression on academic, social, and physical functioning. *Pediatrics, 124*(4), e596–e605.

Kaufman, N., Rohde, P., Seeley, J., Clarke, G., & Stice, E. (2005). Potential mediators of cognitive-behavioral therapy for adolescents with comorbid major depression and conduct disorder. *Journal of Consulting and Clinical Psychology, 73*, 38–46.

Kendler, K., Thornton, L., & Gardner, C. (2001). Genetic risk, number of previous depressive episodes, and stressful life events in predicting onset of major depression. *The American Journal of Psychiatry, 158*(4), 582–586.

Kessler, R. C., Foster, C. L., Saunders, W. B., & Stang, P. E. (1995). Social consequences of psychiatric disorders, I: Educational attainment. *American Journal of Psychiatry, 152*(7), 1026–1032.

Klerman, G. K., Weissman, M. M., Rounsaville, B. J., & Chevrson, E. S. (1984). *Interpersonal psychotherapy of depression: A brief, focused, specific strategy.* Northvale, NJ: Jason Aronson.

Kolko, D., Brent, D., Baugher, M., Bridge, J., & Birmaher, B. (2000). Cognitive and family therapies for adolescent depression: Treatment specificity, mediation, and moderation. *Journal of Consulting and Clinical Psychology, 68*(4), 603–614.

Kratochvil, C., May, D., Silva, S., Madaan, V., Puumala, S., Curry, J. F., . . . March, J. S. (2009). Treatment response in depressed adolescents with and without co-morbid attention-deficit/hyperactivity disorder in the treatment for adolescents with depression study. *Journal of Child and Adolescent Psychopharmacology, 19*(5), 519–527.

Lewinsohn, P. M. (1975). Engagement in pleasant activities and depression level. *Journal of Abnormal Psychology, 84*(6), 729–731.

Lewinsohn, P. M., Allen, N., Seeley, J., & Gotlib, I. (1999). First onset versus recurrence of depression: Differential processes of psychosocial risk. *Journal of Abnormal Psychology, 108*(3), 483–489.

Lewinsohn, P. M., Clarke, G. N., Rohde, P., Hops, H., & Seeley, J. R. (1996). A course in coping: A cognitive-behavioral approach to the treatment of adolescent depression. In E. D. Hibbs & P. S. Jensen (Eds.), *Psychosocial treatments for child and adolescent disorders: Empirically based strategies for clinical practice* (pp. 109–135). Washington, DC: American Psychological Association. doi: 10.1037/10196-005

Lewinsohn, P. M., & MacPhillamy, D. (1974). The relationship between age and engagement in pleasant activities. *Journal of Gerontology, 29*(3), 290.

Lewinsohn, P. M., Roberts, R., Seeley, J., Rohde, P., Gotlib, I., & Hops, H. (1994). Adolescent psychopathology: II. Psychosocial risk factors for depression. *Journal of Abnormal Psychology, 103*(2), 302–315.

Lewis, C., Simons, A., Nguyen, L., Murakami, J., Reid, M., Silva, S. G., & March, J. S. (2010). Impact of childhood trauma on treatment outcome in the treatment for adolescents with depression study (TADS). *Journal of the American Academy of Child & Adolescent Psychiatry, 49*(2), 132–140.

Mash, E. J., & Wolfe, D. A. (2016). Depressive and bipolar disorders. *Abnormal Child Psychology* (6th ed.) (pp. 318). Boston, MA: Cengage Learning.

Mufson, L., Dorta, K., Wickramaratne, P., Nomura, Y., Olfson, M., & Weissman, M. M. (2004). A randomized effectiveness trial of interpersonal psychotherapy for depressed adolescents. *Archives of General Psychiatry, 61*(6), 577–584.

Mufson, L., Dorta, K., Moreau, D., & Weissman, M. M. (2011). *Interpersonal psychotherapy for depressed adolescents* (2nd ed.). New York: Guilford Press.

Mufson, L., Weissman, M., Moreau, D., & Garfinkel, R. (1999). The efficacy of interpersonal psychotherapy for depressed adolescents. *Archives of General Psychiatry, 56*(6), 573–579.

National Institute of Mental Health; University of Pittsburgh. (2000). Family based interpersonal psychotherapy (FB-IPT) for depressed preadolescents. In ClinicalTrials.gov [Internet]. Bethesda, MD: National Library of Medicine (US). Available from https://clinicaltrials.gov/ct2/show/study/NCT02054312 NLM Identifier: NCT02054312.

Prinz, R. J. (1977). *The assessment of parent-adolescent relations: Discriminating distressed and nondistressed dyads* (Doctoral dissertation, ProQuest Information & Learning).

Rao, U., Weissman, M. M., Martin, J. A., & Hammond, R. W. (1993). Childhood depression and risk of suicide: A preliminary report of a longitudinal study. *Journal of the American Academy of Child & Adolescent Psychiatry, 32*, 21–27.

Reynolds, W. M. (1987). *Professional manual for the Reynolds Adolescent Depression Scale*. Lutz, FL: Psychological Assessment Resources.

Rice, F., Lifford, K. J., Thomas, H. V., & Thapar, A. (2007). Mental health and functional outcomes of maternal and adolescent reports of adolescent depressive symptoms. *Journal of the American Academy of Child & Adolescent Psychiatry, 46*(9), 1162–1170. doi: 10.1097/chi.0b013e3180cc255f

Rohde, P., Clarke, G. N., Mace, D. E., Jorgensen, J. S., & Seeley, J. R. (2004). An efficacy/ effectiveness study of cognitive-behavioral treatment for adolescents with comorbid major depression and conduct disorder. *Journal of the American Academy of Child & Adolescent Psychiatry, 43*(6), 660–668.

Rohde, P., Seeley, J., Kaufman, N., Clarke, G., & Stice, E. (2006). Predicting time to recovery among depressed adolescents treated in two psychosocial group interventions. *Journal of Consulting and Clinical Psychology, 74*, 80–88. doi: 10.1037/0022-006X.74.1.80

Rossello, J., Bernal, G., & Rivera-Medina, C. (2008). Individual and group CBT and IPT for Puerto Rican adolescents with depressive symptoms. *Cultural Diversity and Ethnic Minority Psychology, 14*(3), 234–245. doi: 10.1037/1099-9809.14.3.234

Rude, S., & Rehm, L. (1991). Response to treatments for depression: The role of initial status on targeted cognitive and behavioral skills. *Clinical Psychology Review, 11*(5), 493–514.

Shaffer, D., Gould, M. S., Brasic, J., Ambrosini, M. D., Fisher, Pl., Bird, H., & Aluwahlia, S. (1983). A children's global assessment scale (CGAS). *Archives of General Psychiatry, 40*(11), 1228–1231.

Shamseddeen, W., Asarnow, J., Clarke, G., Vitiello, B., Wagner, K. D., Birmaher, B., . . . Brent, D. A. (2011). Impact of physical and sexual abuse on treatment response in the treatment of resistant depression in adolescent study (TORDIA). *Journal of the American Academy of Child & Adolescent Psychiatry, 50*(3), 293–301.

Simonoff, E., Pickles, A., Meyer, J. M., Silberg, J. L., Maes, H. H., Loeber, R., . . . & Eaves, L. J. (1997). The Virginia Twin Study of Adolescent Behavioral Development: Influences of age, sex, and impairment on rates of disorder. *Archives of General Psychiatry, 54*(9), 801–808.

Skinner, H. A., Steinhauer, P., & Santa-Barbara, J. (1983). The family assessment measure. *Canadian Journal of Community Mental Health, 2*, 91–105.

Spanier, G. B. (1976). Measuring dyadic adjustment: New scales for assessing the quality of marriage and similar dyads. *Journal of Marriage and the Family, 38*, 15–28.

Stice, E., Rohde, P., Gau, J., & Wade, E. (2010). Efficacy trial of a brief cognitive-behavioral depression prevention program for high-risk adolescents: Effects at 1- and 2-year follow-up. *Journal of Consulting and Clinical Psychology, 78*(6), 856–867.

Treatment for Adolescents with Depression Study Team. (2003). Treatment for Adolescents with Depression Study (TADS): Rationale, design, and methods. *Journal of the American Academy of Child and Adolescent Psychiatry, 42*(5), 531.

Treatment for Adolescents with Depression Study Team. (2004). Fluoxetine, cognitive-behavioral therapy, and their combination for adolescents with depression. *Journal of the American Medical Association, 292*(7), 807–820.

Tompson, M., Pierre, C., Boger, K., McKowen, J., Chan, P., & Freed, R. D. (2010). Maternal depression, maternal expressed emotion, and youth psychopathology. *Journal of Abnormal Child Psychology, 38*, 105–117.

Vitiello, B., Emslie, G., Clarke, G., Wagner, K., Asarnow, J., . . . Brent, D. A. (2011). Long-term outcome of adolescent depression initially resistant to selective serotonin reuptake inhibitor treatment: A follow-up study of the TORDIA sample. *The Journal of Clinical Psychiatry, 72*(3), 388–396.

Vostanis, P., Feehan, C., Grattan, E., & Bickerton, W. (1996). Treatment for children and adolescents with depression: Lessons from a controlled trial. *Clinical Child Psychology and Psychiatry, 1*(2), 199–212. doi: 10.1177/1359104596012003.

Weersing, V. R., & Gonzalez, A. (2009). Effectiveness of interventions for adolescent depression: reason for hope or cause for concern? In S. Nolen-Hoeksema & L. M. Hilt (Eds.), *Handbook of depression in adolescents* (pp. 589–616). New York: Routledge.

Weersing, V. R., Rozenman, M., & Gonzalez, A. (2009). Core components of therapy in youth: Do we know what to disseminate? *Behavior Modification, 33*, 24–47.

Weissman, M. M., Orvaschel, H., & Padian, N. (1980). Children's symptom and social functioning self-report scales: Comparison of mothers' and children's reports. *Journal of Nervous and Mental Disease, 168*(12), 736–740.

Weisz, J., McCarty, C., & Valeri, S. (2006). Effects of psychotherapy for depression in children and adolescents: A meta-analysis. *Psychological Bulletin, 132*, 132–149.

Wood, A., Harrington, R., & Moore, A. (1996). Controlled trial of a brief cognitive-behavioural intervention in adolescent patients with depressive disorders. *Journal of Child Psychology and Psychiatry, 37*(6), 737–746.

Young, J., Mufson, L., & Davies, M. (2006). Efficacy of interpersonal psychotherapy-adolescent skills training: An indicated preventive intervention for depression. *Journal of Child Psychology and Psychiatry, 47*(12), 1254–1262.

5

Moderators and Mediators of Treatments for Youth Who Show Externalizing Problem Behavior

MAJA DEKOVIĆ AND SABINE STOLTZ ■

INTRODUCTION

Externalizing problem behavior (EPB), broadly defined as oppositional behavior (non-compliance, disruptive behavior) and conduct problems (antisocial behavior, aggression, delinquency), is one of the most common reasons for referral to inpatient and outpatient child and adolescent mental health clinics. A large body of longitudinal research conducted in the past 30 years has shown that EPB is relatively stable and, if left untreated, leads to adverse outcomes such as school failure, unemployment, crime involvement, and serious pathology such as antisocial personality disorder later in life (Kimonis & Frick, 2011). The high prevalence, chronic course, and serious risk for later adverse outcomes have led to the development of different treatments aimed to decrease these problems. Among these treatments, approaches that involve parents, parental training for younger children, and multisystemic therapy for adolescents, have been most extensively studied, and their effectiveness has been demonstrated in a number of controlled outcome studies (e.g., Eyberg, Nelson, & Boggs, 2008; McCart, Priester, Davies, & Azen, 2006).

   In this chapter, we begin with a brief definition of externalizing problems and we provide an overview of developmental trajectories and the most important factors that play a role in the development and maintenance of such problems. Next, we describe the theoretical background, assumptions, and approaches of two evidence-based treatments for these problems: behavioral and cognitive behavioral parental training (PT) and multisystemic therapy (MST). Although other treatments, such as child-focused individual and group-based cognitive behavioral trainings, have been identified as evidence based as well (see Eyberg et al., 2008), they are not reviewed here, due to the lack of studies on moderators and mediators of these treatments. In subsequent sections, we review the empirical literature on moderators and mediators of effects of PT and MST. We present some illustrative examples of such work and the most important findings up to now. Finally, we identify gaps in our knowledge regarding how, for whom, and under what circumstances these treatments produce their effects; we offer suggestions for future research and discuss the implications of the findings for clinical practice.

Externalizing Problem Behaviors: Brief Description and Developmental Course

Externalizing problem behaviors (EPBs) are common in children and adolescents. These problem behaviors typically include disobedience, disruptive and aggressive behaviors, troublesome and conflictive relations with others, rule-breaking behavior, and lack of consideration for others. Within a *dimensional approach*, EPBs are seen as existing on a continuum of severity, with, at one end, children who do not show such behavior or show only mild forms of such behavior, infrequently and only in some situations (at home, with peers, or at school), and at the other end, children who show serious forms, frequently and in different situations (Furlong, McGilloway, Bywater, Hutchings, Smith, & Donnelly, 2012). Within a *categorical approach*, that is, that of the *Diagnostic and Statistical Manual of Mental Disorders*, fifth edition (*DSM-5*; American Psychiatric Association, 2013), children who show the most severe behaviors may be diagnosed with oppositional defiant disorder (ODD) or conduct disorder (CD). Common features of ODD include disregard for authority, excessive (often persistent) anger, irritable mood, and frequent temper tantrums or angry outbursts. Children and adolescents with ODD often purposely annoy others, blame others for their own mistakes or misbehaviors, and are touchy, argumentative or easily annoyed by others, spiteful or vindictive. CD is diagnosed based on a prolonged pattern of antisocial behavior such as serious violation of laws and social norms and rules. Symptoms of CD include aggression to people and animals, destruction of property, deceitfulness or theft, and serious violations of rules.

In the research literature, these problems are often studied within a dimensional, rather than a categorical, approach, and also frequently are labeled as "aggression," or "disruptive behavior," and at older ages, "antisocial behavior" or "delinquency." Although it is possible to distinguish these different types conceptually, in the present chapter, we do not make such differentiation, and we combine studies that focus on treatment of such problems under a common label "externalizing problem behavior" (EPB). We are aware that this may result in loss of information, as subtyping in different kind of problems is relevant for moderation analysis. However, up to now, a body of research on moderators and mediators is still too small to make such differentiation.

In a developmental-ecological framework, EPB is conceptualized as resulting from stacking sets of child personal, familial, and extra-familial factors (Loeber, Burke & Pardini, 2009). The developmental trajectory leading toward serious and chronic antisocial behavior later in life often starts with physical aggression and non-compliance in infancy and preschool years. Family factors such as socioeconomic disadvantage, low parental education, family stress, and, especially, inadequate parenting skills (i.e., inconsistent, harsh discipline; lack of warmth, encouragement, and support; and disengaged parenting) place children at particularly high risk for the development and maintenance of EPB (Broidy et al., 2003). If left untreated, early risk factors tend to accumulate and escalate over time. In early and middle childhood, increasingly oppositional children are likely to experience social isolation and rejection by peers, and to receive more negative reactions from teachers, which might not only hamper their academic progress, but also reduce their opportunities to learn appropriate social skills and effective problem-solving. By early adolescence, these children tend to become more susceptible to deviant peer group influences, setting the stage for further escalation of problems, high likelihood of school failure, disengagement from society, and involvement in criminal activities in later adolescence and adulthood (Odgers et al., 2008). Obviously, given these serious negative consequences for the child and her or his environment, treatments to interrupt this developmental trajectory are necessary.

State-of-the-art Treatments for EPB

Findings on the characteristics and development of chronic EPB offer insight into which risk and protective factors at the level of the child and the level of the child's social environment should be targeted in treatments for EPB. Notwithstanding the importance of child-level genetic and biological risk factors, as well as risk factors in the broader social environment, the factors within the child's family, especially the quality of parenting, are often seen as a major influence in child development. Indeed, considerable empirical evidence has been produced over the past several decades showing that inadequate parenting, such as harsh and inconsistent discipline, poor monitoring, and lack of warmth, is one of the most important predictors of (early) onset and maintenance of EPB (Grusec, 2011). It is then not surprising that many efforts to change child EPB have focused on changing parenting, with the idea that improvements in parenting will lead to improvement in child outcomes. In the next paragraphs we briefly discuss two treatments that have been often used and that have proven effective in decreasing child and adolescent EPB: PT for younger children and MST for adolescents.

PT, that is, treatment designed to enhance parental role performance through training, support, or education, is today generally accepted as evidence-based intervention for child EPB (e.g., Matthys & Lochman, 2010). Several meta-analyses, synthesizing the results of an increasing amount of studies on effectiveness of PT, showed that PTs generally do succeed in changing both parenting and child outcomes (Kaminski, Vallew, Filene, & Boyle, 2008; Lundahl, Risser, & Lovejoy, 2006; Piquero, Farrington, Welsh, Tremblay, & Jennings, 2009). Although there are differences among various forms of PT regarding the content and delivery settings (group, individual, self-administered), in most PTs parents are trained in using more effective parenting skills for managing child behavior. These skills include conveying clear expectations to the child, enhancing positive interactions, reducing harsh discipline, and enforcing rules by consistent and appropriate use of rewards and punishment.

PTs are mostly based on social learning theory (Bandura, 1997) and use principles of operant, classical, and social learning, alongside techniques derived from cognitive therapy. Parents are taught to focus on the child's positive behavior and to reinforce it through praising and rewards. Typically, the child's undesirable behaviors are dealt with by ignoring or using a mild form of punishment, such as "time out." In addition to principles and techniques of positive and negative reinforcement, parents learn the importance of modeling appropriate behavior that the child can learn by observing and imitating. This principle of learning by observing and imitation applies also for the parents. The trainers themselves model appropriate behavior and parenting skills that the parents can practice during the sessions in role-play. This practice then extends to the home situation and the parents receive homework assignments that are discussed in the following session. Traditionally, PTs are mastery based, that is, there is a strong emphasis on the acquisition of parental skills (behavior), but in some programs there is explicit attention for parental cognitions. The cognitive components of PT include dealing with problematic thinking patterns, such as inadequate attributions for child behavior ("he is doing this to hurt me"), overgeneralization ("he is a bad child"), and low sense of competence regarding parenting ("I can do nothing about it"). The parents learn how to reframe these negative cognitions and how to use positive problem-solving strategies.

Among many other parenting programs (see Murrihy, Kidman, & Ollendick, 2011, for review), Parent Management Training Oregon (PMTO) and Incredible Years are two examples of leading and noteworthy programs. PMTO, developed by Patterson and colleagues (Patterson, Reid, Jones, & Conger, 1975), is based on the social interaction learning model and on coercion theory and is one of the most thoroughly studied parent interventions. Families of children aged 3–13 years with serious conduct problems are seen individually for weekly sessions. In the treatment, parental skills that may affect parent-child interactions, such as monitoring, positive parenting, and limit setting, are increased. The effectiveness of PMTO as a treatment method in reducing antisocial behavior has been demonstrated (Patterson, DeGarmo, & Forgatch, 2004; Patterson, Forgatch, & DeGarmo, 2010).

Incredible Years (Webster-Stratton, 2006) targets conduct problems in young children aged 2–8 years and consists of modules for parents, teachers, and children. The parent treatment is delivered in a group format (8–12 parents), which enables parents to support each other during the sessions. Incredible Years also focuses on strengthening parent-child interactions and teaching parents to use positive discipline and skills to promote their child's social, emotional, and language development. Many studies have established the effectiveness of Incredible Years as a treatment method (e.g., Gardner, Hutchings, Bywater, & Whitaker, 2010; Webster-Stratton & Reid, 2010).

PT is often employed at earlier ages (early and middle childhood), because at this age children are more dependent on their parents and have not yet developed the more abstract social cognitive skills that are necessary for most child-focused therapies (McCart et al., 2006). Moreover, intervening at earlier ages can prevent a child's problems from reaching clinical levels. In adolescents, problems have often persisted across many years, and this pattern might be more difficult to alter (Bernazzani, Cothe, & Tremblay, 2001). Also, adolescents spend more time outside the home and, from mid-adolescence forward, other socialization agents (i.e., peers) become increasingly more salient. One of the evidence-based treatments for adolescents with serious EPB that target multiple domains (i.e., factors within the family, school, peer group, and neighborhood) is MST. It is an intensive home- and community-based treatment, grounded on social ecological and family systems theories and on research on the causes and correlates of serious antisocial behavior. Although MST aims to address multiple risk factors associated with EPB, its underlying assumption is that parents are still central for adolescent behavior change (Henggeler, 2011). Consistent with this assumption, MST therapists use a strength-focused approach and aim to empower parents to change factors within or outside the family that promote and maintain adolescent antisocial behavior. Parents are trained in using more effective parenting skills, including reducing harsh discipline, employing more consistent discipline and monitoring, and enhancing supportive, positive interactions. Previous effectiveness studies of MST conducted in the United States (Timmons-Mitchell, Bender, Kishna, & Mitchell, 2006), Norway (Ogden & Halliday-Boykins, 2004), the United Kingdom (Butler, Baruch, Hickey, & Fonagy, 2011), and The Netherlands (Asscher, Deković, Manders, Van der Laan, Prins, & the Dutch MST Cost-Effectiveness Study Group, 2013) showed positive effects: juveniles treated with MST showed less delinquent behavior and recidivism than juveniles from the control groups.

THEORETICAL MODELS FOR MODERATION AND EMPIRICAL RESULTS OF MODERATION STUDIES FOR EPB

There is an increasing awareness that the expectation that a treatment will have the same effects on all participants is quite naïve and that it is much more realistic to expect that some participants would benefit more than others from the same treatment. Treatment moderators clarify for whom and under what conditions a treatment works (Kraemer, Frank, & Kupfer, 2006; see also Chapter 1 of this volume). In most evaluation studies, identified moderators are based on routinely obtained information (Kazdin, 2007), such as age or initial level of problems. However, when selecting variables that can be considered as possible moderators, it is important that this selection is theoretically based. Clinical trials that do include theoretically based moderators are often guided in their choice of moderators by previous field studies on risk factors for child externalizing problems (Gardner et al., 2010). These risk factors are then expected to predict poor treatment outcome as well. Most of these risk factors can be conceptualized within an ecological framework. From an ecological perspective, externalizing problem behavior is a result of interactions between risk factors at multiple levels: individual child risk factors (e.g., gender, temperament) and environmental risk factors (e.g., marital status of parents, parental psychopathology; Bronfenbrenner, 1979; Sameroff, 2010).

In the following sections we discuss frequently studied or theoretically relevant moderators. In general, these moderators can be classified into three main categories at multiple levels (see Figure 5.1): child characteristics, family/parent characteristics, and program characteristics. The first two categories address the question "for whom does this treatment work?" whereas the last category deals with the question "under what circumstances does this treatment work?"

With respect to PTs, we make use of two meta-analyses (Lundahl et al., 2006; Reyno & McGrath, 2006) that combined findings on moderators of outcomes of a large number of trials to the effectiveness of PT (61 versus 31 trials, respectively), but we also discuss the findings of some individual studies as well.

Often, the examined moderators of treatment effects concern *child characteristics*, although it is still not yet clear which child characteristics (and why) deserve the most attention. Many trials include *child age* as potential predictor (i.e., a variable that affects treatment outcome) or moderator (i.e., a variable that is differentially related to treatment outcome dependent on the type of treatment) of program outcomes. Mainly, the expectation is that interventions that begin early in development will result in larger benefits than those that begin later, as evidence indicates that children with EPBs become increasingly resistant

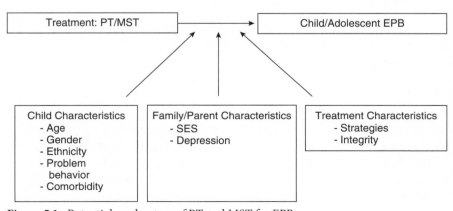

Figure 5.1. Potential moderators of PT and MST for EPB.

to change with age (Bernazzani et al., 2001). Moreover, it is expected that younger children may benefit especially from PT, because of their dependency on parents. Although some trials indeed found greater benefits for younger children (for a meta-analysis, see Deković, Slagt, Asscher, Boendermaker, Eichelsheim, & Prinzie, 2011), several meta-analyses did not find significant effects of age (Cedar & Levant, 1990; Lundahl et al., 2006). Moreover, another meta-analysis reported even a positive correlation between child age and effects of PT on EPBs (Serketic & Dumas, 1996).

There is still insufficient evidence regarding the question of whether programs work equally well for *boys and girls* (Hippwell & Loeber, 2006). Male gender is found to be a risk factor for EPB and can therefore be seen as a marker for severity of problem behavior, and in turn as a moderator of (better) intervention outcomes. However, in previous studies (Beauchaine, Webster-Stratton, & Reid, 2005; CPPRG, 2002; McGilloway et al., 2012), these proposed effects were not found.

Research has shown that *ethnic background* is an important child characteristic to consider because of different cultural values and traditions, challenges of acculturation processes, negative experiences with discrimination, or different parental socialization practices (Yasui & Dishion, 2007). Recently, some studies have examined ethnicity as a potential *predictor* of changes in externalizing problem behavior that result from PTs. For example, in an evaluation of the Incredible Years program, with a sample of Caucasian, African-American, Latino and Asian-American mothers, no significant ethnic differences in treatment effects on EBPs were found (Reid, Webster-Stratton, & Beauchaine, 2001). These universal effects were supported by a study in which the effectiveness of the Schools and Homes Partnership program (including parent training as a component of the program) was evaluated in Latino and Caucasian families (Barrera et al., 2002). In another trial on the efficacy of a universal parent and child prevention program for child behavior problems, moderator analyses indicate similar intervention effects on externalizing behavior for Black and Latino families (Brotman et al., 2011). It may be that PTs are simply robust against ethnicity effects; however, more studies that actually test interaction effects (i.e., ethnicity as moderator) are necessary.

Severity of initial child problem behavior has often been suggested to predict effect sizes of treatments. Curiously, the expectations go both ways. On the one hand, it is expected that children showing more severe problem behaviors also have a larger scope for improvement (Leijten, Raaijmakers, de Castro, & Matthys, 2013). On the other hand, it is expected that more severely troubled children show more ingrained problem behaviors that are less easy to change. Some studies indeed found severity of child problem behavior to be associated with lower effect sizes of treatments. Other studies, however, found opposite results (for review, see McMahon, Wells, & Kotler, 2006). When findings are synthesized in meta-analyses (Lundahl et al, 2006; Reyno & McGrath, 2006), it can be concluded that children with more severe problem behaviors show better outcomes from PT. This was replicated in two other recent meta-analyses regarding treatments for younger children (Deković, et al., 2011; Leijten et al., 2013): highly disruptive children benefit most from such interventions.

Related to severity of problem behavior is *comorbidity of problem behavior*. For example, it can be expected that children with comorbid conduct problems and ADHD may be less responsive to interventions, because they are particularly non-compliant (Beauchaine et al., 2005). In a review on comorbidity as moderator of treatment outcome in youth with oppositional/conduct disorders (Ollendick, Jarrett, Grills-Taquechel, Hovey, & Wolff, 2008) it was found that only one of the 28 reviewed studies examined comorbidity as a moderator of treatment outcome. In this study it was found that co-occurring symptoms of anxiety/depression were slightly associated with less beneficial outcomes of PT (Beauchaine et al., 2005). In general, it was concluded in this review (also based on predictor studies) that comorbidity has little or no effect on the treatment of child conduct problems (Ollendick et al., 2008).

With respect to *family/parent characteristics*, it appears that children of low-income parents, lower educated parents, and single parents showed poorer treatment outcomes compared to children from less disadvantaged parents (Lundahl et al., 2006; Reyno & McGrath, 2006). These socially and/or economically disadvantaged families have more psychological, financial, or social stressors (which place stress on the parent-child relationship) and are, as a result, less responsive to positive change. From another meta-analysis (Leijten et al., 2013), including 75 trials on PT effectiveness to reduce disruptive child behavior, the same conclusion was drawn. Disadvantaged samples, based on socioeconomic status (SES), benefited less from parent training in the longer term.

Maternal depression is often included as family risk factor to predict poor treatment outcome. Parental psychopathology exerts a strong influence on a child's behavior and therefore may also impact response to PT (i.e., depression has been associated with more disruptions in parent-child interactions; for results in outcome studies, see Baydar, Reid, & Webster-Stratton, 2003). From meta-analyses it can indeed be concluded that children with parents who have higher levels of depressive symptoms do not benefit as much from an intervention as children from non-depressed parents (Reyno & McGrath, 2006). However, some large trials on the effectiveness of PT for EPBs found opposite moderating effects: children of depressed parents did better with intervention (Beauchaine et al., 2005; Gardner et al., 2010).

As previously stated, different PT programs share some features, but they also differ in intensity, duration, target domain (i.e., parenting skills, general support), and format (individual vs. group). All of these *program characteristics* might be related to the intervention's effectiveness. From a recent meta-analysis (Kaminski et al., 2008) it can be concluded that *strategies of PTs* that focus on problem-solving, teaching parents to promote children's cognitive academic or social skills, and providing an array of additional services resulted in smaller effect sizes compared to programs that used strategies that focus on increasing positive parent-child interaction and communication, teaching time out and the importance of parenting consistency, and requiring parents to practice new skills with their child during parent training sessions.

It is important to realize that some large trials did not find specific moderator effects on intervention outcomes as described above. It seems plausible that more individualized programs show less moderating effects, because the intervention can be tailored to the specific needs of subgroups. The notion that studies of individualized treatments show the lack of significant moderator effects seems to be supported by research on MST. Several studies that examined the effectiveness of MST also included the test of potential moderators of effectiveness. The examined moderators were most often demographic *adolescent characteristics*: gender, ethnicity, and age (Asscher et al., 2013; Schaeffer & Borduin, 2005, Sundell, Hansson, Löfholm, Olsson, Gustle, & Kadesjö, 2008). In general, these studies did not find any or found only few moderator effects, leading to the conclusion that the effects of MST do not vary as a consequence of demographic characteristics, which might not be surprising given that this is a highly individualized treatment.

In addition to demographic characteristics, adolescent psychopathy, defined as a multidimensional construct with callous/unemotional traits (lack of feelings of guilt, a poor conscience, poor empathic skills, and poverty in emotional expression), narcissism, and impulsiveness as dimensions, has been recently examined as potential moderator of MST effectiveness (Manders, Deković, Asscher, Van der Laan, & Prins, 2013). Antisocial adolescents who also show psychopathic traits have been found to be particularly at risk for developing a severe and stable form of antisocial behavior (Frick, Blair, & Castellanos, 2012). In addition to being a risk factor for the development of severe and stable antisocial behaviour, these adolescents might also be less responsive to environmental influence, including treatment. Indeed, it was found that the effect of MST on EPB varies with the level of psychopathic traits, with MST showing advantage above treatment as usual for the lower, but not for the higher levels of psychopathic traits, suggesting that MST needs to be tailored specifically to meet the needs of adolescent with psychopathic traits to achieve the same treatment gains as with the adolescents with lower levels of psychopathy. For example, it has been suggested that these adolescents might be more responsive to the reward-based strategies (e.g., use of praise) of PT and less responsive to the disciplinary strategies (e.g., time-out) (Manders et al., 2013).

Regarding *family/parent characteristics*, there are some indications, although not replicated in all studies, that low parental education and low income are positively related to both treatment outcome and treatment integrity (Schoenwald, Halliday-Boykins, & Henggeler, 2003).

Finally, *the program characteristics*, in this case treatment integrity, have been suggested as a moderator of MST effectiveness. The US studies showed that higher levels of treatment integrity are related to better outcomes, both primary outcomes (adolescent EPB, recidivism) and secondary outcomes (family functioning, parental monitoring, involvement with deviant peers) (Huey, Henggeler, Brondino, & Pickrel, 2000; Schoenwald, Carter, Chapman, & Sheidow, 2008).

However, the studies outside the United States did not replicate these findings: in Sweden (Sundell et al., 2008), Canada (Cunningham, 2002) and The Netherlands (Manders et al., 2011), there was no convincing evidence that higher treatment integrity led to better treatment outcomes. One explanation for these findings is a relatively high level and low variation in treatment integrity score. Another explanation is that the instrument used to asses treatment integrity does not function well outside the US context. This instrument, the Therapist Adherence Measure, a monthly telephone interview with the parents, assesses therapist adherence to the nine principles of MST, rather than assessing whether a specific component or a specific intervention technique is implemented with a particular level of quality. A more specific measure of treatment integrity might have produced different results.

To conclude, there is more awareness today that studying moderator effects of treatment for EPB is important. Even the most effective interventions are only effective for two-thirds of the children; dropout rates are often high (40%–60% in child mental health clinics; Dumas, Moreland, Gitter, Pearl, & Nordstrom, 2008), and effect sizes of treatment are still small to moderate. Understanding which children/adolescents benefit from treatment, through moderator analyses, can be helpful in refining the inclusion and exclusion criteria and can lead to further refinement of treatments for subgroups who are less responsive to a treatment.

Unfortunately, the findings up to now are far from conclusive. This is especially the case for child characteristics of age and gender. Obviously, more research is needed to provide more clarity on the role of these child characteristics. A tentative conclusion is that specific child risk factors, such as comorbidity and ethnic background, do not necessarily lead to less beneficial treatment effects. In contrast, it seems that some child risk factors, for example severity of externalizing problem behavior, may result in greater benefits of PTs. In general, PTs seem to be less successful in reducing externalizing problem behavior for children from more disadvantaged families. However, with respect to parental psychopathology as a moderator (i.e., depression), findings are again mixed.

Specific program strategies and better implementation of a program seem to lead to larger intervention effects. For more individualized treatments, such as MST, less moderating effects on intervention outcomes were found, because interventions are more tailor-made to participants' needs. However, for youth with psychopathic traits, MST appears to be less effective. Also for MST, there are indications that better implementation of the program results in better treatment outcomes. In short, although a body of research on moderators of EPB treatments is increasing, it is still too early to pinpoint the most promising moderators, as the findings are far from consistent across studies. Moreover, most of the work is led by pragmatic reasons (i.e., ad hoc, using variables already available in the data set to check moderation), rather than choosing moderators a priori and based on theory.

THEORETICAL MODELS FOR MEDIATION AND EMPIRICAL RESULTS OF MEDIATION STUDIES FOR EPB

In order to understand how a treatment works and why it does or does not produce the desired effects, it is important to specify and test potential mediators of treatment outcomes. The treatment mediators are processes, suggested by theoretical models on which the treatment is based, that lead to and cause therapeutic change (see also Chapter 1 of this volume). In the theoretical background of both PT and MST, parenting is seen as the most important risk and protective factor in the etiology and maintenance of child EPB. Consequently, these treatments attempt to change parenting, assuming that the changes in parenting will lead to improvements in child behavior (i.e., decrease in EPB).

Although there are differences between PTs in content (for example, the emphasis that is put on the decrease in coercive processes versus the increase in reinforcement of child positive behavior), or in the strategies that are used to change parenting (for example, more or less emphasis on role-playing), all evidence-based PTs use largely the same theories and focus on the same factors that have been identified in the literature as important risk and protective in the etiology and maintenance of child EPB (see paragraphs above). These theories about the development and maintenance of EPB serve also as the basis of MST. Given the fact that PTs and MST focus on different developmental periods, there is a slightly different emphasis in the type of child behavior and the dimensions of parenting behaviors that are targeted in the treatment. Whereas in PTs for younger children, the emphasis is on child non-compliance/oppositionality and on parental discipline management, in MST the emphasis is on adolescent antisocial behavior/delinquency and on parental monitoring, communication, and problem-solving skills. Despite these—developmentally appropriate—differences in the dimensions of parenting that are hypothesized to be important risk factors and thus also important targets of the treatment, it is possible to group the most often proposed mediators into three global dimensions. These dimensions have often been used in the literature to organize much of the variation in parenting (Prinzie, Stams, Deković, Reijntjes, & Belsky, 2009).

The first dimension, *negative discipline,* involves harsh and punitive parenting, or lax parenting and lack of control. The second dimension, *positive parenting,* refers to parents' limit setting, enforcement of predictable rules, consistent discipline, and monitoring of child behavior. Both of these dimensions refer to strategies that the parents use to control the child behavior, whether reactively (i.e., as a reaction to the child misbehaviors) or proactively (i.e., with the aim to prevent child misbehavior). The third dimension is a more affective one and refers to the *quality of the parent-child relationship*: open communication, support, positive interaction with the child, constructive problem-solving, and conflict management. In both PTs and MST, consistent with their theoretical underpinning, there is a strong emphasis on both dealing with discipline and on

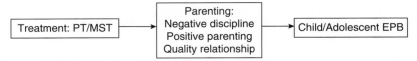

Figure 5.2. Potential mediators of PT and MST for EPB.

affective aspects of parenting, and thus at least some attention is given to each of these three global dimensions (see Figure 5.2).

In the empirical research on the effects of these treatments, however, not all of the above dimensions have been systematically assessed. Moreover, although the evaluation studies of these treatments have almost always assessed changes in parenting from pre-test to post-test, the changes in parenting have been seen as just one of the outcomes. It is only in recent years that researchers have tried to link these changes in parenting to changes in child EPB and to actually test the mediational role of parenting (Kazdin, 2007; Sandler, Schoenfelder, Wolchik, & MacKinnon, 2011). We highlight the few studies, for the purpose of illustration, that have used formal mediational analyses to investigate the processes that account for the effects of treatment. Table 5.1 shows an overview of these studies, containing information regarding design, conditions, number of assessment of both mediator(s) and outcome(s), and whether a formal test of mediation is used.

One of the first studies that examined and formally tested the mediating role of parenting was a study by Degarmo, Patterson, and Forgatch (2004). In this study it was found that the improvement in effective parenting, assessed as a composite of both positive (involvement, skill encouragement, problem-solving, monitoring) and negative (inept discipline, negative reciprocity, negative reinforcement) parenting behaviors mediated the effects of PMTO on boys' EPBs across a period of 30 months. Interestingly, they also tested a mediational model for child internalizing problems, but found that the treatment effects on internalizing problems were only partly mediated by changes in parental behavior. More recently, Hagen, Ogden and Bjørnebekk (2011) examined whether parenting measured at treatment termination mediated the effects of an individually delivered version of PMTO on child behavior 1 year later. They found that effective discipline (appropriate and contingent use of mild sanctions and providing child with clear boundaries for acceptable behavior) acted as the mediator of treatment effects on child aggression, although the indirect effects for other child outcomes (opposition, social skills, and observed child behavior) were only marginally significant.

Several studies examined the mediators of effectiveness of the Incredible Years parenting program. Beauchaine and colleagues (2005) combined the data from six RCTs and tested whether different dimensions of parenting acted as mediators of effects on child EPB at 1 year follow-up. They found that the decreases in verbal criticism, harsh parenting, and ineffective parenting mediated treatment outcome. No such effect was found for supportive parenting (labeled praise, reflective statements, reasoning). Gardner and colleagues evaluated the same

Table 5.1. OVERVIEW OF THE REVIEWED MEDIATION STUDIES

	Design	Conditions	Number of assessments	Mediator(s) and Outcome(s) Assessed at Each Assessment?	Significance of Mediation Effect Tested?	Temporal Precedence Requirement Met?[a]
PT						
Beauchaine et al. (2005)	RCT/single condition	Only treatment condition examined	3 (pre-, post-, and 1-year FU)	yes	yes	no
Degarmo et al. (2004)	RCT	PT vs. no intervention	5 (pre-, post-, and 3 FUs: at 12, 18, and 30 months)	yes	yes	no
Gardner et al. (2006)	RCT	PT vs. wait list	2 (pre-, and post-)	yes	yes	no
Gardner et al. (2010)	RCT	PT vs. wait list	2 (pre-, and post-)	yes	yes	no
Hagen et al. (2011)	RCT	PT vs. TAU	3 (pre-, post-, and 1-year FU)	yes	yes	yes
MST						
Deković et al. (2012)	RCT	MST vs. TAU	5 (monthly, during treatment)	yes	yes	no
Henggeler et al. (2009)	RCT	MST vs. TAU	3 (pre-, post-, and 1-year FU)	yes	yes	no
Huey et al. (2000)	RCT	MST vs. TAU	2 (pre-, and post-)	yes	no	no

NOTE: [a]YES = CHANGES in mediating variable were tested before the changes in outcome variable. RCT = Randomized Controlled Trial; PT = Parental training; MST = Multisystemic Therapy; TAU = Treatment as usual; FU = Follow-up.

program, but found somewhat different results. Gardner, Burton, and Klimes (2006) hypothesized that changes in positive parenting (positive affect, use of praise) would mediate the effects of this program on child EPB 6 months after the start of the program, and found support for this hypothesis. In a later study with a different sample (clinically referred children with conduct problems), Gardner and colleagues (2010) examined not only changes in positive parenting, but also changes in negative parenting (criticism, harsh commands) as putative mediators. They replicated the findings of their first study and showed that improvement in positive parenting, rather than reduction in harsh or negative parenting, is a key factor mediating change in child ODD behaviors, such as non-compliance and aggressive, destructive behavior.

That improvements in parenting explain positive changes in adolescent behavior was also shown in MST trials: effects of MST on adolescent antisocial behavior appear to be mediated by improvements in parental monitoring (Huey et al., 2000) and parental use of consistent discipline (Henggeler, Letourneau, Chapman, Borduin, Schewe, & McCart, 2009). However, the first study (Huey et al., 2000) had several important methodological limitations (i.e., small sample size, only two assessment points, lack of control group, and no formal mediational tests), whereas the second study (Henggeler et al., 2009) focused on a specific group, that is, juvenile sexual offenders. Deković, Asscher, Manders, Prins, and Van der Laan (2012) tested sequential mediation models (i.e., models including two mediators that influence each other in a sequence; see also Chapter 1 of this volume) using the data of a Dutch RCT on the effectiveness of MST for adolescents who show chronic antisocial behaviors. Such sequential models allow researchers to investigate whether the change would emerge in an orderly sequence as hypothesized, starting with the targeted mechanism of parental cognitions, followed by changes in parental behavior, and eventually resulting in changes in adolescent behavior. The hypothesis was that improvements in parental sense of competence during MST (changes in Mediator 1) would lead to positive changes in parenting (changes in Mediator 2), which in turn would lead to a decrease of adolescent EPB (changes in treatment outcomes). Mediational models were tested separately for three dimensions of parenting (positive discipline, inept discipline, and relationship quality) that are targeted in MST. The results supported a sequential pattern of change for positive discipline: changes in parental sense of competence predicted changes in positive discipline, which in turn predicted decrease in adolescent externalizing problems. However, no support was found for mediated effects of inept discipline and relationship quality. Interestingly, the results of this Dutch study are quite consistent with the results of the previous US studies on mediators of change in MST (Henggeler et al., 2009), regardless of the important differences between the studies in study population, design, and the test of mediation (sequential vs "single" mediation). The consistency in the results across these studies provides strong support for the assumption stated by the MST theory of change that improvement in parenting, especially more consistent discipline, is one of the core working elements of this complex intervention.

To conclude, the studies reviewed above represent an important step toward elaborating the mechanisms through which PT and MST operate. First, the findings so far indicate that parenting, as hypothesized, is indeed the "active ingredient" or "working mechanism" behind the treatment effects, and thus provide legitimization for focusing on parenting in order to reduce child EPB. Second, it appears that similar mechanisms are at work in treatment for both younger children and adolescents: improvement in positive parenting, rather than reduction in negative harsh discipline, appears to be the key mechanism of change. It is possible that change in positive parenting is more salient than change in harsh discipline, as positive parenting does not occur often in families with children or adolescents who show EPB. However, it is also possible that the instruments used to assess different parenting behaviors are not equally sensitive to capture changes in parenting (i.e., negative harsh discipline might be more difficult to assess, as the parents might be reluctant to admit that they use such practices and tend not to show such behavior during observation). Third, a more affective dimension, that is, quality of the parent-child relationship, has not been extensively studied, although in both treatments there is at least some attention for quality of communication and/or positive non-disciplinarian interaction, such as playing with the child. When it has been tested (Beauchaine et al., 2005; Deković et al., 2012), no evidence was found that it functions as a mediator. These findings suggest that the change in affective quality of the parent-child relationship might not be crucial for producing changes in child behavior, and that positive changes in parental controlling behaviors might be the most salient ingredient of effective treatments for EPB. However, more research is needed before this tentative conclusion can be accepted.

CHALLENGES AND RECOMMENDATION FOR FUTURE MODERATOR/MEDIATOR RESEARCH

Moderators

Although PTs and MST are widely accepted and implemented as evidence-based interventions for child EPB, these treatments, of course, do not work equally well for all children. Nowadays, besides examining direct effects, researchers are increasingly interested in moderating effects of interventions to determine for whom and under what circumstances a treatment exerts its effects. Studying moderators of treatments is not only relevant for clinical practice to inform clinicians which particular treatments are beneficial for particular subpopulations. For scientific goals, studying moderators can contribute to developmental theory by elucidating whether developmental processes can be changed under certain conditions (Kellam & Rebok, 1992).

Based on a large number of empirical studies testing moderating effects of PT and MST, we can conclude that there is a clear need for the PT/MST field to develop testable theoretical models of moderator effects. This is especially true since demographic characteristics such as gender, age, or ethnicity do not have very large or straightforward influences on intervention effects. More recently, researchers became interested in testing risk factors for the development of severe and stable EPB as moderators of treatments for EPB, such as adolescents' psychopathy (Manders et al., 2013), youth callous/unemotional traits (Frick, Ray, Thornton, & Kahn, 2014), and child personality (Stoltz, Prinzie, De Haan, Van Londen, De Castro, & Deković, 2012). Moreover, it has been suggested that neurocognitive characteristics, such as reward processing, punishment processing, and cognitive control, could also influence intervention effects in youth (Matthys, Vanderschuren, Schutter, & Lochman, 2013). PT and MST are based on social learning, and limited effectiveness of interventions may be caused by difficulties in social learning by youth with ODD and CD (Matthys et al., 2013). In future studies, more attention should be paid to these more substantive child characteristics to enhance intervention effects for specific subgroups of children. For example, from empirical studies we know that children with ODD/CD may have impairments in neurocognitive functions, such as low reward and punishment sensitivity (Matthys et al., 2013). Many parent trainings are based on the principles of reward and punishment. It is possible that children with these specific neurocognitive impairments are not sensitive to the proposed working mechanism (i.e., teach parents how to use reward and punishment) of the parent training. Moderated mediation analyses can expand our current knowledge on these child factors that may affect treatment working mechanisms, and in turn intervention effects.

Besides examining more theoretically based moderator effects, we need to gain more knowledge of how *mechanisms* might vary by moderator groups (moderated mediation) (Tein, Sandler, MacKinnon, & Wolchik, 2004). More specifically, working mechanisms of an intervention can differ as a function of specific child characteristics. Very few intervention studies tested this "moderated mediation." In a study on the effects of a preventive *child* intervention for children with EPB, it was found that child personality moderated mediation effects (Stoltz, Van Londen, Deković, De Castro, & Prinzie, 2013): the child personality factor of extraversion moderated the mediating effect of parental involvement. In other words, the intervention worked through different mechanisms, depending on differences in personality characteristics. Pointing to subgroups for which mediating mechanisms might be different (Hinshaw, 2002) can perhaps lead to more insight for tailoring treatments to meet the specific needs of less responding youth (Chorpita, Daleiden, & Weisz, 2005).

A second direction for future research on moderators of PT and MST may be to develop and include a more specific measure of treatment integrity. To date, it is not exactly clear whether treatment integrity, as an indication of quality of implementation of a treatment, influences intervention outcomes of PT and MST. Knowledge about treatment integrity, and in turn assuring treatment integrity, is important for dissemination of evidence-based treatments and for quality improvement of already implemented treatments.

Finally, there is a lack of studies on PT/MST testing comorbidity of problem behavior as a potential moderator. Especially children with EPB are at increased risk for the presence of other emotional or behavioral problems, such as ADHD, anxiety, and depression (Nock, Kazdin, & Hiripi, & Kessler, 2007). There are indications that comorbid problem behavior may result in poorer treatment outcomes. Therefore, future studies should include a measure of comorbidity as moderator, not only as predictor, of treatment outcomes (Ollendick et al., 2008).

Mediators

In the recent years the number of studies that examined whether changes in parenting targeted in treatments for child EPB account for changes that occurs in child behavior is steadily increasing. Although significant progress has been made, our knowledge of the processes by which these treatments have effects is limited (Sandler et al., 2011). In this section we attempt to identify the gaps in our knowledge and offer some suggestion for the future studies.

Both PTs and MST address many different mediators, and we do not know which aspects of these multi-component interventions produce positive results. An important condition for identifying the treatment mediators is that the theoretical basis of the treatment is explicitly worked out. This means that, ideally, the following questions need to be answered before the treatment (and before the evaluation study) starts: What is the problem to be targeted in the treatment: what aspects of child EPB need to be changed? What are theory-based expectations regarding working mechanisms: which aspects of parenting are relevant for child behavior that the treatment attempts to alter? What is the desired outcome? Not all child EPBs are equally troublesome and/or require the same approach, not all parenting behaviors have equal salience in impacting child EPBs, and some levels or intensity of EPB might be considered acceptable or even developmentally appropriate. Only when the theoretical rationale of a program is explicitly stated is it possible to tailor the treatment to the most powerful mediators of the desired behavior changes and to assess hypothesized mediators of its effectiveness (Deković, Stoltz, Schuiringa, Manders, & Asscher, 2012).

There is, however, a lack of information regarding the specificity of mediational effects. Parenting behavior in the mediational studies has often been assessed as a broad category of "positive" or "negative" parenting, rather than as *specific* parenting behaviors that have been targeted in the parenting programs, such as limit setting, praising the child, ignoring child negative behaviors, and rewarding child appropriate behavior. In order to better identify the specific mechanisms of change, there is need for a tighter link between what is assessed in the evaluation studies and what is targeted in the parenting programs. Moreover, although the need to include multiple putative mediators within the same study has been stressed (Kazdin & Nock, 2003), there are still very few studies that have tested mediational models for different parental behaviors within the same study.

One important limitation in the present body of research on mediational effects is that parenting behavior is often assessed through parental reports only. Given the fact that parents invest a lot by following parental training, one should be aware of possible bias in their reports. Parents *want* to see the improvement in their own behavior, they want to believe that they have acquired the parenting skills targeted in the programs, and they might not be aware that they still might miss some of the targeted skills. Therefore, the use of a more objective, observational measure of parenting change would improve confidence in the findings regarding effectiveness. Such measures are still infrequently found, especially in studies with older children. Although this is understandable given the time-consuming nature of collecting this type of data and the possible reluctance of participants to take part in data collection involving observations, more efforts should be made to obtain more objective information on parenting. In addition, and maybe even more important, the child perspective on (change in) parenting should be assessed. Especially in the case of older children with more developed social cognitive skills, one might assume that the children do not just automatically react on different "input" from their parents, but that they also assess and interpret this input. The awareness of the child that the change in parenting took place and/or the change in child's interpretation of parental behavior ("she does this in order to protect, rather than to frustrate me"), might be crucial for the child's reaction to changes in parenting. Even if the observable change in parenting did take place, but the child fails to perceive it or keeps interpreting it in a negative way, it is likely that no change in child behavior would occur. Thus, the inclusion of child assessment of parenting might be important to the interpretation of both positive and negative findings regarding the effectiveness of treatment for EPB.

Similar lack of attention to cognitive processes within the *parent* can be seen in the literature. The emphasis in many treatments for EPB is on altering parental behavior, and typically little attention is being paid to parental cognition and affect. The implicit assumption seems to be that the treatment affects parenting directly through instruction, modeling of appropriate behavior, rehearsal, and feedback. But it is logical to assume that, as a result of participation in a treatment, change occurs not only in parenting behavior, but also in the way in which parents think about the child, themselves, and their parental role as a result of participation in a treatment (Teti & Cole, 2011). In our own research program, we identified the parental sense of competence (i.e., parents' belief in their ability to effectively manage parenting tasks) as an important determinant of (changes in) parental behavior. Other potential candidate mediators are parental attributions, implicit theories, parental goals, and parental readiness for change.

IMPLICATIONS FOR THE CLINICAL PRACTICE

How can current findings on moderators of PT/MST inform clinical practice? Knowledge of different child characteristics can lead to personalized mental healthcare or modular protocols, by adapting programs to the child's specific needs, which in turn can produce stronger intervention effects (Chorpita et al., 2005). Although implications should be considered tentative, because of inconclusive findings, different approaches may be necessary to treat subgroups of children with specific risk factors, such as children from more disadvantaged families or youth with psychopathic traits, because of potential distinct causal pathways leading to their problem behavior (e.g., Frick et al., 2014). Perhaps for these children, PT can be combined with a cognitive behavioral child training that seems to be effective for youth with EPB (McCart et al., 2006). Or maybe, for these children and their parents, a more individualized and intensive program is needed. Moreover, for clinicians working with parents of children with EPB, it is important to realize that specific strategies in PT and MST work better (see also mediation) and that the quality of implementation of their interventions is related to the effectiveness of the intervention. Higher quality of implementation of interventions in everyday clinical practice can be reached when more intensive training is provided to clinicians (Lochman, Boxmeyer, Powell, Qu, Wells, & Windle, 2009).

Regarding the mediators, for clinicians it is important to know whether their focus on certain precursor risk and protective factors really contributed to the positive outcomes. Both PT and MST are multi-component treatments that address many different mediators, and we still do not know *why* these treatment work. By specifying concrete parenting behaviors targeted within the program and by comparing mediational models for different parenting behaviors, information could be obtained regarding which specific parenting behavior should be targeted in the parenting program (those that function as working mechanisms of the interventions) and which specific parenting behaviors play a lesser role in decreasing child EPB (those that do not explain the link between the intervention and a decrease in child problems). Such information will help to focus treatment on parenting skills that are truly important (i.e., most likely to impact child EPB) and to identify the components of PT that can be left out. This is especially important in the light of findings showing that it is difficult to motivate parents to attend and to participate in a meaningful way in PT, which results in high dropout rates (Dumas et al., 2008). Moreover, two meta-analyses on the effectiveness of PT (Kaminski et al., 2008; Lundahl et al., 2006) both point out that the commonly held assumption "the more, the better" does not hold and that adding more components and/or offering additional services might actually impede parental ability to focus on learning parenting skills and thus can lead to less positive outcomes. To decrease the burden on both parents and practitioners, the PT should be as short and as focused as possible, containing only those components that do actually work.

Our results suggest that the process of change in parenting behavior starts with change in parental thinking (Deković, Asscher, Hermanns, Reitz, & Prinzie, 2010; Deković et al., 2012). Although these findings need to be replicated in future studies with different treatments, they are in line with the conclusions of Mah and Johnston (2008) that the benefits of addressing parental social cognitions may be greatest in the early stages of the treatment process. This is not surprising. Many parents who enter treatment for child EPB have an extremely low sense of competence. To change their parenting behaviors, the parents must first believe that they are able to change it. If parents keep believing they have no impact on their child's behavior, that they have no control over their own parental behavior, or if they believe that they cannot learn other ways of behaving, it is quite likely that they will not even try or that they will give up as soon as they encounter child resistance to change. Dealing with this low sense of competence immediately at the start of treatment might be crucial for proceeding toward real change in parenting behaviors. In later phases of treatment, when the parents experience that learned skills indeed do have the desired effect on child behavior, a positive feedback loop is likely to occur: the successes in the interactions with the child and increased sense of competence can reinforce each other in a natural way (Coleman & Karraker, 1998). In addition to potential benefits in terms of increased motivation and better engagement in treatment, the focus on parental intrapersonal processes (cognition, affect) might also increase the long-term effectiveness of treatment. There are indications in the literature that without improvement in parental well-being, the beneficial effects of parenting interventions may be likely to dissipate over time (Hutchings, Lane, & Kelly, 2004).

To conclude, the work on moderators and mediators of treatment outcomes for EPBs is very much "work in progress." Although compared to the treatments for other child problems (for example, anxiety), the field of EPB is relatively well researched (Forehand, Jones, & Parent, 2013), there are not (yet) enough studies that have examined the moderators and mediators to allow for a definite answer to the questions regarding how, for whom, and under what circumstances these treatments produce their effects. Such studies are very much needed to improve the effectiveness of treatments by better identification of children who are likely to respond and children who are not helped by these treatments (i.e., moderators) and by refining current treatment by enhancing ingredients that do work (i.e., mediators) and discarding those that do not work.

REFERENCES

American Psychiatric Association. (2013). *Diagnostic and statistical manual of mental disorders* (5th ed.). Arlington, VA: American Psychiatric Publishing.

Asscher, J. J., Deković, M., Manders, W. A., Van der Laan, P., Prins, P. J. M., & the Dutch MST Cost-Effectiveness Study Group. (2013). A randomized controlled trial of the effectiveness of Multisystemic Therapy in the Netherlands: Post-treatment changes and moderator effects. *Journal of Experimental Criminology, 9,* 169–187.

Bandura, A. (1997). *Self-efficacy: The exercise in control.* New York: Freeman.

Barrera, M. Jr., Biglan, A., Taylor, T. K., Gunn, B. K., Smolkowski, K., et al. (2002). Early elementary school intervention to reduce conduct problems: A randomized trial with Hispanic and non-Hispanic children. *Prevention Science, 3,* 83–94.

Baydar, N., Reid, M. J., & Webster-Stratton, C. (2003). The role of mental health factors and program engagement in the effectiveness of a preventive parenting program for Head Start mothers. *Child Development, 74,* 1433–1453.

Beauchaine, T. P., Webster-Stratton, C., & Reid. M. J. (2005). Mediators, moderators, and predictors of 1-year outcomes among children treated for early-onset conduct problems: A latent growth curve analysis. *Journal of Consulting and Clinical Psychology, 73,* 371–388.

Bernazzani, O., Cothe, C., & Tremblay, R. E. (2001). Early parent training to prevent disruptive behavior problems and delinquency in children. *The Annals of the American Academy of Political and Social Science, 578,* 90–103.

Broidy, L. M., Nagin, D. S., Tremblay, R. E., Bates, J. E., Brame, B., Dodge, K. A., et al. (2003). Developmental trajectories of childhood disruptive behaviors and adolescent delinquency: A six-site, cross-national study. *Developmental Psychology, 39,* 222–245.

Bronfenbrenner, U. (1979). Contexts of child rearing. *American Psychologist, 34,* 844–858.

Brotman, L. M., Calzada, E., Huang. K. Y., Kingston, S., Dawson-McClure, S., . . . & Petkova, E. (2011). Promoting effective parenting practices and preventing child behavior problems in school among ethnically diverse families from underserved, urban communities. *Child Development, 82,* 258–276.

Butler, S., Baruch, G., Hickey, N., Fonagy, P. (2011). A randomized controlled trial of multisystemic therapy and a statutory therapeutic intervention for young offenders. *Journal of the American Academy of Child & Adolescent Psychiatry, 50,* 1220–1235.

Cedar, B., & Levant, R. F. (1990). A meta-analysis of the effects of parent effectiveness training. *The American Journal of Family Therapy, 18,* 373–384.

Chorpita, B. F., Daleiden, E. L., & Weisz, J. R. (2005). Modularity in the design and application of therapeutic intervention. *Applied and Preventive Psychology, 11,* 141–156.

Coleman, P. K., & Karraker, K. H. (1998). Self-efficacy and parenting quality: Findings and future applications. *Developmental Review, 18,* 47–85.

Conduct Problems Prevention Research Group. (2002). Evaluation of the first 3 years of the Fast Track prevention trial with children at high risk for adolescent conduct problems. *Journal of Abnormal Child Psychology, 30,* 19–35.

Cunningham, A. J. (2002). One step forward: lessons learned from a randomized study of Multisystemic Therapy in Canada. *Praxis: Research from the Centre for Children & Families in the Justice System,* Accessed June 2, 2013 at., at: http://www.lfcc.on.ca/One_Step_Forward.pdf

DeGarmo, D. S., Patterson, G. R., & Forgatch, M. S. (2004). How do outcomes in a specified parent training intervention maintain or wane over time? *Prevention Science, 5,* 73–89.

Deković, M., Asscher, J. J., Hermanns, J., Reitz, E., & Prinzie, P. (2010). Tracing changes in families who participated in Home-Start parenting program: Parental competence as mechanism of change. *Prevention Science, 11,* 263–274.

Deković, M., Asscher, J. J., Manders, W.A., Prins, P. J. M., & Van der Laan, P. (2012). Within-intervention change: Mediators of intervention effects during Multisystemic Therapy. *Journal of Consulting and Clinical Psychology, 80,* 574–587.

Deković, M., Slagt, M. I., Asscher, J. J., Boendermaker, L., Eichelsheim, V. I., & Prinzie, P. (2011). Effects of early prevention programs on adult criminal offending: A meta-analysis. *Clinical Psychology Review, 31,* 532–544.

Deković, M., Stoltz, S., Schuiringa, H., Manders, W., & Asscher, J. J. (2012). Testing theories through evaluation research: Conceptual and methodological issues embedded in evaluations of parenting programmes. *European Journal of Developmental Psychology, 9*, 61–74.

Dumas, J. E., Moreland, A. D., Gitter, A. H., Pearl, A. M., & Nordstrom, A. H. (2008). Engaging parents in preventative parenting groups: Do ethnic, socio-economic, and belief match between parents and group leaders matter? *Health Education & Behaviour, 35*, 619–633.

Eyberg, S. M., Nelson, M. M., & Boggs, S. R. (2008). Evidence-based psychosocial treatments for children and adolescents with disruptive behavior. *Journal of Clinical Child & Adolescent Psychology, 37*, 215–237.

Forehand, R., Jones, D. J., & Parent, J. (2013). Behavioral parenting interventions for child disruptive behaviors and anxiety: What's different and what's the same. *Clinical Psychology Review, 33*, 133–145.

Frick, P. J., Blair, R. J. R., & Castellanos, F. X. (2012). Callous-unemotional traits and developmental pathways to the disruptive behavior disorders. In P. H. Tolan, & B. L. Leventhal (Eds). *Advances in child and adolescent psychopathology, Vol. I: Disruptive behavior disorders* (pp. 69–102). New York: Springer.

Frick, P. J., Ray, J. V., Thornton, L. C., & Kahn, R. E. (2014). Annual Research Review: A developmental psychopathology approach to understanding callous-unemotional traits in children and adolescents with serious conduct problems. *Journal of Child Psychology and Psychiatry, 55*, 532–548.

Furlong, M., McGilloway, S., Bywater, T., Hutchings, J., Smith, S. M., & Donnelly, M. (2012). Behavioural and cognitive-behavioural group-based parenting programmes for early-onset conduct problems in children aged 3 to 12 years. *Cochrane Database for Systematic Reviews, 2*, 1–344.

Gardner, F., Burton, J., & Klimes, I. (2006). Randomized controlled trial of a parenting intervention in the voluntary sector for reducing child conduct problems: outcomes and mechanisms of change. *Journal of Child Psychology and Psychiatry, 47*, 1123–1132.

Gardner, F., Hutchings, J., Bywater, T, & Whitaker, C. (2010). Who benefits and how does it work? Moderators and mediators of outcome in an effectiveness trial of a parenting intervention. *Journal of Clinical Child and Adolescent Psychology, 39*, 568–580.

Grusec, J. E. (2011). Socialization processes in the family: Social and emotional development. *Annual Review of Psychology, 62*, 243–269.

Hagen, K. A., Ogden, T., & Bjørnebekk, G. (2011). Treatment outcomes and mediators of parental management training: A one-year follow-up of children with conduct problems. *Journal of Clinical Child and Adolescent Psychology, 40*, 165–178.

Henggeler, S. W. (2011). Efficacy studies to large-scale transport: The development and validation of multisystemic therapy programs. *Annual Review of Clinical Psychology, 7*, 351–381.

Henggeler, S. W., Letourneau, E. J., Chapman, J. E., Borduin, C. M., Schewe, P. A., & McCart, M. R. (2009). Mediators of change for multisystemic therapy with juvenile sexual offenders. *Journal of Consulting and Clinical Psychology, 77*, 451–462.

Hinshaw, S. P. (2002). Intervention research, theoretical mechanisms, and causal processes related to externalizing behavior patterns. *Development and Psychopathology, 14*, 789–818.

Huey, S. J. J., Henggeler, S. W., Brondino, M. J., & Pickrel, S. G. (2000). Mechanisms of change in multisystemic therapy: Reducing delinquent behavior through therapist adherence and improved family and peer functioning. *Journal of Consulting and Clinical Psychology, 68,* 451–467.

Hutchings, J., Lane, E., & Kelly J. (2004). Comparison of two treatments of children with severely disruptive behaviours: A four year follow up. *Behavioural and Cognitive Psychotherapy, 32,* 15–30.

Kaminski, J. W., Vallew, L. A., Filene, J. H., & Boyle, C. L. (2008). A meta-analytic review of components associated with parent training program effectiveness. *Journal of Abnormal Child Psychology, 36,* 567–589.

Kazdin, A. E. (2007). Mediators and mechanisms of change in psychotherapy research. *Annual Review of Clinical Psychology, 3,* 1–27.

Kazdin, A., & Nock, M. (2003). Delineating mechanisms of change in child and adolescent therapy: Methodological issues and research recommendations. *Journal of Child Psychology and Psychiatry, 44,* 1116–1130.

Kellam, S. G., & Rebok, G. W. (1992). Building developmental and etiological theory through epidemiologically based preventive intervention trials. In J. McCord & R. E. Tremblay (Eds.), *Preventing antisocial behavior: Intervention from birth through adolescence* (pp. 162–195). New York: Guilford.

Kimonis, E.R., & Frick, P.J. (2011). Etiology of oppositional defiant disorder and conduct disorder: Biological, familial and environmental factors identified in the development of Disruptive Behavior Disorders. In R. C. Murrihy, A. D. Kidman, & T. H. Ollendick (Eds.), *Clinical handbook of assessing and treating conduct problems in youth* (pp. 49–76). New York: Springer.

Kraemer, H. C., Frank, E., & Kupfer, D. J. (2006). Moderators of treatment outcomes: Clinical, research, and policy importance. *The Journal of American Medical Association, 296,* 1286–1289.

Leijten, P., Raaijmakers, M. A. J., De Castro, B. O., & Matthys, W. (2013). Does socioeconomic status matter? A meta-analysis on parent training effectiveness for disruptive child behavior. *Journal of Clinical Child & Adolescent Psychology, 42,* 384–392.

Lochman, J. E., Boxmeyer, C., Powell, N., Qu, L., Wells, K., & Windle, M. (2009). Dissemination of the coping power program: Importance of intensity of counselor training. *Journal of Consulting and Clinical Psychology, 77,* 397–409.

Loeber, R., Burke J. D., & Pardini, D. A. (2009). Development and etiology of disruptive and delinquent behavior. *Annual Review of Clinical Psychology, 5,* 291–310.

Lundahl, B., Risser, H. J., & Lovejoy, M. C. (2006) A meta-analysis of parent training: Moderators and follow-up effects. *Clinical Psychology Review, 26,* 86–104.

Mah, J. W. T., & Johnston, C. (2008). Parental social cognitions: Considerations in the acceptability of and engagement in behavioral parent training. *Clinical Child and Family Psychology Review, 11,* 218–236.

Manders, W. A., Deković, M., Asscher, J. J., Laan, P. H. van der, & Prins, P. J. M. (2011). De implementatie van multisysteem therapie in Nederland: De invloed van behandelintegriteit en nonspecifieke factoren op behandeluitkomsten [Implementation of MST in The Netherlands: The effects of treatment integrity and non-specific factors on treatment outcomes]. *Gedragstherapie, 44,* 327–340.

Manders, W. A., Deković, M., Asscher, J. J., Van der Laan, P., & Prins, P. J. M. (2013). Psychopathy as predictor and moderator of multisystemic therapy outcomes among adolescents treated for antisocial behavior. *Journal of Abnormal Child Psychology, 41,* 1121–1132.

Matthys, W., & Lochman, J. E. (2010). *Oppositional defiant disorder and conduct disorder in childhood.* Chichester, UK: Wiley-Blackwell.

Matthys, W., Vanderschuren, L. J. M. J., & Schutter, D. J. L. G. (2013). Impaired neurocognitive functions affect social learning processes in oppositional defiant disorder and conduct disorder: Implications for interventions. *Clinical Child and Family Psychology Review, 15,* 234–246.

McCart, M. R., Priester, P. E., Davies, W. H., & Azen, R. (2006). Differential effectiveness of behavioral parent-training and cognitive-behavioral therapy for antisocial youth: A meta-analysis. *Journal of Abnormal Child Psychology, 34,* 525–541.

McGilloway, S., Mhaille, G. N., Bywater, T., Furlong, M., Leckey, Y., . . . & Donnelly, M. (2012). A parenting intervention for childhood behavior problems: A randomized controlled trial in disadvantaged community-based setting. *Journal of Consulting and Clinical Psychology, 80,* 116–127.

McMahon, R. J., Wells, K. C., & Kotler, J. S. (2006). Conduct problems. In E. J. Mash & R. A. Barkley (Eds.), *Treatment of childhood disorders.* New York: Guilford.

Murrihy, R. C., Kidman, A. D., & Ollendick, T. H. (Eds.) (2011). *Clinical handbook of assessing and treating conduct problems in youth.* New York: Springer.

Nock, M. K., Kazdin, A. E., Hiripi, E., & Kessler, R. C. (2007). Lifetime prevalences, correlates and persistence of oppositional defiant disorder: Results from the National Comorbidity Survey Replication. *Journal of Child Psychology and Psychiatry, 48,* 703–713.

Odgers, C. L., Moffitt, T. E., Broadbent, J. M., Dickson, N., Hancox, R. J., Harrington, H., et al. (2008). Female and male antisocial trajectories: From childhood origins to adult outcomes. *Development and Psychopathology, 20,* 673–716.

Ogden, T., & Halliday-Boykins, C. A. (2004). Multisystemic treatment of antisocial adolescents in Norway: Replication of clinical outcomes outside of the US. *Child and Adolescent Mental Health, 9,* 77–83.

Ollendick, T. H., Jarrett, M. A., Grills-Taquechel, A. E., Hovey, L. D., & Wolff, J. C. (2008). Comorbidity as a predictor and moderator of treatment outcome in youth with anxiety, affective, attention deficit/hyperactivity disorder, and oppositional/conduct disorders. *Clinical Psychology Review, 28,* 1447–1471.

Patterson, G. R., Reid, J. B., Jones, R. R., & Conger, R. E. (1975). *A social learning approach to family intervention: Families with aggressive children,* Vol. 1. Eugene, OR: Castalia.

Patterson, G. R., DeGarmo, D. S., & Forgatch, M. S. (2004). Systematic changes in families following prevention trials. *Journal of Abnormal Psychology, 32,* 621–633.

Patterson, G. R., Forgatch, M. S., & DeGarmo, D. S. (2010). Cascading effects following intervention. *Development and Psychopathology, 22,* 949–970.

Piquero, A. R., Farrington, D. P., Welsh, B. C., Tremblay, R., & Jennings, W. G. (2009). Effects of early family/parent training programs on antisocial behavior and delinquency. *Journal of Experimental Criminology, 5,* 83–120.

Prinzie, P., Stams, G. J., Deković, M., Reijntjes, A. H. A., & Belsky, J. (2009). The relations between parents' Big Five personality factors and parenting: A meta-analytic review. *Journal of Personality and Social Psychology, 97,* 351–362.

Reid, M. J., Webster-Stratton, C., & Beauchaine, T. P. (2001). Parent training in Head Start: a comparison of program response among African American, Asian American, Caucasian, and Hispanic mothers. *Prevention Science, 2*, 209–227.

Reyno, S. M., & McGrath, P. J. (2006). Predictors of parent training efficacy for child externalizing behavior problems: A meta-analytic review. *Journal of Child Psychology and Psychiatry, 47*, 99–111.

Sameroff, A. J. (2010). A unified theory of development: A dialectic integration of nature and nurture. *Child Development, 81*, 6–22.

Sandler, I. N., Schoenfelder, E. N., Wolchik, S. A., & MacKinnon, D. P. (2011). Long-term impact of prevention programs to promote effective parenting: Lasting effects, but uncertain processes. *Annual Review of Psychology, 62*, 299–329.

Schaeffer, C. M., & Borduin, C. M. (2005). Long-term follow-up to a randomized clinical trial of multisystemic therapy with serious and violent juvenile offenders. *Journal of Consulting and Clinical Psychology, 73*, 445–453.

Schoenwald, S. K., Carter, R. E., Chapman, J. E., & Sheidow, A. J. (2008). Therapist adherence and organizational effects on change in youth behavior problems one year after multisystemic therapy. *Administration and Policy in Mental Health and Mental Health Services Research, 35*, 379–394.

Schoenwald, S. K., Halliday-Boykins, C. A., & Henggeler, S. W. (2003). Client-level predictors of adherence to MST in community service settings. *Family Process, 42*, 345–359.

Serketic, W. J., & Dumas, J. E. (1996). The effectiveness of behavioral parent training to modify antisocial behavior in children: A meta-analysis. *Behavior Therapy, 27*, 171–186.

Stoltz, S., Van Londen, M., Deković, M., Castro, B.O., de, Prinzie, P. (2013). What works for whom, how and under what circumstances? Testing moderated mediation of intervention effects on externalizing behavior in children. *Social Development, 22*, 406–425.

Stoltz, S., Prinzie, P., Haan, A. D., de, Londen, M., van, Castro, B. O., de, & Deković, M. (2012). Child personality as moderator of outcome in a school-based intervention for preventing externalising behaviour. *European Journal of Personality, 27*, 271–279.

Sundell, K., Hansson, K., Löfholm, C. A., Olsson, T., Gustle, L. H., & Kadesjö, C. (2008). The transportability of multisystemic therapy to Sweden: Short-term results from a randomized trial of conduct-disordered youths. *Journal of Family Psychology, 22*, 550–560.

Tein, J., Sandler, I. N., MacKinnon, D. P., & Wolchik, S. A. (2004). How did it work? Who did it work for? Mediation in the context of a moderated prevention effect for children of divorce. *Journal of Consulting and Clinical Psychology, 74*, 617–624.

Teti, D. M., & Cole, P. M. (2011). Parenting at risk: New perspectives, new approaches. *Journal of Family Psychology, 25*, 625–634.

Timmons-Mitchell, J., Bender, M. B., Kishna, M. A., & Mitchell, C. C. (2006). An independent effectiveness trial of Multisystemic therapy with juvenile justice youth. *Journal of Clinical Child & Adolescent Psychology, 35*, 227–236.

Webster-Stratton, C. H. (2006). *The Incredible Years: A trouble-shooting guide for parents of children aged 3–8.* Seattle, WA: Incredible Years Press.

Webster-Stratton, C. H., & Reid, J. M. (2010). The Incredible Years Program for children from infancy to pre-adolescence: Prevention and treatment of behavior problems. In R. C. Murrihy, A. D. Kidman, & T. H. Ollendick (Eds.) (2010). *Clinical handbook of assessing and treating conduct problems in youth* (pp. 117–138). New York: Springer.

Yasui, M., & Dishion, T. J. (2007). The ethnic context of child and adolescent problem behaviour: Implications for child and family interventions. *Clinical Child and Family Psychology Review, 10,* 137–179.

6

Moderators and Mediators of Treatments for Youth With ADHD

SASKIA VAN DER OORD AND DAVID DALEY ■

INTRODUCTION

ADHD (attention deficit hyperactivity disorder) is a neurodevelopmental psychiatric disorder, which consists of a pervasive and developmentally inappropriate pattern of inattention and hyperactivity/impulsivity symptoms (*DSM-5*, American Psychiatric Association, 2013). Prevalence rates of ADHD in the United States are around 9%–11% of the 4–17-year-old children and adolescents (Visser et al., 2014). There is variability in prevalence rates across countries, but this is mainly accounted for by methodological factors of the studies and not geographical location (Polanczyk, de Lima, Horta, Biederman, & Rohde, 2007). ADHD is observed more in boys than girls, with a ratio of 3:1 in population-based samples (Gerson, 2002).

There are three subtypes of ADHD, the predominantly inattentive, the predominantly hyperactive/impulsive, and the combined subtype. In childhood, the combined subtype is most prevalent, while in adolescence and adulthood the inattentive subtype is most prevalent (Wilcutt et al., 2012). This is in line with the notion that there is a different developmental trajectory of the two symptom dimensions; the inattentive symptoms are relatively stable, while the hyperactive/impulsive symptoms decline from childhood to adulthood (Biederman, Mick, & Faraone, 2000). The hyperactive/impulsive subtype is rare, and is mostly observed in preschool children (Daley, 2006).

In a large proportion of the individuals with ADHD, there are comorbid conditions, both in the internalizing (mood, anxiety disorders) and externalizing domains of psychopathology, with the most prevalent comorbid condition in childhood being oppositional defiant disorder (ODD). Often there is more than one comorbid condition, and in clinical samples the "pure" ADHD is rare

(Yoshimashu et al., 2012). With regard to gender differences, girls tend to have more comorbid internalizing disorders than boys, while boys with ADHD are at higher risk for externalizing psychiatric comorbidities than girls (Yoshimashu et al., 2012).

Next to comorbid conditions, individuals with ADHD have impairments in school, social, and academic functioning (Fabiano et al., 2006). Also, compared to parents of children without ADHD, parents of children with ADHD feel less competent in parenting, have more parenting stress, and display less positive (rewarding) and more negative (punishing) parenting behavior toward their child (Deault, 2010; Johnston & Mash, Miller, & Ninowski, 2012). Further, parents of children with ADHD show elevated rates of depression, anxiety, conduct, substance use, and ADHD (Harvey, Danforth, McKee, Ulaszek, & Friedman, 2003; Johnston & Mash, 2001). Thus, as such, ADHD is highly impairing not only for the child with ADHD, but also for the parents of the child.

TREATMENTS FOR ADHD

To date, the two prevailing treatments for ADHD are medication (mostly stimulants) and behavioral interventions. Medication shows robust short- and middle-term effects on the reduction of ADHD symptoms (Faraone, Biederman, Spencer, & Aleardi, 2006). However, there are a number of limitations. First, a proportion of individuals with ADHD show only limited or no response to medication. Second, there may be adverse effects of medication on sleep, appetite, and growth. Third, long-term effects of medication still need to be determined (Molina et al., 2009). And fourth, although effects on the reduction of ADHD behavior are well established, the effects of medication on related areas of impairment, such as academic functioning, may be limited (Van der Oord, Prins, Oosterlaan, & Emmelkamp, 2008). Also, many parents and clinicians may have reservations about the use of medication for their child (Berger, Dor, Nevo, & Goldzweig, 2008). Therefore, in clinical guidelines often the combination of medication and behavioral interventions is recommended (Taylor et al., 2004).

Behavioral treatment is defined as all interventions employing learning principles to target ADHD or ADHD-related behaviors (Sonuga-Barke et al., 2013). These interventions can be directed specifically to the child (e.g., in the case of skills training interventions such as organizational skills or social skills training interventions), but are commonly conducted indirectly via an adult, in most cases in the form of parent training. In these interventions, parents or other "facilitators" such as teachers learn to use basic operant learning principles in order to reduce the child's non-adaptive or negative behavior, and to shape and reward more adaptive behavior. Thus, through reinforcement learning the child learns more adaptive behavior. Also, adapting and structuring of daily life is part of the program, to reduce the chance of occurrence of non-adaptive behavior. Further, as the challenging behavior of the child is thought to be a result of a negative coercive interactional cycle with parents, transforming this cycle into a positive cycle by enhancing enjoyable parenting is also a part of the program.

Recently, two meta-analyses using similar methodology examined the effectiveness of behavioral interventions compared to control conditions/interventions for children and adolescents with ADHD. They examined not only ADHD outcomes (Sonuga-Barke et al., 2013), but also common comorbid conditions, associated areas of impairment, parenting practices and competence, and parental mental health (Daley et al., 2014). Evidence was analyzed separately for what was referred to as the *most proximal rater* and *the probably blind rater*. The most proximal rater was in most cases the parent. The interventions examined were mainly behavioral parent training programs; thus the parent was not blind to the intervention, was involved in giving the intervention, and probably was biased for favorable outcome of the behavioral intervention. *The probably blind rater* was the rater of behavior who was blind to treatment allocation, was not involved in giving the intervention, and thus was the more objective rater of the child's behavior.

These meta-analyses show small and for the blinded rater non-significant effects of behavioral treatment on the reduction of core ADHD symptoms (Daley et al., 2014; Sonuga-Barke et al., 2013). On reduction of comorbid ODD symptoms, the improvement of social skills, academic performance, and parenting practices and competence, there are significant effects of behavioral treatment as rated by the *most proximal rater*. Using the *blinded most objective rating*, there were significant moderate effects of behavioral treatment on improving positive parenting and reducing the use of more negative parenting (Daley et al., 2014). Moreover, conduct problems were significantly reduced (small effect size). In sum, evidence from both subjective and objective measures of behavior shows that although there are limited effects on reduction of core ADHD behaviors, behavior interventions may have a number of benefits with regard to the improvement of parenting and comorbid conditions and impairments.

For a long time, behavioral interventions were the most frequently investigated non-pharmacological treatments for ADHD. In the last decade, following the work of Klingberg et al. (2005), there has been an increase in the use and research into the effectiveness of other forms of non-pharmacological interventions, such as computerized cognitive-based intervention approaches, aimed at targeting executive functioning in children with ADHD (Rapport et al., 2013; Sonuga-Barke et al., 2013).

Ample research shows that individuals with ADHD have deficits in executive functioning (Martinussen, Hayden, Hogg-Johnson & Tannock, 2005; Wilcutt et al., 2005). Executive functions (EF) allow individuals to regulate their behavior, thoughts, and emotions, and thereby enable self-control. The problems that children with ADHD display in daily life are thought to be the result of EF deficits (e.g., Nigg, 2006), although motivational deficits are also thought to be underlying ADHD behavior (Sagvolden, Aase, Johansen & Russell, 2005; Sonuga-Barke, 2003). With regard to EF, meta-analyses demonstrate that children with ADHD particularly show impairment in the executive function working memory (Martinussen et al., 2005). In particular, visuospatial working memory is impaired in ADHD, which is described as the ability to maintain and manipulate/reorganize visuospatial information (e.g., Martinussen et al., 2005). Due to an impaired visuospatial working memory, a child has trouble remembering what he or she was doing or what she or he needs to do to reach a current goal.

Computerized cognitive training is aimed at strengthening these deficient underlying neuropsychological processes through adaptive training. Most of these cognitive training programs are focused on enhancing the executive function working memory, and, in particular, visuospatial working memory. It is thought that the maturation and/or efficiency of neural circuitry underlying targeted executive functions such as working memory can be accelerated by means of protracted training, practice, and feedback (Klingberg, 2010). Through training of these neuropsychological processes, the transfer of training effects is expected not only to improve related cognitive functions, such as inhibition or reasoning (near transfer; thus transfer of effects to the trained cognitive functions or related cognitive functions), but also to affect ADHD-related behavior in daily life (far transfer; i.e., thus transfer beyond the trained cognitive or related cognitive function to daily life behavior such as levels of inattention and/or hyperactivity/impulsivity).

Recently, several meta-analyses and reviews have shown that, although near transfer to related cognitive functions is generally accomplished after cognitive training, there is little evidence of far transfer effects of cognitive training to daily life ADHD behavior and associated problem areas (e.g., Rapport et al., 2013; Sonuga-Barke et al., 2013).

In this chapter we will focus on evidence for moderators and mediators for these non-pharmacological interventions of ADHD, and in particular for behavioral and cognitive interventions.

THEORETICAL MODELS FOR MODERATION OF BEHAVIORAL TREATMENT OUTCOME FOR ADHD

Considering the high prevalence rates of ADHD and the impairments associated with the disorder, the question of "which intervention works for whom, and why does it work" is highly relevant for clinical practice. However, there is limited research with regard to moderators and mediators of treatment outcome in ADHD. Also, theoretical models with regard to moderation and mediation of behavioral treatment outcomes specifically for ADHD are lacking. To date, most research has consisted more of a non-theoretically based test of different potential moderators. Even after some significant moderators have been found, there often has been no theoretical explanation for these significant moderators.

The main aim of most traditional behavioral parent training programs is reducing the externalizing and behavioral impairments that often co-occur with ADHD symptomatology. As mentioned above, this is often accomplished by, on the one hand, adapting/changing the environment of the child (e.g., by setting clear rules) and, on the other hand, by teaching parents to use operant techniques to change the behavior of their child (e.g., rewarding desired behavior and ignoring non-desired behavior).

One may hypothesize that the (psychological) availability of and possibility for parents to provide such techniques is important for moderation of outcome, given that behavioral interventions rely on parents implementing the behavioral techniques at home. Important moderators may be parental psychopathology and other factors influencing the availability, confidence, and possibilities of parents to provide the intervention (e.g., education level of parents, parenting efficacy). Further, the challenging behavior targeted in the behavioral parent training programs is thought to be the result of a long-lasting negative coercive interactional cycle between parents and child (the coercion theory; Patterson, 1982). One of the aims of the intervention is turning this interactional cycle into a positive one. The more rooted this cycle is, the more difficult it may be to turn this cycle, thus pointing to age of the child as a hypothetical moderator of behavioral intervention. Also, in young children patterns of learned defiant behavior are less rooted, while the brain is highly plastic; thus it may be easier for parents of young children to ameliorate behavior through operant procedures (Sonuga-Barke & Halperin, 2010).

Relatedly, the more problem behavior a child displays, the more negative this coercive cycle may be, which may suggest that for those children with more severe comorbidity it may be more difficult to change the behavior of the child through behavioral interventions than for children with no or less severe comorbidity (see Figure 6.1).

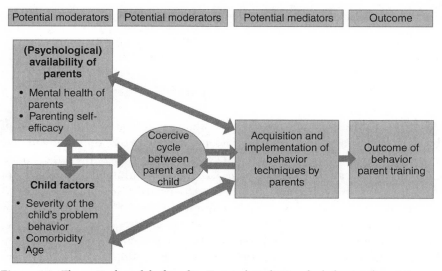

Figure 6.1. Theoretical model of moderation and mediation for behavioral parent training.

With regard to moderators of outcome of cognitive training, cognitive dysfunction may be a potential moderator. There are different underlying psychopathological pathways toward ADHD behavior (Sonuga-Barke, 2003), the motivational and the executive functioning pathways. Some children with ADHD have motivational deficits or other executive functioning and working memory deficits, and some children have both motivational and executive functioning deficits (Dovis et al., in press; Solanto et al., 2001). With regard to a moderation model for computerized cognitive training interventions, one could hypothesize that, given that training is aimed at strengthening these deficient underlying neuropsychological processes, those children displaying more deficits in a particular executive function problem would benefit more from the training of this cognitive function than children displaying less deficits in this cognitive function. Although intuitive, unfortunately to date no studies have directly assessed this hypothesis within ADHD samples (Rapport, Orban, Kofler, & Friedman, 2013). Other potential moderators of cognitive training outcome may be the degree to which participants are intrinsically motivated for the cognitive training and their pre-treatment beliefs regarding whether cognitive deficits can be modulated by training (Jaeggi, Buschkuehl, Jonides, & Shah, 2011; Jaeggi, Buschkuehl, Shah, & Jonides, 2014). Within non-ADHD samples these factors have been suggested to moderate treatment outcome; those participants who were more intrinsically motivated and had the belief that cognitive deficits could be modulated had better outcomes than those who were less intrinsically motivated and did not believe that cognitive deficits could be modulated (Jaeggi et al., 2011; Jaeggi et al., 2014). To date, these moderators of cognitive training have not been explored within ADHD samples, although given the motivational functioning deficits within individuals with ADHD, intrinsic motivation may be a potent moderator of cognitive training outcome.

EMPIRICAL RESULTS OF MODERATION OF BEHAVIORAL TREATMENT OUTCOME FOR ADHD

Moderators of Treatment Response in the MTA Study

As mentioned earlier, there are very few studies with regard to moderation of behavioral and cognitive treatment outcome in ADHD. The only study to date that was a priori powered for these moderation analyses was the largest treatment study to date in children with ADHD: the Multimodal Treatment of ADHD (MTA) study (Hinshaw, 2007; MTA Cooperative Group, 1999a, 1999b).

The MTA study, which was conducted in the United States, compared four treatment arms in 579 children 9–11-year-old children with ADHD: first, medication management (methylphenidate); second, an intense multimodal behavior therapy consisting of a school-based intervention, an intensive parent training program, and a summer treatment program for the child; third, a combination of both treatments; and, finally, standard community care, in which almost 70% of the children received stimulant treatment. Primary analyses of the MTA study showed that all conditions showed significant reductions in core ADHD and related symptoms after treatment. Especially, the medication management and combined condition showed significant improvements in ADHD and related symptoms, compared to standard community care and multimodal behavioral treatment. The medication management and combined condition did not differ significantly (MTA Cooperative Group, 1999a). However, several secondary analyses and subsequent papers did suggest some effect of adding behavioral intervention to medication. First, secondary outcome analyses using composite measures showed significant differences in effect sizes between the medication management and combined condition, in favor of the latter (Conners et al., 2001). Also, children in the combined condition received lower doses of medication at post-test than those in the medication management condition (MTA Cooperative Group, 1999a). Further, the combined condition showed more excellent responders than the other conditions. Also, parents preferred both conditions including behavioral treatments above the medication management condition (MTA Cooperative Group, 1999a; Swanson et al., 2001). Within the MTA study, several moderators of treatment outcome have been explored in a series of studies (Arnold et al., 2004; Jensen et al., 2001; Jones et al., 2010; March et al., 2000; MTA Cooperative Group, 1999b; Owens et al., 2003). Significant moderators emerged for behavioral and combined interventions, in particular, comorbid anxiety disorder, patterns of comorbidity, family public assistance, and ethnicity/race. Moderators that were not significant for outcome of behavioral intervention were gender, comorbid ODD/CD, a history of stimulant treatment, severity of ADHD, parental depressive symptomatology, and child IQ.

With regard to the significant moderators specifically for the behavioral intervention condition, the most important one was anxiety of the child; on parent reported outcomes of ADHD and internalizing symptoms, children with comorbid anxiety disorders showed better outcome to behavioral intervention than those without comorbid anxiety disorders. The children with ADHD and comorbid anxiety who received behavioral intervention had similar outcomes as children with ADHD only receiving the medication intervention. Those children with comorbid anxiety who received the combined intervention had even better outcomes (MTA Cooperative Group, 1999b). Few explanations are given for these results. However, it may be that enhancing parenting skills, providing structure in daily life, and positive parenting in the behavioral intervention conditions may have more impact on reduction of ADHD symptoms for the anxious subgroup of children with ADHD than for the non-anxious group of children with ADHD. The finding of more significant improvement in internalizing behavior in this anxious group due to behavioral ADHD interventions may indicate that behavioral treatment of ADHD may also ameliorate anxiety in some way. It may well be that at least some of the anxiety these children experience flows from the stress of ADHD-related problems and impairments (MTA Cooperative Group, 1999b).

Also, there were indications that patterns of double comorbidity were related to outcome; it was tested whether children with both comorbid anxiety and conduct disorder showed differential response than children with only comorbid anxiety. Those children with comorbidity with anxiety without conduct disorder showed better response to behavioral interventions, while moderator effects in those with double comorbidity (both comorbid conduct disorder and anxiety) were less robust and on only one outcome (parent-rated hyperactivity/impulsivity). In general, those with double comorbidity showed better response to the combined treatment of medication with behavioral intervention (Jensen et al., 2001; March et al., 2000). This differential response may be related to the fact that those with double comorbidity had more severe ADHD, and more general problem behavior symptomatology than those with single comorbidity (March et al., 2000). It may well be that for these more severe cases, a single treatment modality is not effective enough, and both treatment with medication and behavioral treatment are necessary.

With regard to the effects of combined intervention of behavioral and medication interventions, children with low-income families showed relatively larger response to the combined intervention, as rated by teachers on improvement of social skills (MTA Cooperative Group, 1999b). Also, ethnicity was a moderator of treatment outcome; ethnic minority children showed relatively better response to combined intervention on the improvement of child ADHD and ODD behavior, as rated by parents and teachers, than did Caucasian children (Arnold et al., 2003; for an extensive review, see Hinshaw, 2007). This effect remained significant after controlling for socioeconomic status variables. However, only parent- and teacher-rated ADHD and ODD behavior was examined as an outcome, while parents and teachers were not blind to treatment status. In a further analysis, it was tested whether ethnicity (i.e., Caucasian, Latino, or African American) was also a moderator of treatment outcome when blinded observed parenting and child behavior were used as outcomes (Jones et al., 2010). Although at baseline parenting practices differed by ethnicity, ethnicity did not moderate treatment outcome using these objective measures as outcomes. This suggests, in contrast to the former study (Arnold et al., 2003), that ethnicity may not be an important factor in differential treatment effectiveness.

Moderators of Treatment Response in Other Treatment Studies

To our knowledge, there is only one other study that assesses moderators for outcome of behavioral intervention in ADHD samples in a series of studies using data of the same treatment outcome study (Van den Hoofdakker et al., 2010; Van den Hoofdakker et al., 2012; Van den Hoofdakker et al., 2014). This treatment study, conducted in The Netherlands, randomized 94 4–12-year-old children with ADHD to either a behavioral parent training plus routine clinical care or to routine clinical care alone. The group behavioral parent training was a 12-week outpatient intervention focusing on structuring the environment, giving instructions, setting rules, anticipating misbehaviors, reinforcing positive behavior, ignoring, employing punishment, and implementing token systems. The routine clinical care was defined as care as usual, provided by psychiatrists, which could consist of supportive counseling, psycho-education, pharmacotherapy, and crisis management whenever necessary.

The primary results of this study showed that children randomized to routine clinical care and those randomized to additive behavior therapy showed improvements over time on ADHD symptoms, externalizing and internalizing behavior, and parenting stress as rated by parents, but that only children who received additional behavioral parent training showed significantly less behavioral (conduct) and parent-rated internalizing symptoms, although the children randomized to only routine clinical care received significantly more poly-pharmaceutical treatment (additional medication treatment next to stimulant treatment). There were no differences between groups in the reduction of core ADHD symptoms and parenting stress (Van den Hoofdakker, Van der Veen-Mulders, Sytema, Emmelkamp, Minderaa, & Nauta, 2007).

In the first moderation analysis (Van den Hoofdakker et al., 2010), IQ, age, comorbidity, maternal ADHD, depression, and parenting self-efficacy were assessed as moderators, and behavioral problems and ADHD symptoms were used as outcomes. This analysis showed that especially those children with no or just one comorbidity (anxiety/depression or oppositional deviant/conduct disorder) had superior response to behavioral parent training. Also, when mothers had high parenting self-efficacy, the children had superior response to behavioral parent training. This suggests that adjunctive behavioral intervention is most useful when mothers have high parenting self-efficacy and in children with no or just a single type of comorbidity.

From the rationale that there may be a differential genetic susceptibility toward parenting interventions (e.g., Bakermans-Kranenburg & Van IJzendoorn, 2011), in a subsequent moderator study Van den Hoofdakker et al. (2012) investigated whether genetic factors could also be a moderator of treatment response in children with ADHD. Ample evidence shows that genetic factors contribute to the etiology of ADHD (Thapar, Langley, Asherhon & Gill, 2007), and that certain susceptibility genes interact with environment in a complex ways. These susceptibility genes may also interact with the developmental pathway of ADHD (Thapar et al., 2007) and the susceptibility children have toward environmental adversity or manipulations such as behavioral or pharmacological interventions (Thapar et al., 2007).

One of the genes that in previous research has been associated with differential susceptibility toward pharmacological treatment response in children with ADHD is the dopamine transporter gene DAT1 (McGough, 2005). Van den Hoofdakker et al. (2012) explored whether this dopamine transporter gene was also involved in susceptibility toward behavioral treatments in children with ADHD, given that the dopamine transporter has a crucial role in regulating dopamine levels in areas of the brain that are associated with motivation, learning, and operant conditioning (Waelti, Dickinson, & Schutlz, 2001).

Thus, Van den Hoofdakker et al. (2012) assessed whether the dopamine transporter gene (SCL6A3/DAT1; supposedly involved in motivation and learning) was a moderator of behavioral treatment response to behavioral parent training using a subsample ($N = 50$) of the 94 children of the formerly described intervention study (Van den Hoofdakker et al., 2007). From the rationale that reinforcement learning is an important element of behavioral intervention for ADHD and given the typical heterogeneity of reinforcement sensitivity within ADHD samples (Dovis, Van der Oord, Wiers, & Prins, 2012; Luman, Oosterlaan, & Sergeant, 2005; Luman, Tripp, & Scheres, 2010), it was hypothesized that there might be differential susceptibility to parenting interventions, as shown by individual differences in dopamine functioning assessed by genetic polymorphisms of this dopamine transporter gene DAT1. The children were divided in two groups with different polymorphisms of DAT1 (those children with 2 versus children with no or 1 DAT1 10-repeat alleles). Results of the study show that this dopamine transporter gene DAT1 moderated treatment response; those children with no or 1 DAT1 10-repeat allele showed superior treatment effects to additive behavioral intervention, but this was not the case for children with 2 DAT1 10-repeat alleles. Although preliminary and not yet replicated, these results suggest that genetic differences in the dopamine transporter gene DAT1 in children with ADHD may influence their susceptibility to a behavioral intervention directed at shaping their environment through their parents.

As research concerning the influence of paternal factors and psychopathology on treatment outcome is scarce, in a recent study Van den Hoofdakker et al. (2014) explored whether paternal ADHD symptoms, depressive symptoms, and parenting self-efficacy were moderators of treatment outcome. For this analysis they used the same data set as described in Van den Hoofdakker et al. (2007; see above). Treatment outcomes were parent-rated ADHD and behavioral symptoms. Results showed that paternal ADHD symptoms and paternal parenting self-efficacy were moderators of treatment outcome on behavioral symptoms. For those fathers with high levels of ADHD symptoms, additional behavioral parent training is most beneficial on reduction of behavioral symptoms of their child. For the ADHD outcome there were no significant moderators. The authors note that the results that fathers with high levels of ADHD symptoms benefit most from additional behavioral parent training are in contrast to studies reporting maternal ADHD symptoms to be a predictor (*note*: not moderator) of worse outcome to behavioral parent training (Sonuga-Barke et al., 2002).

The authors have several explanations for this moderating effect. They propose that the fathers with ADHD may benefit more from the behavioral management techniques, such as setting clear rules, and applying consistent rewards and unambiguous rules, as it guards them against their more impulsive parenting style (i.e., they have more room for improvement in parenting skills than fathers with low levels of ADHD behavior). Also, a more indirect pathway is proposed in which teaching fathers new parenting skills together with their wives, and coaching fathers and mothers to operate together as a team, may positively affect their marital relationship, especially for those fathers with high ADHD symptoms (as high levels of parental ADHD are often associated with increased marital discord; Asherson, Manor, & Huss, 2014). This improved marital relationship may in turn have a positive influence on the child's behavioral problems.

Summary of Moderation Results

Bringing all the moderator results together, there are only two studies assessing moderation for behavioral intervention within ADHD samples. The intensity and scope of both these interventions differ: the MTA behavioral intervention is multi-modal and intense, and the other intervention resembles behavioral parent interventions often used in clinical practice, that is, outpatient, short term, and uni-modal.

For outpatient short-term behavioral parent interventions, comorbidity and parenting self-efficacy (of both mother and father) and paternal ADHD symptoms are important indicators of treatment success. Parents with high self-efficacy, fathers with high levels of ADHD symptoms, and children with only one or no comorbid condition are most likely to benefit from these parent interventions. With regard to our hypothesized theoretical model and clinical implications, those parents who are *confident* in providing parenting techniques may gain the most benefit from behavioral parent training. Also, with regard to the possibility of breaking the coercive cycle, for those with the *least* comorbid problem behavior, it may be easier to break the coercive cycle. Somewhat counterintuitively, children with fathers with high levels of ADHD symptoms respond best to additive behavioral treatment, which may be related to the fact that there is more room for improvement for the behavioral techniques taught in the interventions for these fathers. Given the small sample size, the genotype transporter gene results need further replication to be able to give any clinical implications.

In sum, for long-term and multi-modal interventions, there were few significant moderators. Only the presence of *specific* comorbidity seems important; in particular, those with comorbid anxiety have a better chance of intervention success with behavioral interventions for ADHD, as reported by parents, while for those children with *both* comorbid anxiety and ODD, a combination of medication and behavioral intervention is indicated.

THEORETICAL MODELS FOR MEDIATION OF ADHD TREATMENT OUTCOMES

Again, there is very little written with regard to theoretical models for mediation *specific* for interventions of ADHD. Often these models are based on theoretical models of behavioral interventions for generic behavioral problems in children; the theoretical notion here is that the more change in parenting (less negative, more positive parenting), the more it will reduce the behavioral problems the child displays (thus breaking the coercive cycle more easily) (see Figure 6.1). Although there is no formal test of mediation, the meta-analysis of Daley et al. (2014) supports this notion, given that it shows a significant improvement of these supposed mechanisms of change of behavioral intervention, that is, more positive parenting and less negative parenting in behavioral parent training than in control conditions as assessed by objective and non-biased measures of parenting. Also, for some of the symptom domains (although not on ADHD symptoms) there is a significant improvement after behavioral interventions.

For more skills-based training, such as organizational skills training or social skills training, one could assume that the more skills the child acquires during the training, the more effective the training will be in reduction of symptoms (De Boo & Prins, 2007). Further, it would seem intuitive to assume that for all interventions there may be a dose-response relationship between exposure to (e.g., attendance) or participation in (e.g., completing homework) the intervention and effectiveness. Another candidate mediator may be that effective parenting mediates the acquisition of the learned skill, as parents can facilitate, reward, and enhance on the spot practicing of the learned skill (De Boo & Prins, 2007). Thus enhanced parental effectiveness in contingency management of socially adaptive behavior may enhance effectiveness of the skills training. However, it may also be that more indirect factors contribute to mediation of treatment outcome in skills training. For example, parental involvement in skills training may enhance parent-child interaction, which in turn may mediate skills training outcomes (De Boo & Prins, 2007). There is no test of mediational effects, but there is one study systematically assessing the additive value of parental involvement in skills training (Pfiffner & McBurnett, 1997), by comparing the effectiveness of social skills training with and without a parent generalization module. Opposing the hypothesis of mediation of effective parenting, this study did not find an additive effect of involving parents in social skills training for the child.

With regard to mediators of outcome of computerized cognitive training, one could argue that the more the executive function improves during training, the more effective the training will be in the reduction of symptoms and associated impairments. This is reflected in the idea that near transfer (i.e., the improvement in the cognitive function trained or a related cognitive function) eventually would lead to far transfer (i.e., improvement in the ADHD behavior of the child) (Klingberg, 2010).

Again, although intuitive, there is no direct test of this mediational mechanism within ADHD samples. However, there is indirect evidence opposing this hypothesis. Using a meta-analytic approach of 25 cognitive training interventions, Rapport et al. (2013) investigated whether the type of cognitive training (i.e., the cognitive function trained) was related to outcome on near transfer (a measure of the trained cognitive function) and far transfer (ADHD symptoms and related impairments). The results revealed that, although the type of training was related to near transfer, it was not related to far transfer. This suggests that other processes (illusory effects, non-specific effects) than improvement in the executive function may account for the benefits in impairments and symptoms. Also opposing this hypothesis, several recent placebo-controlled studies find near transfer effects of cognitive training, but do not find far transfer effects (e.g., Chacko, Bedard, Marks Feirson, Uderman, et al., 2014; Dovis, Van der Oord, Wiers, & Prins, in press; Egeland, Aarlien, & Saunes, 2013; Van Dongen-Boomsma, Vollebregt, Buitelaar, & Slaat-Willemse, 2014). Moreover, Van Dongen-Boomsma et al. (2014) also *directly* investigated whether improvement in the training program was correlated with near transfer (e.g., effects on working memory measures) and far transfer (e.g., effects on ADHD behavior), and they did not find significant cognitive training effects, which suggests that the mediational hypothesis that improvement in the trained cognitive function leads to near transfer and eventually far transfer cannot be supported.

EMPIRICAL RESULTS FOR MEDIATION OF BEHAVIORAL TREATMENT OUTCOME FOR ADHD

Mediation Analyses in the MTA Study

The formerly described MTA study conducted mediator analyses for behavioral and combined interventions, and showed that attendance levels did not influence outcome for behavioral interventions. However, it may well be that another variable related to adherence to the principles and skills taught in the intervention process (e.g., amount of homework completed) would mediate outcome (Hinshaw, 2007). However, this was not tested in the MTA study.

Also, based on the ideas that the MTA behavioral treatments targeted parenting behavior directly and parent-child relationship indirectly, and that, following the coercion theory (Patterson, 1982), changes in the parental practices and in parent-child interaction would affect the child's behavioral improvement, it was hypothesized that changes in family discipline practices from pre- to post-test, as rated by parents, would mediate outcome, especially for the combined and behavioral intervention conditions (Hinshaw et al., 2000). Three parenting factors were tested: positive parenting, monitoring, and negative/ineffective parenting. Results showed that those parents with the greatest reduction of negative/ineffective discipline showed relatively greater improvement on teacher-rated behavioral problems and social skills than those parents without this reduction. This effect was specific for the combined treatment condition of medication and behavioral treatment. For these children, at post-test the teacher-rated behavioral and social skills problems were even in the normal range. How this mediation worked is speculative; it may be that stimulant medication alters the child's behavioral problems, leading to less harsh discipline of the parents, which may allow the child to advance more from the taught skills-based techniques or to learn more from the behavioral and operant techniques provided by parents, which in turn improves self-regulation and improved functioning at school (Hinshaw et al., 2000). Or it may be possible that improvements in school behavior (facilitated by medication) may enable parents to use less harsh discipline at home when the behavioral parent training procedures of the combined treatment are being implemented (Hinshaw et al., 2000). These results suggest that in combined interventions, the reduction of negative/ineffective parenting is an import target of intervention.

Mediation Analyses in Other Studies

To our knowledge, only one other study assessed mediation of change of behavioral intervention through parenting factors, while also assessing the effects of a potent predictor of outcome (*note*: predictor, not moderator): parental ADHD (Chronis-Tuscano et al., 2008; Chronis-Tuscano et al., 2011). Parental ADHD has been shown to be a predictor of reduced response to behavioral parent training (Sonuga-Barke, Daley, & Thompson, 2002), while the MTA study showed that the reduction of negative and ineffective discipline may be crucial for intervention success. Combining these results, Chronis-Tuscano et al. (2008) assessed whether the relation between maternal ADHD symptoms and improvement in child behavior following behavioral parent training was mediated by change in parenting. In this study, 70 mothers of 6–10-year-old children with ADHD followed a brief five-session parent-training program for ADHD. The parent training consisted of psycho-education, teaching parents to reward prosocial behavior and to ignore minor or irritating behaviors, to give effective commands, and to use the "time-out" disciplinary strategy. Results of this study showed that the relation between maternal ADHD symptomatology and improvement in the child's behavior was mediated by pre- to post-test change in observed maternal negative parenting (and not positive parenting). Thus, it may be that mothers with ADHD have worse treatment outcome because they do not manage to reduce or inhibit the negative reactions to their child after behavioral intervention.

One other study assessed the mediators of outcome of a collaborative school-home behavioral intervention for ADHD. In a non-randomized study of 57 school-aged children with ADHD, Pfiffner, Villodas, Kaiser, Rooney, and McBurnett (2013) assessed whether outcomes of a 12-week behavioral intervention were mediated by improvement in organizational skills. The behavioral intervention consisted of several components. The teacher intervention consisted of implementing a daily school-home report card system and a homework plan. The parental intervention included teaching parents effective use of commands, rewards, and discipline, and strategies for managing areas of organizational and social difficulty. The child skills program targeted enhancing social functioning and independence (such as homework skills, completing chores/tasks). There were large improvements from pre- to post-test on all outcome measures, both as indicated by parent and teacher reports, and by academic indicators such as school grades and achievement tests. Notably, on teacher ratings, the relationship between improvement in ADHD and academic skills (grade report of teacher) after treatment was fully explained by improvement in organizational skills (as objectified by the difference in pre-post teacher-rated organizational skills).

In the home situation, the improvements in organizational skills (as objectified by the difference in pre-post parent-rated organizational skills) partially explained the relationship between improvement in ADHD symptom severity and improvement in homework problems. This indicates that improvements in academic skills related to improvements in ADHD symptom severity may be attributed to improvements in organizational skills. However, for the home situation, the mediation was partial, and other mediators, such as negative and ineffective discipline, shown to be significant in other mediation studies (Chronis et al., 2011; Hinshaw et al., 2000), were not tested. It does support the notion that for teachers, parents, and children, enhancing organization skills through behavioral intervention may be an important focus of intervention.

Summary of Mediation Results

In sum, the reduction of ineffective and negative parenting appears to be an important mediator of behavioral intervention outcome and thus may need to be targeted and monitored specifically during intervention, especially for parents with ADHD. For improvement of academic skills of children with ADHD through behavioral intervention, enhancing organization skills during intervention is important, especially to be able to achieve better academic functioning at school.

CHALLENGES AND RECOMMENDATIONS FOR FUTURE MODERATOR AND MEDIATOR RESEARCH WITHIN ADHD TREATMENT OUTCOME

Our literature review for this chapter shows the lack of research in moderator and mediators for treatment outcomes in ADHD samples. Moreover, with the exception of the MTA study, the studies are often underpowered and are not replicated, which heightens the probability of chance findings. A challenge for the future is to conduct adequately powered intervention studies, which are able to detect these moderator and mediator effects of intervention outcome.

With regard to theoretical underlying mechanisms of moderators and mediators of the interventions, there is a clear lack of theoretical focus of the intervention or translation of the significant results to a theoretical framework of the treatment intervention of the disorder. This is a clear challenge for the future: in order to be able to ultimately modify and develop effective treatments, there must be an empirical and theoretical framework of the *mechanism (mediator)* of the intervention for the disorder (Emmelkamp et al., 2014; Wittchen et al., 2014). This implies more fundamental research into the mechanisms of change of behavioral interventions for ADHD and a close cooperation of fundamental researchers with clinical researchers to test the moderation and mediation of these fundamental processes in large-scale randomized controlled trials.

ADHD is a highly heterogeneous disorder, and there is accumulating evidence that there are several distinct subgroups within the ADHD population (e.g., Dovis et al., in press; Sjöwall, Roth, Lindqvist & Thorell, 2013; Sonuga-Barke et al., 2010), marked by distinct neuropsychological dysfunction and proposed different underlying neuropathophysiological pathways toward this dysfunction. Given the distinctiveness of these subgroups with regard to neuropathophysiology and behavior, these subgroups may be highly relevant for moderator and mediator research and ultimately intervention development. Several subgroups are identified, for example those marked by dysfunction in motivation and those marked by dysfunction in executive functioning (Sonuga-Barke et al., 2010). Treatment effectiveness may be specific for these subgroups (moderators), and amelioration of a dysfunctional process may be a potent mediator of treatment outcome. Further, specifically targeting intervention to underlying deficit processes may enhance general effectiveness (Sonuga-Barke & Halperin, 2010).

Unfortunately, all the behavioral intervention studies reviewed in this chapter did not specifically target intervention to dysfunctional process, nor did they assess distinct neuropsychological processes as moderators or mediators of intervention outcome. In contrast, cognitive intervention is specifically targeted at ameliorating one of these distinct neuropsychological processes: executive functioning. However, to date executive functioning or change in executive functioning during intervention was not assessed as a moderator or as a mediator, thereby leaving room for interpretation on mechanism of change and specificity of effectiveness for subgroups of children.

Clinical Implications

Given the limited amount of studies into moderation and mediation, combined with lack of generalizability of the MTA behavioral interventions to behavioral interventions for ADHD in regular clinical practice, it is hard to distill clear-cut clinical implications for treatment of children with ADHD. The following implications are therefore offered with caution.

For outpatient, short-term behavioral parent interventions, comorbidity and parenting self-efficacy (of mothers and fathers) and paternal ADHD are indicators of treatment success (Van den Hoofdakker et al., 2010) and screening for these factors before allocating to additional behavioral intervention next to treatment as usual may be indicated; parents with high self-efficacy, fathers with high levels of ADHD symptoms, and children with only one or no comorbid condition have the best chance for success. Those parents with low self-efficacy and children with more comorbid conditions may need more intense behavioral interventions or focused interventions to enhance parental self-efficacy and reduce comorbidity of their child.

Although it is unclear how the results of the behavioral arm of the MTA study generalize to regular clinical practice, it seems that presence of *specific* comorbidity is important; in particular, those with comorbid anxiety have a better chance of intervention success to behavioral interventions for ADHD, as reported by parents, while for those children with *both* comorbid anxiety and ODD, a combination of medication and behavioral intervention is indicated (Jensen et al., 2001; March et al., 2000).

With regard to mediators of behavioral intervention outcome, reduction of ineffective and negative parenting is a mediator of behavioral intervention outcome and thus may need to be targeted and monitored specifically during intervention (Chronis-Tuscano et al., 2011; Hinshaw et al., 2000), and may be a specific target for behavioral treatment, especially for those parents who also have a diagnosis of ADHD.

Furthermore, to enhance academic functioning at school through behavioral interventions, there is initial evidence that focusing on improving organizational skills is crucial (Pfiffner et al., 2013). Thus if the child displays impairments in academic functioning, behavioral intervention may need to include modules that teach organizational skills.

To conclude, there are very few studies on moderation and mediation of behavioral treatment and cognitive training outcome in children with ADHD. For cognitive training, to our knowledge, no studies have assessed mediation and moderation. The few moderation studies of behavioral interventions did show child factors (anxiety, comorbidity) and parental factors (self-efficacy, paternal ADHD) as moderators of behavioral treatment outcome. Also, in two studies, reduction of negative parenting was a mediator of behavioral treatment outcome. ADHD is prevalent, very impairing, and a highly heterogeneous disorder in underlying deficits, symptomatology, comorbidity, and associated problems. Moreover, behavioral treatment for ADHD is also very heterogeneous with regard to content, length, focus, and scope. Given this heterogeneity in both ADHD and behavioral treatment, more research is needed into moderators and mediators of behavioral treatment outcome.

REFERENCES

American Psychiatric Association (2013). *Diagnostic and statistical manual of mental disorders* (5th ed.). Arlington, VA: American Psychiatric Publishing.

Arnold, L. E., Chuang, S., Davies, M., Abikoff, H. B., Conners, C. K., Elliot, G. R., Greenhill, L. L., Hechtman, L., Hinshaw, S. P., Hoza, B., Jensen, P. S., Kraemer, H. C., Langworthy-Lam, K. S., March, J. S., Newcorn, J. H., Pelham, E. E., Severe, J. B., Swanson, J. M., Vitiello, B., Wells, K. C., & Wigal, T. (2004). Nine months of multicomponent behavioral treatment for ADHD and effectiveness of MTA fading procedures. *Journal of Abnormal Child Psychology, 32,* 39–51.

Asherson, P., Manor, I., & Huss, M. (2014). Attention-deficit/hyperactivity disorder in adults: Update on clinical presentation and care. *Neuropsychiatry, 4,* 109–128.

Bakermans-Kranenburg, M. J., & Van IJzendoorn, M. H. (2011). Differential susceptibility to rearing environment depending on dopamine-related genes: New evidence and a meta-analysis. *Development and Psychopathology, 23,* 39–52.

Berger, I., Dor, T., Nevo, Y., & Goldzweig, G. (2008). Attitudes toward attention-deficit hyperactivity disorder (ADHD) treatment: Parent's and children's perspectives. *Journal of Child Neurology, 23*, 1036–1042.

Biederman, J., Mick, E., & Faraone, S. V. (2000). Age-dependent decline of symptoms of attention- deficit hyperactivity disorder and related disorders. *American Journal of Psychiatry, 157*, 816–818.

Chacko, A., Bedard, A. C., Marks, D. J., Feirsen, N., Uderman, J. Z., et al. (2014) A randomized clinical trial of Cogmed Working Memory Training in school-age children with ADHD: A replication in a diverse sample using a control condition. *Journal of Child Psychology and Psychiatry, 55*, 247–255.

Chronis-Tuscano, A., O'Brien, K. A., Johnston, C., Jones, H. A., Clarke, T. L., Raggi, V. L., Rooney, M. E., Diaz, Y., Pian, J., & Seymour, K. E. (2011). The relation between maternal ADHD symptoms and improvement in child behavior following brief behavioral parent training is mediated by change in negative parenting. *Journal of Abnormal Child Psychology, 39*, 1047–1057.

Chronis-Tuscano, A., Raggi, V. L., Clarke, T. L., Rooney, M. E., Diaz, Y., & Pian, J. (2008). Associations between maternal attention-deficit/hyperactivity disorder symptoms and parenting. *Journal of Abnormal Child Psychology, 36*, 1237–1250.

Conners, C. K., Epstein, J. N., March, J. S., Angold, A., Wells, K. C., Klaric, J., Swanson, J. M., Arnold, L. E., Abikoff, H. B., Elliot, G. R., Greenhill, L. L., Hechtman, L., Hinshaw, S. P., Hoza, B., Jensen, P. S., Kraemer, H. C., Newcorn, J. H., Pelham, W. R., Severe, J. B., Vitiello, B., & Wigal, T. (2001). Multimodal treatment of ADHD in the MTA: An alternative outcome analysis. *Journal of the American Academy of Child and Adolescent Psychiatry, 40*, 159–167.

Daley, D. (2006). Attention deficit hyperactivity disorder: A review of the essential facts. *Child Care Health and Development, 32*, 193–204.

Daley, D., Van der Oord, S., Ferrin, M., Danckaerts, M., Doepfner, M., Cortese, S., & Sonuga-Barke, E. (2014). Behavioural interventions in Attention-Deficit/ Hyperactivity Disorder: A meta-analysis of randomised controlled trials across multiple outcome domains. *Journal of the American Academy of Child and Adolescent Psychiatry, 53*, 835–847.

Deault, L. C. (2010). A systematic review of parenting in relation to the development of comorbidities and functional impairments in children with attention-deficit/ hyperactivity disorder (ADHD). *Child Psychiatry and Human Development, 41*, 168–192.

De Boo, G. M., & Prins, P. J. M. (2007). Social incompetence in children with ADHD: Possible moderators and mediators in social skills training. *Clinical Psychology Review, 27*, 78–97.

Dovis, S., Van der Oord, S., Huizinga, H., Wiers, R., & Prins, P. (2013) Not all children with ADHD are the same: Prevalence and diagnostic validity of motivational impairments and deficits in visuospatial short-term memory and working memory in ADHD subtypes (in press). *European Child and Adolescent Psychiatry.* doi: 10.1007/s00787-014-0612-1.

Dovis, S., Van der Oord, S., Wiers, R., & Prins, P. (2012). Can motivation normalize working memory and task persistence in children with attention-deficit/hyperactivity disorder? The effects of money and computer-gaming. *Journal of Abnormal Child Psychology, 40*, 669–681.

Dovis, S., Van der Oord, S., Wiers, R., & Prins, P. (in press). Improving executive functioning in children with ADHD: Training multiple executive functions within the context of a computer game. A randomized double-blind placebo controlled trial. *PLoS one*.

Egeland J., Aarlien, A. K., Saunes, B. K. (2013) Few effects of far transfer of working memory training in ADHD: A randomized controlled trial. PloS one 8: e75660. Available: http://www.plosone.org/article/info:doi/10.1371/journal.pone.0075660#pone-0075660-g001 (accessed November 27, 2013).

Emmelkamp, P., David, D., Beckers, T., Muris, P., Cuijpers, P., Lutz, W., Andersson, G., Araya, R., Banos Rivera, R., Barkham, M., Berking, M., Berger, T., Botella, C., Carlbring, P., Colom, F., Essau, C., Hermans, D., Hofmann, S., Knappe, S., Ollendick, T., Raes, F., Rief, W., Riper, H., Van der Oord, S., Vervliet, B. (2014). Advancing psychotherapy and evidence-based psychological interventions. *International Journal of Methods in Psychiatric Research*, 23, 58–91.

Fabiano, G. A., Pelham, W. E., Waschbusch, D. A., Gnagy, E. M., Lahey, B. B., Chronis, A. M., Onyango, A. N., Kipp, H., Lopez-Williams, A., & Burrows-Maclean, L. (2006). A practical measure of impairment: Psychometric properties of the impairment rating scale in samples of children with attention deficit hyperactivity disorder and two school-based samples. *Journal of Clinical Child and Adolescent Psychology*, 35, 369–385.

Faraone, S. V., Biederman, J., Spencer, T. J., & Aleardi, M. (2006). Comparing the efficacy of medications for ADHD using meta-analysis. *Medscape General Medicine*, 8, 4.

Gerson, J. (2002). A meta-analytic review of gender differences in ADHD. *Journal of Attention Disorders*, 5, 143–154.

Harvey, E., Danforth, J. S., McKee, T. E., Ulaszek, W. R., & Friedman, J. L. (2003). Parenting of children with attention-deficit/hyperactivity disorder (ADHD): The role of parental ADHD symptomatology. *Journal of Attention Disorders*, 7, 31–42.

Hinshaw, S. (2007). Moderators and mediatiors of treatment outcome for youth with ADHD: Understanding for whom and how interventions work. *Journal of Pediatric Psychology*, 32, 664–675.

Hinshaw, S. P., Owens, E. B., Wells, K., Kraemer, H. C., Abikoff, H. B., Arnold, L. E., Conners, C. K., Elliot, G., Greenhill, L. L., Hechtman, L., Hoza, B., Jensen, P. S., March, J. S., Newcorn, J. H., Pelham, W. E., Swanson, J. M., Vitiello, B., & Wigal, T. (2000). Family processes and treatment outcome in the MTA: Negative/ineffective parenting practices in relation to multimodal treatment. *Journal of Abnormal Child Psychology*, 28, 555–568.

Jaeggi, S. M., Buschkuehl, M., Jonides, J., & Shah, P. (2011). Short- and long-term benefits of cognitive training. *Proceedings of the National Academy of Sciences*, 108, 10081–10086.

Jaeggi, S. M., Buschkuehl, M., Shah, P., & Jonides, J. (2014). The role of individual differences in cognitive training and transfer. *Memory and Cognition*, 42, 464–480.

Jensen, P. S., Hinshaw, S. P., Kraemer, H. C., Lenora, N., Newcorn, J. H., Abikoff, H. B., March, J. S., Arnold, L. E., Cantwell, D. P., Conners, C. K., Elliot, G. R., Greenhill, L. L., Hechtman, L., Hoza, B., Pelham, W. E., Severe, J. B., Swanson, J. M., Wells, K. C., Wigal, T., & Vitiello, B. (2001). ADHD comorbidity findings from the MTA study: Comparing comorbid subgroups. *Journal of the American Academy of Child and Adolescent Psychiatry*, 40, 147–158.

Johnston, C., & Mash, E. J. (2001). Families of children with Attention-deficit/hyperactivity disorder: Review and recommendations for future research. *Clinical Child and Family Psychology Review, 4*, 183–207.

Johnston, C., Mash, E. J., Miller, N., & Ninowski, J. R. (2012). Parenting in adults with attention/deficit hyperactivity disorder (ADHD). *Clinical Psychology Review, 32*, 215–228.

Jones, H. A., Epstein, J. N., Hinshaw, S. P., Owens, E. B., Chi, T. C., Arnold, L. E., Hoza, B., & Wells, K. C. (2010). Ethnicity as moderator of treatment effects on parents-child interaction for children with ADHD. *Journal of Attention Disorders, 13*, 592–600.

Klingberg, T. (2010). Training and plasticity of working memory. *Trends in Cognitive Science, 14*, 317–324.

Klingberg, T., Fernell, E., Olesen, P. J., Johnson, M., Gustafsson, P., Dahlström, K., et al. (2005). Computerized training of working memory in children with ADHD: A randomized, controlled trial. *Journal of the American Academy of Child and Adolescent Psychiatry, 44*, 177–186.

Luman, M., Oosterlaan, J., & Sergeant, J. A. (2005). The impact of reinforcement contingencies on AD/HD: A review and theoretical appraisal. *Clinical Psychology Review, 25*, 183–213.

Luman, M., Tripp, G., & Scheres, A. (2010). Identifying the neuropathology of altered reinforcement sensitivity in ADHD: A review and research agenda. *Neuroscience and Biobehavioral Reviews, 34*, 744–754.

March, J. S., Swanson, J. M., Arnold, L. E., Hoza, B., Conners, K. C., Hinshaw, S. P., Hechtman, L., Kraemer, H. C., Greenhill, L. L., Abikoff, H. B., Elliot, L. G., Jensen, P. S., Newcorn, J. H., Vitiello, B., Severe, J., Wells, K. C., & Pelham, W. E. (2000). Anxiety as a predictor and outcome variable in the multimodal treatment study of children with ADHD. *Journal of Abnormal Child Psychology, 28*, 527–541.

Martinussen, R., Hayden, J., Hogg-Johnson, S., & Tannock, R. (2005). A meta-analysis of working memory impairments in children with attention-deficit/hyperactivity disorder. *Journal of the American Academy of Child and Adolescent Psychiatry, 44*, 377–384.

McGough, J. J. (2005). Attention-deficit/hyperactivity disorder pharmacogenomics. *Biological Psychiatry, 57*, 1367–1373.

Molina, B. A., Hinshaw, S. P., Swanson, J. M., Arnold, L. E., Vitiello, M. D., Jensen, P. S., et al. (2009). The MTA at 8 years: Prospective follow-up of children treated for combined-type ADHD in a multisite study. *Journal of the American Academy of Child and Adolescent Psychiatry, 48*, 484–500.

MTA Cooperative Group. (1999a). A 14-month randomized clinical trail of treatment strategies for attention deficit hyperactivity disorder. *Archives of General Psychiatry, 56*, 1073–1086.

MTA Cooperative Group. (1999b). Moderators and mediators of treatment response for children with attention-deficit/hyperactivity disorder. *Archives of General Psychiatry, 56*, 1088–1097.

Nigg, J. T. (2006). *What causes ADHD?: Understanding what goes wrong and why.* New York: Guilford Press.

Owens, E. B., Hinshaw, S. P., Kraemer, H. C., Arnold, L. E., Abikoff, H. B., Cantwell, D. P., Conners, C. K., Elliott, G., Greenhill, L. L., Hechtman, L., Hoza, B., Jensen, P. S., March, J. S., Newcorn, J. H., Pelham, W. E., Severe, J. B., Swanson, J. M., Vitiello, B., Wells, K. C., &

Wigal, T. (2003). Which treatment for whom with ADHD? Moderators of treatment response in the MTA. *Journal of Consulting and Clinical Psychology, 71*, 540–552.

Pfiffner, L. J., & McBurnett, K. (1997). Social skills training with parent generalization: Treatment effects for children with attention deficit disorder. *Journal of Consulting and Clinical Psychology, 65*, 749–757.

Pfiffner, L. J., Villodas, M., Kaiser, N., Rooney, M., & McBurnett, K. (2013). Educational outcomes of a collaborative school-home behavioral intervention for ADHD. *School Psychology Quaterly, 28*, 25–36.

Rapport, M. D., Orban, S. A., Kofler, M. J., & Friedman, L. M. (2013). Do programs designed to train working memory, other executive functions, and attention benefit children with ADHD? A meta-analytic review of cognitive, academic, and behavioral outcomes. *Clinical Psychology Review, 33*, 1237–1252.

Patterson, G. R. (1982). *Coercive family process.* Eugene, OR: Castalia.

Polanczyk, G., de Lima, M. S., Horta, B. L., Biederman, J., & Rohde, L. A. (2007). The worldwide prevalence of ADHD: A systematic review and metaregression analysis. *American Journal of Psychiatry, 164*, 942–948.

Sagvolden, T., Aase, H., Johansen, E. B., & Russell, V. A. (2005). A dynamic developmental theory of attention deficit/hyperactivity disorder (ADHD) predominantly hyperactive/impulsive and combined subtypes. *Behavioral and Brain Sciences, 28*, 397–468.

Sjowall, D., Roth, L., Lindqvist, S., & Thorell, L. B. (2013). Multiple deficits in ADHD: Executive dysfunction, delay aversion, reaction time variability, and emotional deficits. *Journal of Child Psychology and Psychiatry, 54*, 619–627.

Solanto, M., Abikoff, H., Sonuga-Barke, E., Schachar, R., Logan, G. D., Wigal, T., Hechtman, L., Hinshaw, S., & Turkel, E. (2001). The ecological validity of delay aversion and response inhibition as measures of impulsivity in AD/HD: A supplement to the NIMH Multimodal Treatment Study of AD/HD. *Journal of Abnormal Child Psychology, 29*, 215–228.

Sonuga-Barke, E. J. S. (2003). The dual pathway model of AD/HD: An elaboration of neuro-developmental characteristics. *Neuroscience and Biobehavioral Reviews, 27*, 593–604.

Sonuga-Barke, E. J. S., Bitsakou, P., & Thompson, M. (2010). Beyond the dual pathway model: Evidence for the dissociation of timing, inhibitory, and delay-related impairments in attention-deficit/hyperactivity disorder. *Journal of the American Academy of Child and Adolescent Psychiatry, 49*, 345–355.

Sonuga-Barke, E., Brandeis, D., Cortese, S., Daley, D., Ferrin, M., Holtmann, M., Stevenson, J., Danckaerts, M., Van der Oord, S., Dopfner, M., Dittmann, R., Simonoff, E., Zuddas, A., Banaschewski, T., Buitelaar, J., Coghill, D., Hollis, C., Konofal, E., Lecendreux, M., Wong, I., Sergeant, J. (2013). Nonpharmacological interventions for ADHD: Systematic review and meta-analyses of randomized controlled trials of dietary and psychological treatments. *American Journal of Psychiatry, 170*, 275–289.

Sonuga-Barke, E., Daley, D., & Thompson, M. (2002). Does maternal ADHD reduce the effectiveness of parent training for preschool children's ADHD? *Journal of the American Academy of Child and Adolescent Psychiatry, 41*, 696–702.

Sonuga-Barke, E. J. S., & Halperin, J. M. (2010). Developmental phenotypes and causal pathways in attention deficit/hyperactivity disorder: Potential targets for early intervention? *Journal of Child Psychology and Psychiatry, 51*, 368–398.

Swanson, J. M., Kraemer, H. C., Hinshaw, S. P., Arnold, L. E., Conners, K. C., Abikoff, H. B., Clevenger, W., Davies, M., Elliot, G. R., Greenhill, L. L., Hechtman, L., Hoza, B., Jensen, P. S., March, J. S., Newcorn, J. H., Owens, E. B., Pelham, W. E., Schiller, E., Severe, J. B., Simpson, S., Vitiello, B., Wells, K., Wigal, T., & Wu, M. (2001). Clinical relevance of the primary findings of the MTA: Success rates based on severity of ADHD and ODD symptoms at the end of treatment. *Journal of the American Academy of Child and Adolescent Psychiatry, 40*, 168–179.

Taylor, E., Döpfner, M., Sergeant, J., Asherson, P., Banaschewski, T., Buitelaar, J., Coghill, D., Danckaerts, M., Rothenberger, A., Sonuga-Barke, E., Steinhausen, H.-Ch., & Zuddas, A. (2004). European clinical guidelines for hyperkinetic disorder-first upgrade. *European Child & Adolescent Psychiatry, 13*, 7–30.

Thapar, A., Langley, K., Asherson, P., & Gill, M. (2007). Gene–environment interplay in attention-deficit hyperactivity disorder and the importance of a developmental perspective. *British Journal of Psychiatry, 190*, 1–3.

Van den Hoofdakker, B., van der Veen-Mulders, L., Sytema, S., Emmelkamp, P., Minderaa, R. B., & Nauta, M. H. (2007). Effectiveness of behavioral parent training for children with ADHD in routine clinical practice: A randomized controlled study. *Journal of the American Academy of Child and Adolescent Psychiatry, 46*, 1263–1271.

Van den Hoofdakker, B., Nauta, M. H., van der Veen-Mulders, L., Sytema, S., Emmelkamp, P., Minderaa, R. B., & Hoekstra, P. J. (2010). Behavioral parent training as an adjunct to routine care in children with attention-deficit/hyperactivity disorder: Moderators of treatment response. *Journal of Pediatric Psychology, 35*, 317–326.

Van den Hoofdakker, B., Nauta, M. H., Dijck-Brouwer, D. A., van der Veen-Mulders, L., Sytema, S., Emmelkamp, P. M., Minderaa, R. B., & Hoekstra, P. J. (2012). Dopamine transporter gene moderates response to behavioral parent training in children with ADHD: a pilot study. *Developmental Psychology, 48*, 567–574.

Van den Hoofdakker, B., Hoekstra, P. J., Van der Veen-Mulders, L., Sytema, S., Emmelkamp, P. M. G., Minderaa, R. B., & Nauta, M. H. (2014). Paternal influences on treatment outcome of behavioral parent training in children with attention-deficit/hyperactivity disorder. *European Child and Adolescent Psychiatry, 23*, 1071–1079.

Van der Oord, S., Prins, P. J. M., Oosterlaan, J., & Emmelkamp, P. (2008). Efficacy of methylphenidate, psychosocial treatments and their combination in school-aged children with ADHD: A meta-analysis. *Clinical Psychology Review, 28*, 783–800.

Van Dongen-Boomsma, M., Vollebregt, M. A., Buitelaar, J. K., & Slaat-Willemse, D. (2014). Working memory training in young children with ADHD: A randomized placebo-controlled trial. *Journal of Child Psychology and Psychiatry, 55*, 886–896.

Visser, S. N., Danielson, M. L., Bitsko, R. H., Holbrook, J. R., Kogan, M. D., Ghandour, R. M., Perou, R., & Blumberg, S. J. (2014). Trends in the parent-report of health care provider diagnosed and medicated attention-deficit/hyperactivity disorder: United States, 2003–2011. *Journal of the American Academy of Child and Adolescent Psychiatry, 53*, 34–46.

Waelti, P., Dickonson, A., & Schultz, W. (2001). Dopamine responses comply with basic assumptions of formal learning theory. *Nature, 412*, 43–48.

Wittchen, H., Knappe, S., Andersson, G., Araya, R., Banos Rivera, R., Barkham, M., Bech, P., Beckers, T., Berger, T., Berking, M., Berrocal, C., Botella, C., Carlbring, P., Chouinard, G., Colom, F., Csillag, C., Cujipers, P., David, D., Emmelkamp, P., Essau, C., Fava, G., Goschke, T., Hermans, D., Hofmann, S., Lutz, W., Muris, P., Ollendick, T., Raes, F., Rief, W., Riper, H., Tossani, E., Van der Oord, S., Vervliet, B., Haro, J., Schumann, G. (2014). The need for a behavioural science focus in research on mental health and mental disorders. *International Journal of Methods in Psychiatric Research, 23,* 28–40.

Moderators and Mediators of Treatments for Youth With Autism Spectrum Disorders

MATTHEW D. LERNER AND SUSAN W. WHITE ■

INTRODUCTION

Autism spectrum disorder (ASD) is a heterogeneous disorder, usually first diagnosed in childhood. The diagnosis is made on the basis of chronic and impairing symptoms expressed across social, communication, and functional/behavioral domains (American Psychiatric Association, 2013). Though descriptions of features have varied over time, the cardinal deficit of ASD exists in the domain of effective reciprocal social interactions. This deficit is thought to be both chronic across the lifespan and pervasive—impairing multiple domains of functioning—and is thus often the primary target of interventions for youth with these disorders. Notably, while many interventions delivered in early childhood have demonstrated considerable evidence of efficacy (Vismara & Rogers, 2010), these interventions are usually intensive, highly targeted behavioral approaches focused on basic communication and cognitive functioning, with often collateral effects on complex social outcomes. Meanwhile, social deficits in ASD often maintain and become more prominent and impactful as youth move into middle childhood and adolescence, when normative elements of social functioning become yet more complex and important. Thus, interventions for social competence in this population, often called *social skills interventions* (SSIs), have proliferated in the literature in recent years (McMahon, Lerner, & Britton, 2013; White, Keonig, & Scahill, 2007). As some of these interventions establish consistent evidence for efficacy, it becomes increasingly important to elucidate those factors that influence strength of their effects (i.e., moderators) and the mechanisms responsible for those effects (i.e., mediators) (Kazdin, 2007; Lerner, White, &

McPartland, 2012). Such evidence has only recently accumulated (Reichow, Steiner, & Volkmar, 2013), and so intervention mechanism research in SSIs for ASD are in their infancy. Thus, this chapter aims to review existing evidence in this area, while also highlighting *theorized* and *implied* mechanisms that may be fruitful for future study.

Although we focus on moderators and mediators of SSI for children with ASD in this chapter, we must note that the last decade has witnessed a proliferation of treatments targeting frequently co-occurring problems in young people with ASD, often using cognitive behavioral therapy (CBT) approaches (e.g., White, Albano, et al., 2010; Wood et al., 2009). While these approaches are indeed well grounded in established intervention technologies for such problems, they tend to address concerns that are peripheral (if common) among youth with ASD. Given that the focus of the present chapter is on ASD and the centrality of social skill deficits, we will restrict ourselves to the examination of intervention approaches to promote improved social behavior.

BRIEF DESCRIPTION OF THE PROBLEM/DISORDER

ASD is classified as a neurodevelopmental disorder. As such, in the *DSM-5* (APA, 2013) it is grouped with Intellectual Disabilities, Communication Disorders, Attention-Deficit/Hyperactivity Disorder, Specific Learning Disorder, and Motor Disorders. By definition, neurodevelopmental disorders have their onset early in development and are characterized by developmental deficits that impair the individual's functioning across domains (e.g., academic and social). Although ASD tends to be first identified and diagnosed during childhood, for most affected individuals the diagnosis is life course persistent (Cederlund, Hagberg, Billstedt, Gillberg, & Gillberg, 2008).

ASD specifically is expressed as a pattern of both excesses and deficits (e.g., heightened rigidity and social aloofness, respectively). Children and adults with ASD present with terrific phenotypic heterogeneity; diagnosed individuals vary greatly in cognitive ability, verbal expression, and ASD severity. This diversity in presentation poses challenges to the identification of evidence-based treatments for ASD. Indeed, most pharmacological (Malone, Maislin, Choudhury, Gifford, & Delaney, 2002) and psychosocial treatments (e.g., White et al., 2013) target specific secondary problems (e.g., anxiety, irritability), rather than ASD core symptoms such as social disability.

The disorder affects approximately 1 in 68 children (US CDC, 2014). Some of the earliest markers of the disorder include any behavioral regression or loss of language skills; lack of cooing, babbling, or other socially meaningful gestures by around 12 months of age; no single-word speech by 16 months; and a lack of two-word spontaneous phrase speech by 24 months (Johnson & Myers, 2007). These deficits are often noted during pediatric well-child visits, prompting referral for clinical diagnostic evaluation. Evaluation for possible ASD often begins with completion of paper and pencil screening measures, completed by the parent, such as the Social Communication Questionnaire (Rutter, Bailey, & Lord, 2005) or Social Responsiveness Scale-2 (Frazier et al., 2014). A full diagnostic evaluation for ASD should include measures specifically designed and validated for ASD assessment, including the Autism Diagnostic Observation Schedule (ADOS-2; Lord et al., 2012), and usually the Autism Diagnostic Interview—Revised (ADI-R; Lord, Rutter, & Le Couteur, 1994). The ADOS-2 is a direct observational assessment conducted by a trained examiner. The ADI-R is a lengthy diagnostic interview completed with the child's caregiver. A full assessment would also include cognitive testing, and assessment of the client's speech and adaptive behavior.

While social challenges are central to the diagnosis of ASD, they are also not unique to ASD. Other child populations also experience social challenges, with those deficits often arising from characteristic features of that population. Youth with ADHD, for instance, also experience significant social problems, with these problems often arising from impulsivity and inattention in social scenarios (Mikami, Jack, & Lerner, 2009). Nonetheless, social disability is arguably more pronounced and more central to the phenotype in ASD than it is in other disorders. Not only are social impairments common in many of the neurodevelopmental disorders, the social disability that is seen in children with ASD is highly complex and variable in presentation across individuals on the spectrum (Koenig, De Los Reyes, Cicchetti, Scahill, & Klin, 2009). Severely affected children with ASD may display a profound lack of social interest; such children are often described as aloof or asocial. Less affected, often "higher functioning" children may be extremely socially motivated yet awkward and imprecise in their attempts to interact. Additionally, the particular types of skill deficits are diverse and include, among others, poorly modulated eye contact, lack of communicative gestures, and presence of ill-timed or overly intrusive personal comments.

Given that social functioning is not a target upon which one can intervene directly (i.e., one cannot directly *make* a child well liked and socially skilled), the features thought to contribute to complex social deficits and interpersonal rejection are often implicit or explicit targets of interventions. Impulsive children are trained to be less impulsive, with the goal of this producing improved social relations; children with lack of understanding of effective social behaviors (social knowledge) are taught what those behaviors might be (Gresham, 1997). Thus, SSIs are often designed based upon the *type* of deficit a given population is thought to manifest, with content adjusted accordingly (Spence, 2003). However, given the heterogeneity within ASD, the impact of such customized content may vary across individuals for whom underlying social deficits differ, with implications for how and for whom a given intervention may work. Thus, such features are important for the exploration of treatment moderation and mediation in ASD.

Ample literature, most of which has been published in the last 5 years, suggests that people with ASD possess characteristic neurocognitive and neurophysiological atypicalities that may manifest as social disability (McPartland & Pelphrey, 2012; Pelphrey, Shultz, Hudac, & Vander Wyk, 2011). Such differences have primarily been explored with reference to the neural processing of social information, with evidence suggesting possible delays and inefficiencies in processing faces (especially facial emotions) in the fusiform gyrus, attenuated amygdala response to varied scenarios, differences in processing of socially salient reward stimuli, and atypical connectivity depending on regional specificity (e.g., local prefrontal overconnectivity; underconnectivity across long-distance neural tracts between prefrontal and other areas of the brain) (for reviews, see McPartland & Pelphrey, 2012; Pelphrey et al., 2011). Although such research is in its infancy, it importantly informs deficit models that may impact interventions. As our methods of directly targeting these underlying mechanisms improves (e.g., real-time fMRI; electrophysiology), we will be better able to establish temporal, mediating relationships between a given causal mechanism and manifest social difficulty. Alterations in the generalized neural pathways related to visual and auditory social information processing (SIP), as well as basic eye-tracking research indicating early deficits in social orienting (Jones & Klin, 2013), suggest the value of social-perceptual and social-cognitive models considering the role of SIP in ASD. Such models often focus on multiple levels of social-cognitive abilities, such as facial emotion recognition (FER), and social perspective-taking processes, such as Theory of Mind (ToM). Impaired SIP may impact coordinated, appropriate behavioral responding. If interventions affecting these abilities impact social behavior, it may provide important evidence supporting the mechanistic role of social cognition and perception in social deficits in ASD. Such interventions may involve specifically targeting and training association of specific social stimuli with normative labels (e.g., identifying a face as happy; noting that an individual holds a false belief).

Differences in low-level social reward processing may also inform models suggesting that social deficits arise from limited social motivation in ASD (Chevallier, Kohls, Troiani, Brodkin, & Schultz, 2012). Such models suggest that individuals with ASD do not experience social interactions as intrinsically rewarding in the way that typically developing individuals do, and may help to differentiate whether withdrawn social behavior arises from aloofness or active avoidance. Interventions focusing on these behaviors are thought to exert downstream effects on social behavior via otherwise intact capacities to engage socially when sufficiently motivated. Such intervention may involve repeatedly embedding motivating activities in social scenarios or shaping social situations to increase overall motivation.

Likewise, limitations in distributed network connectivity with prefrontal cortex suggest a model in which social deficits arise from limitations in explicit social knowledge, as well as ineffective social planning and execution (e.g., Pelphrey et al., 2011). This suggests that individuals with ASD may not be aware of correct social behaviors and may not be able to organize and plan their reactions effectively. Interventions focusing on such deficits may explicitly teach correct social behaviors, and/or provide stepwise planning strategies for engagement in them, with the expectation that such teaching will directly produce such behaviors.

Overall, each of these sets of models of neurophysiological and behavioral deficits suggests substantial chronicity of ASD across the life span, including early onset derailment of basic, undergirding processes of social communication. With development and experience, the underlying mechanisms and the manifest social deficits become increasingly canalized (cf., Jones & Klin, 2013). As such, these models also suggest the need for intensive and often ongoing or repeat interventions from early childhood through adulthood to address the ever-evolving manifestations of the underlying social challenges.

DESCRIPTION OF STATE-OF-THE-ART TREATMENT OUTCOME FOR THIS PROBLEM/DISORDER

SSIs for youth with ASD vary widely in their content, type, structure, and therapeutic targets (McMahon, Lerner, et al., 2013; White et al., 2007). Both the heterogeneity of social functioning across the ASD spectrum and the complex, often ill-defined nature of the indicators of social deficits contribute to this variability (Koenig et al., 2009; McMahon, Vismara, & Solomon, 2013). While a full accounting of the range of interventions used to target social deficits in ASD is beyond the scope of the current chapter, we highlight the most common broad approaches seen in the literature with evidence for efficacy: group-based, individually administered, and contextual interventions. Then, in the following section, we will highlight moderators and mediators that have been specifically theorized to contribute to outcomes, both within and across intervention types, as well as the (often limited) empirical investigations that have been undertaken for each.

Group-Based Training

By far the most common SSI type is the group-based approach (Barnhill, Cook, Tebbenkamp, & Myles, 2002; Barry et al., 2003; DeRosier, Swick, Davis, McMillen, & Matthews, 2011; Koenig et al., 2010; Laugeson, Frankel, Gantman, Dillon, & Mogil, 2012; Lerner, Mikami, & Levine, 2011; Lopata et al., 2010; McMahon, Vismara, et al., 2013; White, Koenig, & Scahill, 2010; White et al., 2013). These groups sometimes contain typically developing similar-age peers (Barnhill et al., 2002; Barry et al., 2003; Mesibov, 1984; Tse, Strulovitch, Tagalakis, Meng, & Fombonne, 2007), and are often (though not always; Solomon, Goodlin-Jones, & Anders, 2004) of mixed gender composition (Laugeson et al., 2012; Laugeson, Frankel, Mogil, & Dillon, 2009; Lopata, Thomeer, Volker, Nida, & Lee, 2008; Lopata et al., 2010). These peers almost always involve other children with ASD, though they may also include other peers with social deficits (such as those with ADHD; Lerner & Levine, 2007). Groups are usually led by one to three adults, with the range of training of these adults varying widely, from bachelor's-level counselors (Lerner et al., 2011) to doctoral-level psychologists (Laugeson et al., 2009;

Laugeson et al., 2012; White et al., 2013; White, Ollendick, Scahill, Oswald, & Albano, 2009). Frequency and duration of meetings vary as well, ranging from 1 to 2 hours per week, once a week for several weeks (Lerner & Mikami, 2012), to every day for several hours per day throughout the summer (Lopata et al., 2008; Lopata et al., 2010), to regular sessions over more than a year (Legoff & Sherman, 2006). Content of these groups is often driven by the theory of the intervention, but usually involves specific skill instruction (though for exceptions see Guli et al., 2013; Lerner et al., 2011), behavior modeling, in vivo practice, role-playing, and homework.

Intervention targets in group SSIs may provide clues for potential mechanisms. Some interventions target posited underlying cognitive abilities such as ToM (Ozonoff & Miller, 1995), FER (Lopata et al., 2008), or social motivation (Legoff & Sherman, 2006), with the suggestion that change in these abilities may contribute to change in broader social outcomes. Others may more directly target and train enactment of social behavior or prosocial engagement (Kroeger, Schultz, & Newsom, 2007), while still others may attempt to structure, engineer, and support opportunities for friendship-making (Laugeson et al., 2009; Laugeson et al., 2012); such interventions may be more agnostic about processes that may underlie social difficulties, highlighting instead the importance of specific skills knowledge or behavioral engagement in activities as potential contributors to outcomes. Notably, most group SSIs contain elements of each of these approaches (McMahon, Lerner, et al., 2013), rendering the identification of discrete mechanistic elements especially challenging.

Non-Group Approaches

Many SSIs are not group-delivered, but rather are individually focused. Such SSIs range in both form and content, and involve teaching or training specific capacities thought to underlie social competence, rather than directly training social interaction or friendship-making per se. They may be delivered in clinical settings or at home, with intervention providers ranging from doctoral-level clinicians to non-human interfaces (e.g., computer screen, video), and with frequency and duration ranging from several sessions of 20 or more minutes to regular administration over months.

One form of SSI within this class that has received considerable attention in recent years is individually administered CBT. While often used to address traditional CBT target symptoms such as anxiety in this population (Fujii et al., 2013), this approach has also been used to directly address and train social behavior in youth with ASD (Bauminger, 2002, 2007), as well as, most recently, the combination of internalizing and social symptoms (White et al., 2013). Another individually based SSI is the social story (Kokina & Kern, 2010). Such stories aim to visually present, outline, and break down specific tasks and social activities into concrete elements, to facilitate learning and repetition. They can be delivered by individuals, video, or computerized means (Sansosti & Powell-Smith, 2008).

Yet another form of SSI within this class is video modeling (Sancho, Sidener, Reeve, & Sidener, 2010; Wilson, 2013). Specific social behaviors and positive peer interactions are video-recorded so that the skills can be segmented and taught in chunks. Usually with video modeling, the child with ASD is then asked to enact or mimic the viewed skill. Video modeling has met with considerable treatment success for children with ASD (Wang & Parrila, 2011). This approach can be highly tailored to a child's unique skill deficiencies and training needs and, once a video is developed, it can be viewed repeatedly to increase the "dose" of training without any added cost.

Computer-Based Approaches

While many group and non-group approaches aim to address processes theorized to underlie social deficits in the context of (peer or therapist) social contact, there is also a class of interventions that attempts to act on these processes directly, without the aid of human interaction. Most prominent among these are computer-based approaches, which, similar to neurocognitive interventions for other populations, are designed to intensively highlight, rehearse, and train key capacities involved in FER and ToM in a game-like format. These computer programs are delivered in front of computers, with participants completing them for discrete, often unassisted, sessions ranging from 10 minutes to 2 hours at a time for anywhere from 5 to 20 consecutive weeks. Several different computerized interventions have been developed to target proposed mechanisms underlying social deficits, such as holistic processing of facial cues, impaired ToM, and increased visual attending to the eye region of others' faces and emotion recognition (Golan & Baron-Cohen, 2006; Hopkins et al., 2011; Tanaka et al., 2010). However, with few exceptions (e.g., Hopkins et al., 2011), these interventions have not examined or have not demonstrated that change in the targeted mechanism translates into improved social behavior. Nevertheless, their mechanistic focus and ease of translation make this class of SSI promising, and more translational research is warranted.

Contextual Approaches

A third category of SSI aims to address the context in which social deficits manifest. That is, in accordance with recent literature suggesting that contextual (i.e., peer and classroom-level) influences may contribute significant variance to the onset and maintenance of social challenges such as peer rejection (Mikami, Lerner, & Lun, 2010), these approaches target these influences in lieu of, or in addition to, focusing on developing individual child behaviors. The two elements common across contextual approaches are environmental restructuring and use of instruction that aligns with the target child's interests and behaviors (Kohler, Anthony, Steighner, & Hoyson, 2001). For instance, the classroom might be arranged such that the child must initiate with a teacher in order to access materials needed for a desirable activity and, once the child is engaged in that activity, the teacher joins in socially with the child to perform the activity. These approaches tend to be naturalistic and child-initiated, so that the child is not passive or mand-dependent (i.e., not requiring a specific prompt). Prelinguistic milieu training (PMT; Yoder & Warren, 1998) is a contextually based SSI useful for nonverbal or pre-verbal children with ASD. PMT occurs in the child's natural environment and involves adults using natural prompts to facilitate nonverbal social interaction (e.g., directed vocalizations, eye gaze). Research on PMT has supported its efficacy; children who receive PMT tend to show increased intentional communication (Franco, Davis, & Davis, 2013). There is evidence that naturalistic (contextual) SSI can be conducted in the classroom by the classroom teacher; however, the teacher will likely require direct instruction in implementation and some level of ongoing support, and more impaired students likely require more intensive skills training, first to take full benefit of this less intensive approach (Kohler et al., 2001).

Peer-mediated SSIs, in which typically developing peers are trained to either teach specific skills (e.g., sharing) or to provide a more inclusive context to students with ASD and to support the student's social integration, have also been found to be effective (Kamps et al., 2002; Kasari, Rotheram-Fuller, Locke, & Gulsrud, 2012; Wang, Cui, & Parrila, 2011). SSI can be implemented entirely in the classroom, often with consultation from ASD experts. The Collaborative Model for Promoting Competence and Success (COMPASS; Ruble, McGrew, Toland, Dalrymple, & Jung, 2013), for instance, is a manual-based teacher training and consultation model. Briefly, in COMPASS individualized teaching plans are developed to address a child's particular deficits (in social and communication domains) and these plans are then integrated into the child's individualized educational program (the IEP) and implemented by the child's teacher, who receives consultation throughout the school year. In a three-arm RCT (placebo control, COMPASS with in-person coaching, and COMPASS with web-based teacher coaching), Ruble and colleagues (2013) found large effects for the two active conditions (web-based or in-person) on child outcomes, relative to placebo.

THEORETICAL MODELS AND EMPIRICAL RESULTS OF MODERATION STUDIES FOR TREATMENT OUTCOMES FOR YOUTH WITH AUTISM SPECTRUM DISORDERS

Theoretical Model of Moderators

Moderators refer to those (usually stable) baseline (or pre-treatment) variables that predict individual differences in intervention response (Kazdin, 2007;

Lerner, White, et al., 2012). Such variables provide important information about who is likely to benefit from an intervention, and under what conditions. Beyond the pursuit of "what works for whom," identification of moderators of treatment response can directly inform what mechanisms (mediators) are evaluated (Lerner, White, et al., 2012). If we establish that group-based SSI is more effective for children with co-occurring anxiety compared to co-occurring depression or ADHD, for example, we might posit that group SSI directly affects anxiety that impedes social skill expression (performance). Here, we enumerate the putative SSI moderators.

GENDER

Males with ASD generally outnumber females in the population roughly 4:1 (US CDC, 2012). Given differences in social norms across genders, it makes good sense that there would be differences in the effects of SSIs across genders. Notably, males and females are often included or excluded from SSIs with one another without substantial theoretical or empirical consideration.

AGE

As noted above, SSIs for youth with ASD vary widely in the age range they target. Given the heterogeneity of social skills, norms, and knowledge found in typically developing children across childhood, it is highly plausible that age differences may emerge across SSIs.

VERBAL ABILITY

Many SSIs for ASD involve activities (e.g. reading, discussion of social choices, etc.) requiring considerable verbal ability. As such, it makes sense that efficacy of some of these approaches may vary by individuals' verbal ability.

COGNITIVE ABILITY

Similar to the relation with verbal ability, general cognitive ability (IQ) may also moderate the effects of SSIs. While youth with ASD exhibit a wide range of cognitive ability, SSIs are generally focused on those with average (or above) cognitive ability (McMahon, Lerner, et al., 2013). However, above this threshold, a wide range of abilities is evinced.

ANXIETY/DEPRESSION/ADHD COMORBIDITY

Although only recently acknowledged in the *DSM-5* (APA, 2013), comorbidities between ASD and other psychiatric conditions have long been considered fairly common (White, Albano, et al., 2010). Indeed, as noted above, several SSIs have recently been adapted to directly address comorbidities such as anxiety symptoms in ASD (White, Albano, et al., 2010; White et al., 2013; Wood et al., 2009). Given the importance of matching underlying deficits to strategies in SSIs, exploring whether such comorbidities influence responsiveness to SSIs in ASD is crucial.

Insight

To translate social skills learned in SSIs into social behaviors, it is likely that individuals with ASDs must be able to agree with others on the presence of their social deficits, reflect on their own enactment of social behavior, or both. Thus, insight into one's own social challenges may predict responsiveness to SSIs.

Medication Status

Often due to the aforementioned comorbidities, youth with ASD are often prescribed psychopharmacological medications (Malone et al., 2002). Given the often parallel goals of psychopharmacological medications and SSIs, it is important to know whether the presence of such medications potentiates or attenuates intervention response.

Other Factors for Considerations

Several other factors may be important to consider as potential SSI moderators given either their prevalence in ASD, SSIs, or both. These include stress of the parents, previous skill and training of interventionist, context of treatment (e.g., school, clinic), previous child experience with SSIs, and developmental level.

Empirical Results

Gender

Few studies have empirically examined the effects of gender on outcomes, with one group SSI study evincing greater group interactions among girls with ASD relative to boys; these differences decreased over time (McMahon, Vismara, & Solomon, 2013).

Age

In three different group SSIs, older participants showed relatively greater decreases in communication problems (age range 8–19) (Herbrecht et al., 2009) and depression symptoms (age range 8–12) (Solomon et al., 2004), and more early-in-treatment and dyadic interaction (age range 10–13) (McMahon, Vismara, & Solomon, 2013). In this latter study, however, younger children showed steeper increase in peer interaction, and more group interaction overall. Finally, in a computer-based study training emotion recognition in slightly younger children (age 4–7), older age correlated with short- and long-term improvements in affect recognition and ToM (Williams, Gray, & Tonge, 2012). Thus, interestingly, while much is made of the importance of earlier intervention in this population, in group- and computer-based modalities it appears that slightly older children may be better responders. However, these effects may not apply to all SSIs, as a recent meta-analysis of single-case design studies of video modeling and peer-mediated approaches in a slightly younger age group (4–15; mean = 6.49) showed evidence that these approaches may be more effective for younger participants (Wang et al., 2011). As such, there is some evidence that some SSIs may be best delivered in younger versus older age groups.

VERBAL ABILITY
Results of several group SSIs support this contention, with some approaches supporting an association of verbal ability with improvements in parent-reported social skills (Herbrecht et al., 2009), adaptive behavior (Legoff & Sherman, 2006), and teacher-reported cooperation (Bauminger, 2002); however, we note that several of the group-based approaches have not found moderating effects of verbal ability (McMahon, Vismara, et al., 2013; Solomon et al., 2004; Tyminski & Moore, 2008). Additionally, two computer-assisted SSIs have evinced associations between verbal ability and improvements in ToM and FER (Golan & Baron-Cohen, 2006; Williams et al., 2012).

COGNITIVE ABILITY
Little research has examined the predictive role of cognitive ability. While one study found no effects (Legoff & Sherman, 2006), another found potentially contradictory effects, wherein, among a cognitively "intact" sample (IQ > 75), more cognitively able children evidenced greater improvement in emotion perception, but less cognitively able showed a greater decrease in depression (Solomon et al., 2004).

ANXIETY/DEPRESSION/ADHD COMORBIDITY
One study has thus far examined the relation of comorbidity to SSI outcome, finding that anxiety comorbidity potentiated changes in parent-reported social skills, while ADHD comorbidity blunted such effects (Antshel et al., 2011).

INSIGHT
One study has considered the possible role of insight, finding that greater differences between their own and their parents' perception of their social skills predicted decreases in social anxiety in a group SSI (Lerner, Calhoun, Mikami, & De Los Reyes, 2012).

MEDICATION STATUS
Interestingly, effects of medication have been inconsistent, with a parent-assisted individual SSI showing greater improvements in an unmedicated group (Frankel, Myatt, & Feinberg, 2007), and a group SSI showing greater improvements in a medicated group (Herbrecht et al., 2009). While these effects are too preliminary to bear conclusions, they do suggest that there may be consonance between pharmacological interventions and some (but not all) SSIs.

OTHERS FOR CONSIDERATION
While theoretically important, the other potential moderators mentioned here have not yet been subject to empirical scrutiny.

THEORETICAL MODELS AND EMPIRICAL RESULTS OF MEDIATION STUDIES FOR TREATMENT OUTCOMES FOR YOUTH WITH AUTISM SPECTRUM DISORDERS

Theoretical Models of Mediation

Mediators are those processes that occur *during the course* of a treatment that contribute to change in target outcomes. As noted above, direct treatment of social competence is often not possible; as such, mediators are often the indirect pathways upon which one must directly intervene to achieve the ultimate goal of improved social functioning. We note that the criteria for consideration as a true statistical mediator (i.e., an intermediate factor responsible for most of the variance in the relation between a predictor and outcome) are appropriately quite stringent; at present, there has yet to be a single study examining true mediation in SSIs for ASD. However, we herein review processes that have been strongly theorized, have received some empirical scrutiny for contribution to outcomes, or both.

Importantly, therapeutic mediators may be either *non-specific* (i.e., existing across approaches) or *specific* (i.e., native to a specific approach) to an SSI. That is, some potential mediators may be present simply by virtue of engaging in an intervention with this population, an intervention for social skills, or both. We will first review these putatively *non-specific* factors, outlining the theoretical justification and evidence for each. Other putative mediators may be *specific* to individual interventions or treatment targets. We will review those in the subsequent section.

NON-SPECIFIC MEDIATORS
Engagement/Involvement
One of the most basic factors that may contribute to change in a given intervention is child engagement in the activities of that intervention (McLeod, Southam-Gerow, Tully, Rodríguez, & Smith, 2013). While the specific activities of each intervention may differ, engagement is a non-specific factor that can be considered content neutral: it may contribute to change irrespective of what the activities are. In other words, just being in an SSI and doing *something* should help social functioning by providing children the opportunity for sustained involvement in an activity with some level of consistency. Engagement may sometimes be posited to exhibit a dose-response relationship to outcomes (i.e., if a child is more engaged, she should demonstrate improved outcomes).

In some respects, all SSIs posit engagement as a mechanism of change; to conduct activities in an intervention implies suspicion that those activities may be helpful. Some interventions posit this more explicitly, noting that the design of the intervention is such that it is meant to be enticing to participants, and to become more so over time, thus targeting engagement (Hillier, Greher, Poto, & Dougherty, 2012; Legoff & Sherman, 2006; Lerner & Levine, 2007).

Alliance

Perhaps the most-studied non-specific factor in child-focused interventions is the working therapeutic relationship between therapist and child (McLeod, 2011). The alliance is thought to be composed of a shared bond, as well as agreement on therapeutic tasks and goals, between the child and the therapist. Given that the goal of SSIs is to improve social connectedness, the alliance is a plausible social learning mechanism for such outcomes. Nonetheless, very few SSIs speak to the importance of facilitating the alliance between children and therapists (Lerner & Levine, 2007; Lerner et al., 2011; Marriage, Gordon, & Brand, 1995).

Group Cohesion/Connection With Peers

Similar to the alliance, group cohesion is the sense of connectedness of members of a (therapy) group with one another. This represents another potential social learning mechanism, as youth in SSIs may become connected with peers in the group and thereby transfer (e.g., via self-efficacy) that capacity into the broader peer group; indeed, the connections made in SSIs may represent the initial achievement of target social outcomes unto themselves (Lerner & Mikami, 2012).

Dose-Response Relationship

Related to engagement, an important mechanism posited in most interventions is some sort of dose-response relationship between intervention and outcomes (McLeod et al., 2013). That is, there may be a minimum amount (i.e., frequency or intensity) of a given intervention required to achieve outcomes, and effects on outcomes may vary as a function (e.g., linear, exponential, polynomial) of that amount. Such relations are often theorized in SSIs (Turner-Brown, Perry, Dichter, Bodfish, & Penn, 2008).

Fidelity

Treatment fidelity is the degree to which an intervention is carried out as intended (integrity), and differs from other interventions (specifcity; McLeod et al., 2013).

Parent Participation and Buy-in

As is often the case in child-focused interventions, youth with ASD are rarely self-referred, and parents often wish to play an active role in treatment. Thus, it is often posited that their support and involvement in treatment may facilitate outcomes (e.g., by ensuring that assigned homework is completed). While this is especially the case for SSIs with formal parent-training components (White et al., 2013), it is not exclusively so. Indeed, many SSI models posit that parental buy-in is crucial (DeRosier et al., 2011; Frankel et al., 2007; Fujii et al., 2013; Laugeson et al., 2009; Laugeson et al., 2012; Minne & Semrud-Clikeman, 2012; Rocha, Schreibman, & Stahmer, 2007).

PUTATIVELY SPECIFIC FACTORS

Facial Emotion Recognition

As noted above, deficits in FER are often considered key (though see Harms, Martin, & Wallace, 2010) and noted to be contributors to social problems in ASD. As such, they are often targeted theoretically (Domitrovich, Cortes, & Greenberg, 2007), though not always directly assessed, in interventions showing significant effects (Bauminger, 2002).

Theory of Mind

Like FER, ToM deficits have often been considered associated with social deficits in ASD, and, as such, are often theorized to represent active elements of SSIs.

Social Motivation

The study of social motivation represents an active area of study in current ASD research, with substantial interest in discovering the degree to which differences in reward processing related to social stimuli represent early and/or accruing factors underlying social dysfunction in this population. It makes good sense, then, that this is a variable whose increase has frequently been targeted in SSIs, and which may increase prosocial behavior. Again, however, while often theorized as an active ingredient (Beaumont & Sofronoff, 2008; Guli, Semrud-Clikeman, Lerner, & Britton, 2013; Hillier et al., 2012; Kroeger et al., 2007; Legoff & Sherman, 2006; Lerner et al., 2011; Minne & Semrud-Clikeman, 2012; Owens, Granader, Humphrey, & Baron-Cohen, 2008), it has been rarely examined.

Social Knowledge

Since the earliest SSIs for ASD (Mesibov, 1984), it has been considered essential that interventions increase individuals' understanding of specific correct responses to social scenarios, such as via the use of scripted behavioral responses. This has been thought to not only make social interactions more manageable, but also to capitalize on the rules-based approach to social behavior often preferred among youth with ASD. Interestingly, though training of social knowledge has long been included in (primarily group-based) SSIs as a theorized mechanism (Barnhill et al., 2002; Barry et al., 2003; Dykstra, Boyd, Watson, Crais, & Baranek, 2012; Franco et al., 2013; Herbrecht et al., 2009; Koenig et al., 2010; McMahon, Vismara, et al., 2013; Ozonoff & Miller, 1995; Stichter, O'Connor, Herzog, Lierheimer, & McGhee, 2012; Tse et al., 2007; Webb, Miller, Pierce, Strawser, & Jones, 2004), actual changes in acquisition of knowledge of social behaviors have rarely been examined.

Decreased Arousal in Social Situations

Due to known differences in amygdala response to social scenarios (McPartland & Pelphrey, 2012) and general hyperarousal in this population, it has often been theorized that SSIs may provide an avenue for desensitizing social contact, which in turn may be an essential prerequisite for learning and enacting prosocial behaviors.

Empirical Results

NON-SPECIFIC MEDIATORS
Engagement/Involvement

Few studies have directly measured this variable. A small number of studies have measured engagement by either videotaped examination of level of child participation (Sancho et al., 2010) or therapist rating (White et al., 2013), but have not considered its relation to outcomes. Only one known study (Nelson, McDonnell, Johnston, Crompton, & Nelson, 2007) has assessed child engagement with respect to outcomes, finding that an individually focused visual intervention strategy related to increased engagement in child play groups and, concurrently, increased initiations with peers. However, this single-case design study examined only four children, and could not assess true mediation status.

Alliance

While promising investigations into alliance in SSIs for ASD have been described (Lerner, White, et al., 2012), they have yet to appear in the published literature.

Group Cohesion/Connection With Peers

Many SSIs posit within-group connections as being valuable elements of the intervention (Kamps et al., 2002; Laugeson et al., 2009; Laugeson et al., 2012; Lopata et al., 2012; Owens et al., 2008), though none has directly assessed it. Interestingly, one recent randomized controlled trial provides indirect support for this non-specific mechanism (Hesselmark, Plenty, & Bejerot, 2014), finding comparable effects of group recreation and group CBT for adults with ASD, suggesting that simple connection with a group of similar peers may be of benefit. However, this bears replication.

Dose-Response Relationship

There is some evidence that multiple SSIs may exhibit a threshold below which some effects (e.g., parent report of generalization) may not replicate (Lerner & Mikami, 2012). Also, two known SSIs have examined the relation between dose and outcomes. First, in a computer-based study of a ToM intervention, Golan and Baron-Cohen (2006) found that the amount of time using the software predicted the degree of improvement on a vocal emotion recognition and a film-based ToM task. Second, McMahon, Vismara, et al. (2013) found that, in a group SSI, greater session attendance predicted increased dyadic interaction with peers. However, neither of these was subjected to formal mediation analysis. Thus, while there is some promise that there may be dose-response mediation in SSIs, more evidence is needed.

Fidelity

For many years there was very little formal fidelity assessment in the SSI literature. Promisingly, more recent studies have shown an increase in assessment of fidelity by either observer- or therapist self-report of adherence to treatment manuals or therapeutic principles (Dykstra et al., 2012; Franco et al., 2013; Koenig et al., 2010; Laugeson et al., 2012; Lopata et al., 2008; Lopata et al., 2010; Lopata et al., 2012; Rocha et al., 2007; Ruble et al., 2013; Sansosti & Powell-Smith, 2008; White, Koenig, et al., 2010; White et al., 2013; Wilson, 2013). These studies have largely shown that the tested intervention met a minimum threshold of integrity, and that, when compared to one another, similarly targeted SSIs can be differentiated (Lerner & Mikami, 2012). Thus far, one small-scale, multiple-baseline study suggests that providing a brief intervention to increase fidelity of teacher implementation of integration tactics in a classroom may increase child social interaction (Kohler et al., 2001), though these findings are highly preliminary.

Parent Participation and Buy-in
No systematic assessment of whether parental involvement relates to efficacy has yet taken place.

PUTATIVELY SPECIFIC FACTORS
Facial Emotion Recognition
Results with respect to FER have been inconsistent. In several group SSIs, *no change* in FER has been found in several SSIs targeting ToM (Begeer et al., 2011; Gevers, Clifford, Mager, & Boer, 2006; Lopata et al., 2008), social motivation (Beaumont & Sofronoff, 2008; Lerner et al., 2011), or general behaviors (Barnhill et al., 2002; Stichter et al., 2012). Conversely, several computer- (Golan & Baron-Cohen, 2006) and group-based interventions (Corbett et al., 2011; Solomon et al., 2004) *have* revealed effects on FER, with theorized (though not tested) impact on social behaviors; however, others have found change in FER, but *no change* in social skills (Williams et al., 2012). Finally, a small but promising subset of group- (Lopata et al., 2012; Stichter et al., 2010) and computer-based (Hopkins et al., 2011) SSIs have evinced improvements in FER and parent-reported social skills. Thus, it is unclear whether the inconsistency in this literature emerges from differences in intervention methods, populations, or perhaps other non-specific factors. Nonetheless, it cannot currently be claimed that improved FER mediates improvements in social functioning in ASD.

Theory of Mind
Like FER, results have been inconsistent. Sometimes, ToM is assessed, but actual social enactment is not (Corbett et al., 2011), or vice versa. In several instances, both individual (Fisher & Happe, 2005) and group-based (Begeer et al., 2011; Ozonoff & Miller, 1995; Turner-Brown et al., 2008) interventions evinced change in ToM, but no change in social behavior. Indeed, only two group-based SSIs focused on CBT, both by Stichter et al (2010; 2012), have shown changes in ToM and social behavior, suggesting it as a promising venue for future study.

Social Motivation

One known study, which examined a small group SSI, directly observed change in social motivation (White, Koenig, et al., 2010); however, this was found in the context of examining parent-report Social Responsiveness Scale subscales, and only for some participants; nonetheless, its correspondence to improved parent- and teacher-report social initiation suggests further exploration of ingredients to potentiate motivation may be valuable.

Social Knowledge

Change in social knowledge has been measured (and found) in recent years (Koenig et al., 2010; Laugeson et al., 2009; Laugeson et al., 2012; Lopata et al., 2012; Solomon et al., 2004; White et al., 2009); however, it has not been assessed in terms of its concordance with broader social outcomes. That said, while direct mediational or predictive assessment of social knowledge is lacking, several recent studies have capitalized on a type of component control comparative design called "dismantling," in which elements of an intervention that represent discrete, theorized mechanisms are taken apart and compared to provide clues as to which ones may be "active ingredients" (Lerner, White, et al., 2012). In this way, such an approach provides a proxy route to potential mediation. These studies compared SSIs that primarily target social knowledge to similar interventions, each with the ultimate goal of improving social functioning. First, Kroeger et al. (2007) found that both knowledge- and motivation-focused group SSIs yielded improved observed social behavior, though the knowledge-focused group showed greater improvements. Second, Lerner and Mikami (2012) found that both knowledge- and motivation-focused group SSIs yielded improved peer-reported friendship-making and social liking, observer-reported prosocial behavior, and instructor-reported social skills, but that the motivation-focused group achieved these outcomes as a *faster* rate. Finally, Kasari et al. (2012) compared a direct-instruction knowledge-training approach to a peer-mediated approach in an inclusion classroom context; they found positive effects for both approaches in terms of being included in peer-nominated social networks, but greater improvements in this variable (and related variables, such as friendship nominations and decreased isolation) in the peer-mediated group. Overall, these findings suggest subtle differences between knowledge-focused and other approaches, suggesting a potential mediating role, and bearing deeper scrutiny.

Decreased Arousal in Social Situations

Few studies have directly assessed this variable. However, Corbett et al. (2011) found attenuated cortisol reactivity over time in a pilot group SSI, providing some support for this mechanism.

Summary and Evaluation of Empirical Results

In considering the above literature, it is important to note that empirical examination of mechanisms of SSIs for ASD is in its infancy, and so few firm conclusions can be drawn. Indeed, not a single statistically formal test of moderation or mediation is found in the literature. Most of the studies referenced in our synthesis on moderation in this field, for example, have examined predictors of pathology and outcome. Likewise, the empirical literature on mediation has examined change in associated processes but has not established temporal precedence of change in the underlying mechanism prior to change in the target outcome. Nonetheless, some initial evidentiary support can be gleaned. Broadly, one may consider the level of support as falling into one of four hierarchical categories: (1) consistent, replicated support across studies; (2) multiple studies linking mechanism to outcome, but inconsistent results; (3) some initial studies of relation to outcomes, but an insufficient number (< 3–4) to draw inferences; and (4) no empirical examination in the literature (see Figure 7.1).

In terms of moderators, none of the proposed variables falls in the second (multiple studies, but inconsistent results) or fourth (no previous research) category. Both age and verbal ability appear to evince well-replicated support consistent with the first category, though the pattern for each one differs. Thus, they may be considered the most important in terms of future directions. For age, preliminary results suggest that group- and computer-based SSIs may be especially effective for older children and adolescents, while video-modeling and typical peer-mediated approaches may be most effective for younger school-aged and preschool children. Meanwhile, multiple modalities appear to be best

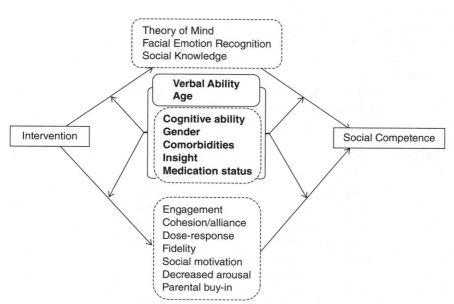

Figure 7.1. Theoretical model of mediators (in curved boxed with regular type) and moderators (in curved boxes with bold type) of social competence interventions for ASD. Variables enclosed in solid lines are those that have been empirically supported by at least two separate studies. Those variables in dashed lines are those that, at present, are less well-supported.

understood by those with at least average verbal ability. In terms of the third category, general cognitive ability, gender, presence of comorbidities, insight in social deficits, and medication status have each been subjected to only a few investigations as moderators, though each shows potential promise in terms of directions for future and ongoing investigation.

Among potential mediators, no variables meet criteria for the first category. In terms of the second category, FER, ToM, and social knowledge have all been subjected to several examinations, but the effects appear to vary across (sometimes similar) studies; this suggests that further investigation into the conditions under which these may be linked to outcomes is warranted. For the third category, engagement, cohesion, dose-response relationship, fidelity, social motivation, and decreased arousal have each only been considered with respect to outcomes a handful of times, and further study is needed to make inferences. Finally, both alliance and parental buy-in have yet to be examined in relation to outcomes; such an examination may be especially valuable to assess whether these theorized mechanisms are truly relevant in SSIs for ASD.

CHALLENGES AND RECOMMENDATIONS FOR FUTURE MODERATOR AND MEDIATOR RESEARCH

In addition to the need for more research in this area, we must try to determine the specificity of identified mechanisms. In other words, we have yet to fully understand the underlying processes that give rise to the observed social disabilities in people who have ASD. If there are some basic pathological mechanisms that are present across individuals, regardless of how specific deficits are manifested, targeting these mechanisms might be cost-efficient and clinically efficacious. This is similar to how most treatments for childhood anxiety target reduction of behavioral avoidance, regardless of the form the anxiety takes, and can be useful for linking phenotypic heterogeneity to common core processes (Pelphrey et al., 2011).

Related to the pursuit of core underlying mechanisms, there also exists a need for more theoretically derived, additive treatment approaches (e.g., Lerner & Mikami, 2012). Ideally, these psychosocial interventions will be tethered to neurobiological understanding of social disability in ASD, such that we can demonstrate some movement at a basic level (e.g., neuroplasticity) that is translated into improved social/daily function. ASD treatment literature is top-heavy with comprehensive approaches, often involving multiple simultaneous steps. We need to examine more closely which aspects of these comprehensive approaches are actually "active ingredients." This refined examination will promote identification of core processes that should be targeted across intervention (Lerner, White, et al., 2012). In addition, we might be able to discern non-essential aspects of existing interventions, which will help us hone and refine *what works*, while jettisoning that which does not.

Although we must pursue identification of outcome moderators and core mediators, we must not lose sight of the vast clinical heterogeneity seen in ASD. The diversity in deficits and abilities seen in children with ASD poses challenges to identifying a small set of mediators or moderators, common across presentation. Along these lines, with respect to moderators, we need to grapple with how we address them in treatment. For those more "central" to ASD, such as heightened arousal or poor emotion regulation, we must determine if it is more effective to treat it (i.e., address the moderator directly to improve outcome) or work around it, so to speak, if direct intervention is unlikely to be productive.

Finally, as we pursue this line of research, we will need to consider methodological considerations such as sample sizes required to attain sufficient power for accurate assessment of moderated effects. ASD, though more common now than ever in the past, affects only approximately 1 in 88 children and, as mentioned previously, is very diverse. Most SSIs target specific ASD subtypes (e.g., those without intellectual disability, and who are at least some minimum age). As such, it will be necessary to combine samples across sites (and, likely, intervention approaches) to statistically examine moderation. And for mediation, the early onset and chronic nature of ASD pose fairly unique challenges. Specifically, most children have had multiple prior treatments and, during SSI implementation, home-based and other concurrent treatments (e.g., medications) are common.

Implications for Clinical Practice

Readers of this volume may open this chapter in hopes of receiving answers to the pressing clinical question, "what works for *whom, how,* and *under what conditions*" (Lerner, White, et al., 2012). Unfortunately, as the study of treatment mechanisms in SSIs for youth with ASD remains yet nascent, conclusive answers regarding these questions remain elusive. However, it is hoped that even these preliminary results may be useful to practitioners in several ways. First, clinicians are encouraged to simply review the list of potential mediators and moderators identified here when planning to implement a given intervention, and apply best-practices clinical judgment to assess whether they have adequately considered each of them in their chosen modality of intervention. Second, we urge clinicians to likewise take qualitative and/or quantitative data on as many of these potential mechanisms as possible, to test underlying clinical assumptions about treatment processes. For instance, one may be implementing a complex group SSI package that appears to have broad-based social outcomes, yet find that one of the putative ingredients (e.g., increased ToM) is not seen among best treatment responders. This may represent an ideal time to use practice as a "natural laboratory," and consider implementation of a modified model without this element to see if effects are attenuated.

Third, we hope this chapter will provide clinicians an opportunity to think carefully about what "counts" as an outcome. That is, if changes in FER or social knowledge or parent-reported social skills, for example, are seen, but friendship-making is not (or is not assessed), practitioners may rightly wonder whether these proximal targets are, indeed, mechanistically related to desired (distal) social functioning. Such assumption-questioning is key to the practice of clinical science, and can provide a venue for innovative thinking about treatment design.

Fourth, we hope that our consideration of moderators can be useful for potentially matching participants to correct treatments now based on what is already known. Although some of the fairly strong effects (e.g., greater efficacy of video modeling for younger participants) in the extant literature can be translated immediately based on extant evidence, others (e.g., determining how much to promote insight into social deficits) may at least provide a foundation for intake assessment that clinicians may use in decisions about group construction and/or referral. In sum, our hope is that this initial foray into mechanisms of change in SSIs for ASD may advance the goal of developing customized, optimized interventions for this population. Such interventions would be tailored to each individual's needs and abilities, efficient in their components and delivery approach, evolving in response to ongoing data collection, yet grounded in an emerging literature that highlights treatment mechanisms as an invaluable area of inquiry as the field embraces the notion of a parsimonious link between mechanisms of social deficit and mechanisms of change for ASD.

AUTHORS' NOTE

We are thankful for Heather Garman's invaluable assistance with organization and collation of references for this chapter.

REFERENCES

Antshel, K. M., Polacek, C., McMahon, M., Dygert, K., Spenceley, L., Dygert, L., ... Faisal, F. (2011). Comorbid ADHD and anxiety affect social skills group intervention treatment efficacy in children with autism spectrum disorders. *Journal of Developmental and Behavioral Pediatrics, 32*(6), 439–446. doi: 10.1097/DBP.0b013e318222355d

Association, American Psychiatric. (2013). *Diagnostic and statistical manual of mental disorders* (5th ed.). Arlington, VA: American Psychiatric Publishing.

Barnhill, G. P., Cook, K. T., Tebbenkamp, K., & Myles, B. S. (2002). The effectiveness of social skills intervention targeting nonverbal communication for adolescents with Asperger syndrome and related pervasive developmental delays. *Focus on Autism and Other Developmental Disabilities, 17*(2), 112–118. doi: 10.1177/10883576020170 020601

Barry, T. D., Klinger, L. G., Lee, J. M., Palardy, N., Gilmore, T., & Bodin, S. D. (2003). Examining the effectiveness of an outpatient clinic-based social skills group for high-functioning children with autism. *Journal of Autism and Developmental Disorders*, *33*(6), 685–701. doi: 10.1023/B:JADD.0000006004.86556.e0

Bauminger, N. (2002). The facilitation of social-emotional understanding and social interaction in high-functioning children with autism: Intervention outcomes. *Journal of Autism and Developmental Disorders*, *32*(4), 283–298. doi: 10.1023/A:1016378718278

Bauminger, N. (2007). Brief report: Individual social-multi-modal intervention for HFASD. *Journal of Autism and Developmental Disorders*, *37*(8), 1593–1604. doi: 10.1007/s10803-006-0245-4

Beaumont, R., & Sofronoff, K. (2008). A multi-component social skills intervention for children with Asperger syndrome: The Junior Detective Training Program. *Journal of Child Psychology and Psychiatry*, *49*(7), 743–753. doi: 10.1111/j.1469-7610.2008.01 920.x

Begeer, S., Gevers, C., Clifford, P., Verhoeve, M., Kat, K., Hoddenbach, E., & Boer, F. (2011). Theory of mind training in children with autism: A randomized controlled trial. *Journal of Autism and Developmental Disorders*, *41*(8), 997–1006. doi: 10.1007/s10803-010-1121-9

Cederlund, M., Hagberg, B., Billstedt, E., Gillberg, I. C., & Gillberg, C. (2008). Asperger syndrome and autism: A comparative longitudinal follow-up study more than 5 years after original diagnosis. *Journal of Autism and Developmental Disorders*, *38*(1), 72–85.

Chevallier, C., Kohls, G., Troiani, V., Brodkin, E. S., & Schultz, R. T. (2012). The social motivation theory of autism. *Trends in Cognitive Sciences*, *16*(4), 231–239. doi: 10.1016/j.tics.2012.02.007

Corbett, B. A., Gunther, J. R., Comins, D., Price, J., Ryan, N., Simon, D., . . . Rios, T. (2011). Brief report: Theatre as therapy for children with autism spectrum disorder. *Journal of Autism and Developmental Disorders*, *41*(4), 505–511. doi: 10.1007/s10803-010-1064-1

DeRosier, M. E., Swick, D. C., Davis, N. O., McMillen, J. S., & Matthews, R. (2011). The efficacy of a social skills group intervention for improving social behaviors in children with high functioning autism spectrum disorders. *Journal of Autism and Developmental Disorders*, *41*(8), 1033–1043. doi: 10.1007/s10803-010-1128-2

Domitrovich, C. E., Cortes, R. C., & Greenberg, M. T. (2007). Improving young children's social and emotional competence: A randomized trial of the preschool 'PATHS' curriculum. *The Journal of Primary Prevention*, *28*(2), 67–91. doi: 10.1007/s10935-007-0081-0

Dykstra, J. R., Boyd, B. A., Watson, L. R., Crais, E. R., & Baranek, G. T. (2012). The impact of the Advancing Social-communication And Play (ASAP) intervention on preschoolers with autism spectrum disorder. *Autism*, *16*(1), 27–44. doi: 10.1177/1362361311408933

Fisher, N., & Happe, F. G. E. (2005). A training study of theory of mind and executive function in children with autistic spectrum disorders. *Journal of Autism and Developmental Disorders*, *35*(6), 757–771.

Franco, J. H., Davis, B. L., & Davis, J. L. (2013). Increasing social interaction using prelinguistic milieu teaching with nonverbal school-age children with autism.

American Journal of Speech-Language Pathology, 22(3), 489–502. doi: 10.1044/1 058-0360(2012/10-0103)

Frankel, F., Myatt, R., & Feinberg, D. (2007). Parent-assisted friendship training for children with autism spectrum disorders: Effects of psychotropic medication. *Child Psychiatry and Human Development, 37*(4), 337–346. doi: 10.1007/s10578-007-0053-x

Frazier, T. W., Ratliff, K. R, Gruber, C., Zhang, Y., Law, P. A, & Constantino, J. N. (2014). Confirmatory factor analytic structure and measurement invariance of quantitative autistic traits measured by the Social Responsiveness Scale-2. *Autism, 18*(1), 31–44. doi: 10.1177/1362361313500382.

Fujii, C., Renno, P., McLeod, B. D., Lin, C. E., Decker, K., Zielinski, K., & Wood, J. J. (2013). Intensive cognitive behavioral therapy for anxiety disorders in school-aged children with autism: A preliminary comparison with treatment-as-usual. *School Mental Health, 5*(1), 25–37. doi: 10.1007/s12310-012-9090-0

Gevers, C., Clifford, P., Mager, M., & Boer, F. (2006). Brief report: A theory-of-mind-based social-cognition training program for school-aged children with pervasive developmental disorders: An open study of its effectiveness. *Journal of Autism and Developmental Disorders, 36*(4), 567–571. doi: 10.1007/s10803-006-0095-0

Golan, Of., & Baron-Cohen, S. (2006). Systemizing empathy: Teaching adults with Asperger syndrome or high-functioning autism to recognize complex emotions using interactive multimedia. *Development and Psychopathology, 18*(2), 591–617. doi: 10.1017/S0954579406060305

Gresham, F. M. (1997). Social competence and students with behavior disorders: Where we've been, where we are, and where we should go. *Education and Treatment of Children, 20*(3), 233–249.

Guli, L. A., Semrud-Clikeman, M., Lerner, M. D., & Britton, N. (2013). Social Competence Intervention Program (SCIP): A pilot study of a creative drama program for youth with social difficulties. *The Arts in Psychotherapy, 40*(1), 37–44. doi: 10.1016/j.aip.2012.09.002

Harms, M. B., Martin, A., & Wallace, G. L. (2010). Facial emotion recognition in autism spectrum disorders: A review of behavioral and neuroimaging studies. *Neuropsychology Review, 20*(3), 290–322. doi: 10.1007/s11065-010-9138-6

Herbrecht, E., Poustka, F., Birnkammer, S., Duketis, E., Schlitt, S., Schmötzer, G., & Bölte, S. (2009). Pilot evaluation of the Frankfurt Social Skills Training for children and adolescents with autism spectrum disorder. *European Child & Adolescent Psychiatry, 18*(6), 327–335. doi: 10.1007/s00787-008-0734-4

Hesselmark, E., Plenty, S., & Bejerot, S. (2014). Group cognitive behavioural therapy and group recreational activity for adults with autism spectrum disorders: A preliminary randomized controlled trial. *Autism, 18*(6), 672–683. doi: 10.1177/1362361313493681.

Hillier, A., Greher, G., Poto, N., & Dougherty, M. (2012). Positive outcomes following participation in a music intervention for adolescents and young adults on the autism spectrum. *Psychology of Music, 40*(2), 201–215. doi: 10.1177/0305735610386837

Hopkins, I. M., Gower, M. W., Perez, T. A., Smith, D. S., Amthor, F. R., Wimsatt, F. C., & Biasini, F. J. (2011). Avatar assistant: Improving social skills in students with an ASD through a computer-based intervention. *Journal of Autism and Developmental Disorders, 41*(11), 1543–1555. doi: 10.1007/s10803-011-1179-z

Johnson, C. P., & Myers, S. M. (2007). Identification and evaluation of children with autism spectrum disorders. *Pediatrics, 120*(5), 1183–1215.

Jones, W., & Klin, A. (2013). Attention to eyes is present but in decline in 2-6-month-old infants later diagnosed with autism. *Nature, 504*, 427–431. doi: 10.1038/nature12715.

Kamps, D., Royer, J., Dugan, E., Kravits, T., Gonzalez-Lopez, A., Garcia, J., . . . Kane, L. G. (2002). Peer training to facilitate social interaction for elementary students with autism and their peers. *Exceptional Children, 68*(2), 173–187.

Kasari, C., Rotheram-Fuller, E., Locke, J., & Gulsrud, A. (2012). Making the connection: Randomized controlled trial of social skills at school for children with autism spectrum disorders. *Journal of Child Psychology and Psychiatry, 53*(4), 431–439. doi : 10.1111/j.1469-7610.2011.02493.x

Kazdin, A. E. (2007). Mediators and mechanisms of change in psychotherapy research. *Annual Review of Clinical Psychology, 3*, 1–27.

Koenig, K., De Los Reyes, A., Cicchetti, D., Scahill, L., & Klin, A. (2009). Group intervention to promote social skills in school-age children with pervasive developmental disorders: Reconsidering efficacy. *Journal of Autism and Developmental Disorders, 39*(8), 1163–1172.

Koenig, K., White, S. W., Pachler, M., Lau, M., Lewis, M., Klin, A., & Scahill, L. (2010). Promoting social skill development in children with pervasive developmental disorders: A feasibility and efficacy study. *Journal of Autism and Developmental Disorders, 40*(10), 1209–1218. doi: 10.1007/s10803-010-0979-x

Kohler, F. W., Anthony, L. J., Steighner, S. A., & Hoyson, M. (2001). Teaching social interaction skills in the integrated preschool: An examination of naturalistic tactics. *Topics in Early Childhood Special Education, 21*(2), 93–103. doi: 10.1177/027112140102100203

Kokina, A., & Kern, L. (2010). Social Story™ interventions for students with autism spectrum disorders: A meta-analysis. *Journal of Autism and Developmental Disorders, 40*(7), 812–826.

Kroeger, K. A., Schultz, J. R., & Newsom, C. (2007). A comparison of two group-delivered social skills programs for young children with autism. *Journal of Autism and Developmental Disorders, 37*(5), 808–817. doi: 10.1007/s10803-006-0207-x

Laugeson, E. A., Frankel, F., Gantman, A., Dillon, A. R., & Mogil, C. (2012). Evidence-based social skills training for adolescents with autism spectrum disorders: The UCLA PEERS program. *Journal of Autism and Developmental Disorders, 42*(6), 1025–1036. doi: 10.1007/s10803-011-1339-1

Laugeson, E. A., Frankel, F., Mogil, C., & Dillon, A. R. (2009). Parent-assisted social skills training to improve friendships in teens with autism spectrum disorders. *Journal of Autism and Developmental Disorders, 39*(4), 596–606. doi: 10.1007/s10803-008-0664-5

Legoff, D. B., & Sherman, M. (2006). Long-term outcome of social skills intervention based on interactive LEGO© play. *Autism, 10*(4), 317–329. doi: 10.1177/1362361306064403

Lerner, M. D., Calhoun, C. D., Mikami, A. Y., & De Los Reyes, A. (2012). Understanding parent–child social informant discrepancy in youth with high functioning autism spectrum disorders. *Journal of Autism and Developmental Disorders, 42*(12), 2680–2692. doi: 10.1007/s10803-012-1525-9

Lerner, M. D., & Levine, K. (2007). The Spotlight Method: An integrative approach to teaching social pragmatics using dramatic principles. *Journal of Developmental Processes, 2*(2), 91–102.

Lerner, M. D., & Mikami, A. Y. (2012). A preliminary randomized controlled trial of two social skills interventions for youth with high-functioning autism spectrum disorders. *Focus on Autism and Other Developmental Disabilities, 27*(3), 147–157. doi: 10.1177/1088357612450613

Lerner, M. D., Mikami, A. Y., & Levine, K. (2011). Socio-dramatic affective-relational intervention for adolescents with Asperger syndrome & high functioning autism: Pilot study. *Autism, 15*(1), 21–42. doi: 10.1177/1362361309353613

Lerner, M. D., White, S. W., & McPartland, J. C. (2012). Mechanisms of change in psychosocial interventions for autism spectrum disorders. *Dialogues in Clinical Neuroscience, 14*(3), 307.

Lopata, C., Thomeer, M. L., Volker, M. A., Lee, G. K., Smith, T. H., Smith, R. A., . . . Toomey, J. A. (2012). Feasibility and initial efficacy of a comprehensive school-based intervention for high-functioning autism spectrum disorders. *Psychology in the Schools, 49*(10), 963–974. doi: 10.1002/pits.21649

Lopata, C., Thomeer, M. L., Volker, M. A., Nida, R. E., & Lee, G. K. (2008). Effectiveness of a manualized summer social treatment program for high-functioning children with autism spectrum disorders. *Journal of Autism and Developmental Disorders, 38*(5), 890–904. doi: 10.1007/s10803-007-0460-7

Lopata, C., Thomeer, M. L., Volker, M. A., Toomey, J. A., Nida, R. E., Lee, G. K., . . . Rodgers, J. D. (2010). RCT of a manualized social treatment for high-functioning autism spectrum disorders. *Journal of Autism and Developmental Disorders, 40*(11), 1297–1310. doi: 10.1007/s10803-010-0989-8

Lord, C., Rutter, M., DiLavore, P. C., Risi, S., Gotham, K., & Bishop, S. L. (2012). *Autism diagnostic observation schedule* (2nd ed.) *(ADOS-2). Manual (Part 1): Modules 1–4.* Torrance, CA: Western Psychological Services.

Lord, C., Rutter, Mi., & Le Couteur, A. (1994). Autism Diagnostic Interview-Revised: A revised version of a diagnostic interview for caregivers of individuals with possible pervasive developmental disorders. *Journal of Autism and Developmental Disorders, 24*(5), 659–685.

Malone, R. P, Maislin, G., Choudhury, M. S., Gifford, C., & Delaney, M. A. (2002). Risperidone treatment in children and adolescents with autism: short-and long-term safety and effectiveness. *Journal of the American Academy of Child & Adolescent Psychiatry, 41*(2), 140–147.

Marriage, K. J., Gordon, V., & Brand, L. (1995). A social skills group for boys with Asperger's syndrome. *Australian and New Zealand Journal of Psychiatry, 29*(1), 58–62. doi: 10.3109/00048679509075892

McLeod, B. D. (2011). Relation of the alliance with outcomes in youth psychotherapy: A meta-analysis. *Clinical Psychology Review, 31*(4), 603–616.

McLeod, B. D, Southam-Gerow, M. A, Tully, C. B., Rodríguez, A., & Smith, M. M. (2013). Making a case for treatment integrity as a psychosocial treatment quality indicator for youth mental health care. *Clinical Psychology: Science and Practice, 20*(1), 14–32.

McMahon, C. M., Lerner, M. D., & Britton, N. (2013). Group-based social skills interventions for adolescents with higher-functioning autism spectrum disorder: A review and looking to the future. *Adolescent Health, Medicine, and Therapeutics, 4*, 23–38.

McMahon, C. M., Vismara, L. A., & Solomon, M. (2013). Measuring changes in social behavior during a social skills intervention for higher-functioning children and adolescents with autism spectrum disorder. *Journal of Autism and Developmental Disorders, 43*(8), 1843–1856. doi: 10.1007/s10803-012-1733-3

McPartland, J. C., & Pelphrey, K. A. (2012). The implications of social neuroscience for social disability. *Journal of Autism and Developmental Disorders, 42*(6), 1256–1262. doi: 10.1007/s10803-012-1514-z

Mesibov, G. B. (1984). Social skills training with verbal autistic adolescents and adults: A program model. *Journal of Autism and Developmental Disorders, 14*(4), 395–404.

Mikami, A. Y., Jack, A., & Lerner, M. D. (2009). Attention-deficit/hyperactivity disorder. In J. L. Matson (Ed.), *Social behavior and skills in children* (pp. 159–186). New York: Springer.

Mikami, A. Y., Lerner, M. D., & Lun, J. (2010). Social context influences on children's rejection by their peers. *Child Development Perspectives, 4*(2), 123–130. doi: 10.1111 /j.1750-8606.2010.00130.x

Minne, E. P., & Semrud-Clikeman, M. (2012). A social competence intervention for young children with high functioning autism and Asperger syndrome: A pilot study. *Autism, 16*(6), 586–602. doi: 10.1177/1362361311423384

Nelson, C., McDonnell, A. P., Johnston, S. S., Crompton, A., & Nelson, A. R. (2007). Keys to play: A strategy to increase the social interactions of young children with autism and their typically developing peers. *Education and Training in Developmental Disabilities, 42*(2), 165–181.

Owens, G., Granader, Y., Humphrey, A., & Baron-Cohen, S. (2008). LEGO® therapy and the social use of language programme: An evaluation of two social skills interventions for children with high functioning autism and Asperger syndrome. *Journal of Autism and Developmental Disorders, 38*(10), 1944–1957. doi: 10.1007/ s10803-008-0590-6

Ozonoff, S., & Miller, J. N. (1995). Teaching theory of mind: A new approach to social skills training for individuals with autism. *Journal of Autism and Developmental Disorders, 25*(4), 415–433. doi: 10.1007/BF02179376

Pelphrey, K. A., Shultz, S., Hudac, C. M., & Vander Wyk, B. C. (2011). Research review: Constraining heterogeneity: The social brain and its development in autism spectrum disorder. *Journal of Child Psychology and Psychiatry, 52*(6), 631–644. doi: 10.1111/j.1469-7610.2010.02349.x

Reichow, B., Steiner, A. M., & Volkmar, F. (2013). Cochrane Review: Social skills groups for people aged 6 to 21 with autism spectrum disorders (ASD). *Evidence-Based Child Health: A Cochrane Review Journal, 8*(2), 266–315.

Rocha, M. L., Schreibman, L., & Stahmer, A. C. (2007). Effectiveness of training parents to teach joint attention in children with autism. *Journal of Early Intervention, 29*(2), 154–172. doi: 10.1177/105381510702900207

Ruble, L. A., McGrew, J. H., Toland, M. D., Dalrymple, N. J., & Jung, L. A. (2013). A randomized controlled trial of COMPASS web-based and face-to-face teacher coaching in autism. *Journal of Consulting and Clinical Psychology, 81*(3), 566–572. doi: 10.1037/a0032003

Rutter, M., Bailey, A., & Lord, C. (2005). *SCQ: The social communication questionnaire manual.* Los Angeles, CA: Western Psychological Services.

Sancho, K., Sidener, T. M., Reeve, S. A., & Sidener, D. W. (2010). Two variations of video modeling interventions for teaching play skills to children with autism. *Education & Treatment of Children, 33*(3), 421–442. doi: 10.1353/etc.0.0097

Sansosti, F. J., & Powell-Smith, K. A. (2008). Using computer-presented social stories and video models to increase the social communication skills of children with high-functioning autism spectrum disorders. *Journal of Positive Behavior Interventions, 10*(3), 162–178. doi: 10.1177/1098300708316259

Solomon, M., Goodlin-Jones, B. L., & Anders, T. F. (2004). A social adjustment enhancement intervention for high functioning autism, asperger's syndrome, and pervasive developmental disorder NOS. *Journal of Autism and Developmental Disorders, 34*(6), 649–668. doi: 10.1007/s10803-004-5286-y

Spence, S. H. (2003). Social skills training with children and young people: Theory, evidence and practice. *Child and Adolescent Mental Health, 8*(2), 84–96.

Stichter, J. P., Herzog, M. J., Visovsky, K., Schmidt, C., Randolph, J., Schultz, T., & Gage, N. (2010). Social competence intervention for youth with Asperger syndrome and high-functioning autism: An initial investigation. *Journal of Autism and Developmental Disorders, 40*(9), 1067–1079. doi: 10.1007/s10803-010-0959-1

Stichter, J. P., O'Connor, K. V., Herzog, M. J., Lierheimer, K., & McGhee, S. D. (2012). Social competence intervention for elementary students with Aspergers syndrome and high functioning autism. *Journal of Autism and Developmental Disorders, 42*(3), 354–366. doi: 10.1007/s10803-011-1249-2

Tanaka, J. W., Wolf, J. M., Klaiman, C., Koenig, K., Cockburn, J., Herlihy, L., . . . Schultz, R. T. (2010). Using computerized games to teach face recognition skills to children with autism spectrum disorder: The Let's Face It! program. *Journal of Child Psychology and Psychiatry, 51*(8), 944–952.

Tse, J., Strulovitch, J., Tagalakis, V., Meng, L., & Fombonne, E. (2007). Social skills training for adolescents with Asperger syndrome and high-functioning autism. *Journal of Autism and Developmental Disorders, 37*(10), 1960–1968. doi: 10.1007/s10803-006-0343-3

Turner-Brown, L. M., Perry, T. D., Dichter, G. S., Bodfish, J. W., & Penn, D. L. (2008). Brief report: Feasibility of social cognition and interaction training for adults with high functioning autism. *Journal of Autism and Developmental Disorders, 38*(9), 1777–1784. doi: 10.1007/s10803-008-0545-y

Tyminski, R. F., & Moore, P. J. (2008). The impact of group psychotherapy on social development in children with pervasive development disorders. *International Journal of Group Psychotherapy, 58*(3), 363–379. doi: 10.1521/ijgp.2008.58.3.363

Vismara, L. A., & Rogers, S. J. (2010). Behavioral treatments in autism spectrum disorder: What do we know? *Annual Review of Clinical Psychology, 6*, 447–468.

Wang, S.-Y., Cui, Y., & Parrila, R. (2011). Examining the effectiveness of peer-mediated and video-modeling social skills interventions for children with autism spectrum disorders: A meta-analysis in single-case research using HLM. *Research in Autism Spectrum Disorders, 5*(1), 562–569.

Webb, B. J., Miller, S. P., Pierce, T. B., Strawser, S., & Jones, W. P. (2004). Effects of social skill instruction for high-functioning adolescents with autism spectrum disorders. *Focus on Autism and Other Developmental Disabilities, 19*(1), 53–62. doi: 10.1177/10883576040190010701

White, S. W., Albano, A. M., Johnson, C. R., Kasari, C., Ollendick, T., Klin, A., . . . Scahill, L. (2010). Development of a cognitive-behavioral intervention program to treat anxiety and social deficits in teens with high-functioning autism. *Clinical Child and Family Psychology Review, 13*(1), 77–90. doi: 10.1007/s10567-009-0062-3

White, S. W., Keonig, K., & Scahill, L. (2007). Social skills development in children with autism spectrum disorders: A review of the intervention research.

Journal of Autism and Developmental Disorders, 37(10), 1858–1868. doi: 10.1007/s10803-006-0320-x

White, S. W., Koenig, K., & Scahill, L. (2010). Group social skills instruction for adolescents with high-functioning autism spectrum disorders. *Focus on Autism and Other Developmental Disabilities, 25*(4), 209–219. doi: 10.1177/1088357610380595

White, S. W., Ollendick, T., Albano, A. M., Oswald, D., Johnson, C., Southam-Gerow, M. A., . . . Scahill, L. (2013). Randomized controlled trial: Multimodal anxiety and social skill intervention for adolescents with autism spectrum disorder. *Journal of Autism and Developmental Disorders, 43*(2), 382–394. doi: 10.1007/s10803-012-1577-x

White, S. W., Ollendick, T., Scahill, L., Oswald, D., & Albano, A. M. (2009). Preliminary efficacy of a cognitive-behavioral treatment program for anxious youth with autism spectrum disorders. *Journal of Autism and Developmental Disorders, 39*(12), 1652–1662. doi: 10.1007/s10803-009-0801-9

Williams, B. T., Gray, K. M., & Tonge, B. J. (2012). Teaching emotion recognition skills to young children with autism: A randomised controlled trial of an emotion training programme. *Journal of Child Psychology and Psychiatry, 53*(12), 1268–1276. doi: 10.1111/j.1469-7610.2012.02593.x

Wilson, K. P. (2013). Teaching social-communication skills to preschoolers with autism: Efficacy of video versus in vivo modeling in the classroom. *Journal of Autism and Developmental Disorders, 43*(8), 1819–1831. doi: 10.1007/s10803-012-1731-5

Wood, J. J., Drahota, A., Sze, K., Har, K., Chiu, A., & Langer, D. A. (2009). Cognitive behavioral therapy for anxiety in children with autism spectrum disorders: A randomized, controlled trial. *Journal of Child Psychology and Psychiatry, 50*(3), 224–234.

Yoder, P. J., & Warren, S. F. (1998). Maternal responsivity predicts the prelinguistic communication intervention that facilitates generalized intentional communication. *Journal of Speech, Language and Hearing Research, 41*(5), 1207.

Moderators and Mediators of Treatments for Youth With Substance Abuse

LYNN HERNANDEZ, ANDREA LAVIGNE,
MARK WOOD, AND REINOUT W. WIERS ■

INTRODUCTION

Adolescence is a developmental period during which profound changes occur. Adolescents' gradual adoption of broader social roles and their experimentation with new behaviors, attitudes, and ways of defining themselves bring not only new opportunities, but also increased risks and vulnerabilities. One particular risk is the development of substance use disorders (SUDs), which are among the most common psychiatric disorders among adolescents, with a prevalence of 11.4% and 5- to 11-fold increases from ages 13–18 (Merikangas et al., 2010). Given the prevalence and potential life-course altering effects of substance abuse, substantial research emphasis has been placed on the development of efficacious universal, selective, and indicated adolescent substance abuse preventive interventions. Increasingly, it is recognized that the identification of factors that affect outcomes (moderators), as well as mechanisms of effects (mediators), are critical considerations in furthering the scope and impact of substance abuse treatment efforts. This chapter focuses on moderators and mediators of selective and indicated preventive interventions to reduce substance abuse from early (beginning at age 13) to late (age 18–21) adolescence. After a brief discussion of the developmental progression of alcohol and other drug use and disorders in adolescence and a brief review of the etiologic foundations upon which current treatment efforts are based, the empirical literature base on moderation and mediation of adolescent preventive intervention research is systematically reviewed, with an emphasis on randomized controlled trials (RCTs).

The chapter concludes with identification of conceptual and methodological challenges in the examination of substance abuse treatment moderators and mediators, as well as discussion of implications for research and clinical practice.

SUBSTANCE USE AND USE DISORDERS IN ADOLESCENCE

Alcohol and other drug use are typically initiated during early adolescence, increase substantially across this developmental epoch, and tend to decrease in the third decade of life. Indeed, this pattern is so typical that some theorists have described substance use disorders as "developmental disorders" (Masten, Faden, Zucker, & Spear, 2008; Sher& Gotham, 1999). In the United States, alcohol use tends to be heaviest between the ages of 19 and 21, while marijuana use tends to peak between the ages of 19 and 22 (Chen & Kandel, 1995). According to the Monitoring the Future study (MTF; Johnston, O'Malley, Bachman, & Schulenberg, 2013), a significant proportion (29.5%) of adolescents have already initiated alcohol use by the time they reach the age of 13, and 13% report having experienced being drunk. These national data, coupled with similar data on drinking rates in Europe (Beccaria & White, 2012), demonstrate that most adolescents report at least some experience with alcohol by the time they reach ages 17–18 (69.4% in the US vs. 90% in Europe). Similar trends are seen in marijuana use among adolescents, the second most commonly used substance. For instance, according to MTF, 45.2% of adolescents report marijuana use by the time they turn 17–18 years old, while 13% of European students (11% of the girls and 15% of the boys) report marijuana use. A recent comparison of the European School Survey Project on Alcohol and Other Drugs (ESPAD) and MTF data concluded that American youth are less likely to use cigarettes and alcohol than European youth, but are more likely to use illicit drugs (Wadley, 2012).

Underage drinking is associated with a wide range of problems for adolescents and society at large, including motor vehicle accidents, suicide, homicide, injuries, unplanned or unprotected sexual experiences, and social and academic problems (Hingson & Kenkel, 2004). In the United States, nearly 2,000 drivers between the ages of 15 and 20 died in motor vehicle crashes in 2011 (National Highway Traffic Safety Administration, 2013), and approximately one-third of these drivers had consumed alcohol. Regarding marijuana, chronic use initiated during adolescence has been related to reductions in cognitive performance. In the longitudinal Dunedin study of 1,037 individuals, Meier et al. (2012) administered cognitive testing to adolescent participants between the ages of 7 and 13 who had not initiated marijuana use, and then followed these participants into middle adulthood. Participants who met criteria for cannabis use disorder at three of the follow-up assessments were found to have a 6-point lower full scale IQ score. These differences were not observed in participants with adult-onset marijuana use, suggesting that adolescent onset of heavy marijuana use may be associated with long-term deleterious cognitive effects. Findings such as these highlight the importance of identifying successful substance abuse intervention approaches geared toward adolescents and young adults.

According to the *Diagnostic and Statistical Manual of Mental Disorders* (5th ed., *DSM-5*; American Psychiatric Association, 2013), substance use is considered problematic when an individual exhibits multiple maladaptive behaviors and symptoms that relate to substance use in one or more domains. The first of these domains comprise behaviors associated with loss of control, such as frequently using more of the substance than originally planned. The second domain comprises social difficulties resulting from substance use, and includes persistent interpersonal problems caused by or exacerbated by the substance. The third domain of problematic behaviors includes risky behaviors, such as continuing to use a substance despite recurrent physical or psychological problems. The final domain refers to pharmacological changes that result from use of a substance, such as the development of tolerance, the need to use in greater amounts to achieve the same effects experienced during initial use, and withdrawal, the symptoms experienced when an adolescent reduces or eliminates the use of a substance after a period of regular use. There are questions regarding the suitability of including symptoms related to pharmacological changes for adolescent diagnoses. For instance, Winters, Martin, and Chung (2011) and Kaminer and Winters (2012) argue that symptoms such as tolerance may be developmentally normative for adolescents and young adults as they move from experimental use to regular use, while symptoms such as withdrawal and craving may need further clarification as to how they manifest during adolescence.

Despite the potential lack of developmental sensitivity of the revised criteria in the *DSM-5*, the revised criteria do include some positive changes for diagnosing substance use disorders among adolescents and young adults. For instance, one notable revision is that substance abuse and dependence are no longer distinct categories. Currently, a single diagnosis of substance use disorder may be obtained if an individual exhibits at least two symptoms across domains within a 12-month period. Additional specification may be provided to indicate the severity of the disorder, such as mild (e.g., 2–3 symptoms are present), moderate (e.g., 4–5 symptoms are present), or severe (e.g., 6 or more symptoms are present). The *DSM-5* also eliminates the "legal problems" symptom. Given the lack of relevance for females and early adolescents (Winters, 2013) and its correlation to driving violations and comorbid conduct disorder (Kaminer & Winters, 2012), elimination of this symptom increases the developmental congruency between substance use disorder criteria and adolescence.

There are numerous substances for which these diagnostic criteria may be applied and a diagnosis of substance use disorder reached, including alcohol, cannabis, hallucinogens, inhalants, opioids, sedatives/hypnotics/anxiolytics, stimulants, tobacco, and other/unknown substances. According to the *DSM-5*, 12-month prevalence estimates for alcohol and cannabis use disorders among 12–17 year olds are 4.6% and 3.4%, respectively. The National Comorbidity Survey-Adolescent study (NCS-A), a large-scale study assessing prevalence and comorbidity of mental health disorders in adolescents between the ages of 13 and

18, yielded slightly higher estimates, with 6.4% of the sample meeting diagnostic criteria for an alcohol use disorder and 8.9% meeting criteria for a substance use disorder (Merikangas et al., 2010).

There is substantial comorbidity, both within substance use disorders and across broader classes of disorders. Lifetime comorbidity estimates of alcohol use and cannabis use disorders exceeds 50%, and 74% of people seeking treatment for cannabis use disorder report additional problems with one or more additional substances (American Psychiatric Association, 2013). In addition to the increased likelihood of problems with multiple substances, adolescents with alcohol and other substance use disorders are more likely to suffer from comorbid psychiatric disturbance. According to findings from the NCS-A, approximately 40% of adolescents meeting criteria for one disorder also meet lifetime criteria for another, while 25% of adolescents who meet criteria for one disorder meet criteria for two additional classes of disorders (Merikangas et al., 2010). Community-based studies of adolescents with diagnosed substance abuse or dependence showed that these adolescents were 2.2 times more likely to meet diagnostic criteria for concurrent depression, and 3.3 more likely to meet criteria for depression in their lifetime (Armstrong & Costello, 2002). The comorbidity of substance use disorders appears to be highest with disruptive behavior disorders, including conduct disorder, oppositional defiant disorder, and attention deficit hyperactivity disorder (ADHD), with odds ratios varying greatly but averaging about 4, indicating that these individuals are four times more likely to also have a diagnosis of substance use disorders. Similar levels of comorbidity were reported for lifetime post-traumatic stress disorder (PTSD) and SUD, with odds ratio of 4. Comorbidity estimates appear greater within the inpatient adolescent population. In their review, Deas and Thomas (2002) report that 73% of their adolescent inpatient sample who used alcohol or other drugs also met diagnostic criteria for depressive disorder. Anxiety disorders, particularly social anxiety disorder and PTSD, were frequently reported to be coexisting, with 60% of adolescents with substance use problems also meeting criteria for social anxiety disorder. Adolescents with alcohol use problems were found to be up to 12 times more likely to have a history of physical abuse, and up to 21 times more likely to have a history of sexual abuse. While conduct disorder was described as frequently co-occurring with SUD in this sample, ADHD was not. Given the very high levels of comorbidity, there is a clear need for research that can elucidate moderators and mediators of multicomponent or hybrid preventive interventions.

THEORETICAL MODELS INFORMING ADOLESCENT PREVENTIVE INTERVENTIONS

Several theoretical models describing the processes underlying both the etiology and maintenance of adolescents' and young adults' substance abuse behaviors have guided the design and implementation of adolescent substance abuse preventive interventions, and the selection of moderators and mediators of intervention effects. Next, we review the two most influential models of adolescent substance abuse: biopsychosocial and dual process models.

Biopsychosocial Models

It is widely recognized that substance use and misuse are influenced by the interplay of a wide array of biological, psychological, and social factors (Sher, Grekin, & Williams, 2005; Sher & Slutske, 2003).This complexity is further heightened by the dramatic maturational processes that occur during adolescence (Hollenstein & Lougheed, 2013), and the manner in which these processes interact with risk, promotive, and protective factors known to affect developmental trajectories of substance use. Risk factors, such as affiliation with substance-using peers, are associated with increased substance use. Promotive factors (Sameroff, 2000) reflect the more advantageous end of a risk factor (e.g., high parental monitoring) and are associated with less substance use. Protective factors are distinct from promotive factors in that they interact with risk factors to mitigate their effects. For example, in addition to a promotive role, parental monitoring may be considered protective if it reduces the influence of a risk factor, such as peer influences (see Fairlie, Wood, & Laird, 2012). While a comprehensive review is beyond the scope of this chapter (see Brown et al., 2008; Hawkins, Catalano, & Miller, 1992; Wiers, Fromme, Latvala, & Stewart, 2012; Windle et al., 2008), we briefly review etiologic research with an emphasis on the most robust and malleable factors that have been targeted in the preventive interventions reviewed subsequently.

Current etiologic thinking incorporates personality traits as important components of larger biopsychosocial models (Sher et al., 2005), and consistent associations with personality assessed in childhood and adolescence and subsequent substance use and misuse have been observed (Caspi, Moffitt, Newman, & Silva, 1996; Cloninger, Sigvardsson, & Bohman, 1988). Of greatest relevance for the development of substance use and misuse are "externalizing" traits such as disinhibition, impulsivity, sensation seeking, novelty seeking, and psychoticism, which appear to be linked to substance use in order to enhance positive affect (Sher, Trull, Bartholow, & Vieth, 1999; Wiers et al., 2012). Indeed, alcohol and substance use disorders have been characterized as "disorders of impulse control" (Sher & Slutske, 2003) with the extreme end of these personality traits overlapping with commonly co-occurring psychiatric disorders such as antisocial personality disorder and conduct disorder. "Internalizing" traits, such as neuroticism, harm avoidance, and negative affectivity, have also been theorized as etiologically relevant to the development of substance use, with the extreme end of these trait continua associated with comorbid substance use–anxiety diagnoses. Relief of negative affect and maladaptive coping are putative mechanisms in relations between internalizing traits and substance abuse. While less well established than externalizing traits, prospective research has shown that neuroticism predicts the progression from adolescent drinking to alcohol problems in young adulthood (Jackson & Sher, 2003). More recently, researchers have examined relations between additional internalizing traits of anxiety sensitivity and introversion-hopelessness. Anxiety sensitivity has demonstrated consistent associations with alcohol problems in young adulthood and has been shown to moderate relations between anxiety symptoms and increasing alcohol use over time (Mackie, Castellanos-Ryan, & Conrod, 2011).

Two distinct alcohol-related cognitions have been the focus of a great deal of research: alcohol-related expectancies (herein referred to as *expectancies*) and drinking motives (herein referred to as *motives*). Expectancies, defined as the expected effects of drinking alcohol (positive or negative) correlate strongly with concurrent drinking levels in adolescents and young adults (explaining up to 50% of variance in drinking), while prospective prediction after accounting for previous use typically yielded much more modest levels of prediction (1%–5%; see Goldman, Del Boca, & Darkes, 1999; Jones, Corbin, & Fromme, 2001, for reviews). This has led to research that identified reciprocal relations; expectancies predict later drinking, and drinking predicts later expectancies (Sher, Wood, Wood, & Raskin, 1996; Smith, Goldman, Greenbaum, & Christiansen, 1995). Children's expectancies can be measured before they start drinking, with some evidence pointing to prospective prediction of onset of drinking (Christiansen, Smith, Roehling, & Goldman, 1989), although it should be mentioned that there are some measurement issues with the assessment of expectancies in general (Leigh, 1989) and with children in particular (Wiers, Sergeant, & Gunning, 2000). While early research only investigated positive expectancies (Brown, Goldman, & Christiansen, 1985), later research has also assessed negative expectancies (Fromme, Stroot, & Kaplan, 1993) and has demonstrated that negative expectancies account for unique variance in use. In addition, dose-specific expectancies have been found to predict unique variance, especially in adolescents (the only group where positive expectancies of a high dose of alcohol were found to do so; Wiers, Hoogeveen, Sergeant, & Gunning, 1997). As detailed later, expectancies, as robust and proximal correlates of substance use and problems, have been targeted in interventions, in order to test their role as putative mediators of heavy drinking.

Drinking motives have also been studied extensively. Cooper (1994) developed a widely used scale, the Drinking Motives Questionnaire—Revised (DMQ-R), which has also been used in many studies of underage drinkers, both in North America and in Europe (Kuntsche, Stewart, & Cooper, 2008). The scale combines two types of reinforcement (positive/negative) with an internal or external drive, leading to four motives to drink: enhancement (internal, positive reinforcement, for example drinking to increase positive affect); social (external, positive reinforcement, drinking to affiliate), coping (internal, negative reinforcement, drinking to manage negative emotional states); and conformity (external, negative reinforcement, drinking to fit in). The scales have been replicated across countries, and enhancement and coping drinking motives have been found to be primary predictors of excessive underage drinking and alcohol-related problems. Across countries, enhancement and coping motives were positively related to heavier alcohol use, and coping motives were additionally related to alcohol problems (Kuntsche et al., 2008). Motives to drink, particularly those related to coping, are also often targeted in cognitive behavioral and motivational interventions, as detailed subsequently.

Peer influences are among the most widely studied psychosocial constructs in adolescent substance use and misuse. Peer–substance use relations are also best construed as a reciprocal influence process comprising both selection (substance-using individuals seeking out similar others) and socialization (substance use is facilitated in environments where it is more accepted and prevalent). Research support for reciprocal influences exists in both early adolescent (Curran, Stice, & Chassin, 1997) and late adolescent (Read, Wood, & Capone, 2005) samples, although there is evidence that the relative importance of these processes varies across adolescence. Specifically, Burk, van der Vorst, Kerr, and Stattin (2011) found peer selection to be more robust than socialization in early adolescence, with relatively equal contributions in middle and late adolescence. Consistent with social learning theory, in early and late adolescent samples, unique effects have been observed for both direct/active (e.g., explicit substance offers) and indirect (social modeling, descriptive, and injunctive norms) peer influences (Graham, Marks, & Hanson, 1991; Read et al., 2005), suggesting additional targets for cognitive behavioral and motivational interventions.

As the primary agents of socialization, parents influence the development of substance use and misuse in a number of direct and indirect ways. Reflecting genetic, environmental, and gene x environment interactions, offspring of parents with substance use disorders are at enhanced risk for the development of substance use disorders (Bucholz, Heath, & Madden, 2000; Lieb et al., 2002; Walden, Iacono, & McGue, 2007). Parental modeling of heavy drinking and both positive alcohol attitudes and expectancies have also shown prospective associations with adolescent substance use (Andrews, Hops, Ary, & Tildesley, 1993; Chassin, Pillow, Curran, Molina, & Barrera, 1993). Several conceptually distinct parenting styles and practices, which can be subsumed within overall parental investment/involvement, have been highlighted as important in the development of adolescent alcohol use (Windle et al., 2008). These include parental warmth/nurturance, parental monitoring/knowledge/rule enforcement, time spent together, and parent-adolescent communication. These parenting domains have demonstrated both promotive and protective effects in studies spanning early to late adolescence (Crawford & Novak, 2002; Fairlie et al., 2012; Marshal & Chassin, 2000; Wood, Read, Mitchell, & Brand, 2004). For example, Wood et al. (2004) found that parental monitoring demonstrated both promotive and protective relations with alcohol-related consequences. Higher monitoring was associated with lower levels of alcohol problems (a promotive effect) and also interacted with peer influences, reducing their association with alcohol problems (a protective effect).

Adolescent development is embedded in a set of contexts, each interacting with one another to influence adolescents' developmental trajectories. According to ecological systems theory (Bronfenbrenner & Morris, 1998), culture is one of these prominent contexts that affect development. Well-investigated cultural processes that are associated with substance use risk among adolescents include acculturation, cultural identity, perceived discrimination, and immigration status. Most research attempting to identify cultural influencesof adolescents' alcohol use has focused on acculturation. Adolescents classified as "more acculturated" demonstrate higher rates of alcohol use than their "less acculturated" counterparts in studies where acculturation has been operationalized as a composite of language, media preference, and social relationships (Caetano & Raspberry, 2000), nativity and length of time in the host culture (Gil et al., 2000), and as predominant use of host rather than native language (Epstein, Botvin, & Diaz, 2001). Further, a well-established finding is that adolescents born in the United States have significantly higher rates of regular alcohol use, tobacco use, and drug use, abuse, or dependency than immigrants (e.g., Gfroerer & Tan, 2003; Gil, Wagner, & Vega, 2000; Vega & Gil, 2005; Warner, Canino, & Colon, 2001), with similar findings generated in Western European countries, such as The Netherlands (related to lower drinking rates in adolescents with Muslim background; van Tubergen & Poortman, 2010). Associations have also been documented between self-reported discrimination and various forms of substance use, including smoking (Bennett, Wolin, Robinson, Fowler, & Edwards, 2005), alcohol consumption (Kwate, Valdimarsdottier, Guevarra, & Bovbjerb, 2003), and use and abuse of other drugs (Minior, Galea, Stuber, Ahern, & Ompad, 2003). Similarly, weakened ethnic, racial, and cultural identity (Holley, Kulis, Marsiglia, & Keith, 2006; Vega, Alderete, Kolody, & Aguilar-Gaxiola, 1998) and lower levels of ethnic/racial pride (Castro, Stein, & Bentler, 2009) have been identified as correlates of alcohol use among ethnic/racial minority adolescents and young adults. Taken together, these findings highlight the importance of examining how these cultural processes influence adolescents' and young adults' amenability to treatment, as well as how interventions could be designed to target these cultural risk, promotive, and protective factors.

Dual Process Models

The past two decades witnessed a surge of dual process models in psychology (e.g., Evans, 2008; Gawronski & Bodenhausen, 2006; Kahneman, 2003; Smith & DeCoster, 2000; Strack & Deutsch, 2004). On the most general level, these models distinguish between two qualitatively different types of processes: impulsive or associative processes, and reflective or symbolic processes. The stronger version claims that there are two or more separable systems, a postulate that has been criticized (Keren & Schul, 2009; for further discussion, see Evans and Stanovich [2013] and subsequent commentaries). Note that a different theoretical perspective is possible, in which the reflective and impulsive cognitive processes are emergent properties of the dynamic, unfolding interplay between different neural systems (Cunningham, Zelazo, Packer, & Van Bavel, 2007; Gladwin, Figner, Crone, & Wiers, 2011; Hazy, Frank, & O'Reilly, 2006). These general dual process models have been applied to health psychology (e.g., Hofmann, Friese, & Wiers, 2008), and more specifically to the etiology of addiction (Bechara, 2005; Stacy, Ames, & Knowlton, 2004;

Wiers & Stacy, 2006; Wiers et al., 2007). Several studies in adolescents have now demonstrated that impulsive processes (memory associations, automatically triggered tendencies to approach the substance) are especially important in the prediction of addictive behaviors in adolescents with relatively poorly developed executive control abilities (Grenard et al., 2008; Peeters et al., 2012; Peeters et al., 2013; Thush et al., 2008).

From this perspective, interventions should either address reflective processes (e.g., ability and motivation to control impulses) and/or interfere with the sensitized impulsive processes (Wiers et al., 2007; Wiers et al., 2013). Indeed, several studies have reported that implicit cognitive processes can be successfully changed, with positive effects on treatment in adult alcohol-dependent patients (Eberl et al., 2013; Schoenmakers et al., 2010; Wiers et al., 2011) and in adult problem drinkers (Fadardi & Cox, 2009). Most relevant here is research reported by Eberl and colleagues (2013), who found that the effect on treatment outcome (10% less relapse one year after treatment discharge, following retraining of automatic alcohol-approach tendencies, compared with treatment as usual without training) was mediated by the change in alcohol-approach bias. Moreover, moderation was also reported: patients with relatively strong alcohol-approach tendencies profited most of the additional cognitive training. Although these findings are clearly promising for the treatment of addiction in adults, these approaches have not been tested yet in adolescents. One issue with such applications is that participants have to be motivated to repeatedly do the training, which is one of the major obstacles in the treatment of adolescent substance use disorders. Two potential solutions to this challenge are to increase both motivation to change and motivation to take part in the training and/or to develop and validate more "game-like" varieties of training for adolescents with substance use problems (see also Wiers et al., 2013).

Consistent with the basic tenets of prevention science, interventions have attempted to target etiologically relevant psychological, social, and, increasingly, biological factors associated with substance use and misuse. Particular emphasis has been placed on factors that are malleable and proximal to substance use. Building on our brief etiologic overview and discussion on theoretical models, we next describe both commonly used and emerging preventive intervention approaches that have been used in adolescent populations.

ADOLESCENT SUBSTANCE ABUSE PREVENTIVE INTERVENTIONS

Commonly Used Approaches

COGNITIVE BEHAVIORAL THERAPY (CBT)

In both the United States and much of Europe, including The Netherlands, CBT is the most widely used and empirically supported treatment approach for adults and adolescents with substance use disorders. According to Waldron and

Kaminer (2004, p. 2), "Cognitive–behavioral models conceptualize substance use and related problems as learned behaviors that are initiated and maintained in the context of environmental factors." Accordingly, CBT is an approach that is informed by learning perspectives, including classical and operant conditioning, and social learning theory. A wide variety of interventions are utilized in CBT, including managing exposure to triggers within the environment and changing the contingencies that maintain use, skill building in the areas of problem-solving, coping and related motives for drinking, and emotion regulation, modifying cognitive distortions, and relapse prevention, among many others (Waldron & Kaminer, 2004). Reviews of RCTs testing the efficacy of CBT with adolescent substance abusers indicate that CBT is effective in reducing substance use and related problems when delivered individually or within a group format (Waldron & Kaminer, 2004; Waldron & Turner, 2008).

Motivational Enhancement Therapy (MET)
Motivational enhancement is a treatment approach that is based on the principles of Motivational Interviewing, defined as "a client-centered, directive method for enhancing intrinsic motivation to change by exploring and resolving ambivalence" (Miller & Rollnick, 2002, p. 25). In an effort to enhance an individual's motivation for behavior change, therapists seek to elicit change talk from the clients themselves, which is a putative mediator of treatment effects (Miller & Rose, 2009). Guiding principles to motivational enhancement include conveying empathy, helping clients develop discrepancy between their present behavior and their goals, viewing resistance for change as a signal to the interventionist to change the approach rather than as an obstacle to treatment, and fostering feelings of self-efficacy in clients (Miller & Rollnick, 2002). The basic tenets of motivational enhancement may make this approach especially appealing and effective with adolescent substance abusers, given that adolescents may be forced into treatment, may present with limited motivation to reduce their substance use, and may react defensively to an authoritarian approach (Tevyaw & Monti, 2004). Motivational enhancement has received substantial research attention in the area of substance misuse, both as a stand-alone approach and as an adjunct to other treatment approaches. Reviews of controlled studies with adolescent substance abusers have shown motivational enhancement to be effective in reducing substance-related problems and use with a variety of substances, often with the intervention delivered in only one session (Jensen et al., 2011; Tevyaw & Monti, 2004).

Family and Parent-Based Interventions
Family- and parent-based approaches to prevention and intervention for alcohol and other drug use have received widespread support (Becker & Curry, 2008; Weinberg et al., 1998). The literature has demonstrated that programs that promote behavior management skills and strong parent-adolescent relationships reduce substance use in adolescence (Dishion & McMahon, 1998; Henggeler, Melton & Smith, 1992). Further, affecting family processes seems to be critical

in reducing the escalation of substance use during adolescence (Borduin et al., 1995; Dishion & Andrews, 1995).

Family therapy has received the most research support in the treatment of adolescent substance abuse and dependence (Becker et al., 2008; Weinberg et al., 1998). Waldron (1997) and Williams and Chang (2000) reviewed family therapy studies for adolescent substance use and found consistent significant reductions in substance use from pre- to post-treatment. When family therapy was compared to group therapy, family education, individual therapy, or individual tracking through schools/courts, family therapy resulted in greater reductions in substance use in 7 of 8 studies (Waldron, 1997). Further, after reviewing family-based interventions for adolescent substance use, Kumpfer et al. (2003) concluded that family-based interventions have average effect sizes 2 to 9 times larger than adolescent-only programs. In a more recent review of adolescent outpatient substance abuse treatments, Becker and Curry (2008) found ecological family therapy (i.e., multisystemic therapy, multidimensional family therapy [MDFT], family systems network, ecologically based family therapy) to be the most evaluated therapy, with seven studies examining its effects, and three demonstrating superior outcomes to other active treatment conditions. However, they also note that three other studies found ecological models to have comparable outcomes with those of treatment as usual in the community as well as those of integrated models of CBT and motivational enhancement therapy.

In MDFT, treatment focuses not only on the adolescent patient but also on the individuals and systems that intersect to exert a meaningful influence in the adolescent's life. Application of this approach results in individual and family therapy sessions, with the therapist working as a liaison between homes and schools, religious organizations, courts and juvenile systems, and community organizations (Liddle & Hogue, 2001). A therapist working from the MDFT framework will focus on several areas, including the adolescent, the adolescent's parents and family, interactions between the adolescent and the family, and outside systems. Across each of these areas, the goal is to improve communication and foster collaboration (Liddle & Hogue, 2001). In a randomized study comparing MDFT, multifamily educational intervention, and adolescent group treatment with substance abusing adolescents between the ages of 13 and 18, MDFT was found to have the strongest effects in terms of lowered substance use and improved family and academic functioning (Liddle et al., 2001). Additional randomized controlled research comparing MDFT and CBT with drug-using adolescents who were, on average, 15 years old, found that both treatments reduced substance use problem severity and cannabis use at 1-month follow-up, but MDFT showed stronger lasting effects at 6- and 12-month follow-up periods (Liddle, Dakof, Turner, Henderson, & Greenbaum, 2008). Hendriks, van der Schee, & Blanken (2011) also compared MDFT and CBT in a Dutch sample of 109 adolescents with a cannabis use disorder, and found the two interventions to be equally effective, with substantial reductions during the first 3 months, but no further reductions in the 9 months to follow. Treatment intensity and retention were significantly higher in MDFT than in CBT.

Building on our discussion of theoretical models describing the processes underlying both the etiology and maintenance of adolescents' and young adults' substance abuse behaviors and our brief overview of the preventive interventions that have been informed by these theoretical models, we now review the literature on moderators and mediators of adolescent and young adult treatment outcomes. Each discussion is organized by the two theoretical models we have discussed, as well as the developmental domains that fall under each of these theoretical models.

EMPIRICAL RESULTS OF MODERATION AND MEDIATION STUDIES IN ADOLESCENT SUBSTANCE ABUSE PREVENTIVE INTERVENTION STUDIES

Evidence for Moderators of Substance Use Treatment Outcomes

By and large, research on moderators for adolescent substance abuse preventive interventions is scant (Kazdin, 2001; Strada, Donohue, &Lefforge, 2006). When moderators are examined, analyses have typically been limited to examining the effects of demographic variables, including age, gender, and race/ethnicity, with mixed results observed for each of these variables. For ethnicity and race, Robbins et al. (2008) reported that structural ecosystems therapy, a family-based ecological approach, was more effective than control groups in reducing drug use in Hispanic-American but not African-American adolescents. In a meta-analysis of evidence-based psychosocial treatments for adolescent substance abuse, Waldron and Turner (2008) suggested that family-based interventions may be more efficacious than CBT interventions for Hispanic substance using participants. Further, Clair et al. (2013) investigated the moderating effects of ethnicity on outcomes of a motivational enhancement therapy (MET) intervention for substance-using incarcerated adolescents and found that Hispanic adolescents who received MET reported significant reductions in drinking but not marijuana use as compared to Hispanic adolescents in the control condition. Contributing to these mixed findings, Liddle and colleagues (2009) compared MDFT to a peer group intervention with 130 adolescents between the ages of 11 and 15 years who had been referred for outpatient substance abuse treatment. While results demonstrated superior effectiveness of MDFT over the 12-month follow-up in reducing substance use frequency and problems, delinquency, and internalized distress, and in reducing risk in family, peer, and school domains, these findings were not moderated by ethnicity or age or gender.

Findings are similarly mixed for age and gender. For instance, Henggeler, Pickrel, and Brondino (1999) examined whether demographic variables moderated the outcomes of multisystemic therapy (MST). Moderator analyses revealed that MST was highly effective for female adolescents in decreasing drug use from pre- to post-treatment when compared to treatment as usual. Yet, by 6 months post-treatment, while drug use among female adolescents in family-based therapy had decreased substantially, no such effects were evident for males in either condition or females in the comparison condition. Monti et al. (1999) found no interaction effects between gender and treatment condition when examining the potential moderating role of gender in the outcomes of an RCT conducted in emergency rooms for 18- and 19-year-olds with an alcohol-related event. Similarly, gender also did not moderate the outcomes of an RCT testing the effectiveness of MET to reduce smoking among 81 adjudicated adolescents (Helstrom, Hutchison, & Bryan, 2007). Across a number of indicated preventive intervention studies in college samples, MET has generally demonstrated equivalent effectiveness for men and women (Carey, Henson, Carey, & Maisto, 2009, Marlatt et al., 1998; Wood, Capone, Laforge, Erickson, & Brand, 2007).

In a review conducted by Wagner (2008), only three published studies examining the effect of age on adolescents' response to treatment were identified, with all three reporting no differences among adolescents between the ages of 12 and 19 years (Kelly, Meyers, & Brown, 2000; Blood & Cornwall, 1994; Winters, Stinchfield, Opland, Weller, & Latimer, 2000).Yet, when comparing the efficacy of CBT to MDFT among cannabis abusing or dependent adolescents in The Netherlands, Hendriks, van der Schee, and Blanken (2012) conducted analysis to examine moderators of between groups effects and found that older adolescents (17–18 years old) showed greater mean reductions in cannabis use days from CBT compared to MDFT, while younger adolescents (13–16 years old) showed greater reductions in MDFT than in CBT conditions. Given these inconsistent findings, some have argued that age is an inaccurate proxy of developmental status given that adolescents of the same chronological age may vary greatly in terms of emotional, physical, social, and cognitive functioning (Holmbeck et al., 2003; Wagner, 2003; Wagner et al., 2008). The same can be said regarding race and ethnicity, with proponents of culturally adapted treatments stressing the importance of considering variables that both acknowledge within-group heterogeneity and explain relations between ethnicity/race and treatment outcomes (Alvidrez, Azocar, & Miranda, 1996). Consequently, more recent treatment outcome studies have begun to examine variables that go beyond demographic variables (e.g., age, gender, and race/ethnicity) and are developmentally appropriate to examine with adolescents. These include constructs within the biological, psychological, and social/contextual domains of adolescent development (Wagner, 2008).

Biopsychosocial Moderators

BIOLOGICAL MODERATORS

With the exception of the fetal/neonatal period of development, adolescence is a time of unsurpassed physical growth and change (Hollenstein & Lougheed, 2013). Potential developmental variables that may influence adolescents' response to substance abuse interventions include pubertal status and timing, hormonal changes, and neurological and brain development (Holmbeck & Updegrove, 1995; Wagner, 2008). Unfortunately, potential moderators within this developmental domain have received virtually no attention in the adolescent substance abuse treatment literature, with most studies focusing on the associations between these variables and adolescent substance use involvement rather than adolescent intervention response (Wagner 2008).

NEUROCOGNITIVE DEVELOPMENT

Recently, interest in examining how pre-existing individual differences in adolescent neurocognitive capacities influence substance abuse intervention outcomes has grown. While the literature in this area is very limited, one study investigated whether individual variation in neurobiological mechanisms associated with substance abuse moderated outcomes of a brief preventive intervention, Positive Adolescent Choice Training, when compared to an assessment-only condition among a sample of male adolescents (Fishbein et al., 2006). Neurocognitive and emotional regulatory functions, as well as conduct disorder, moderated adolescents' social competency skills (e.g., emotional composure, interpersonal communication, and conflict-resolution skills). Specifically, within this sample of male adolescents, those who exhibited lower levels of specific executive cognitive function abilities and emotional perception responded less favorably to the preventive intervention, that is, they demonstrated lower social competency skills at follow-up, when compared to adolescents with higher levels of function. These initial findings support the hypothesis that pre-existing neurocognitive proficiency may enhance intervention outcomes, whereas neurocognitive deficiencies may temper intervention effects.

PSYCHOLOGICAL MODERATORS

Perhaps receiving more research attention than biological developmental factors are the potential moderating effects of adolescent cognitive and psychological factors on the efficacy and effectiveness of substance abuse intervention outcomes. Constructs within this domain of adolescent development include but are not limited to cognitive development and problem-solving, severity of substance use, self-regulation, personality, and other psychiatric disorders. The effect of cognitive development as well as problem-solving variables are particularly relevant given the popularity of CBT and the growing popularity of motivational interventions for addressing substance use among adolescents (e.g., D'Amico et al., 2005). As previously discussed, CBT and motivational interventions are based on assumptions that individuals are capable of choosing their response to circumstances and, with the appropriate guidance and motivation, will be able to make adaptive changes in their lives. Because the self provides the impetus for change in these interventions, it may be assumed that such interventions require some degree of self-development that allows adolescents to assume responsibility for self-directed change, and requires some degree of cognitive processing that will allow adolescents to evaluate self-relevant information and help them make choices in their health-related behaviors (Grimley, Prochaska, Velicer, Blais, &

DiClemente, 1994; Kellogg, 1993). These assumptions then pose the question as to whether CBT and motivational interventions are appropriate for adolescents who have yet to fully develop such skills. For which adolescents do these interventions actually work—or work best?

PERSONALITY

An area that has received a little bit more attention is that of adolescent personality and temperament. Using data from the RCT comparing CBT to psycho-education mentioned above, Burleson and Kaminer (2008) examined the moderating role of adolescents' temperament on treatment outcomes, and found that adolescents with a more difficult temperament (poor regulation of sleep, appetite, and daily activity) who were assigned to the psycho-education condition showed relatively more reduction in alcohol but not in psychological distress or other substance use. Those with better levels of rhythmicity (e.g., the regularity/irregularity of biological functioning such as eating, sleeping, and daily activity) showed improvement for psychological function with CBT. In recognition of the moderating role of personality, researchers have begun developing and implementing adolescent-based personalized substance abuse prevention programs based on selected adolescent risk profiles (Conrod et al., 2006). Conrod and colleagues suggest that while this personality-targeted intervention may not result in changes in personality traits (e.g., impulsivity, sensation seeking, anxiety), it does seem to change how personality risk factors influence substance use. This work builds on prior research on demonstrating a moderating role for personality and provides evidence that adolescents may be more amenable to interventions that are tailored to their specific personality-related risks (Conrod, Castellanos-Ryan, & Strang, 2010).

READINESS TO CHANGE

An individual's readiness to change as a potential moderator has become the focus of attention with the increased popularity of motivational interventions. Barnett et al. (2010) found that young adults' readiness to change their alcohol use moderated the results of an MET intervention delivered in an emergency department. Specifically, young adults who demonstrated low or moderate levels of readiness to change had better alcohol use outcomes if they received the MET intervention rather than a feedback-only control condition. Further, in examining the efficacy of a web-based brief alcohol intervention among a sample of Dutch college students, Voogt, Poelen, Kleinjan, Lemmers, and Engels (2013) found no significant main effects of the web-based intervention on any of the indicators of alcohol use at follow-up. However, they were able to identify specific subgroups of college students who benefited from the web-based intervention more than others through moderator analyses. These analyses demonstrated that heavy drinking college students with higher levels of readiness to change benefited the most from the web-based intervention when compared to their control counterparts.

DRINKING AND DRUG USE SEVERITY

Researchers have recommended using substance use severity as a potential variable for matching adolescents and young adults to substance abuse interventions (Winters, 1999) given studies demonstrating its predictive effect on intervention outcomes (Henderson, Dakof, Greenbaum, & Liddle, 2010; Spirito et al., 2011). Yet, findings from moderator analyses have been inconsistent. As mentioned above, drinking severity moderated the effects of a web-based intervention among a sample of Dutch college students (Voogt et al., 2013). Similarly, among a sample of severe cannabis users, adolescents with high baseline substance use problem severity and high psychiatric severity showed greater reductions of cannabis use with MDFT than CBT (Hendriks et al., 2011). In contrast, Winters et al. (2012) compared the efficacy of two brief school-based substance use interventions (brief intervention with adolescent versus brief intervention with adolescent and parent) to an assessment-only condition and found no significant interactions with the two active treatment conditions and baseline drug use severity. Some have speculated that these inconsistent findings may be due to variation in definitions of severity and sample selection issues with regard to alcohol and drug problem severity (Blow et al., 2009). As a result, the literature remains unclear as to the extent to which baseline substance use problem severity may moderate a young person's response to an intervention.

COMORBIDITY

Research indicates that adolescents with comorbid substance use and psychiatric disorders are at increased risk of not completing treatment (Kaminer, Burleson, Goldston, & Burke, 2006; Kaminer, Tartar, Bukstein, & Kabene, 1992; Myers, Stewart, & Brown, 1998) and have poorer treatment outcomes (Grella, Hser, Joshi, & Rounds-Bryant, 2001; White et al., 2004). Yet, findings on the moderating effects of comorbid conditions have been inconsistent. For example, Kaminer and others (1992) found poorer outcomes for individuals with comorbid diagnosis of substance use and conduct disorders than those with adjustment disorders and affective disorders, while another study suggested that CBT may be beneficial for adolescents with a comorbid diagnosis of a substance use disorder and depression (Birmaher et al., 2000). In an RCT with dually diagnosed adolescent substance abusers, Kaminer, Burleson, Blitz, Sussman, and Rounsaville (1998) hypothesized that patients with externalizing disorders would have better substance use outcomes in a group CBT, whereas those with internalizing disorders without co-occurring externalizing disorders would benefit more from interactional group treatment. Contrary to these hypotheses, no significant matching effects were identified. In another RCT, neither externalizing disorders nor internalizing disorders moderated CBT intervention outcomes (Kaminer et al., 2002). In a direct comparison RCT of the effectiveness of MDFT and CBT for adolescent drug abusers, Rowe, Liddle, Greenbaum, and Henderson (2004) compared outcomes of four adolescent groups: (1) adolescents with only a substance use diagnosis; (2) adolescents with a comorbid internalizing disorder; (3) adolescents with a comorbid externalizing disorder;

and (4) adolescents with both a comorbid internalizing and externalizing disorder. While the shape of the substance use change trajectories from baseline to 12-month follow-up differed substantially among the comorbidity subgroups, these effects were not moderated by treatment condition, age, or gender. In order to determine whether baseline characteristics predicted treatment outcomes, Hendriks, van der Schee, and Blanken (2012) re-examined data from a previous RCT (Hendriks et al., 2011) that demonstrated no significant differences between MDFT to CBT in adolescents who met criteria for cannabis abuse or dependence. Results from this study demonstrated that along with age, conduct disorder/oppositional defiant disorder and internalizing problems differentially moderated baseline to 12-month changes in cannabis use. Specifically, younger adolescents (13–16 years old) and adolescents with conduct disorder/ oppositional defiant disorder or internalizing problems in MDFT demonstrated greater reductions in cannabis use. Conversely, greater cannabis use reductions were seen in older adolescents (17–18 years old) and adolescents without conduct disorder/oppositional defiant disorder or internalizing problems in CBT. These inconsistent findings highlight the need for additional research involving adolescents with psychological comorbidity to better identify the treatments most effective for them.

SOCIAL AND CONTEXTUAL MODERATORS

Most cognitive behavioral and motivational interventions seek to present individuals with essential skills to change their problem behaviors. Those developed for adolescents also have broader goals of fostering the comprehensive changes needed to work against the robust social influences that support problem behaviors in adolescents' lives, including their peer networks, families, and social contexts.

FAMILIAL CONTEXTS

An individual's social context undergoes many changes during adolescence, and these changes may influence an adolescent's response to treatment. For instance, an adolescent's familial context shifts from dependence to interdependence, with the adolescent increasingly participating in family decision-making processes. However, most research has focused on understanding the mediating role that family context plays on adolescent substance abuse treatment outcomes, rather than the moderating role. One RCT examining the efficacy of Familias Unidas, a Hispanic-specific family-based intervention for externalizing behavior problems, substance use, and sexual risk-taking, found that family context moderated Hispanic adolescents' outcomes. Specifically, Prado et al. (2013) clustered adolescents into three risk subgroups (i.e., low, moderate, and high risk) according to the number of baseline contextual risk factors. Results demonstrated that Familias Unidas was efficacious, relative to a community practice control condition, for Hispanic adolescents in the high-risk group, that is, those reporting poor parent-adolescent communication, low parental involvement, poor family cohesion, and low family support, but not for Hispanic adolescents in the moderate- or low-risk groups. Prado et al.'s (2013) results suggest that classifying adolescents according to level of contextual risk may not only be an effective strategy for examining moderators of family-based preventive interventions but also could provide information for tailoring these interventions to be congruent with adolescents' risk levels.

CULTURAL CONTEXTS

Variables that go beyond race and ethnicity and capture within-group variability as well as help explain the inconsistent findings regarding race and ethnicity as moderators of treatment outcomes include levels of acculturation, language, perceived discrimination, and racial/ethnic identity, salience, and pride. Santisteban et al. (1996) found that non-acculturated Cuban Hispanic families were significantly more likely to engage in treatment than more acculturated Cuban Hispanic families. Gil, Wagner, and Tubman (2004) found that among US-born Hispanic youth in Miami, baseline levels of ethnic orientation and ethnic pride were associated positively with greater reductions in alcohol use. Another study found that therapist-client ethnic matching moderated treatment outcomes for Hispanic adolescents, but not for white, non-Hispanic adolescents (Flicker, Waldron, Turner, Brody, & Hops, 2008). Given that most of these studies have been conducted among Hispanic populations, research focusing on other ethnic/racial groups is warranted so that interventions can be refined to not only be developmentally appropriate but also culturally appropriate.

Summary

Despite research on moderators of adolescent substance abuse treatment outcomes being scant, new research findings have begun to emerge. As researchers begin to consider the inclusion of developmentally appropriate variables in substance abuse treatment efficacy studies, the potential for understanding and identifying which adolescents benefit most (or least) from participating in substance abuse preventive interventions and under what conditions will grow as well. For instance, literature identifying moderator variables that go beyond the typical age, gender, and race/ethnicity-related variables has begun to emerge. To date, these include variables within adolescents' cognitive development, social and cultural context, psychological development, and, most recently, neurocognitive capabilities. However, while identifying moderators that are non-malleable to intervention are important (Kraemer et al., 1997) given that they can be used to select a subpopulation that is at risk or can inform the adaptation of existing interventions, identifying mediating factors that are amenable to interventions is equally important because they can be targeted as important mechanisms for facilitating treatment-related change.

EVIDENCE FOR MEDIATORS OF SUBSTANCE USE TREATMENT OUTCOMES

Like the literature on moderators, extant knowledge of mediators of adolescent substance abuse treatment outcomes is modest. Below we review this small but growing body of work, with a particular emphasis on mediators informed by theoretical models of adolescent substance use and related to adolescent development. Given the importance of consideration of temporal sequencing for drawing strong inferences about mediated effects, we include information about the timing of measurement from intervention to mediator(s) to outcomes.

Biopsychosocial Variables

PSYCHOLOGICAL MEDIATORS

Recent evidence demonstrates that changes in young people's cognitive representations often mediate changes in substance use. Winters, Fahnhorst, Botzet, Lee, and Lalone (2012) recruited 315 high school students who had been identified as engaging in substance use and randomized them into one of three conditions: (1) a two-session adolescent-only brief MET; (2) a two-session adolescent brief MET plus a one-session parent MET addressing their teen's substance use, parent monitoring and supervision, and healthy parent drug use behaviors and attitudes; or (3) an assessment-only condition. The majority of the adolescents in this sample met *DSM-IV* criteria for alcohol use disorder, cannabis use disorder, or both. While results showed that the two active conditions demonstrated significant reductions in substance use from pre-test to 6-month follow-up when compared to the assessment-only control condition, the group that received the additional parent session exhibited greater and more consistent intervention effects at 6-month follow-up, yet parenting practices assessed at 6 months *did not* mediate adolescent outcomes at the same follow-up point. However, adolescent problem-solving and seeking additional services assessed at 6-month follow-up *did* mediate 6-month treatment outcomes in both active conditions. Therefore, changes in adolescents' problem-solving from baseline to post-intervention seemed to be an important mechanism for intervention-related change among this adolescent sample.

Motivation has also been identified as a putative mediator of adolescents' response to substance abuse interventions. For instance, in a cluster-randomized trial aimed at increasing motivation to quit smoking, McCuller et al. (2006) found that changes in motivation from pre- to post-intervention mediated intervention effects on adolescent smoking outcomes at 3-month follow-up, with 26% of the intervention effect accounted for by increases in motivation to quit smoking. Similarly, Kelly, Myers, and Brown (2000) found that relations between 12-step meeting attendance in the 3 months following inpatient treatment and abstinence at 6-month follow-up were mediated by changes in changes in baseline to

3-month motivation for abstinence. However, changes in self-efficacy and coping did not mediate relations between 12-step meeting attendance and 6-month abstinence. These studies suggest that maintaining and enhancing motivation for change is an important aim for substance use interventions.

While Kelly et al. (2000) found no evidence for self-efficacy as a mediator, a cluster randomized trial conducted in 50 public high schools ($N = 2,151$) examined a number of social cognitive mediators of a motivational intervention (MI) and cognitive behavioral skills training (CBST) telephone-delivered intervention on smoking cessation among 17–18-year-old smokers (Bricker, Liu, Comstock, Peterson, Kealey, & Marek, 2010). Results demonstrated that the intervention led to increased levels of self-efficacy to resist smoking in social and stressful situations at 12-month follow-up, which in turn predicted increased levels of smoking cessation at the same follow-up. Specifically, self-efficacy to resist smoking in stressful situations statistically mediated 56.9% of the intervention's effect.

Social and Contextual Mediators

FAMILIAL CONTEXT

A number of effective prevention and treatment models have been developed based on the core assumption that changes in family environment can prompt reductions in adolescent substance abuse behaviors. In fact, research has demonstrated that parenting and family factors respond to intervention (Steinberg, Fletcher, & Darling, 1994), and parenting can have an impact even after substance abuse behaviors have been initiated or have become established (Connell, Dishion, Yasui, & Kavanagh, 2007), thus making parenting variables important intervention targets for reducing adolescent substance abuse.

To examine whether parenting practices mediated results from an earlier RCT, Henderson, Rowe, Dakof, Hawes, and Liddle (2009) re-examined data collected from 83 adolescents who were randomized to receive either MDFT or a peer group treatment condition to determine whether the effects of MDFT on increased abstinence from substance use at 6- and 12-month follow-up were mediated by improvements in parental monitoring from intake to treatment discharge. Despite the small sample size, mediation analyses indicated a marginally significant indirect effect for parental monitoring on MDFT–substance use abstinence relations, suggesting, consistent with prior research on MDFT effects on delinquency (Huey, Henggeler, Brondino & Pickrel, 2000), that parental monitoring and family functioning more generally are important mechanisms of change in MDFT. In a universal preventive intervention study of 2,937 Dutch early adolescents, Konining, van den Eijnden, Engles, Verdurmen and Vollebergh (2011) examined whether changes in parental attitudes and rules about alcohol from baseline to 10-month follow-up mediated the effects of a parent, student, or combined parent-student intervention on the onset of drinking at 22-month follow-up. For both the parent and combined intervention, parent rules about alcohol were significant mediators. Of note, for the combined condition, adolescent-reported self-control at 10 months also mediated intervention effects. Alternatively, a parent-based universal intervention targeting alcohol onset and growth in drinking over 22 months among late adolescents ($N = 1,014$ matriculating US college students) found no support for intervention-targeted mediators of parental permissiveness for drinking, parental disapproval of drinking, parental monitoring, or alcohol-related communication assessed at baseline and 10-month follow-up (Wood et al., 2010).

SOCIAL SUPPORT

In secondary analyses of post-treatment substance use and problems, self-help group participation and the degree of social support from family, friends, and professionals have been identified as potential mediators of treatment response (Godley, Kahn, Dennis, Godley, & Funk, 2005). Similarly, in a study of 162 treated adolescents 4 years after discharge, Brown, D'Amico, McCarthy, and Tapert (2001) found that adolescents who were classified as *abstainers* or *users* (no heavy episodic drinking or major relapse episodes) were significantly more likely to have higher and more appropriate levels of social support (family and peers) than the more substance-involved groups (slow *improvers, worse with time,* and *continuous heavy use* groups). Similarly, Chi, Kaskutas, Sterling, Campbell, and Weisner (2009) conducted a secondary analysis of longitudinal data collected from 419 adolescents between the ages of 13 and 18 entering chemical dependency treatment. The authors examined 12-step affiliation and its association with substance use outcomes 3 years post-treatment intake, as well as the potential mediating effects of social support and religious service attendance, also assessed 3 years post-treatment, on 12-step affiliation and substance use abstinence relations. Results of mediation analyses indicated that social support mediated both alcohol and drug abstinence outcomes, while religious service attendance only mediated the drug abstinence outcome. It is important to note that the studies reviewed in this subsection, while informative regarding the potential role of social support as a mediator of adolescent treatment outcomes, do not constitute empirical support. More definitive conclusions require the examination of changes in social support in response to interventions that target this construct, measuring it at intervening period(s), and conducting explicit tests of mediation for subsequent outcomes.

Social Cognitive Variables

In recognition of the important role that alcohol expectancies play in adolescent and young adults' drinking, Wood, Capone, Laforge, Erickson, and Brand (2007) examined the unique and combined effects of a motivational intervention (MI) and an alcohol expectancy challenge (AEC) on heavy drinking college students' ($N = 335$) alcohol-related use and problem trajectories at 1-, 3-, and 6-month follow-ups. Putative mediators were measured at baseline and 1-month follow-up and included perceived norms, self-regulation, and motivation to change (for MI) and alcohol expectancies (for AEC). MI intervention effects were mediated by changes in perceived norms but not self-regulation or motivation to change. AEC intervention effects were significant at 1 and 3 months but exhibited decay by 6-month follow-up. Alcohol expectancies were not altered by the AEC intervention and did not mediate observed intervention effects. Wiers, van de Luitgaarden, van den Wildenberg, and Smulders (2005) conducted an alcohol expectancy challenge with 92 heavy-drinking college students and found, for men, AEC reduced drinking at one of the four weekly follow-ups (week 3) and this effect was mediated by changes in pre- to post- (1 week) alcohol expectancies. Given the generally modest, inconsistent, and relatively transient direct and mediated effects of AEC (see Scott-Sheldon, Terry, K. Carey, Garey, and M. Carey, 2012) and consistent with the emergence of dual process approaches detailed earlier, research examining the direct and indirect effects of interventions targeting adolescents' implicit cognitions could constitute an important advancement.

Summary

Our review of the literature on mediators of adolescent substance abuse treatment outcomes clearly demonstrates that this area of research is still in its very early stages. While *some* research has provided clues to mechanisms of change associated with adolescents' self-efficacy, motivation, problem-solving, and substance-related expectancies and their social context, including their peer networks, familial context, and social support, basic questions regarding the process, mechanism, or means of treatment-related change remain unaddressed (Kazdin, 2001). However, as briefly detailed next, this provides a number of opportunities for future research to identify mechanisms of change, which in turn can inform the development and implementation of interventions by intensifying and refining active ingredients which can yield greater effects (Kraemer, Wilson, Fairburn, & Agras, 2002).

CHALLENGES AND RECOMMENDATIONS

In contrast to the adult addictions literature, adolescent substance abuse treatment outcomes research to date has paid relatively little attention to identifying potential moderators and mediators of treatment-related change, with more attention focused on demonstrating direct intervention effects on key substance abuse outcomes. While identifying treatments that work with this developmentally vulnerable population is an important and necessary first step, problems emerge when there is a sole focus on treatment outcomes, particularly short-term outcomes (Kazdin, 1998, 2001). For instance, research demonstrates that 60%–70% of young people relapse 1 year after completing treatment (Brown, Vik, & Creamer, 1989; Godley, Godley, Dennis, Funk, & Passetti, 2002; White,

2008), and over half of adolescents who receive residential care return within 1 month of treatment completion (Chung & Maisto, 2006). Therefore, without better understanding of factors that make a young person more or less amenable and responsive to treatment and what therapeutic mechanisms lead to change, it is unlikely that treatments that may have proven to be successful in producing short-term outcomes will be able to maintain such outcomes in the longer term (Wagner, 2008). Second, given individual differences in adolescents' and young adults' risk profiles and the developmental variation that may exist, no one substance abuse intervention will be universally effective. Therefore, it is essential to gain an understanding of factors that will help explain which interventions work best for whom, and what active intervention ingredients could be refined or enhanced to yield behavioral change in specific individuals. As was demonstrated in Prado et al.'s (2013) study, given that certain active ingredients may actually produce benefits for different adolescents and young adults exhibiting different risk profiles, research on both moderators and mediators cannot be understood independently from one another. Identifying moderators and the mechanisms through which moderators may operate can improve treatment outcomes by providing better triage of adolescents and young adults to treatments from which they are most likely to benefit (Kazdin, 2003).

CONCLUSIONS AND CLINICAL IMPLICATIONS

Research into treatment effects on adolescent substance use disorders and their moderators and mediators is an emerging field, in which little consistent findings can be reported. Nonetheless, we present some tentative conclusions and clinical implications, with the recognition that they are not strongly supported by the literature, and should primarily be seen as guiding hypotheses for future research that can replicate and extend the nascent literature on moderators and mediators of adolescent preventive interventions. First, both in prevention (e.g., Koning et al., 2009; Koning et al., 2011) and in treatment research (e.g., Hendriks et al., 2011, 2012; Winter et al., 2011), there is evidence that including parents in the intervention is especially beneficial with early to mid-adolescents, which is consistent with developmental theory and research on adolescent substance use. In older adolescents, individual-focused CBT and/or MET might be more (cost-)efficient (Hendriks et al., 2011, 2012). In this group, there is also some evidence pointing to an enhancing effect of peer-group sessions (as provided in AA), provided that they include same-age peers (Kelly et al., 2005). Second, explicit alcohol-related cognitions (expectancies, motives) are generally discussed in MET/CBT, but relatively little is known about the potential mediating role of these variables in adolescent treatment outcome studies. As noted, interventions targeting automatically activated or implicit cognitive processes, which can be addressed using varieties of cognitive bias modification paradigms, have demonstrated success in adults (Wiers et al., 2011; Wiers et al., 2013). The direct and indirect effects of these types of interventions remain to be tested in adolescents, which may be a group that are less amenable to this type of cognitive training, given the weak motivation to change that they often exhibit. Third, motivation to change, self-efficacy, and problem-solving have received some support as mediators of adolescent interventions for SUDs. Thus, interventions that focus on enhancing motivation for change and self-efficacy seem promising for adolescents and young adults. Fourth, social context, including peer networks, familial context, and social support have been shown to be important correlates of substance use outcomes, thus suggesting a need for post-discharge treatment plans or aftercare to maintain treatment gains, along with explicit tests of these factors as mediators of longer term intervention effects. Apart from age, little is known about moderators of adolescent treatment for SUDs. There is emerging research into the study of developmentally appropriate and cultural moderators, which constitutes an important development in this field. Interestingly, the adjacent field of targeted intervention has shown promising results with a personality-based approach (Conrod et al., 2010; Conrod et al., 2011), which may be successfully extended to adolescent treatment. Similarly, emerging findings demonstrating that pre-existing neurocognitive proficiencies or deficiencies may alter intervention effects highlight the need for further research to be conducted in this area to further inform which intervention modalities may be most cognitively appropriate for use with adolescents (Lopez, Schwartz, Prado, Campo, & Pantin, 2008). In addition to the central role of theory, as discussed in the earlier chapters of this book and elsewhere (Hoyle & Robinson, 2004; MacKinnon, 2008), careful consideration of design, measurement, and analysis issues are also critical for optimizing tests of moderation and mediation to maximally advance current knowledge. We hope this chapter will help to stimulate this needed conceptual and methodological development in the area of adolescent substance abuse preventive interventions.

ACKNOWLEDGMENTS

During the production process of this chapter, our co-author Prof. Dr. Mark Wood unexpectedly passed away. The remaining authors would like to dedicate this chapter to our fond memories of a great colleague, collaborator, mentor and most of all a true friend.

REFERENCES

Alvidrez, J., Azocar, F., & Miranda, J. (1996). Demystifying the concept of ethnicity for psychotherapy researchers. *Journal of Consulting and Clinical Psychology, 64*(5), 903–908.

American Psychiatric Association. (2013). *Diagnostic and statistical manual of mental disorders* (5th ed.). Arlington, VA: American Psychiatric Publishing.

Andrews, J. A., Hops, H., Ary, D., Tildesley, E., & Harris, J. (1993). Parental influence on early adolescent substance use specific and nonspecific effects. *The Journal of Early Adolescence, 13*(3), 285–310.

Armstrong, T. D., & Costello, E. J. (2002). Community studies on adolescent substance use, abuse, or dependence and psychiatric comorbidity. *Journal of Consulting and Clinical Psychology, 70*(6),1224–1239.

Barnett, N. P., Apodaca, T., Magill, M., Colby, S. M., Gwaltney, C., Rohsenow, D. J., & Monti, P. M. (2010). Moderators and mediators of two brief interventions for alcohol in the emergency department. *Addiction, 105*, 452–465.

Beccaria, F., & White, H. R. (2012). Underage drinking in Europe and North America. In P. D. Witte & M. C. Mitchell (Eds.), *Underage drinking: A report on drinking in the second decade of life in Europe and North America* (pp. 21–78). Louvain-la-Neuve, Belgium: Presses Universitaires de Louvain.

Bechara, A. (2005). Decision making, impulse control and loss of willpower to resist drugs: A neurocognitive perspective. *Nature Neuroscience, 8*(11), 1458–1463.

Becker, S. J., & Curry, J. F. (2008). Outpatient interventions for adolescent substance abuse: A quality of evidence review. *Journal of Consulting and Clinical Psychology, 76*(4), 531–543.

Bennett, G. G., Wolin, K. Y., Robinson, E. L., Fowler, S., & Edwards, C. L. (2005). Perceived racial/ethnic harassment and tobacco use among African American young adults. *American Journal of Public Health, 95*(2), 238–240.

Birmaher, B., Brent, D. A., Kolko, D., Baugher, M., Bridge, J., Holder, D., . . . Ulloa, R. E. (2000). Clinical outcome after short-term psychotherapy for adolescents with major depressive disorder. *Archives of General Psychiatry, 57*(1), 29–36.

Blood, L., & Cornwall, A. (1994). Pretreatment variables that predict completion of an adolescent substance abuse treatment program. *Journal of Nervous and Mental Disease, 182*(1), 14–19.

Blow, F. C., Ilgen, M. A., Walton, M. A., Czyz, E. K., McCammon, R., Chermack, S. T., . . . & Barry, K. L. (2009). Severity of baseline alcohol use as a moderator of brief interventions in the emergency department. *Alcohol and Alcoholism, 44*(5), 486–490.

Borduin, C. M., Mann, B. J., Cone, L. T., Henggeler, S. W., Fucci, B. R., Blaske, D. M., & Williams, R. A. (1995). Multisystemic treatment of serious juvenile offenders: long-term prevention of criminality and violence. *Journal of Consulting and Clinical Psychology, 63*(4), 569.

Bricker, J. B., Liu, J., Comstock, B. A., Peterson, A. V., Kealey, K. A., & Marek, P. M. (2010). Social cognitive mediators of adolescent smoking cessation: Results from a large randomized intervention trial. *Psychology of Addictive Behaviors, 24*(3), 436–445.

Bronfenbrenner, U., & Morris, P. A. (1998). The ecology of developmental processes. *Handbook of Child Psychology, 1*, 993–1028.

Brown, S. A., D'Amico, E. J., McCarthy, D., & Tapert, S. F. (2001). Four year outcomes from adolescent alcohol and drug treatment. *Journal of Studies on Alcohol, 62*(3), 381–388.

Brown, S. A., Goldman, M. S., & Christiansen, B. A. (1985). Do alcohol expectancies mediate drinking patterns of adults? *Journal of Consulting and Clinical Psychology, 53*(4), 512.

Brown, S. A., McGue, M., Maggs, J., Schulenberg, J., Hingson, R., Swartzwelder, S., . . . Murphy, S. (2008). A developmental perspective on alcohol and youths 16 to 20 years of age. *Pediatrics, 121*, S290–S310.

Brown, S. A., Vik, P. W., & Creamer, V. A. (1989). Characteristics of relapse following adolescent substance abuse treatment. *Addictive Behaviors, 14*(3), 291–300.

Bucholz, K. K., Heath, A. C., & Madden, P. A. (2000). Transitions in drinking in adolescent females: Evidence from the Missouri adolescent female twin study. *Alcoholism, Clinical and Experimental Research, 24*(6), 914–923.

Burk, W. J., Vorst, H. V. D., Kerr, M., & Stattin, H. (2011). Alcohol use and friendship dynamics: Selection and socialization in early-, middle-, and late-adolescent peer networks. *Journal of Studies on Alcohol and Drugs, 73*(1), 89.

Burleson, J. A., & Kaminer, Y. (2008). Does temperament moderate treatment response in adolescent substance use disorders? *Substance Abuse, 29*, 89–95.

Caetano, R., & Raspberry, K. (2000). Drinking and DSM-IV alcohol and drug dependence among white and Mexican-American DUI offenders. *Journal of Studies on Alcohol and Drugs, 61*(3), 420.

Carey, K. B., Henson, J. M., Carey, M. P., & Maisto, S. A. (2009). Computer versus in-person intervention for students violating campus alcohol policy. *Journal of Consulting and Clinical Psychology, 77*, 74–87.

Caspi, A., Moffitt, T. E., Newman, D. L., & Silva, P. A. (1996). Behavioral observations at age 3 years predict adult psychiatric disorders: Longitudinal evidence from a birth cohort. *Archives of General Psychiatry, 53*(11), 1033–1039.

Castro, F. G., Stein, J. A., & Bentler, P. M. (2009). Ethnic pride, traditional family values, and acculturation in early cigarette and alcohol use among Latino adolescents. *The Journal of Primary Prevention, 30*(3–4), 265–292.

Chassin, L., Pillow, D. R., Curran, P. J., Molina, B. S., & Barrera, M., Jr. (1993). Relation of parental alcoholism to early adolescent substance use: A test of three mediating mechanisms. *Journal of Abnormal Psychology, 102*(1), 3–19.

Chen, K., & Kandel, D. B. (1995). The natural history of drug use from adolescence to the mid-thirties in a general population sample. *American Journal of Public Health, 85*(1), 41–47.

Chi, F. W., Kaskutas, L. A., Sterling, S., Campbell, C. I., &Weisner, C. (2009). Twelve-step affiliation and 3-year substance use outcomes among adolescents: social support and religious service attendance as potential mediators. *Addiction, 104*, 927–939.

Christiansen, B. A., Smith, G. T., Roehling, P. V., & Goldman, M. S. (1989). Using alcohol expectancies to predict adolescent drinking behavior after one year. *Journal of Consulting and Clinical Psychology, 57*(1), 93–99.

Chung, T. A., & Maisto, S. A. (2006). Relapse to alcohol and other drug use in treated adolescents: Review and reconsideration of relapse as a change point in clinical course. *Clinical Psychology Review, 26*, 149–161.

Clair, M., Stein, L. A., Soenksen, S., Martin, R. A., Lebeau, R., & Golembeske, C. (2013). Ethnicity as a moderator of motivational interviewing for incarcerated adolescents after release. *Journal of Substance Abuse Treatment, 45*(4), 370–375.

Cloninger, C. R., Sigvardsson, S., & Bohman, M. (1988). Childhood personality predicts alcohol abuse in young adults. *Alcoholism: Clinical and Experimental Research, 12*(4), 494–505.

Connell, A., Dishion, T., Yasui, M., & Kavanagh, K. (2007). An adaptive approach to family intervention: Linking engagement in family-centered intervention to reductions in adolescent problem behavior. *Journal of Consulting and Clinical Psychology, 75*, 568–579.

Conrod, P. J., Castellanos-Ryan, N., & Mackie, C. (2011). Long-term effects of a personality-targeted intervention to reduce alcohol use in adolescents. *Journal of Consulting and Clinical Psychology, 79*(3), 296–306.

Conrod, P. J., Castellanos-Ryan, N., & Strang, J. (2010). Brief, personality-targeted coping skills interventions and survival as a non-drug user over a 2-year period during adolescence. *Archives of General Psychiatry, 67*(1), 85–93.

Conrod, P. J., Stewart, S. H., Comeau, N., & Maclean, A. M. (2006). Efficacy of cognitive–behavioral interventions targeting personality risk factors for youth alcohol misuse. *Journal of Clinical Child and Adolescent Psychology, 35*(4), 550–563.

Cooper, M. L. (1994). Motivations for alcohol use among adolescents: Development and validation of a four-factor model. *Psychological Assessment, 6*, 117–128.

Crawford, L. A., & Novak, K. B. (2002). Parental and peer influences on adolescent drinking: The relative impact of attachment and opportunity. *Journal of Child & Adolescent Substance Abuse, 12*(1), 1–26.

Cunningham, W. A., Zelazo, P. D., Packer, D. J., & Van Bavel, J. J. (2007). The iterative reprocessing model: A multilevel framework for attitudes and evaluation. *Social Cognition, 25*(5), 736–760.

Curran, P. J., Stice, E., & Chassin, L. (1997). The relation between adolescent alcohol use and peer alcohol use: A longitudinal random coefficients model. *Journal of Consulting and Clinical Psychology, 65*(1), 130.

D'Amico, E. J., Ellickson, P. L., Wagner, E. F., Turrisi, R., Fromme, K., Ghosh-Dastidar, B., . . . Wright, D. (2005). Developmental considerations for substance use interventions from middle school through college. *Alcoholism: Clinical and Experimental Research, 29*(3), 474–483.

Deas, D., & Thomas, S. (2002). Comorbid psychiatric factors contributing to adolescent alcohol and other drug use. *Alcohol Research and Health, 26*(2), 116–121.

Dishion, T. J., & Andrews, D. W. (1995). Preventing escalation in problem behaviors with high-risk young adolescents: Immediate and 1-year outcomes. *Journal of Consulting and Clinical Psychology, 63*(4), 538.

Dishion, T. J., & McMahon, R. J. (1998). Parental monitoring and the prevention of child and adolescent problem behavior: A conceptual and empirical formulation. *Clinical Child and Family Psychology Review, 1*(1), 61–75.

Eberl, C., Wiers, R. W., Pawelczack, S., Rinck, M., Becker, E. S., & Lindenmeyer, J. (2013). Approach bias modification in alcohol dependence: Do clinical effects replicate and for whom does it work best? *Developmental Cognitive Neuroscience, 4*, 38–51.

Epstein, J. A., Botvin, G. J., & Diaz, T. (2001). Linguistic acculturation associated with higher marijuana and polydrug use among Hispanic adolescents. *Substance Use & Misuse, 36*(4), 477–499.

Evans, J. S. B. (2008). Dual-processing accounts of reasoning, judgment, and social cognition. *Annual Review of Psychology, 59*, 255–278.

Evans, J. S. B., & Stanovich, K. E. (2013). Dual-process theories of higher cognition advancing the debate. *Perspectives on Psychological Science, 8*(3), 223–241.

Fadardi, J. S., & Cox, W. M. (2009). Reversing the sequence: Reducing alcohol consumption by overcoming alcohol attentional bias. *Drug and Alcohol Dependence, 101*(3), 137–145.

Fairlie, A. M., Wood, M. D., & Laird, R. D. (2012). Prospective protective effect of parents on peer influences and college alcohol involvement. *Psychology of Addictive Behaviors, 26*(1), 30–41.

Fishbein, D. H., Hyde, C., Eldreth, D., Paschall, M. J., Hubal, R., Das, A., & Yung, B. (2006). Neurocognitive skills moderate urban male adolescents' response to preventative intervention materials. *Drug and Alcohol Dependence, 82*(1), 47–60.

Flicker, S. M., Waldron, H. B., Turner, C. W., Brody, J. L., & Hops, H. (2008). Ethnic matching and treatment outcome with Hispanic and Anglo substance-abusing adolescents in family therapy. *Journal of Family Psychology, 22*(3), 439–447.

Fromme, K., Stroot, E. A., & Kaplan, D. (1993). Comprehensive effects of alcohol: Development and psychometric assessment of a new expectancy questionnaire. *Psychological Assessment, 5*(1), 19–26.

Gawronski, B., & Bodenhausen, G. V. (2006). Associative and propositional processes in evaluation: An integrative review of implicit and explicit attitude change. *Psychological Bulletin, 132*, 692–731.

Gfroerer, J. C., & Tan, L. L. (2003). Substance use among foreign-born youths in the United States: Does the length of residence matter? *American Journal of Public Health, 93*(11), 1892–1895.

Gil, A. G., Wagner, E. F., & Tubman, J. G. (2004). Young adult consequences of early adolescent substance use: Substance use and psychiatric disorders in a multiethnic sample of males. *American Journal of Public Health, 94*(9), 1603–1609

Gil, A. G., Wagner, E. F., & Vega, W. A. (2000). Acculturation, familism, and alcohol use among Latino adolescent males: Longitudinal relations. *Journal of Community Psychology, 28*(4), 443–458.

Gladwin, T. E., Figner, B., Crone, E. A., & Wiers, R. W. (2011). Addiction, adolescence, and the integration of control and motivation. *Developmental Cognitive Neuroscience, 1*, 364–376.

Godley, M. D., Godley, S. H., Dennis, M. L., Funk, R., & Passetti, L. L. (2002). Preliminary outcomes from the assertive continuing care experiment for adolescents discharged from residential treatment. *Journal of Substance Abuse Treatment, 23*(1), 21–32.

Godley, M. D., Kahn, J. H., Dennis, M. L., Godley, S. H., & Funk, R. R. (2005). The stability and impact of environmental factors on substance use and problems after adolescent outpatient treatment for cannabis use or dependence. *Psychology of Addictive Behaviors, 19*(1), 62–70.

Goldman, M. S., Del Boca, F. K., & Darkes, J. (1999). Alcohol expectancy theory: The application of cognitive neuroscience. *Psychological Theories of Drinking and Alcoholism, 2*, 203–246.

Graham, J. W., Marks, G., & Hansen, W. B. (1991). Social influence processes affecting adolescent substance use. *Journal of Applied Psychology, 76*(2), 291.

Grella, C. E., Hser, Y. I., Joshi, V., & Rounds-Bryant, J. (2001). Drug treatment outcomes for adolescents with comorbid mental and substance use disorders. *Journal of Nervous and Mental Disease, 189*(6), 384–392.

Grenard, J. L., Ames, S. L., Wiers, R. W., Thush, C., Sussman, S., & Stacy, A. W. (2008). Working memory capacity moderates the predictive effects of drug-related associations on substance use. *Psychology of Addictive Behaviors, 22*, 426–432.

Grimley, D., Prochaska, J. O., Valicer, W. F., Blais, L. M., & DiClemente, C. D. (1994). The transtheoretical model of change. In T. M. Brinthaupt & R. P. Lipka (Eds.), *Changing the self: Philosophies, techniques, and experiences* (pp. 201–227). Albany: State University of New York Press.

Hawkins, J. D., Catalano, R. F., & Miller, J. Y. (1992). Risk and protective factors for alcohol and other drug problems in adolescence and early adulthood: Implications for substance abuse prevention. *Psychological Bulletin, 112*(1), 64–105.

Hazy, T. E., Frank, M. J., & O'Reilly, R. C. (2006). Banishing the homunculus: Making working memory work. *Neuroscience, 139*, 105–118.

Helstrom, A., Hutchison, K. E., & Bryan, A. (2007). Motivational enhancement therapy for high-risk adolescent smokers. *Addictive Behaviors, 32*(10), 2404–2410.

Henderson, C. E., Dakof, G. A., Greenbaum, P. E., & Liddle, H. A. (2010). Effectiveness of multidimensional family therapy with higher severity substance-abusing adolescents: Report from two randomized controlled trials. *Journal of Consulting and Clinical Psychology, 78*(6), 885–897.

Henderson, C. E., Rowe, C. L., Dakof, G. A., Hawes, S. W., & Liddle, H. A. (2009). Parenting practices as mediators of treatment effects in an early-intervention trial of Multidimensional Family Therapy. *American Journal of Drug and Alcohol Abuse, 35*, 220–226.

Hendriks, V., van der Schee, E., & Blanken, P. (2011). Treatment of adolescents with a cannabis use disorder: Main findings of a randomized controlled trial comparing multidimensional family therapy and cognitive behavioral therapy in The Netherlands. *Drug and Alcohol Dependence, 119*(1), 64–71.

Hendriks, V., van der Schee, E., & Blanken, P. (2012). Matching adolescents with a cannabis use disorder to multidimensional family therapy or cognitive behavioral therapy: Treatment effect moderators in a randomized controlled trial. *Drug and Alcohol Dependence, 125*(1), 119–126.

Henggeler, S. W., Melton, G. B., & Smith, L. A. (1992). Family preservation using multisystemic therapy: An effective alternative to incarcerating serious juvenile offenders. *Journal of Consulting and Clinical Psychology, 60*(6), 953.

Henggeler, S. W., Pickrel, S. G., & Brondino, M. J. (1999). Multisystemic treatment of substance abusing and dependent delinquents: Outcomes, treatment fidelity, and transportability. *Mental Health Services Research, 1*, 171–184.

Hingson, R., & Kenkel, D. (2004). Social, health, and economic consequences of underage drinking. In R. J. Bonnie & M. E. O'Connell (Eds.), *Reducing underage drinking: A collective responsibility* (pp. 351–382). Washington, DC: National Academies Press. http://www.nap.edu/books/0309089352/html.

Hofmann, W., Friese, M., & Wiers, R. W. (2008). Impulsive versus reflective influences on health behavior: A theoretical framework and empirical review. *Health Psychology Review, 2*, 111–137.

Hollenstein, T., & Lougheed, J. P. (2013). Beyond storm and stress: Typicality, transactions, timing, and temperament to account for adolescent change. *American Psychologist, 68*(6), 444–454.

Holley, L. C., Kulis, S., Marsiglia, F. F., & Keith, V. M. (2006). Ethnicity versus ethnic identity: What predicts substance use norms and behaviors? *Journal of Social Work Practice in the Addictions, 6*(3), 53–79.

Holmbeck, G. N., Greenley, R. N., & Franks, E. A. (2003). Developmental issues and considerations in research and practice. In A. E. Kazdin, (Ed)., *Evidence-based psychotherapies for children and adolescents* (pp. 21–40). New York: Guilford Press.

Holmbeck, G., & Updegrove, A. (1995). Clinical-developmental interface: Implications of developmental research for adolescent psychotherapy. *Psychotherapy*, *32*(1), 16–33.

Hoyle, R. H., & Robinson, J. C. (2004). Mediated and moderated effects in social psychological research: Measurement, design, and analysis issues. In C. Sansone, C. C. Morf, & A. T. Panter (Eds.), *Sage handbook of methods in social psychology* (pp. 213–233). New York: Sage.

Huey, S. J., Henggeler, S. W., Brondino, M. J., & Pickrel, S. G. (2000). Mechanisms of change in multisystemic therapy: Reducing delinquent behavior through therapist adherence and improved family and peer functioning. *Journal of Consulting and Clinical Psychology*, *68*, 451–467.

Jackson, K. M., & Sher, K. J. (2003). Alcohol use disorders and psychological distress: A prospective state-trait analysis. *Journal of Abnormal Psychology*, *112*(4), 599.

Jensen, C. D., Cushing, C. C., Aylward, B. S., Craig, J. T., Sorell, D. M., & Steele, R. G. (2011). Effectiveness of motivational interviewing interventions for adolescent substance use behavior change: A meta-analytic review. *Journal of Consulting and Clinical Psychology*, *79*(4), 433–440.

Johnston, L. D., O'Malley, P. M., Bachman, J. G., & Schulenberg, J. E. (2013). *Monitoring the Future national results on drug use: 2012 overview, key findings on adolescent drug use*. Ann Arbor: Institute for Social Research, The University of Michigan.

Jones, B. T., Corbin, W., & Fromme, K. (2001). A review of expectancy theory and alcohol consumption. *Addiction*, *96*(1), 57–72.

Kahneman, D. (2003). A perspective on judgment and choice: Mapping bounded rationality. *American Psychologist*, *58*, 697–720.

Kaminer, Y., Burleson, J. A., Blitz, C., Sussman, J., & Rounsaville, B. J. (1998). Psychotherapies for adolescent substance abusers: A pilot study. *Journal of Nervous and Mental Disorders*, *186*, 684–690.

Kaminer, Y., Burleson, J. A., Goldberger, R. (2002). Cognitive-behavioral coping skills and psychoeducation therapies for adolescent substance abuse. *Journal of Nervous and Mental Disease*, *190*(11), 737–745.

Kaminer, Y., Burleson, J. A., Goldston, D. B., & Burke, R. H. (2006). Suicidal ideation among adolescents with alcohol use disorders during treatment and aftercare. *American Journal on Addictions*, *15*(S1), 43–49.

Kaminer, Y., Tarter, R. E., Bukstein, O. G., & Kabene, M. (1992). Comparison between treatment completers and noncompleters among dually diagnosed substance abusing adolescents. *Journal of American Academy of Child and Adolescent Psychiatry*, *31*, 1046–1049.

Kaminer, Y., & Winters, K. C. (2012). Proposed DSM-5 substance use disorders for adolescents: If you build it, will they come? *The American Journal on Addictions*, *21*(3), 280–281.

Kazdin, A. E. (1998). *Research design in clinical psychology* (3rd ed.). Needham Heights, MA: Allyn & Bacon.

Kazdin, A. E. (2001). Bridging the enormous gaps of theory with therapy research and practice. *Journal of Clinical Child Psychology*, *30*(1), 59–66.

Kazdin, A. E. (2003). Psychotherapy for children and adolescents. *Annual Review of Psychology*, *54*(1), 253–276.

Kellogg, S. (1993). Identity and recovery. *Psychotherapy*, *30*, 235–244.

Kelly, J. F., Myers, M. G., & Brown, S. A. (2000). A multivariate process model of adolescent 12-step attendance and substance use outcome following inpatient treatment. *Psychology of Addictive Behaviors, 14*(4), 376–389.

Kelly, J. F., Myers, M. G., & Brown, S. A. (2005). The effects of age composition of 12-step groups on adolescent 12-step participation and substance use outcome. *Journal of Child & Adolescent Substance Abuse, 15*(1), 63–72.

Keren, G., & Schul, Y. (2009). Two is not always better than one: A critical evaluation of two-system theories. *Perspectives on Psychological Science, 4*, 533–550.

Koning, I. M., Vollebergh, W. A., Smit, F., Verdurmen, J. E., Van Den Eijnden, R. J., TerBogt, T. F., . . . Engels, R. C. (2009). Preventing heavy alcohol use in adolescents (PAS): Cluster randomized trial of a parent and student intervention offered separately and simultaneously. *Addiction, 104*(10), 1669–1678.

Konining, I. M., van den Eijnden, R. J. J. M, Engles, C. M. E., Verdurm, J. E. E., & Vollebergh, W. A. M. (2011). Why target early adolescents and parents in alcohol prevention? The mediating effects of self-control, rules and attitudes about alcohol use. *Addiction, 106*, 538–546.

Kraemer, H., Kazdin, A., Offord, D., Kessler, R., Jensen, P., & Kupfer, D. (1997). Coming to terms with the terms of risk. *Archives of General Psychiatry, 54*, 337–343.

Kraemer, H. C., Wilson, G. T., Fairburn, C. G., & Agras, W. S. (2002). Mediators and moderators of treatment effects in randomized clinical trials. *Archives of General Psychiatry, 59*(10), 877–883.

Kumpfer, K. L., Alvarado, R., & Whiteside, H. O. (2003). Family-based interventions for substance use and misuse prevention. *Substance Use & Misuse, 38*(11–13), 1759–1787.

Kuntsche, E., Stewart, S. H., & Cooper, M. L. (2008). How stable is the motive-alcohol use link? A cross-national validation of the Drinking Motives Questionnaire Revised among adolescents from Switzerland, Canada, and the United States. *Journal of Studies on Alcohol and Drugs, 69*(3), 388.

Kwate, N. O. A., Valdimarsdottir, H. B., Guevarra, J. S., Bovbjerg, D. H. (2003). Experiences of racist events have negative health consequences for African American women. *National Medical Association, 95*, 450–460.

Leigh, B. C. (1989). In search of the seven dwarves: Issues of measurement and meaning in alcohol expectancy research. *Psychological Bulletin, 105*(3), 361–373.

Liddle, H. A., Dakof, G. A., Parker, K., Diamond, G. S., Barrett, K., Tejeda, M. (2001). Multidimensional family therapy for adolescent drug abuse: Results of a randomized clinical trial. *American Journal of Drug and Alcohol Abuse, 27*(4), 651–688.

Liddle, H. A., Dakof, G. A., Turner, R. M., Henderson, C. E., & Greenbaum, P. E. (2008). Treating adolescent drug abuse: A randomized trial comparing multidimensional family therapy and cognitive behavior therapy. *Addiction, 103*, 1660–1670.

Liddle, H. A., & Hogue, A. (2001). Multidimensional family therapy for adolescent substance abuse. In E. F. Wagner & H. B. Waldron (Eds.), *Innovations in adolescent substance abuse interventions* (pp. 229–261). Oxford: Elsevier.

Liddle, H. A., Rowe, C. L., Dakof, G. A., Henderson, C., & Greenbaum, P. (2009). Multidimensional Family Therapy for early adolescent substance abusers: Twelve month outcomes of a randomized controlled trial. *Journal of Consulting and Clinical Psychology, 77*(1), 12–25.

Lieb, R., Merikangas, K. R., Höfler, M., Pfister, H., Isensee, B., & Wittchen, H. U. (2002). Parental alcohol use disorders and alcohol use and disorders in offspring: A community study. *Psychological Medicine, 32*(1), 63–78.

Lopez, B., Schwartz, S. J., Prado, G., Campo, A., & Pantin, H. (2008). Adolescent neurological development and its implications for adolescent substance use prevention. *Journal of Primary Prevention, 29*, 5–35.

Mackie, C. J., Castellanos-Ryan, N., & Conrod, P. J. (2011). Developmental trajectories of psychotic-like experiences across adolescence: Impact of victimization and substance use. *Psychological Medicine, 41*(1), 47–58.

MacKinnon, D. P. (2008). *Introduction to statistical mediation analysis.* New York: Lawrence Erlbaum.

Marlatt, G. A., Baer, J. S., Kivlahan, D. R., Dimeff, L. A., Larimer, M. E., Quigley, L. A., . . . Williams, E. (1998). Screening and brief intervention for high-risk college student drinkers: Results from a 2-year follow-up assessment. *Journal of Consulting and Clinical Psychology, 66*(4), 604–615.

Marshal, M. P., & Chassin, L. (2000). Peer influence on adolescent alcohol use: The moderating role of parental support and discipline. *Applied Developmental Science, 4*(2), 80–88.

Masten, A. S., Faden, V. B., Zucker, R. A., & Spear, L. P. (2008). Underage drinking: A developmental framework. *Pediatrics, 121*(Supplement 4), S235–S251.

McCuller, W. J., Sussman, S., Wapner, M., Dent, C., & Weiss, D. J. (2006). Motivation to quit as a mediator of tobacco cessation among at-risk youth. *Addictive Behaviors, 31*, 880–888.

Meier, M. H., Caspi, A., Ambler, A., Harrington, H., Houts, R., Keefe, R. S., . . . Moffitt, T. E. (2012). Persistent cannabis users show neuropsychological decline from childhood to midlife. *Proceedings of the National Academy of Sciences, 109*(40), E2657–E2664.

Merikangas, K. R., He, J., Burstein, M., Swanson, S. A., Avenevoli, S., Cui, L., . . . Swendsen, J. (2010). Lifetime prevalence of mental disorders in US adolescents: Results from the National Comorbidity Study-Adolescent Supplement (NCS-A). *Journal of American Academy of Child and Adolescent Psychiatry, 49*(10), 980–989. doi: 10.1016/j.jaac.201.05.017

Miller, W. R., & Rollnick, S. (2002). *Motivational interviewing: Preparing people for change* (2nd ed.). New York: Guildford Press.

Miller, W. R., & Rose, G. S. (2009). Toward a theory of Motivational Interviewing, *American Psychologist, 64*(6), 527–537. doi: 10.1037/a0016830\

Minior, T., Galea, S., Stuber, J., Ahern, J., & Ompad, D. (2003). Racial differences in discrimination experiences and responses among minority substance users. *Ethnicity and Disease, 13*(4), 521–527.

Monti, P. M., Colby, S. M., Barnett, N. P., Spirito, A., Rohsenow, D. J., Myers, M., . . . Lewander, W. (1999). Brief intervention for harm reduction with alcohol-positive older adolescents in a hospital emergency department. *Journal of Consulting and Clinical Psychology, 67*(6), 989–994.

Myers, M. G., Stewart, D. G., & Brown, S. A. (1998). Progression from conduct disorder to antisocial personality disorder following treatment for adolescent substance abuse. *American Journal of Psychiatry, 155*, 479–486.

National Highway Traffic Safety Administration. (2013). Traffic safety facts 2011 data. US Department of Transportation. http://www-nrd.nhtsa.dot.gov/Pubs/811744.pdf

Peeters, M., Wiers, R. W., Monshouwer, K., van de Schoot, R., Janssen, T., & Vollebergh, W. A. (2012). Automatic processes in at-risk adolescents: The role of alcohol-approach tendencies and response inhibition in drinking behavior. *Addiction, 107*, 1939–1946.

Peeters, M., Monshouwer, K., van de Schoot, R. A., Janssen, T., Vollebergh, W. A., & Wiers, R. W. (2013). Automatic processes and the drinking behavior in early adolescence: A prospective study. *Alcoholism: Clinical and Experimental Research, 37*(10), 1737–1744.

Prado, G., Huang, S., Cordova, D., Malcolm, S., Estrada, Y., Cano, N., . . . Brown, C. H. (2013). Ecodevelopmental and intrapersonal moderators of a family based preventive intervention for Hispanic youth: A latent profile analysis. *Prevention Science, 14*(3), 290–299.

Read, J. P., Wood, M. D., & Capone, C. (2005). A prospective investigation of relations between social influences and alcohol involvement during the transition into college [corrected]. *Journal of Studies on Alcohol and Drugs, 66*(1), 23–34.

Robbins, M. S., Szapocznik, J., Dillon, F. R., Turner, C. W., Mitrani, V. B., & Feaster, D. J. (2008). The efficacy of structural ecosystems therapy with drug abusing/dependent African American and Hispanic American adolescents. *Journal of Family Psychology, 22*(1), 51–61.

Rowe, C. L., Liddle, H. A., Greenbaum, P. E., & Henderson, C. E. (2004). Impact of psychiatric comorbidity on treatment of adolescentdrug abusers. *Journal of Substance Abuse Treatment, 26*, 129–140.

Sameroff, A. J. (2000). Developmental systems and psychopathology. *Development and Psychopathology, 12*, 297–312.

Santisteban, D. A., Szapocznik, J., Perez-Vidal, A., Kurtines, W., Murray, E. J., & La Perriere, A. (1996). Efficacy of interventions for engaging youth/families into treatment and some variables that may contribute to differential effectiveness. *Journal of Family Psychology, 10*, 35–44.

Schoenmakers, T., Lux, I., Goertz, A., Van Kerkhof, D., De Bruin, M., & Wiers, R. W. (2010). A randomized clinical trial to measure effects of an intervention to modify attentional bias in alcohol dependent patients. *Drug and Alcohol Dependence, 109*, 30–36.

Sher, K. J., & Gotham, H. J. (1999). Pathological alcohol involvement: A developmental disorder of young adulthood. *Development and Psychopathology, 11*, 933–956.

Sher, K. J., Grekin, E. R., & Williams, N. A. (2005). The development of alcohol use disorders. *Annual Review of Clinical Psychology, 1*, 493–523.

Sher, K. J., & Slutske, W. S. (2003). Disorders of impulse control. In G. Stricker, T. A. Widiger, & I. B. Weiner (Eds.), *Handbook of psychology* (pp. 195–228). New Jersey: John Wiley & Sons.

Sher, K. J., Trull, T. J., Bartholow, B. D., & Vieth, A. (1999). Personality and alcoholism: Issues, methods, and etiological processes. In K. E. Leonard & H. T. Blane (Eds.), *Psychological theories of drinking and alcoholism* (pp. 54–105). New York: Guilford Press.

Sher, K. J., Wood, M. D., Wood, P. K., & Raskin, G. (1996). Alcohol outcome expectancies and alcohol use: A latent variable cross-lagged panel study. *Journal of Abnormal Psychology, 105*(4), 561.

Smith, E. R., & DeCoster, J. (2000). Dual process models in social and cognitive psychology: conceptual integration and links to underlying memory systems. *Personality and Social Psychology Review, 4*, 108–131.

Smith, G. T., Goldman, M. S., Greenbaum, P. E., & Christiansen, B. A. (1995). Expectancy for social facilitation from drinking: The divergent paths of high-expectancy and low-expectancy adolescents. *Journal of Abnormal Psychology, 104*(1), 32.

Spirito, A., Sindelar-Manning, H., Colby, S. M., Barnett, N. P., Lewander, W., Rohsenow, D. J., & Monti, P. M. (2011). Individual and family motivational interventions for alcohol-positive adolescents treated in an emergency department: Results from a randomized clinical trial. *Archives of Pediatric Adolescent Medicine, 165*, 269–274.

Stacy, A. W., Ames, S. L., & Knowlton, B. (2004). Neurologically plausible distinctions in cognition relevant to drug use etiology and prevention. *Substance Use and Misuse, 39*, 1571–1623.

Steinberg, L., Fletcher, A., & Darling, N. (1994). Parental monitoring and peer influences on adolescent substance use. *Pediatrics, 93*, 1060–1063.

Strack, F., & Deutsch, R. (2004). Reflective and impulsive determinants of social behavior. *Personality and Social Psychology Review, 3*, 220–247.

Strada, M. J., Donohue, B., & Lefforge, N. (2006). Examination of ethnicity in controlled treatment outcome studies involving adolescent substance abusers: A comprehensive literature review. *Psychology of Addictive Behaviors, 20*, 11–27.

Tevyaw, T. O., & Monti, P. M. (2004). Motivational enhancement and other brief interventions for adolescent substance abuse: Foundations, applications and evaluations. *Addiction, 99*(Suppl. 2), 63–75.

Thush, C., Wiers, R. W., Ames, S. L., Grenard, J. L., Sussman, S., & Stacy, A. W. (2008). Interactions between implicit and explicit cognition and working memory capacity in the prediction of alcohol use in at-risk adolescents. *Drug and Alcohol Dependence, 94*, 116–124.

Van Tubergen, F., & Poortman, A. R. (2010). Adolescent alcohol use in the Netherlands: the role of ethnicity, ethnic intermarriage, and ethnic school composition. *Ethnicity & Health, 15*(1), 1–13.

Vega, W. A., Alderete, E., Kolody, B., & Aguilar-Gaxiola, S. (1998). Illicit drug use among Mexicans and Mexican Americans in California: The effects of gender and acculturation. *Addiction, 93*(12), 1839–1850.

Vega, W. A., & Gil, A. G. (2005). Revisiting drug progression: Long-range effects of early tobacco use. *Addiction, 100*(9), 1358–1369.

Voogt, C. V., Poelen, E. A. P., Kleinjan, M., Lemmers, L. A. C. J., & Engels, R. C. M. E. (2013). The effectiveness of the "What Do You Drink" web-based brief alcohol intervention in reducing heavy drinking among students. *Alcohol and Alcoholism, 48*, 312–321.

Wadley, J. (2012, June 1). American teens are less likely than European teens to use cigarettes and alcohol, but more likely to use illicit drugs [Online press release]. http://www.ns.umich.edu/new/releases/20420-american-teens-are-less-likely-than-european-teens-to-use-cigarettes-and-alcohol-but-more-likely-to-use-illicit-drugs.

Wagner, E. F. (2003). Conceptualizing alcohol treatment research for Hispanic/Hispanic adolescents. *Alcoholism: Clinical and Experimental Research, 27*, 1349–1352.

Wagner, E. F. (2008). Developmentally informed research on the effectiveness of clinical trials: A primer for assessing how developmental issues may influence treatment responses among adolescents with alcohol use problems. *Pediatrics, 121,* S337–S347.

Walden, B., Iacono, W. G., & McGue, M. (2007). Trajectories of change in adolescent substance use and symptomatology: Impact of paternal and maternal substance use disorders. *Psychology of Addictive Behaviors, 21*(1), 35–43.

Waldron, H. B. (1997). Adolescent substance abuse and family therapy outcome: A review of randomized trials. *Advances in Clinical Child Psychology, 19,* 199–234.

Waldron, H. B., & Kaminer, Y. (2004). On the learning curve: The emerging evidence supporting cognitive-behavioral therapies for adolescent substance abuse, *Addiction, 99*(Suppl. 2), 93–105.

Waldron, H. B., & Turner, C. W. (2008). Evidence-based psychosocial treatments for adolescent substance abuse. *Journal of Clinical Child & Adolescent Psychology, 37*(1), 238–261.

Warner, L. A., Canino, G., & Colón, H. M. (2001). Prevalence and correlates of substance use disorders among older adolescents in Puerto Rico and the United States: A cross-cultural comparison. *Drug and Alcohol Dependence, 63*(3), 229–243.

Weinberg, N. Z., Rahdert, E., Colliver, J. D., & Glantz, M. D. (1998). Adolescent substance abuse: A review of the past 10 years. *Journal of the American Academy of Child & Adolescent Psychiatry, 37*(3), 252–261.

White, W. (2008). *Recovery management and recovery-oriented systems of care: Scientific rationale and promising practices.* Jointly published by the Northeast Addiction Technology Transfer Center, the Great Lakes Addiction Technology Transfer Center, and the Philadelphia Department of Behavioral Health/Mental Retardation Services.

White, V. M., Hill, D. J., & Effendi, Y. (2004). How does active parental consent influence the findings of drug-use surveys in schools? *Evaluation Review, 28,* 246–260.

Wiers, R. W., Bartholow, B. D., van den Wildenberg, E., Thush, C., Engels, R. C. M. E., Sher, K., . . . Stacy, A. W. (2007). Automatic and controlled processes and the development of addictive behaviors in adolescents: A review and a model. *Pharmacology, Biochemistry and Behavior, 86,* 263–283.

Wiers, R. W., Eberl, C., Rinck, M., Becker, E., & Lindenmeyer, J. (2011). Re-training automatic action tendencies changes alcoholic patients' approach bias for alcohol and improves treatment outcome. *Psychological Science, 22*(4), 490–497.

Wiers, R. W., Fromme, K., Latvala, A., & Stewart, S. H. (2012). Risk and protective factors for underage drinking. In P. De Witte & M. C. Mitchell, Jr. (Eds.), *Underage drinking: A report on drinking in the second decade of life in Europe and North America* (pp. 79–146). Louvain-la-Neuve, Belgium: Presses Universitaires de Louvain.

Wiers, R. W., Gladwin, T. E., Hofmann, W. Salemink, E., & Ridderinkhof, K. R. (2013). Cognitive bias modification and control training in addiction and related psychopathology: Mechanisms, clinical perspectives and ways forward. *Clinical Psychological Science, 1*(2), 192–212.

Wiers, R. W., Hoogeveen, K. J., Sergeant, J. A., & Gunning, W. B. (1997). High-and low-dose alcohol-related expectancies and the differential associations with drinking in male and female adolescents and young adults. *Addiction, 92*(7), 871–888.

Wiers, R. W., Sergeant, J. A., & Gunning, W. B. (2000). The assessment of alcohol expectancies in school children: Measurement or modification? *Addiction, 95*, 737–746.

Wiers, R. W., & Stacy, A. W. (Eds.) (2006). *Handbook of implicit cognition and addiction.* Thousand Oaks, CA: SAGE.

Wiers, R. W., van de Luitgaarden, J., van den Wildenberg, E., Smulders, F. T. Y. (2005). Challenging implicit and explicit alcohol-related cognitions in young heavy drinkers. *Addiction, 100*, 806–819.

Williams, R. J., & Chang, S. Y. (2000). A comprehensive and comparative review of adolescent substance abuse treatment outcome. *Clinical Psychology: Science and Practice, 7*(2), 138–166.

Windle, M., Spear, L. P., Fuligni, A. J., Angold, A., Brown, J. D., Pine, D., . . . Dahl, R. E. (2008). Transitions into underage and problem drinking: Developmental processes and mechanisms between 10 and 15 years of age. *Pediatrics, 121*(Supplement 4), S273–S289.

Winters, K. C. (1999). Treating adolescents with substance use disorders: An overview of practice issues and treatment outcomes. *Substance Abuse, 20*(4), 203–225.

Winters, K. (2013). Advances in the science of adolescent drug involvement: Implications for assessment and diagnosis. *Current Opinion in Psychiatry, 26*(4), 318–324.

Winters, K. C., Fahnhorst, T., Botzet, A., Lee, S., & Laione, B. (2012). Brief interventions for drug-abusing adolescents in a school setting: Outcomes and mediating factors. *Journal of Substance Abuse Treatment, 42*, 279–288.

Winters, K. C., Martin, C. S., & Chung, T. (2011). Substance use disorders in DSM-IV when applied to adolescents. *Addiction, 106*(5), 882–884.

Winters, K. C., Stinchfield, R. D., Opland, E., Weller, C., & Latimer W. W. (2000). The effectiveness of the Minnesota Model approach in the treatment of adolescent drug abusers. *Addiction, 95*, 601–612.

Wood, M. D., Capone, C., Laforge, R., Erickson, D. J., & Brand, N. H. (2007). Brief motivational intervention and alcohol expectancy challenge with heavy drinking college students: A randomized factorial study. *Addictive Behaviors, 32*, 2509–2528.

Wood, M. D., Fairlie, A. M., Fernandez, A. C., Borsari, B., Capone, C., Laforge, R. G., & Carmona-Barros, R. (2010). Brief motivational and parent Interventions for college students: A randomized factorial study. *Journal of Consulting and Clinical Psychology, 78*, 349–361. PMID: 2880835.

Wood, M. D., Read, J. P., Mitchell, R. E., & Brand, N. H. (2004). Do parents still matter? Parent and peer influences on alcohol involvement among recent high school graduates. *Psychology of Addictive Behaviors, 18*, 19–30.

Moderators and Mediators of Treatments for Youth With Eating Disorders

STUART B. MURRAY, KATHARINE L. LOEB,
AND DANIEL LE GRANGE ■

INTRODUCTION

Eating disorders are among the most serious and pernicious of psychiatric disorders, and have for many years continued to pose significant challenges for patients, clinicians, and researchers alike. Indeed, while the precise pathogenesis of eating disorders remains elusive, their multifactorial nature spans social, psychological, and biological processes, and current evidence-based treatments are generally thought to fall short of acceptable treatment outcomes (Bulik et al., 2007). However, juxtaposed alongside these difficulties in the treatment of eating disorders, research has demonstrated devastating physical and psychosocial comorbidities, including mortality rates of up to 20% (Steinhausen, 2002), medical complications (Steinhausen, 2002), elevated suicidality (Pompili et al., 2004), impaired quality of life (Mond et al., 2005), and a protracted and relapsing illness course (Treasure & Russell, 2011). Thus, there can be little question that much ongoing research is warranted in further delineating effective treatment components for varying presentations of disordered eating.

In appreciating the complexity and heterogeneity among profiles of disordered eating across the life span, clinical eating disorders broadly fall into five categories among adults and adolescents: anorexia nervosa (AN), bulimia nervosa (BN), binge eating disorder (BED), the subclinical category of "other specified feeding or eating disorder" (OSFED), and the residual atypical category of "unspecified feeding or eating disorder" (UFED). Further presentations of eating disorders typically occurring in pre-adolescence include pica, rumination disorder (RD), and avoidant/restrictive food intake disorder (AFRID). See *DSM-5* for the complete classification and diagnostic criteria for eating disorders (APA, 2013).

EATING DISORDERS IN ADOLESCENCE

Over the last 50 years, eating disorders in adult populations have been plagued by poor rates of full symptom remission (Steinhausen, 2002), high rates of transdiagnostic crossover between eating disorder diagnoses (Eddy et al., 2008), and high rates of relapse (Keel & Brown, 2010). However, despite increasing incidence rates of eating disorders among adolescents (Smink, van Hoeken, & Hoek, 2012), relatively little research has focused on adolescent populations, despite research indicating that the best prognostic outcomes for eating disorders, as in many other psychiatric illnesses, appear to be best afforded by early intervention (Rome et al., 2003). For instance, when treated in adolescence, anorexia nervosa is characterised by lower mortality rates, reduced illness chronicity, and greater rates of recovery and symptom improvement (Steinhausen, 2002). As such, an increasing body of research has been oriented toward the development of treatment interventions for eating disorders in adolescence, given that adolescence is the time in which eating disorders are most likely to develop (Kohn & Golden, 2001).

Evidence-Based Treatment for Anorexia Nervosa in Adolescence

INPATIENT TREATMENT

Inpatient treatment is often a necessary treatment component in the treatment of AN, and is potentially life-saving in the event of serious medical complications (Winston, Paul, & Juanolo-Borrat, 2012). However, while inpatient admissions are generally an established part of treatment in adult presentations, less comprehensive evidence exists in cases of adolescent AN (Winston et al., 2012). For instance, many have documented the detrimental psychosocial consequences of long inpatient admissions for adolescents, often resulting in social dislocation during important developmental stages (Gowers & Bryant-Waugh, 2004; Gowers et al., 2007). Furthermore, emerging evidence points toward elevated rates of relapse following lengthier inpatient admissions, suggesting that shorter adolescent inpatient admissions require continued and prioritized treatment upon discharge, which may be associated with better overall treatment outcome (Madden et al., 2014), and further aligns the clinical emphasis in adolescent treatment toward outpatient interventions.

FAMILY-BASED TREATMENT

The family-based treatment (FBT) of adolescent AN may be characterized by an agnostic stance toward the origin of the illness, alongside the core theoretical tenet that parents themselves represent the primary and most influential resource in their child's recovery (Lock & Le Grange, 2013). FBT postulates that parents instinctively possess the necessary skills and ideas to re-feed their unwell child, but are frequently coerced away from their instincts by the overwhelming presence of AN, which in some instances inadvertently results in a level of accommodation to AN symptoms within family interactions (Eisler, 2005). Thus, treatment is initially focused on mobilizing parental strengths and resources in dismantling the array of behavioral symptoms, in addition to ensuring nutritional rehabilitation and prompt weight restoration in their child. Due to the more severe nature of potential medical complications in adolescent AN (Winston et al., 2012), the focus on weight restoration takes undivided precedence over other areas of adolescent functioning, and parents are encouraged to exercise the necessary parental authority in ensuring that all ecological and individual maintaining factors, such as dietary restraint and compensatory exercise, are abated. Following weight restoration and symptom remission, less parental authority may be required, and the adolescent typically demonstrates more autonomy over food and eating, and may gradually return to age-appropriate adolescent endeavors, which allows for a more central focus on general adolescent issues, away from food and eating (Lock & Le Grange, 2013).

FBT continues to demonstrate encouraging treatment outcome in a number of empirical studies spanning randomized controlled trials (RCTs), meta-analyses, dissemination studies, and case series studies (e.g., Couturier, Kimber, & Szatmari, 2013; Eisler et al., 2000; Ellison et al., 2012; Le Grange, Binford, & Loeb, 2005; Loeb et al., 2007). For instance, 50%–75% of adolescents are weight restored within a year of commencing FBT (Le Grange & Eisler, 2009), and 6- and 12-month follow-ups indicate that treatment gains are indeed robust (Couturier et al., 2013; Lock et al., 2008). Furthermore, FBT has demonstrated a promising capacity to alleviate the cognitive symptoms of AN, such as the drive for thinness, and eating, shape, and weight concerns, comparing favorably with other adolescent treatment interventions (Lock et al., 2010). However, it should be noted that 30%–50% of patients do not fully remit from symptoms during FBT (Fisher et al., 2010), and as such, ongoing research is required in illuminating the moderators and mediators of FBT, which may directly inform attempts to augment this treatment approach.

MULTIFAMILY THERAPY

Multifamily therapy represents an alternative family-based approach to the treatment of adolescent AN, and typically involves the uniting of 6–8 families for several intensive multi-family visits of up to 5 days, alongside weekly individual family therapy meetings. While adopting similar therapeutic aims to that of FBT in empowering the parental development of strategies to offset the maintenance of AN symptomatology and helping the adolescent address any developmental processes that may have been disrupted by AN, multifamily therapy conceptualizes the agent of change somewhat distinctly and relies more centrally on group processes (Dare & Eisler, 2000). For instance, the presence of several families working alongside one another in overcoming AN has been reported to have strong destigmatizing effects for both parents and children alike, in addition to fostering a forum in which ideas can be shared, allowing families the experience of both being helped by other families and acting as consultants to other families, further solidifying one's own sense of efficacy and agency (Dare & Eisler, 2000).

In working toward its therapeutic aims, multifamily therapy for AN typically incorporates the interchangeable use of structural, systemic, and narrative family therapy practices. Examples of such practices may include video-recorded family meals, group feedback, "foster family meals" in which children rotate and eat with different families, psychodrama and family sculpting practices, and psycho-educational information pertaining to the nature of eating disorders and the coercive symptomatology that may emerge in attempting to avoid confronting food-based fears and anxieties (Dare & Eisler, 2000).

Controlled empirical evidence supporting multifamily therapy for AN remains sparse, although preliminary findings report that the majority of families who engage in multifamily therapy are successful in bringing about weight restoration and a stabilization in the eating practices of their child (Dare & Eisler, 2001; Scholz & Asen, 2001). Furthermore, strikingly low rates of treatment dropout have been reported, indirectly indicating that adolescents and parents alike find this treatment beneficial (Dare & Eisler, 2001; Scholz & Asen, 2001). However, it should be noted that at this stage such findings may only be drawn tentatively since the sample sizes in the few existing empirical studies have been modest. Thus, further research is warranted in further illustrating the efficacy of multifamily therapy.

ADOLESCENT-FOCUSED THERAPY

Adolescent-focused therapy (AFT) is an individual treatment for adolescent onset AN, and is a clinically and empirically well-tested alternative to FBT, rendering it a potentially viable option for those whose symptoms do not remit with FBT, alongside those adolescents not nested within their family of origin or for whom there are family-level contraindications for FBT (e.g., physical abuse). Initially based on the principles of ego-oriented self-psychology (Robin et al., 1994; Robin et al., 1999), AFT aims to address the core deficits in adolescent development that brought about the AN, through a continued emphasis on self-exploration and the development of the "self." In the context of AN, self-starvation and preoccupation with food and weight may often be linked to the avoidance of negative affective states associated with one's normative adolescent development, with treatment aiming to facilitate a more adaptive coping style such that one's developmental trajectory is not arrested (Fitzpatrick et al., 2010).

Further to the early development and testing of AFT (Robin et al., 1994; Robin et al., 1999), this treatment approach has now been manualized and takes the form of three distinct therapeutic phases (Fitzpatrick et al., 2010). The first phase of treatment is oriented toward establishing a therapeutic alliance and a preliminary understanding of the ways in which AN serves as a coping strategy for managing or avoiding challenging developmental issues. The second phase is primarily oriented toward adolescent exploration of issues surrounding individuation, which may have been arrested by AN, with a view toward developing age-appropriate independence from one's parents and family. The third and final phase is oriented toward the preparation and initiation of behaviors and strategies that will lead toward more autonomy and independence.

To date, AFT has been the subject of a small number of RCTs for adolescent AN. Such trials, conducting direct comparisons of AFT and family interventions, have generally concluded that AFT is a viable treatment alternative to FBT in the treatment of adolescent AN, noting comparable rates of symptom remission at end of treatment, despite less robust long-term symptom remission for both weight- and cognitive-related symptoms (Le Grange et al., 2014; Lock et al., 2010; Robin et al., 1994; Robin et al., 1999).

ENHANCED COGNITIVE BEHAVIORAL THERAPY

Cognitive behavioral therapy is a well-known treatment modality that demonstrates an impressive evidence base across a range of psychopathologies, and typically consists of therapeutic endeavors to modify irrational cognitions, alongside behavioral experiments that are designed to help generate disconfirmatory evidence to create cognitive dissonance between irrational thoughts and behavioral outcomes. With specific respect to eating disorders, treatment centrally aims to restructure deeply entrenched cognitions surrounding the over-valuation of weight and shape, in addition to modifying behaviors based on such irrational cognitions including the development of food rules and avoidance, feared weight ranges, and compulsive exercise practices (Fairburn, 2008).

While more commonly prescribed in the context of adult presentations of AN, recent evidence has advanced an "enhanced" form of CBT that specifically targets the core maintaining features of eating disorder psychopathology, thought to be perfectionism, low self-esteem, mood intolerance, and interpersonal difficulties, and was recently examined in the context of adolescent presentations of AN (Grave et al., 2013). Such findings reported modest rates of weight gain among adolescents, with approximately 19% of those offered treatment reaching close to their ideal body weight by the end of treatment. However, more impressive findings were indicated by the rates of adolescents self-reporting an absence of eating disordered cognitions and behaviors by end of treatment (Grave et al., 2013), although the limitations of self-report methods of indexing psychopathology in ego-syntonic illnesses have recently been noted (Murray, Loeb, & Le Grange, 2014). Thus, further research is warranted in establishing the efficacy of CBT treatments in adolescent presentations of AN.

PSYCHOPHARMACOLOGICAL TREATMENT

Empirical data demonstrate a recent upsurge in prescriptions of psychotropic medication in the context of adolescent AN (Couturier & Lock, 2007), necessitating an empirical thrust to identify effective psychopharmacological treatment for adolescent AN. In examining the efficacy of psychotropic medication in relation to AN symptomatology, antidepressants, selective serotonin reuptake inhibitors (SSRIs), and antipsychotic drugs have been assessed, with mixed findings emerging thus far (Balestrieri et al., 2013). For instance, studies have reported no significant differences on body mass index (BMI)- and cognitive-related outcomes in adolescent AN when comparing those treated with antidepressant and SSRI medication and those not treated with psychotropic medication (Balestrieri et al., 2013). Somewhat similarly, controlled trials examining antipsychotic medication such as olanzapine demonstrated no significant improvement in weight- and cognitive-related AN psychopathology in those treated with olanzapine compared to those receiving placebo medication (Kafantaris et al., 2011). As such, a recent review reported no benefit of atypical antipsychotic medications for adolescent AN (Brandenburg et al., 2011). This review echoes a recent meta-analysis in adult AN which concluded that atypical antipsychotics do not reliably result in any weight- or cognitive-related improvements in AN symptomatology, although they do alleviate depressive symptomatology (Lebow et al., 2013).

Evidence-Based Treatment for Bulimia Nervosa in Adolescence

COGNITIVE BEHAVIORAL THERAPY

In adult populations with BN, a wealth of empirical evidence points to the efficacy of cognitive behavioral therapy (CBT); however, relatively few studies exist examining the efficacy of CBT in adolescent populations. To date, several advocates have argued for the conceptual modification of adult-oriented CBT for adolescent populations, with one RCT and several case series attempting to illuminate the potential role of CBT in the treatment of adolescent BN (Lock, 2005; Schapman-Williams & Lock, 2006; Schmidt et al., 2007). Such adaptations of CBT in adolescent populations typically emphasize the need to acknowledge normative cognitive and emotional immaturity among adolescents, resulting in greater age-appropriate psycho-education, greater flexibility in homework assignments, and parental involvement to assist in behavioral experiments and modified dietary practices (Lock, 2005).

Treatment findings to date point toward promising findings, suggesting that an adolescent-oriented self-help CBT program may be helpful in alleviating both binge eating and purging episodes (Schmidt et al., 2007). Furthermore, a study of older adolescents revealed that an online CBT intervention was effective in reducing both cognitive and behavioral BN symptomatology, demonstrating similar rates of symptom remission to those found in studies in adult BN populations (Pretorious et al., 2009). However, despite promising preliminary evidence, further controlled studies are warranted in further explicating the efficacy of CBT in adolescent presentations of BN.

FAMILY-BASED TREATMENT

Upon the emergence of family-based interventions for adolescent anorexia nervosa, corresponding work also advanced a family-based treatment model for adolescent cases of bulimia nervosa (Le Grange & Lock, 2007). This model borrows conceptually from the well-established FBT for AN and shares similar core theoretical tenets, taking account of symptomatic similarities, including an over-valuation of weight and shape, elevated eating concerns, and a tendency to under-report symptom severity, thus centrally leveraging parental involvement. However, FBT-BN is somewhat distinct in light of the ego-dystonicity of BN behavioral symptoms, as the primary symptoms of binge eating and purging are almost universally experienced as distressing and contrary to one's aims (and as punctuated failures of rigid dietary restriction). Thus, FBT-BN features a more collaborative stance between parents and the adolescent in collectively devising strategies to overcome the distressing behavioral features of BN (Le Grange & Lock, 2007).

To date, two randomized clinical trials have demonstrated promising results, in that FBT-BN appears efficacious in bringing about symptom remission, which remains robust at both 6- and 12-month follow-up (Le Grange et al., 2007), and demonstrating similar treatment outcome to that of a modified guided self-help program of cognitive behavioral therapy (Schmidt et al., 2007).

PSYCHOPHARMACOLOGICAL TREATMENT

To date only one trial has examined the pharmacological treatment of adolescent BN, demonstrating that adult doses of fluoxetine are not only well tolerated by adolescents, but may also bring about reductions in the frequency of binge and purge episodes when administered alongside psychotherapy (Kotler et al., 2003). Although this finding mirrors the findings of trials conducted in adult populations, further research is undoubtedly warranted in further expanding our understanding of the role of psychopharmacology in adolescent BN.

MODERATORS AND MEDIATORS OF THE TREATMENT OF EATING DISORDERS IN ADOLESCENCE

Across many psychopathologies and treatment modalities in the field of mental health, the continued focus on illuminating moderators and mediators of treatment has been outlined as a crucial endeavor in ascertaining the patient variables and clinical conditions under which treatment interventions may have differing effects, in addition to understanding the manner in which treatment effects may differ (Kraemer et al., 2002). This may be particularly warranted in the study of adolescent eating disorders, because only three studies to date have examined the moderators and mediators of the treatments tested in RCTs (Le Grange et al., 2008; Le Grange et al., 2012; Lock et al., 2005). The dearth of treatment studies incorporating such analyses has precluded the rigorous and replicated testing of theoretical models of the moderation and mediation of interventions for disordered eating in adolescence. Thus, continued exploration of the moderators and mediators of treatment in this population may potentially aid ongoing endeavors in (1) better understanding the etiology of eating disorders, (2) better understanding which treatment interventions are likely to be successful, and

(3) developing augmentative strategies in conditions in which treatments are less likely to be effective (Kraemer et al., 2002), all of which have been outlined as crucial to the development of treatment outcomes in those with eating disorders (Strober & Johnson, 2012). As such, we present a comprehensive outline of the extant evidence base, although sparse, as to the moderators and mediators of treatment outcome in adolescent eating disorders.

Moderators of Treatment in Adolescent Eating Disorders

Several moderators of treatment outcome in adolescent eating disorders have been examined and will be reviewed in detail below. Among them, two relate to the core FBT approach (Le Grange & Lock, 2007; Lock & Legrange, 2013) and intersect case characteristics and treatment modality. Specifically, the age or developmental stage of the patient has been proposed to moderate FBT outcome in that for both pragmatic and clinical reasons, an intervention that places parents as primary agents of change in the renourishment process inherent in the resolution of AN may not be appropriate for older adolescents and emerging adults. Second, familial factors including family structures that deviate from a traditional two-parent household, negative patterns of interpersonal interactions in the family, and parental eating disorder pathology could theoretically undermine hypothesized active mechanisms of FBT (Loeb, Lock, Le Grange, & Greif, 2012), and thereby fare more poorly than intact families, than families with low levels of expressed emotion, and than parents who are free from eating disorder cognitions and behaviors themselves.

AGE OF PATIENT

Though research has indicated that the age in which disordered eating onsets during adolescence (early vs. late adolescence) does not necessarily moderate treatment response (Le Grange et al, 2012; Strober et al., 1997), evidence does suggest that the age of the patient when treated does indeed impart a moderating role on treatment outcome, with early intervention typically yielding better outcomes (Russell et al., 1987). An RCT examining family versus individual treatment for AN found that identical family-based interventions resulted in largely discrepant outcomes in those younger than age 19 versus those older than age 19, with treatment outcome favoring adolescent versus young adult populations (Russell et al., 1987). Alternatively, this trial also found that patients' response to individual treatment also differed according to their age, with greater benefits of individual treatment being reported in young adults as opposed to adolescents. Thus, these findings suggest that FBT may be indicated in adolescents younger than age 19, whereas individual treatment may be indicated in those older than age 19. However, it should be noted that this study did not involve strictly controlled statistical analyses of moderator effects, solely examining clinical outcomes across treatment and clinical groups.

FAMILY FACTORS

Of the research investigating family-based approaches to the treatment of eating disorders, somewhat inconsistent findings have emerged in assessing the potentially moderating role of family structure. For instance, no difference in outcome was noted in families undertaking FBT-BN in both intact and non-intact family structures (Doyle et al., 2009). However, evidence from the family-based treatment of AN suggests that those from non-intact families do not typically respond as well to short-duration treatment as those from intact families, although they do respond more favorably to longer, as opposed to shorter, forms of treatment (Lock et al., 2005). This may possibly reflect the greater ego-syntonicity of symptoms and corresponding emphasis on parental control throughout FBT-AN, which may result in high levels of parental distress, anxiety, and an elevated need for emotional support among parents (Parent & Parent, 2008). Somewhat contrastingly, the more collaborative nature of the parent-adolescent relationship throughout FBT-BN may not be as vulnerable to the impact of non-intact family structures, because the parent and adolescent are typically working toward the same goal, thereby yielding less conflict and distress.

Alongside the structure of the family, reports have indicated that the interactions among family members may also impact upon treatment outcome in those undergoing family-based treatment. For instance, early studies identified that families in which high levels of expressed emotion and criticism were present (from parents to children) did not typically fare very well in traditional FBT delivered in a conjoint format with parents, patient, and siblings all seen together (Le Grange et al., 1992a); alternately, more recent studies have identified that parental warmth is predictive of favorable treatment outcome (Le Grange et al., 2011). Indeed, families characterized by high levels of expressed emotion typically fare better in a separated form of family-based treatment, both at end of treatment and at 5-year follow-up (Eisler et al., 2000; Eisler et al., 2007).

Finally, the presence of eating disordered psychopathology in one or both parents is thought to moderate the efficacy of treatment modalities that centrally implicate parental involvement (Lock & Le Grange, 2013), as parents grappling with their own eating disordered symptom profile may find being charged with the responsibility of their child's recovery particularly challenging.

ILLNESS DURATION

In keeping with adult populations, treatment outcomes in adolescent eating disorders may be particularly impacted by the length of illness, with longer illness durations typically corresponding with poorer treatment outcomes. (However, research is needed to disaggregate time from onset of illness to first treatment and overall duration of illness, variables that are often conflated in the literature [Shoemaker, 1997]). With respect to adolescent populations, this finding is particularly robust, and holds across a range of eating disorder psychopathologies and treatment modalities (Russell et al., 1987). For instance, in cases of adolescent anorexia nervosa, research demonstrated that those with an illness duration of longer than 1 year typically responded less favorably than those whose illness has lasted less than 1 year (Russell et al., 1987). Though illness duration has not been specifically tested in cases of adolescent BN, research from adult populations similarly suggests that length of illness duration may moderate treatment efficacy, with those receiving treatment within the first few years of their illness (typically during adolescence) reporting better outcomes (Reas et al., 2000).

EARLY TREATMENT RESPONSE

Early response to treatment has been found to be a robust predictor of treatment outcome across eating disorder presentations, and in a variety of treatment modalities. For instance, studies in adult populations of BN have demonstrated that treatment response within the first 3–4 weeks of therapy may reliably predict long-term outcome in CBT (Wilson et al., 1999), interpersonal psychotherapy (IPT; Fairburn et al., 2004), and psychopharmacology trials (Walsh et al., 2006). In exploring this relationship in adolescent populations, less comprehensive research exists, although recent evidence similarly suggests that treatment response by session 6 of treatment reliably predicts outcome in FBT and supportive psychotherapy for adolescent BN (Le Grange et al., 2008). In the context of adolescent AN, research from inpatient settings suggests that weight gain during the first 3 weeks of an inpatient admission is highly predictive of discharge weight (Hartmann, Wirth, & Zeeck, 2007). Somewhat similarly, the outpatient treatment of adolescent AN may also be predicted by early response to treatment, with recent evidence suggesting that overall treatment response in FBT-AN and adolescent-focused therapy can be reliably indicated by treatment response as early as session 3–5 (Doyle et al., 2010; Le Grange et al., 2013).

EATING DISORDER SEVERITY

A robust predictor of treatment outcome, spanning a multitude of treatment modalities, is the patient's body mass index (BMI; a standardized score for body weight, based on the adolescent's age, height, and weight), which is broadly assumed to reflect the degree of malnutrition and starvation in the unwell adolescent in the context of eating disorders. For instance, one large-scale longitudinal international study recently examined the relevance of BMI in predicting outcome in adolescent AN across a variety of treatment contexts, finding that lower BMI at intake was significantly predictive of lower BMI and poorer psychosocial functioning at discharge, and at follow-up approximately 8 years later (Steinhausen et al., 2009). Accordingly, higher body weight at admission is associated with greater weight maintenance post discharge (Castro-Fornieles et al., 2007).

Alongside the physiological indicators of illness severity, the cognitive severity of eating disorder symptomatology has also been found to predict treatment outcome in adolescents with eating disorders. As such, lower scores on measures of cognitive and behavioral symptomatology at baseline significantly predict treatment outcome in adolescent BN, regardless of the treatment modality employed (Le Grange, Crosby, & Lock, 2008). Somewhat similarly in adolescent samples of AN, eating-related obsessionality has been found to have a moderating effect on weight-related outcome, in that those reporting high eating-related obsessional-ity are less likely to make progress with shorter FBT interventions, and typi-cally require lengthier treatment to make significant progress (Lock et al., 2005). However, the same study examining short (6 months) versus long (12 months) treatment conditions found that length of treatment also moderates treatment dropout, with lengthier treatment interventions being more predictive of prema-ture treatment dropout, suggesting that adolescents with AN who report high eating-related obsessionality may be particularly vulnerable to poor treatment outcome.

However, in further exploring this moderating effect in the treatment of ado-lescent AN, it has more recently been found that those with high eating disor-der psychopathology and eating-related obsessionality fare more favorably by the end of treatment in family-based treatment as opposed to insight-oriented individual treatment (Le Grange et al., 2012). In instances of more severe eating disorder psychopathology and obsessionality, the sustained focus on behavioral symptoms (i.e., dietary restriction) afforded by FBT may assist in the disrupting of maintaining behaviors, which is central to initiating cognitive change (i.e., drive for thinness) (Le Grange et al., 2012).

PSYCHIATRIC COMORBIDITY

Psychiatric comorbidity is high among adolescents with eating disorders, with up to 55% of those with AN, 88% of those with BN, and 83% of those with binge eating disorder reporting one or more comorbid psychiatric condition, respec-tively (Swanson et al., 2011). Among those with AN, the presence of psychiatric comorbidity has been associated with both greater rates of treatment dropout and poorer rates of symptom remission, as compared to adolescents without comorbid concerns, across a range of treatment modalities (Le Grange et al., 2012; Lock et al., 2007). In the context of adolescent BN, lower baseline scores for depression are also associated with more favorable treatment outcomes in the content of adolescent BN, with those adolescents with higher levels of depressive symptomatology at the outset of treatment typically being less likely to be remit-ted of symptoms (Le Grange et al., 2008).

Mediators of Treatment in Adolescent Eating Disorders

Formal tests of mediation effects in the treatment of adolescent eating disorders are limited and are restricted to clinician factors, reviewed below. However, theo-retical models have been put forward hypothesizing individual- and family-level factors that drive change in FBT for AN (Hildebrandt, Bacow, Markella, & Loeb, 2012; Le Grange & Loeb, 2014; Loeb, Lock, Le Grange, & Grief, 2012). Specifically, FBT is thought to possess explicit corrective techniques to address maladaptive family-level processes. These processes are a result of early attempts to man-age disordered eating in offspring; these family-level processes include secrecy, blame, fear that parental action or lack of intervention will worsen the eating disorder, and internalization of the illness (Le Grange & Loeb, 2014; Loeb et al., 2012). By extension, theoretical mediators include reductions in these parental variables. At the same time, FBT carries implicit corrective mechanisms to address individual processes, such as maladaptive reinforcement patterns like fear conditioning; by functioning as a naturalistic exposure treatment in many ways (e.g., exposing the patient to a wide range of foods across multiple contexts and to feared weight values on the scale), FBT may be mediated by systematic anxiety reduction in the patient (Hildebrandt et al., 2012; Le Grange & Loeb, 2014; Loeb et al., 2012). To date, these mediators have not been subjected to empirical testing.

CLINICIAN FACTORS

One possible mediating factor in the treatment of adolescent eating disorders, which has not been assessed in strict mediator analyses, pertains to the clinical practice of the treating clinicians themselves. Recent evidence has outlined how a large proportion of clinicians face barriers in taking up evidence-based practice in adolescent presentations of AN, citing a multitude of difficulties, including interventional, organizational, interpersonal, and systemic barriers (Couturier et al., 2013). As such, up to 95% of clinicians report feeling as though they require extra training and more support before attempting to undertake evidence-based treatment in the context of adolescent anorexia nervosa (Couturier et al., 2013). Thus, although not formally assessed, it seems plausible that instances in which evidence-based treatment is not adopted and practiced may mediate treatment outcome. Furthermore, of those who do attempt to take up evidence-based practice for eating disorders, a significant proportion have been found to "drift" from the core principles of the treatment they endorse, resulting in a reduced fidelity to the treatment models assessed in controlled research trials (Waller, Stringer, & Meyer, 2012), which may perhaps further mediate treatment effects.

Furthermore, alongside the individual clinician's clinical practice, recent research has called attention to the professional relationship among treating clinicians as a potentially mediating factor in the treatment of adolescent eating disorders (Murray, Thornton, & Wallis, 2012). Indeed, the multifactorial nature of eating disorders often necessitates involvement by a number of clinicians spanning a variety of professional and institutional contexts, and as such, may be oriented toward differing goals or employ differing methods in bringing about shared goals. Research has posited that poor alliance and cohesion in multidisciplinary teams may lead to treatment interventions being undermined and rendered less effective, particularly in the context of eating disorders due to the lack of accepted treatments and high propensity for splitting behaviors among those afflicted (Murray et al., 2012). To date, one pilot study has examined the relationship between collegial alliance and treatment outcome in FBT for adolescent AN. Although no formal mediation tests were conducted, correlational analyses in this clinical study showed that alliance among colleagues may demonstrate predictive value in discriminating between those patients who drop out and those who complete treatment, and is also positively correlated with the remission of cognitive AN symptomatology (Murray, Griffiths, & Le Grange, 2014).

In addition to collegial alliance, therapeutic alliance between the therapist and the patient and the patient's family has also been investigated in the context of eating disorders, with mixed results emerging this far. For instance, in the context of family-based treatment for adolescent AN, while therapeutic alliance is correlated with early treatment response and early treatment non-dropout (Pereira, Lock, & Oggins, 2006), a strong therapeutic alliance alone is not sufficient to bring about full symptom remission, and shows no relationship to sustained illness remission by the end of treatment (Forsberg et al., 2013). Somewhat similarly in CBT-based approaches, despite up to 90% of clinicians endorsing the belief that the strength of the therapeutic relationship is what facilitates symptom remission (Brown, Mountford, & Waller, 2013a), research suggests that therapeutic alliance is predicted by symptom remission and early behavioral change, but not vice versa (Brown, Mountford, & Waller, 2013b). Thus, rather than mediating treatment outcome, emerging evidence suggests, across eating disorder psychopathology and psychotherapies, that treatment outcome mediates therapeutic alliance.

CONCLUDING COMMENTS, CLINICAL IMPLICATIONS, AND DIRECTIONS FOR FUTURE RESEARCH

To date, the empirical work outlining moderating and mediating variables in the treatment of adolescents with eating disorders has yielded important clinical implications, resulting in more informed efforts to improve treatment efficacy. In steering away from generic and homogenous approaches to treatment, current research has been able to identify subgroups of patients for which particular types of treatment may not exert therapeutic effects. For instance, those with high familial expressed emotion may not fare as well as those without high expressed emotion in family-based treatments (Le Grange et al., 1992b). As a result, treatment in such instances has been modified, and the provision of separated family-based treatment has allowed much better treatment outcomes for groups with high familial expressed emotion (Eisler et al., 2000).

Furthermore, in explicating the mediating processes of treatment once it has commenced, important findings have emerged suggesting that several crucial variables that are readily identifiable at early stages of treatment may impact treatment outcome. For instance, the first 4–6 sessions of treatment may be a particularly important time for the treatment of adolescent eating disorders, with early clinical markers during this time reliably predicting outcome (Doyle et al., 2010; Le Grange et al, 2013) and treatment dropout (Murray et al., 2014). This is particularly important in the context of adolescent eating disorders, given that longer illness duration is associated with more severe medical and psychological sequale (Treasure & Russell, 2011), poorer response to treatments, and greater likelihood of chronic illness course (Reas et al., 2000; Russell et al., 1987).

Thus, those whose early indicators suggest treatment non-response may benefit significantly from the early identification of this likely treatment non-response, allowing for alternative treatment or augmentations, as opposed to undergoing lengthy treatment programs, which may be contraindicated by moderating or mediating variables. Thus, all clinicians working with adolescent eating disorders should review treatment progress within the first 4–6 sessions, calculating progress and assessing whether alternative or augmentative interventions are indicated.

Furthermore, in attempting to augment treatment for those who may not respond to standard treatment, a thorough understanding of the mediating variables and processes that bring about favorable treatment response may inform possible augmentations. For instance, empirical research has demonstrated that the core tenets of FBT (i.e., parental control, lack of parental criticism to the adolescent) are directly related to treatment outcome (Ellison et al., 2012), suggesting that augmentations may seek to amplify and not corrupt these active therapeutic processes.

Despite mounting empirical evidence allowing for clinically useful inferences, few trials to date have reported moderating and mediating variables in adolescent eating disorder treatment (Le Grange et al., 2008; Le Grange et al., 2012; Lock et al., 2005). As such, the sparse evidence base to date has precluded the development of an overarching theoretical framework accounting for the interaction of moderating and mediating variables in the treatment of adolescent eating disorders. There can be little question as to the ongoing need for greater illumination of moderators and mediators in the treatment of adolescents with eating disorders. Future research ought to further investigate moderating and mediating variables of treatment, particularly in RCTs, and it has been recommended that all those conducting RCTs conduct moderator and mediator analyses (Kraemer et al., 2002). In addition, future research ought to develop and test possible augmentations to treatment interventions oriented toward adolescents with eating disorders, in light of both (1) moderating variables that may highlight conditions under which treatment may be less effective, and (2) mediating processes that, once treatment has commenced, may undermine active and therapeutic components of treatment. Such endeavors have commenced, illustrating that online parent-support forums (Binford-Hopf et al., 2013) and intensive parent-to-parent consultations (Rhodes et al., 2008) may augment treatment.

REFERENCES

American Psychiatric Association (2013). *Diagnostic and statistical manual of mental disorders* (5th ed.,). Washington, DC: American Psychiatric Publishing.

Balestrieri, M., Oriani, M. G., Simoncini, A., Bellantuono, C. (2013). Psychotropic drug treatment in anorexia nervosa: Search for differences in efficacy/tolerability between adolescent and mixed-age population. *European Eating Disorders Review, 21*, 361–373.

Binford-Hopf, R., Le Grange, D., Moessner, M., & Bauer, S. (2013). Internet-based chat support groups for parents in family-based treatment for adolescent eating disorders: A pilot study. *European Eating Disorders Review, 21*, 215–223.

Brandenburg, B., Lesser, J., Mangham, D., & Crow, S. (2011). Psychopharmacological interventions for adolescents with eating disorders. *Adolescent Psychiatry, 1*, 277–285.

Brown, A., Mountford, V. A., & Waller, G. (2013a). Therapeutic alliance and weight gain during cognitive behavioural therapy for anorexia nervosa. *Behaviour Research and Therapy, 51*, 216–220.

Brown, A., Mountford, V. A., & Waller, G. (2013b). Is the therapeutic alliance overvalued in the treatment of eating disorders? *International Journal of Eating Disorders, 46*, 779–782.

Bulik, C. M., Berkman, N. D., Brownley, K. A., Sedway, J. A., & Lohr, K. N. (2007). Anorexia nervosa treatment: A systematic review of randomized control trials. *International Journal of Eating Disorders, 40*, 310–320.

Castro-Fornieles, J., Casualà, V., Saura, B., Martinez, E., Lazaro, L., Vila, M., Plana, M. T., et al., (2007). Predictors of weight maintenance after hospital discharge in adolescent anorexia nervosa. *International Journal of Eating Disorders, 40*, 129–135.

Couturier, J., Kimber, M., & Szatmari, P. (2013). Efficacy of family-based treatment for adolescents with eating disorders: A systematic review and meta-analysis. *International Journal of Eating Disorders, 46*, 3–11.

Couturier, J., Kimber, M., Jack, S., Niccols, A., Van Blyderveen, S., & McVey, G. (2013). Understanding the update of family-based treatment for adolescents with anorexia nervosa: Therapist perspectives. *International Journal of Eating Disorders, 46*, 177–188.

Couturier, J., & Lock, J. (2007). A review of medication use for children and adolescents with eating disorders. *Journal of the Canadian Academy for Child and Adolescent Psychiatry, 16*, 173–176.

Dare, C., & Eisler, I. (2000). A multi-family group day program treatment programme for adolescent eating disorder. *European Eating Disorder Review, 8*, 4–18.

Doyle, P. M., Le Grange, D., Loeb, K. L., Doyle, A. M., & Crosby, R. D. (2010). Early response to family-based treatment for adolescent anorexia nervosa. *International Journal of Eating Disorders, 43*, 659–662.

Doyle, A. C., McLean, C., Washington, B. N., Hoste, R. R., & Le Grange, D. (2009). Are single-parent families different from two-parent families in the treatment of adolescent bulimia nervosa using family-based treatment? *International Journal of Eating Disorders, 42*, 153–157.

Eddy, K. T., Dojer, D. J., Franko, D. L., Tahilani, K., Thomptson-Brenner, H., & Herzog, D. B. (2008). Diagnostic crossover in anorexia nervosa and bulimia nervosa: Implications for DSM-V. *American Journal of Psychiatry, 165*, 245–250.

Eisler, I. (2005). The empirical and theoretical base of family therapy and multiple family day therapy for adolescent anorexia nervosa. *Journal of Family Therapy, 27*, 104–131.

Eisler, I., Dare, C., Hodes, M., Russell, G. F. M., Dodge, E., & Le Grange, D. (2000). Family therapy for adolescent anorexia nervosa: The results of a controlled comparison of two family interventions. *The Journal of Child Psychology and Psychiatry, 41*, 727–736.

Eisler, I., Simic, M., Russell, G. F. M., & Dare, C. (2007). A randomised controlled treatment trial of two forms of family therapy in adolescent anorexia nervosa: A five-year follow-up. *The Journal of Child Psychology and Psychiatry, 48*, 552–560.

Ellison, R., Rhodes, P., Madden, S., Miskovic, J., Wallis, A., Baillie, A., Kohn, M., & Touyz, S. W. (2012). Do the components of manualised family-based treatment for anorexia nervosa predict weight gain? *International Journal of Eating Disorders, 45*, 609–614.

Fairburn, C. G. (2008). *Cognitive behavior therapy and eating disorders.* New York: Guilford Press.

Fairburn, C. G., Agras, S. W., Walsh, B. T., Wilson, G. T., & Stice, E. (2004). Prediction of outcome in bulimia nervosa by early change in treatment. *American Journal of Psychiatry, 161*, 2322–2324.

Fisher, C. A., Hetrick, S. E., & Rushford, N. (2010). Family therapy for anorexia nervosa. *Cochrane Database Syst Rev, 14*(4), CD004780. doi: 10.1002/14651858.CD004780. pub2.

Fitzpatrick, K. K., Moye, A., Hoste, R., Lock, J., & Le Grange, D. (2010). Adolescent focussed psychotherapy for adolescents with anorexia nervosa. *Journal of Contemporary Psychotherapy, 40*, 31–39.

Forsberg, S., LoTiempo, E., Bryson, S., Fitzpatrick, K. K., Le Grange, D., & Lock, J. (2013). Therapeutic alliance in two treatments for adolescent anorexia nervosa. *International Journal of Eating Disorders, 46*, 34–38.

Gower, S, & Bryant-Waugh, R. (2004). Management of child and adolescent eating disorders: The current evidence base and future directions. *Journal of Child Psychology and Psychiatry, 45*, 63–83.

Gower, S., Clark, A., Roberts, C., Griffiths, A., Edwards, V., Bryan, C., et al. (2007). Clinical effectiveness of treatments for anorexia nervosa in young people: Randomised controlled trial. *The British Journal of Psychiatry, 191*, 427–435.

Grave, R. D., Calugi, S., Doll, H. A., & Fairburn, C. G. (2013). Enhanced cognitive behaviour therapy for adolescents with anorexia nervosa: An alternative to family therapy? *Behaviour, Research and Therapy, 51*, R9–R12.

Hartmann, A., Wirth, C., & Zeeck, A. (2007). Prediction of failure of inpatient treatment of anorexia nervosa from early weight gain. *Psychotherapy Research, 17*, 218–229.

Hildebrandt, T., Bacow, T., Markella, M., & Loeb, K. L. (2012). Anxiety in anorexia nervosa and its management using family-based treatment. *European Eating Disorders Review, 20*, e1–e16.

Kafantaris, V., Leigh, E., Hertz, S., Berest, A., Schebendach, J., Sterling, W. M, et al. (2011). A placebopcontrolled pilot study of adjunctive olanzapine for adolescents with anorexia nervosa. *Journal of Child and Adolescent Psychopharmacology, 21*, 207–212.

Keel, P. K., & Brown, T. A. (2010). Update on course and outcome in eating disorders. *International Journal of Eating Disorders, 43*, 195–204.

Kohn, M., & Golden, N. H. (2001). Eating disorders in children and adolescents: Epidemiology, diagnosis and treatment. *Paediatric Drugs, 3*, 91–99.

Kotler, L. A., Devlin, M. J., Davies, M., & Walsh, B. T. (2003). An open trial of fluoxetine for adolescents with bulimia nervosa. *Journal of Child and Adolescent Psychopharmacology, 13*, 329–335.

Kraemer, H. C., Wilson, G. T., Fairburn, C. G., & Agras, W. S. (2002). Mediators and moderators of treatment effects in randomized control trials. *Archives of General Psychiatry, 59,* 877–883.

Lebow, J., Sim, L. A., Erwin, P. J., Murad, M. H. (2013). The effect of atypical antipsychotic medication in indivuals with anorexia nervosa: A systematic review and meta-analysis. *International Journal of Eating Disorders, 46,* 332–339.

Le Grange, D., Accurso, E., Lock, J., Agras, W. S., & Bryson, S. W. (2013). Early weight gain predicts outcome in two treatments for adolescent anorexia nervosa. *International Journal of Eating Disorders, 47,* 124–129.

Le Grange, D., Binford, R., & Loeb, K. L. (2005). Manualized family-based treatment for anorexia nervosa: A case series. *Journal of the American Academy of Child and Adolescent Psychiatry, 44,* 41–46.

Le Grange, D., Crosby, R., & Lock, J. (2008). Predictors and moderators of outcome in family-based treatment for adolescent bulimia nervosa. *Journal of the American Academy for Child & Adolescent Psychiatry, 47,* 464–470.

Le Grange, D., Doyle, P., Crosby, R. D., & Chen, E. (2008). Early response to treatment in adolescent bulimia nervosa. *International Journal of Eating Disorders, 41,* 755–757.

Le Grange, D., & Eisler, I. (2009). Family interventions in adolescent anorexia nervosa. *Child and Adolescent Psychiatric Clinics of North America, 18,* 159–173.

Le Grange, D., Eisler, I., Dare, C., & Russell, G. F. (1992a). Evaluation of family treatments in adolescent anorexia nervosa: A pilot study. *International Journal of Eating Disorders, 12,* 347–357.

Le Grange, D., Eisler, I., Dare, C., & Hodes, M. (1992b). Family criticism and self-starvation: A study of expressed emotion. *Journal of Family Therapy, 14,* 177–192.

Le Grange, D., & Lock, J. (2007). *Treating bulimia in adolescents: A family-based approach.* New York: Guilford Press.

Le Grange, D., Lock, J., Agras, W. S., Bryson, S. W., Jo, B., & Kraemer, H. C. (2012). Mediators and moderators of remission in family-based treatment and adolescent focussed therapy for anorexia nervosa. *Behavior Research and Therapy, 50,* 85–92.

Le Grange, D., Lock, J., Accurso, E., Agras, W., Darcy, A., Forsberg, S., & Bryson, S. (2014). Relapse from remission at two- to four-year follow-up in two treatments for adolescent anorexia nervosa. *Journal of the American Academy for Child and Adolescent Psychiatry, 53*(11), 1162–1167.

Le Grange, D., & Loeb, K. L. (2014). Family-based treatment for adolescent eating disorders: A transdiagnostic approach. In J. Ehrenreich-May & B. Chu (Eds.), *Transdiagnostic mechanisms and treatment for youth psychopathology.* New York: Guilford Press.

Lock, J. (2005). Adjusting cognitive behaviour therapy for adolescents with bulimia nervosa: Results of a case series. *American Journal of Psychotherapy, 59,* 267–281.

Lock, J., Agras, W. S., Bryson, S., & Kraemer, H. C. (2005). A comparison of short- and long-term family therapy for adolescent anorexia nervosa. *Journal of the American Academy of Child & Adolescent Psychiatry, 44,* 632–639.

Lock, J., Couturier, J., & Agras, W. S. (2008). Costs of remission and recovery using family-based treatment for adolescent anorexia nervosa: A descriptive report. *Eating Disorders: The Journal of Treatment & Prevention, 4,* 322–330.

Lock, J., & Le Grange, D. (2013). *Treatment manual for anorexia nervosa: A family-based approach* (2nd ed.). New York: Guilford Press.

Lock, J., Le Grange, D., Agras, W. S., Moye, A., Bryson, S., & Jo, B. (2010). Randomized control trial comparing family-based treatment with adolescent-focussed individual therapy for adolescents with anorexia nervosa. *Archives of General Psychiatry*, *67*, 1025–1032.

Loeb, K. L., Lock, J., Le Grange, D., & Greif, R. (2012) Transdiagnostic theory and application of family-based treatment for youth with eating disorders. *Cognitive and Behavioral Practice*, *19*, 17–30.

Loeb, K. L., Walsh, B., Lock, J., Le Grange, D., Jones, J., Marcus, S., . . . Dobrow, I. (2007). Open trial of family-based treatment for full and partial anorexia nervosa in adolescence: Evidence of successful dissemination. *Journal of the American Academy of Child & Adolescent Psychiatry*, *46*(7), 792–800.

Madden, S., Miskovic-Wheatley, J., Wallis, A., Kohn, M., Lock, J., Le Grange, D., Jo, B., Clarke, S., Rhodes, P., Hay, P., & Touyz, S. (2014). A randomized controlled trial of inpatient treatment for anorexia nervosa in medically unstable adolescents. *Psychological Medicine*, *14*, 1–13.

Mond, J. M., Hay, P. J., Rodgers, B., Owen, C., & Beumont, P. J. V. (2005). Assessing quality of life in eating disorder patients. *Quality of Life Research*, *14*, 171–178.

Murray, S. B., Griffiths, S., & Le Grange, D. (2014). The role of collegial alliance in family based treatment of adolescent anorexia nervosa: A pilot study. *International Journal of Eating Disorders*, *47*, 418–421.

Murray, S. B., Loeb, K., & Le Grange, D. (2014). Indexing psychopathology throughout family-based treatment for adolescent anorexia nervosa: Are we on track? *Advances in Eating Disorders: Theory, Research and Practice*, *2*, 93–96.

Murray, S. B., Thornton, C., & Wallis, A. (2012). A thorn in the side of evidence-based treatment for adolescent anorexia nervosa. *Australian & New Zealand Journal of Psychiatry*, *46*, 1026–1068.

Parent, B. A., & Parent, T. C. (2008). Anorexia, Maudsley and an impressive recovery: One family's story. *Journal of Paediatrics and Child Health*, *44*, 70–73.

Pereira, T., Lock, J., & Oggins, J. (2006). Role of therapeutic alliance in family therapy for adolescent anorexia nervosa. *International Journal of Eating Disorders*, *39*, 677–684.

Pompili, M., Mancinelli, I., Girardi, P., Ruberto, A., & Tatarelli, R. (2004). Suicide in anorexia nervosa: A meta-analysis. *International Journal of Eating Disorders*, *36*, 99–103.

Pretorious, N., Arcelus, J., Beetham J, et al. (2009). Cognitive-behavioral therapy for adolescents with binge eating syndromes: A case series. *International Journal of Eating Disorders*, *39*, 252–255.

Reas, D. L., Williamson, D. A., Martin, C. K., & Zucker, N. L. (2000). Duration of illness predicts outcome for bulimia nervosa: A long term follow-up study. *International Journal of Eating Disorders*, *27*, 428–434.

Rhodes, P., Baillee, A., Brown, J., &, S. (2008). Can parent-to-parent consultation improve the effectiveness of the Maudsley model of family-based treatment for anorexia nervosa? A randomized control trial. *Journal of Family Therapy*, *30*, 96–108.

Robin, A., Siegal, P., Koepke, T., Moye, A., & Tice, S. (1994). Family therapy versus individual therapy for adolescent females with anorexia nervosa. *Journal of Developmental and Behavioral Pediatrics, 15,* 111–116.

Robin, A., Siegal, P., Moye, A., Gilroy, M., Dennis, A., & Sikand, A. (1999). A controlled comparison of family versus individual therapy fort adolescents with anorexia nervosa. *Journal of the American Academy of Child and Adolescent Psychiatry, 38,* 1482–1489.

Rome, E. S., Ammermann, S., Rosen, D., Keller, R. J., Lock, J., Mammel, K. A., O'Toole, J., et al. (2003). Children and adolescent with eating disorders: The state of the art. *Paediatrics, 111,* e98–e108.

Russell, G. F. M., Szmuckler, G. I., Dare, C., & Eiler, I. (1987). An evaluation of family therapy in anorexia nervosa and bulimia nervosa. *Archives of General Psychiatry, 44,* 1047–1056.

Schapman-Williams, A. M., & Lock, J. (2006). Cognitive-behavioral therapy for adolescents with binge eating syndromes: A case series. *International Journal of Eating Disorders, 39,* 252–255.

Schmidt, U., Lee, S., Beecham, J., Perkins, S., Treasure, J., Yi, I., et al. (2007). A randomized control trial of family therapy and cognitive behavior therapy guided self help care for adolescents with bulimia nervosa and related disorders. *American Journal of Psychiatry, 164,* 591–598.

Scholz, M., & Asen, E. (2001). Multiple family therapy with eating disordered adolescents: Concepts and preliminary results. *European Eating Disorders Review, 9,* 33–42.

Shoemaker, C. (1997). Does early intervention improve the prognosis in anorexia nervosa? A systematic review of the treatment outcome literature. *International Journal of Eating Disorders, 21*(1), 1–15.

Smink, F. R., van Hoeken, D., & Hoek, H. W. (2012). Epidemiology of eating disorder: Incidence, prevalence and mortality rates. *Current Psychiatry Reports, 14,* 406–414.

Steinhausen, H. C. (2002). The outcome of anorexia nervosa in the 20th century. *American Journal of Psychiatry, 159,* 1284–1293.

Steinhausen, H. C., Grigoriou-Serbanescu, M., Boyadjieva, S., Neumärker, K. L., & Metzke, C. W. (2009). The relevance of body weight in the medium-term to long-term course of adolescent anorexia nervosa: Findings from a multisite study. *International Journal of Eating Disorders, 42,* 19–25.

Strober, M., Freeman, R., & Morrell, W. (1997). The long-term course of severe anorexia nervosa in adolescents: Survival analysis of recovery, relapse, and outcome predictors over 10–15 years in a prospective study. *International Journal of Eating Disorders, 22,* 339–360.

Strober, M., & Johnson, C. (2012). The need for complex ideas in anorexia nervosa: Why biology, environment, and psyche all matter, why therapists make mistakes, and why clinical benchmarks are needed for managing weight correction. *International Journal of Eating Disorders, 45,* 155–178.

Swanson, S. A., Crow, S. J., Le Grange, D., Swendsen, J., & Merikangas, K. R. (2011). Prevalence and correlates of eating disorder in adolescents. *Archives of General Psychiatry, 68,* 714–723.

Treasure, J., & Russell, G. (2011). The case for early intervention in anorexia nervosa: Theoretical exploration or maintaining factors. *British Journal of Psychiatry, 199*, 5–7.

Waller, G., Stringer, H., & Meyer, C. (2012). What cognitive behavioural techniques do therapists report using when delivering cognitive behavioural therapy for the eating disorders? *Journal of Consulting and Clinical Psychology, 80*, 171–175.

Walsh, B. T, Sysko, R., Parides, M. K. (2006). Early response to desipramine among women with bulimia nervosa. *International Journal of Eating Disorders, 39*, 72–75.

Wilson, G. T., Loeb, K. L., Walsh, B. T., Labouvie, E., Perkova, E., Liu, X., et al. (1999). Psychological versus pharmacological treatments of bulimia nervosa: Predictors and processes of change. *Journal of Consulting and Clinical Psychology, 67*, 451–459.

Winston, A. P., Paul, M., & Juanola-Borrat, Y. (2012). The same but different? Treatment of anorexia nervosa in adolescents and adults. *European Eating Disorders Review, 20*, 89–93.

Moderators and Mediators of Treatments for Youth With School Refusal or Truancy

DAVID A. HEYNE, FLOOR M. SAUTER, AND
BRANDY R. MAYNARD ■

INTRODUCTION

Going to school is an uncomplicated fact of life for most school-aged youth. In some households, however, school attendance is a source of upset for the young person and possible conflict among family members. In other households there may be no indication that a young person has difficulty going to school, but he or she fails to attend as often as required by law. School absenteeism jeopardizes a young person's development and poses a risk for well-being in late adolescence and adulthood (Heyne, Sauter, Ollendick, van Widenfelt, & Westenberg, 2014). Effective intervention is needed, and the process begins with accurate identification (Contessa & Paccione-Dyszlewski, 1981) and subtyping (Maynard, Salas-Wright, Vaughn, & Peters, 2012).

Accurate identification requires that a distinction be made between non-problematic and problematic absenteeism, paying attention to the legitimacy and the amount of absenteeism. Non-problematic absenteeism includes legitimate absences due to events that are agreed upon by school and parents (e.g., illness, religious holidays) and can be compensated for (e.g., extra classwork). Regarding the amount of absenteeism, Kearney (2008) proposed that problematic absenteeism exists when youth: "(1) have missed at least 25% of total school time for at least 2 weeks, (2) experience severe difficulty attending classes for at least 2 weeks with significant interference in a child's or family's daily routine, and/or (3) are absent for at least 10 days of school during any 15-week period while school is in session" (p. 265). The second criterion indicates that actual absence from school is not a necessary condition for determining that "problematic absenteeism" exists. Indeed, Kearney's (2001) continuum for problematic absenteeism ranges from full attendance but with duress and pleas not to have to go to school, through periodic absences, to complete absence for an extended period.

Subtyping begins with the differentiation between parent-motivated problematic absenteeism (also referred to as school withdrawal) and child-motivated[1] problematic absenteeism (Kearney, 2003). Child-motivated absenteeism, the focus of this chapter, may take the form of truancy or school refusal. Truancy is said to occur when a young person is absent from school and the parents do not know about their child's absence (Kearney, 2002) or whereabouts (Berg et al., 1985). School refusal has been defined by Berg and colleagues (Berg, 1997, 2002; Berg, Nichols, & Pritchard, 1969; Bools, Foster, Brown, & Berg, 1990) as the following: (a) reluctance or refusal to attend school, often leading to prolonged absence; (b) the young person is usually at home during school hours rather than concealing the problem from parents; (c) there is emotional upset at the prospect of attending school (e.g., somatic complaints, anxiety, unhappiness) or more generally (e.g., anxiety or depressive disorder); (d) there is an absence of severe antisocial behavior, beyond the young person's resistance to parental attempts to get them to go to school; and (e) parents have made efforts to secure their child's attendance at school. These criteria help differentiate school refusal from truancy (based on criteria b, c, and d) and school withdrawal (based on criterion e).

Some clinical researchers refer to truancy and school refusal collectively as "school refusal behavior" (e.g., Kearney, 2003; Lyon & Cotler, 2007), while others maintain the distinction between truancy and school refusal (e.g., Goodman & Scott, 2012; Hella & Bernstein, 2012). According to Egger, Costello, and Angold (2003), school refusal and truancy are "distinct but not mutually exclusive" (p. 797). To be sure, a relatively small proportion of youth with school attendance problems display characteristics of both school refusal and truancy (e.g., 5% in Berg et al., 1993; 9% in Bools et al., 1990; 5% in Egger et al., 2003). Differentiation between school refusal, truancy, and the mixed type helps isolate type-specific risk factors and processes warranting attention in treatment. For example, Egger and colleagues found that lax parental supervision was significantly associated with truancy and not with school refusal; being shy with peers and being bullied or teased were significantly associated with school refusal but not with truancy; and moving house multiple times was significantly associated with mixed school refusal and truancy but not with pure school refusal or pure truancy.

The current chapter preserves the distinction between school refusal and truancy and conceptualizes school refusal according to Berg and colleagues' criteria (Berg, 1997, 2002; Berg et al., 1969; Bools et al., 1990). The main emphasis in this chapter is school refusal, but consideration is also given to truancy. Given the differences between school refusal, truancy, and their respective interventions, it is likely that the prediction, moderation, and mediation of outcome will also differ across these two types of problematic absenteeism.

DESCRIPTION

Internalizing Problems

School refusal is not listed as a disorder in the classification system presented in the *Diagnostic and Statistical Manual of Mental Disorders* (5th ed.; *DSM-5*; American Psychiatric Association [APA], 2013). However, one or more of the criteria for the anxiety disorders likely apply in cases of school refusal. By definition, a school refuser displays reluctance or refusal to go to school, which is one of the criteria for separation anxiety disorder. School refusal is also defined by emotional distress associated with school attendance. School refusers may, for example, display marked fear about being in the classroom (specific phobia), marked fear about social interaction at school (social anxiety disorder), and/or excessive worry about academic performance (generalized anxiety disorder). Approximately one-half of referred school refusers meet full diagnostic criteria for one or more of the anxiety disorders (e.g., 47% in Walter et al., 2010; 53% in Bernstein, 1991; 54% in McShane, Walter, & Rey, 2001).

Truancy is not commonly associated with anxiety problems. In a non-clinical study of youth with school attendance problems, Bools et al. (1990) found that none of the truants had an emotional disorder, while half of the school refusers did (usually with anxiety and fearfulness and occasionally with unhappiness). In Egger and colleagues' (2003) community sample, school refusal was significantly associated with anxiety disorders, school-related fears, and performance anxiety, while truancy was not. Further, just 1% of truants experienced headaches and stomachaches associated with separation or school attendance compared with 27% of school refusers.

High rates of depressive disorders have also been reported in referred samples of school refusers (e.g., 52% in Bernstein, 1991; 52% in McShane et al., 2001). In Egger and colleagues' (2003) community sample, depressive disorder was significantly associated with both school refusal (14%) and truancy (8%), although the likelihood of having a depressive disorder was higher for school refusers than truants (odds ratios of 3.4 and 1.2, respectively). At the symptom level, trouble falling or staying asleep was significantly associated with school refusal (32%) but not with truancy (19%), while fatigue was significantly associated with both school refusal (12%) and truancy (10%).

Externalizing Problems

Less severe externalizing problems, such as anger and argumentativeness, may be observed among school refusers when parents try to get them to school (e.g., Berg, 2002). In some school refusal cases, the presence of multiple externalizing behaviors over time will lead to a diagnosis of oppositional defiant disorder (ODD; e.g., 21% in Heyne et al., 2002; 44% in Layne, Bernstein, Egan, & Kushner,

2003; 24% in McShane et al., 2001). In Egger and colleagues' (2003) community sample, 6% of school refusers and 10% of truants were diagnosed with ODD. When comorbidity was accounted for, ODD was significantly associated with truancy but not with school refusal.

The school refusal criteria of Berg and colleagues (see the introduction of this chapter) specify the absence of severe antisocial behavior such as stealing and destructiveness. Numerous authors similarly differentiate between school refusal and truancy on the grounds that school refusal is not associated with serious antisocial behavior (e.g., McShane et al., 2001; Place, Hulsmeier, Davis, & Taylor, 2002; Thambirajah, Grandison, & De-Hayes, 2008). It is thus not surprising that conduct disorder (CD) is typically not observed among samples of school refusers. Even when Egger et al. (2003) defined school refusal without using Berg and colleagues' criteria, few school refusers (5%) were diagnosed with CD. By comparison, CD was diagnosed in 15% of truancy cases, and when comorbidity was accounted for, CD was significantly associated with truancy but not with school refusal. The relationship between truancy and CD will be due, in part, to a definition artifact; one of the criteria for CD is "often truant from school" (APA, 2013, p. 470). However, truancy is just one of 15 criteria for CD (3 are required for diagnosis), and truancy has been found to be highly correlated with myriad severe antisocial behaviors, including attacking others and frequent stealing (Vaughn, Maynard, Salas-Wright, Perron, & Abdon, 2013). Of course, truants will also vary in the extent to which they display externalizing problems. Maynard, Salas-Wright, et al. (2012) found that an "achiever" subgroup of truants reported fewer externalizing behaviors relative to three other truant subgroups.

STATE-OF-THE-ART TREATMENT OUTCOME

Cognitive Behavioral Therapy for School Refusal

Clinicians working with school refusers sometimes use cognitive behavioral therapy (CBT) manuals developed to treat anxiety disorders (e.g., Barrett & Turner, 2000; Kendall & Hedkte, 2006) or depressive disorders (e.g., Lewinsohn, Clarke, Hops, & Andrews, 1990; TADS Team, 2003). However, published anecdotal reports suggest that anxiety-focused treatment and depression-focused treatment fail to address co-occurring school refusal (see Heyne & Sauter, 2013). Standard manuals for anxiety or depression may be insufficient because of the heterogeneity associated with the etiology and presentation of school refusal (Heyne & Sauter, 2013). Moreover, because of the need to efficiently resolve school refusal, parents may have an important role to play in treatment (Heyne et al., 2014; Reynolds, Wilson, Austin, & Hooper, 2012; Tolin et al., 2009), whereas the need to involve parents is less clear in the treatment of anxiety disorders (Breinholst, Esbjørn, Reinholdt-Dunne, & Stallard, 2012; Reynolds et al., 2012) and depressive disorders (Clarke, Rohde, Lewinsohn, Hops, & Seeley, 1999). Evidence also suggests that when anxiety-focused manuals are applied with school refusers, the dropout rate is very high (56%; Beidas, Crawley, Mychailyszyn, Comer, & Kendall, 2010) and certainly higher than dropout rates in studies applying treatment manuals for school refusal (i.e., 0%–27%; Bernstein et al., 2000; Heyne et al., 2002; Heyne, Sauter, van Widenfelt, Vermeiren, & Westenberg, 2013; King et al., 1998; Last, Hansen, & Franco, 1998). According to Beidas et al. (2010), the high dropout from general CBT treatment might occur because of a failure to specifically target school refusal.

Five CBT manuals have been developed to target school refusal (i.e., Heyne & Rollings, 2002; Heyne, Sauter, & van Hout, 2008; Kearney & Albano, 2007; Last, 1993; Tolin et al., 2009). All five involve treatment delivery per case (as opposed to group treatment), consultation with school staff, and an emphasis on the completion of between-session tasks. Graded exposure to school attendance is included in all manuals but receives less attention in Kearney and Albano's (2007) interventions for positively reinforced school refusal behavior. All manuals but one (i.e., Last, 1993) include family work on communication and problem-solving. The manuals also differ in some ways. For example, Kearney and Albano's (2007) programs comprise approximately 8 sessions across 4 to 8 weeks, while Tolin and colleagues' (2009) intensive approach comprises 15 sessions across 3 weeks. The manuals incorporate problem-solving training with the young person as a matter of routine (Heyne & Rollings, 2002; Heyne et al., 2008), as required (Kearney & Albano, 2007; Tolin et al., 2009), or not at all (Last, 1993). Likewise, cognitive therapy (CT) is employed with all clients (e.g., Heyne et al., 2008) or as required (e.g., Tolin et al., 2009). Even when routinely used, CT might be limited to training in coping self-statements to facilitate engagement in exposure tasks (e.g., Last, 1993), or cognitive restructuring might be applied more broadly (e.g., Heyne et al., 2008; Kearney & Albano, 2007). The earliest CBT manual for school refusal (Last, 1993) was standardized, with all cases receiving the same intervention. Newer manuals advocate individualized treatment on the basis of the main function(s) served by the young person's behavior (e.g., Kearney & Albano, 2007) and/or on the basis of a broader case formulation (e.g., Heyne & Rollings, 2002; Heyne et al., 2008; Tolin et al., 2009). The differences across manuals should be borne in mind when interpreting the results of prediction, moderation, and mediation studies.

Outcome of CBT for School Refusal

Currently the most commonly reported treatment for school refusal is CBT. As a stand-alone treatment, CBT for school refusal has been evaluated in group-design studies in the continental United States (Kearney & Silverman, 1999; Last et al., 1998) and Australia (Heyne et al., 2002; King et al., 1998) and in case series from the continental United States (Kearney & Silverman, 1990; Tolin et al., 2009) and The Netherlands (Heyne et al., 2011). As part of a multimodal treatment, CBT for school refusal has been evaluated in the continental United States (Bernstein et al., 2000), Australia (McShane, Walter, & Rey, 2004), Germany (Walter et al., 2010), and China (Wu et al., 2013).

In treatment reviews, CBT for school refusal is described as "useful" (King, Heyne, & Ollendick, 2005, p. 241), "possibly efficacious" (Silverman, Pina, & Viswesvaran, 2008, p. 109), and "promising" (Pina, Zerr, Gonzels, & Oritz, 2009, p. 11). The most recent of these reviews was a narrative synthesis evaluating eight single-case experimental design studies and six group-design studies (Pina et al., 2009). It revealed significant increases in school attendance and reductions in symptoms associated with school refusal (e.g., anxiety, fear, depression, disruptive behavior). The authors suggested that behavioral strategies alone or in combination with cognitive strategies are promising. An examination of effect sizes supported the positive findings. The durability of gains following CBT is observed in King and colleagues' (2001) 3- to 5-year follow-up of school refusers treated in the King et al. (1998) study. Improvements in school attendance were maintained and there was an absence of new psychological problems.

Since Pina and colleagues' (2009) review, two studies of CBT as a stand-alone treatment have appeared. Tolin et al. (2009) reported a multiple baseline case series in which intensive (daily) CBT was conducted with four adolescents. Three adolescents showed post-treatment improvement in school attendance. At 3-year follow-up these three were still improved and engaged in alternative educational programs. Heyne et al. (2011) reported a non-randomized trial of CBT for adolescent school refusal, using a developmentally sensitive modular CBT. Across the 20 school-refusing adolescents, there were significant improvements for primary outcomes (school attendance, school-related fear, anxiety) and secondary outcomes (depression, overall functioning, adolescent and parental self-efficacy). Improvements were maintained at 2-month follow-up, and effect sizes were medium to large. At the same time, only 50% of adolescents were free of anxiety disorder and only 45% were attending school regularly (i.e., at least 80% of the time). While the intervention appears to be more effective than other CBTs when applied with school-refusing adolescents, there is still considerable room for improvement in treatment.

CBT combined with medication has been evaluated in two studies. Bernstein et al. (2000) compared CBT plus imipramine with CBT plus placebo for school-refusing adolescents. Significant improvement in school attendance occurred for the CBT plus imipramine group only, but just half (54%) of those in this group attended school at least 75% of the time by the end of treatment. A one-year follow-up (Bernstein, Hektner, Borchardt, & McMillan, 2001) revealed high continuity of anxiety disorder (64%) and depressive disorder (33%) with no significant difference between the treatment groups. School attendance was not reported at follow-up. Wu et al. (2013) compared CBT plus fluoxetine with CBT alone for school-refusing children and adolescents. Both groups displayed significant reductions in anxiety and depression. One month after treatment there was no group difference with respect to the percentage of youth achieving at least 80% attendance. Longer follow-up was not reported.

Two studies report the outcome of CBT combined with numerous other interventions, thus precluding conclusions about the effectiveness of CBT per se. McShane et al. (2004) reported 6-month and 3-year outcomes following inpatient or outpatient treatment with school-refusing adolescents. Treatment may have included CBT, family therapy, and psychotropic medication. Walter and colleagues (2010) reported on the outcomes for adolescents with "chronic anxious-depressive school absenteeism with or without comorbid disruptive symptoms" (p. 835). Inpatient treatment included CBT and other interventions, such as self-management therapy and access to youth welfare support.

Indicated Interventions for Truancy

Because truancy is a problem recognized among various disciplines—including education, psychology, social work, nursing, criminal justice, sociology, and others—the conceptualizations of truancy and interventions to reduce it are diverse (Kearney, 2008). Truancy interventions target an array of risk factors within various levels of the ecology (i.e., young person, family, school, community), are implemented in a variety of settings (e.g., home, school, clinic, court), and are delivered through various and often multiple modalities (e.g., individual, group, family). Typically the aim is to improve school attendance, although studies also often measure secondary outcomes such as academic performance, externalizing and internalizing problems, attitudes toward school, and self-esteem/self-efficacy (Maynard, McCrea, Pigott, & Kelly, 2012). For the purposes of this chapter, we will focus on indicated interventions intended to improve attendance with truanting youth. As such, the interventions discussed herein are primarily delivered directly to the student and/or parent rather than on a school-wide or community basis.

While there is some consensus and a body of empirical support for the use of CBT in the treatment of school refusal, there is no single intervention that is clearly the preferred or most effective intervention for truancy. Indeed, there are hundreds of truancy interventions in use; however, relatively few rigorous trials of indicated interventions have been conducted (Maynard, McCrea, et al., 2012; Maynard, McCrea, Pigott, & Kelly, 2013). Moreover, much of the small corpus of outcome studies is plagued by low internal validity, small sample size, high overall and differential attrition, lack of long-term follow-up, and poorly explicated interventions. Despite the limitations of the current body of evidence of intervention effects, a recent systematic review and meta-analysis of 16 studies meeting inclusion criteria found that indicated truancy interventions were, overall, effective in improving school attendance among chronic truant students (Hedges's g = .46, CI [.30, .62]; Maynard, McCrea, et al., 2012).

Several different types and modalities of indicated truancy interventions were included in the Maynard, McCrea, et al. (2012) review. Interventions delivered in school settings, commonly referred to as school-based interventions, were the most common indicated truancy interventions evaluated (n = 12). This diverse set of interventions included group counseling, mentoring or tutoring, behavioral interventions with parent training, and alternative education programs. On average, school-based interventions were effective (ES = .47, CI [.26, .68]), but not more or less so than court- or community-based interventions (Maynard et al., 2013). In examining individual school-based intervention studies, positive and significant effects were found for two behavioral interventions, Going to Class Pays, a positive behavior support program (Flanagan, 2006), and a contingency contracting and parent-training program that was examined in two studies (Hess, 1990; Hess, Rosenberg, & Levy, 1990). Not all studies employing a behavioral intervention component, however, were effective (e.g., Herrick, 1992; Tichenor, 1991). Effects of tutoring and mentoring interventions were not significantly different from zero, and mixed effects were found across studies assessing alternative education models. While school-based interventions appear to be, on average, effective in improving school attendance, the interventions employed in schools are quite diverse, and no intervention modality stands out as more effective than others.

Court- and community-based interventions are also widely employed to increase school attendance among truanting youth. However, only three court-based interventions and one community-based intervention met criteria for the Maynard et al. (2013) review. The court-based interventions were found to be, on average, effective in improving school attendance (ES = .49, CI [.20, .79]), but not more or less so than school- or community-based interventions. Effects of two court-based programs, Project Start, a truancy court program, and SToP Truancy Now, a two-hour informational meeting for parents and truanting youth held at the courthouse, were positive and significant. Effects of the third court-based intervention, the School Success Project, a diversion conference with brief assessment, school attendance agreement, and referrals for services, was not significantly different from zero. The one community-based intervention that met inclusion criteria for the review, a brief family systems intervention delivered over 8 weeks, was not significant (ES = .27, CI [−.25, .79]).

PREDICTION AND MODERATION: EMPIRICAL RESULTS AND THEORETICAL MODELS

In Pina and colleagues' (2009) review of psychosocial treatments for school refusal, effect sizes varied markedly across studies and across measures within studies. The authors contended that treatment effects are influenced in important ways, that research needs to determine the conditions under which treatment is more or less efficacious (i.e., moderation of treatment outcome), and that a critical next step is the examination of factors mediating change. There are many potential moderators and mediators of outcome, given the heterogeneity in the etiology and manifestation of school refusal (Heyne, 2006). In this section we summarize the literature on the prediction and moderation of CBT outcome.

We also present several moderation models that include factors related to the school refuser, their social context, and the family context.

Similar to school refusal, truancy is a heterogeneous and developmentally complex problem. Moreover, truancy has been conceptualized in multiple ways: as an externalizing behavior corresponding to delinquency, as an indicator of school engagement, and as a predictor of dropout and low school achievement, to name a few. As such, researchers have examined truancy as both a primary outcome as well as a variable that predicts, moderates, and mediates other outcomes. Research on the outcomes of truancy interventions generally focus on the examination of the main effects of the intervention on the outcome, usually measured in terms of school attendance. Some studies include predictor analyses, and a few have examined moderating variables, as presented later in this section.

Predictors of the Outcome of CBT for School Refusal

Research on factors influencing the outcome of CBT for school refusal has mostly been in the form of predictor analyses. Predictor analyses have been reported in three studies of CBT (Heyne, 1999;[2] Heyne et al., 2011; Last et al., 1998), four studies of CBT combined with other treatment (Bernstein et al., 2000; Bernstein et al., 2001; Layne et al., 2003; Walter et al., 2013), and one study of CBT or other treatments (McShane et al., 2004). Some studies examined the influence of pre-treatment variables on the outcome of a single treatment, and in other studies the predictor analyses were based on data from different treatment groups combined, without taking account of treatment assignment. The question of whether different school refusers respond to alternative treatments was sometimes touched upon, but no studies were dedicated to the investigation of moderation. The longest follow-up period reported in predictor analyses is 3 years (McShane et al., 2004), but caution is required when interpreting the results of this study because of the retrospective design and the fact that 14% of the cases had not received treatment.

AGE AND GENDER

In studies comprising adolescents only, age was unrelated to school attendance at post-treatment (Layne et al., 2003), unrelated to school attendance and mental health problems at post-treatment and 2-month follow-up (Walter et al., 2013), and unrelated to educational and occupational functioning at 6-month and 3-year follow-up (McShane et al., 2004). However, in the two studies including children and adolescents, outcome was superior for younger children (Heyne, 1999; Last et al., 1998). This age-related finding contrasts with the results of Bennett and colleagues' (2013) individual patient data meta-analysis of CBT for children and adolescents with anxiety disorders, in which no significant age effect was found. The different finding for school refusers underscores Berg and colleagues' (1993) contention that school refusal is a problem worth consideration in its own right.

There have been mixed results regarding gender. Layne et al. (2003) found that males had significantly higher post-treatment attendance based on a t-test. However, when gender was entered in a hierarchical regression analysis with variables such as pre-treatment attendance and treatment condition, gender was not found to be a significant predictor of post-treatment attendance. Walter and colleagues (2013) found that gender was significantly correlated with adolescent reports of anxiety and depression at post-treatment but not with other measures of functioning such as school attendance. When they conducted a hierarchical regression analysis, being female and older was significantly associated with high levels of anxiety and depression at post-treatment, but there was no gender effect when other variables were added to the model. In two other studies, gender was found to be unrelated to outcome (Last et al., 1998; McShane et al., 2004).

CHRONICITY AND SEVERITY

A common notion is that the longer the school refuser is away from school, the harder it is for him or her to return. In support of this, a non-CBT study revealed that school refusers who improved following treatment had been absent from school for a significantly shorter period of time (M = 3.5 months) relative to those who did not improve (M = 24.9 months) (Okuyama, Okada, Kuribayashi, & Kaneko, 1999). In the one CBT study addressing chronicity, the outcome of CBT or educational-support therapy (EST) was not predicted by the duration of school refusal (Last et al., 1998). Unfortunately, no information was provided about duration; if there was little variability in the data, then the likelihood of finding a relationship between duration and treatment outcome was reduced.

In the absence of robust empirical findings, we contend that chronic cases (i.e., more than a year's absence) are less likely to be responsive to current CBTs because more problematic individual functioning seems to be typical of these cases. In support of a relationship between individual functioning and chronicity, Okuyama et al. (1999) found that introversion and nervousness were significantly associated with the prolongation of school refusal. Thus, chronicity as a moderating factor might be associated with poorer outcome following CBT, compared to outcome following long-term individual psychotherapy. In our clinical experience, chronic cases are also characterized by more problematic family functioning, and for these cases a CBT intervention that does not contain a strong family focus may be less effective than family therapy interventions.

The severity of school refusal, operationalized as the amount of non-attendance, has been studied as a predictor of outcome in three CBT studies. Last et al. (1998) pooled subjects who received CBT or EST, and Layne et al. (2003) pooled subjects who received CBT plus imipramine or CBT plus placebo. Both studies showed that lower attendance at pre-treatment predicted poorer outcome as measured by attendance. In Walter and colleagues' (2013) study of multimodal treatment, which included CBT, school attendance at pre-treatment did not predict attendance at post-treatment or follow-up.

The severity of co-occurring symptoms has also been studied as a predictor of outcome. Pre-treatment severity of mental health problems was found to predict the severity of mental health problems at post-treatment and follow-up (Walter et al., 2013). In another study, the severity of somatic complaints at pre-treatment was related to the level of depression at 1-year follow-up, but not to anxiety level, the presence of anxiety disorder, or the presence of depressive disorder (Bernstein et al., 2001). McShane et al. (2004) found that comorbid diagnoses at intake predicted poorer educational and occupational functioning 6 months following treatment, but not at 3-year follow-up.

ACADEMIC FUNCTIONING

Academic difficulties, defined by below average academic performance or the need for remedial or special education, were found to be predictive of poorer educational and occupational adjustment 3 years after treatment (McShane et al., 2004). Heyne et al. (2011) evaluated school type (practical vocational training versus higher general education or pre-university education) in relation to the (dis)continuity of social anxiety disorder (SAD) among school-refusing adolescents. Of the adolescents whose SAD remitted by 2-month follow-up, the majority (80%) were enrolled in less academically challenging schools. Of those who retained the diagnosis of SAD, the majority (86%) were enrolled in more academically challenging schools. Walter et al. (2013) found that intelligence and school type (regular versus special or basic level) did not predict school attendance.

CO-OCCURRING PSYCHOPATHOLOGY

Last et al. (1998) found no relationship between school-refusing children's and adolescents' primary diagnosis (one of the anxiety disorders) and post-treatment school attendance. In Bernstein and colleagues' (2001) 1-year follow-up of school-refusing adolescents treated with CBT plus imipramine or CBT plus placebo, the retention rate of disorders was higher for SAD (50% retention) and avoidant disorder of childhood and adolescence (AD; 50% retention) relative to other disorders. In further analysis of data from the original cohort, Layne et al. (2003) found that separation anxiety disorder and AD significantly predicted poorer school attendance at post-treatment [3]; these disorders accounted for 10% and 6% of the variance, respectively. In contrast, Last and Hansen (2001, personal communication as cited in Layne et al., 2003) found greater improvement in post-treatment school attendance for children with a primary diagnosis of separation anxiety disorder relative to children with other anxiety disorders.[4] According to Layne and colleagues (2003), separation anxiety disorder may present adolescents with "a different and more complex set of challenges" relative to children with this disorder (p. 323).

Heyne et al. (2011) reported that adolescent school refusers who still met criteria for SAD 2 months following CBT less commonly had friends in the same class at pre-treatment, relative to adolescents who did not meet criteria for SAD at follow-up (50% versus 80%, respectively). Furthermore, school attendance at follow-up was lower for those who still met criteria for SAD at follow-up (18% of school-time attended) relative to those who had no disorder or a disorder other than SAD (68% of school-time attended). McShane et al. (2004) found that a pre-treatment diagnosis of SAD predicted poorer functional outcomes (i.e., unemployment or home schooling). That is, only 40% of those with SAD at pre-treatment were doing well 3 years after treatment, compared with 79% of those without SAD.

The relationship between depression and treatment outcome was evaluated by Heyne (1999). Children and adolescents were designated responders (≥ 90% school attendance at follow-up) or non-responders (< 90% school attendance). The groups did not differ on pre-treatment depression scores, but the responders reported significantly less depression at post-treatment and follow-up. It is plausible that increased school attendance facilitated a reduction in depressive symptoms in some cases. In other cases, depression may have been more steadfast, making it difficult to resume normal school attendance. Indeed, when McShane et al. (2004) entered disorder-level depression in a regression model, it was found to be associated with poorer functional outcomes 6 months after treatment. No relationship was found between depressive disorders and outcome at 3-year follow-up. However, poorer functioning at 3-year follow-up was associated with higher withdrawal at pre-treatment, and this withdrawal may be associated with depressive disorder and/or with SAD.

FAMILY FACTORS

There is scant support for the influence of family-related factors on treatment outcome. There was no effect on outcome for marital status (Heyne, unpublished data; Last et al., 1998; Walter et al., 2013), family composition, or maternal psychiatric illness (McShane et al., 2004). Bernstein and colleagues (2001) found that a more extreme family type (i.e., problematic family cohesion and adaptability) was a marginally significant predictor ($p = .06$) of higher youth depression at 1-year follow-up. Later in this chapter we speculate further on the influence of family factors on the outcome of CBT for school refusal.

TREATMENT CONDITION

Bernstein et al. (2000) reported that CBT plus imipramine predicted post-treatment remission when remission was based on school attendance (i.e., ≥ 75% attendance) but not when it was based on clinical cutoffs for anxiety and depression. Using data from the same sample, Layne et al. (2003) conducted a hierarchical multiple regression analysis on pre-treatment school attendance, treatment condition, separation anxiety disorder, and AD. Again, CBT plus imipramine was a significant predictor of post-treatment school attendance. While Layne and colleagues' study was focused on the predictors of treatment response, they also included interactions between treatment condition and diagnosis in their analyses. The interactions did not improve the prediction of post-treatment outcome; as such, diagnosis was not found to moderate treatment outcome. In other words, the additional use of imipramine did not change the impact of separation anxiety or of social avoidance on the outcome of CBT for school refusal. In McShane and colleagues' (2004) study, univariate analysis yielded no differences in outcomes for school refusers treated as inpatients and those treated as outpatients.

Moderators of the Outcome of CBT for School Refusal

Following, we describe two studies that can be conceptualized in terms of moderation, even though the authors did not purport to investigate moderation per se. We then review studies that point to the role of social factors and parental factors in school refusal and its treatment, and we propose moderation models that account for these factors. In our models, the outcome variables are assumed to include school attendance and internalizing problems. These are key variables in theoretical discussions of school refusal, and they are primary outcome measures customarily employed in treatment outcome studies (King, Tonge, Heyne, & Ollendick, 2000).

THE FUNCTION OF SCHOOL REFUSAL

Kearney and Silverman (1999) conducted a small controlled study to test the treatment utility of their functional analytic model of school refusal behavior (SRB). The School Refusal Assessment Scale (SRAS; Kearney & Silverman, 1993) was administered to eight youth and their parents to assess reasons for the maintenance of SRB, namely (1) avoidance of school-related stimuli that provoke a sense of general negative affectivity; (2) escape from aversive social and/or evaluative situations at school; (3) pursuit of attention from significant others; and (4) pursuit of tangible reinforcement outside the school setting. Four cases received a prescribed treatment, whereby cognitive and behavioral interventions with the young person and/or parents were matched to the function of the SRB, as indicated by the SRAS. Four other cases received a non-prescribed treatment based on interventions associated with a non-indicated function.

In effect, the researchers studied the moderating influence of the predominant factor maintaining a young person's SRB. That is, youths with Function X at pre-treatment were matched to Treatment X, and youths with Function Y at pre-treatment were matched to Treatment Y. The cases receiving prescribed treatment showed increases in attendance and decreases in anxiety and depression. Across the four cases receiving non-prescribed treatment, there was a decrease in attendance and an increase in anxiety and depression. The results suggest that the function of the young person's refusal to attend school is a potentially important moderating factor in treatment outcome. At the same time, the four functions assessed via the SRAS do not represent the broad range of factors associated with the development and maintenance of school refusal (Heyne & Sauter, 2013). Rather than being based on an etiological model of school refusal, the SRAS was modeled after a scale designed to assess factors maintaining self-injurious behavior in people with developmental disorders (Durand & Crimmins, 1988). As noted by others (e.g., Kearney, 2006), the SRAS is unlikely to be sufficient for determining which treatment is most beneficial for a school refuser.

DEVELOPMENTAL LEVEL

A randomized trial reported by Heyne et al. (2002) involved a comparison between child/adolescent-focused CBT (CH), parent/teacher-focused CBT (PTT), and both (CH + PTT). Post-treatment school attendance was significantly greater for those in the PTT and CH + PTT conditions, relative to those in the CH condition. At 4-month follow-up there was no difference between the groups with respect to school attendance. The study used a combined sample of children and adolescents, which may have obscured developmental differences associated with the benefit of parental involvement. Post hoc analyses reported by Heyne (1999) examined within-group change between post-treatment and 4.5-month follow-up according to the young person's developmental level, crudely differentiated as primary school or secondary school level. There was no significant change in attendance between post-treatment and follow-up for secondary school students in the CH condition, while secondary school students in the PTT condition and the CH + PTT condition manifested significant decreases in attendance. Between post-treatment and follow-up there was a statistically marginal increase in attendance for primary school children in the CH condition, while no change was observed for primary school children in the PTT and CH + PTT conditions. The results suggest that the delayed treatment effect for those in the CH condition is more typical of younger school refusers, and that the gains made by older school refusers whose parents are involved in treatment (i.e., PTT and CH + PTT) are not maintained in the same way that they are for younger school refusers whose parents are involved in treatment. There are thus indications for the potential moderational role of developmental level, but formal tests of moderation are still needed.

SOCIAL FACTORS

A relationship between social factors and school refusal is suggested by numerous studies of referred school refusers. Interviews with the families of 17 school-refusing adolescents revealed difficulty with peer relationships, a sense of isolation (most did not belong to a friendship group when they started secondary school), and bullying and teasing at school (Place et al., 2002). Heyne et al. (1998) assessed 135 school-refusing children and adolescents regarding their perception of their ability to cope with situations related to school attendance. Self-efficacy was lowest for the social-related situation of answering peers' questions about absences from school and highest for the non-social situation of doing schoolwork. In a sample of 25 school-refusing adolescents, Buitelaar, Van Andel, Duyx, and Van Strien (1994) found that the majority had "unsatisfactory or insufficient social relationships" prior to referral, and one of the most common diagnoses at initial contact was AD (p. 251). In two other studies of school-refusing adolescents, SAD was a primary or secondary diagnosis among approximately two-thirds of the sample (Bernstein et al., 2001; Heyne et al., 2011). Furthermore, in the study of Beidas et al. (2010), more of the 27 school-refusing children and adolescents presented with a principal diagnosis of SAD (41%) than with a principal diagnosis of generalized anxiety disorder (26%) or separation anxiety disorder (33%). Of course, local referral behaviors and intake procedures will influence rates of disorders observed. To wit, some studies of clinic-referred school refusers point to relatively low rates of SAD (e.g., 6% in McShane et al., 2001). More robust support for the relationship between social factors and school attendance problems is found in community-based studies. For example, a comparison of high-anxious youth often absent from school and high-anxious youth attending school regularly revealed that those who were often absent from school had higher social anxiety and fewer close friends (Ingul & Nordahl, 2013). (See Blote, Miers, Heyne, & Westenberg [in press] for additional studies.)

The relationship between social factors and school refusal is age-related. Last and Strauss (1990) reported that, at intake, school refusers with SAD were older than school refusers with separation anxiety disorder. Kearney and Albano (2004) reported that youth who refused school to escape from aversive social and/or evaluative situations were typically older; younger school refusers were more likely to endorse other reasons for refusing to attend. The higher prevalence of social anxiety among older school refusers may simply be a reflection of the higher prevalence of SAD among older youth relative to younger youth (e.g., Costello, Mustillo, Erkanli, Keeler, & Angold, 2003). It might also be explained by the increasingly complex and demanding nature of the secondary school environment. At secondary school the student is confronted with a larger and more complex social environment involving multiple teachers, moving between classes, and needing to function more autonomously (Steinberg, 2005, cited in Holmbeck, Devine, Wasserman, Schellinger, & Tuminello, 2012). This, combined with the increasing importance of the peer context during adolescence, may lead some vulnerable youth to become overwhelmed and to escape to the security of the home environment. According to McShane et al. (2004), the "climate of forced and broad social interaction" at school is daunting for socially phobic adolescents and can be expected to lead to poorer response to treatment for school refusal (p. 54).

Indeed, there is accumulating evidence that social factors—especially social anxiety—are related to poor response to treatment (see earlier discussion of the predictors of treatment outcome). Why does social anxiety predict poorer treatment outcome for school refusers? Continued absence from school severely reduces the quality and number of opportunities for socially anxious school refusers to increase social interactions (Albano, 1995), and in this way, school refusal and social anxiety are mutual maintaining factors. The process of school return is thus more challenging for a socially anxious school refuser. From a moderation perspective, socially anxious school refusers are more likely to respond to CBTs that give greater attention to the complex interplay between school refusal and social anxiety. Later in this chapter we summarize suggestions made to enhance treatment outcome for socially anxious school refusers.

Depression co-occurring with social anxiety is also likely to hinder the treatment process. In a treatment study of anxious youth not identified as school refusers, Crawley et al. (2008) found a high retention rate for SAD relative to other disorders. When cases with comorbid SAD and depressive disorder were excluded from analyses, SAD no longer had a significantly higher retention rate. The authors argued that difficulty treating SAD may contribute to the development of depressive symptoms and that the temporal relationship between SAD and depressive disorders warrants investigation. This is especially pertinent in cases of adolescent school refusal because of the high rate of SAD before and after treatment and the high rate of depressive symptoms and disorders among school-refusing adolescents (Heyne & Sauter, 2013). For socially anxious school-refusing adolescents, CBTs are more likely to be effective when they address co-occurring depression.

PARENTAL FACTORS

Psychopathology is frequently observed in the parents of school refusers (e.g., Bernstein & Garfinkel, 1988; Bools et al., 1990; Last, Francis, Hersen, Kazdin, & Strauss, 1987; Martin, Cabrol, Bouvard, Lepine, & Mouren-Simeoni, 1999; McShane et al., 2004). According to Bahali, Tahiroglu, Avci, and Seydaoglu (2011), parent psychopathology has a negative impact on treatment for school refusal and needs to be addressed to increase parent participation in therapy. At the same time, Valles and Oddy (1984) found that psychiatric history in the family was unrelated to the outcome of inpatient treatment for school refusal, and McShane et al. (2004) found that maternal psychiatric illness was unrelated to outcome following school refusal treatment, which may have included CBT. If these two studies had included outcome measures directly related to school refusal—namely school attendance and fear about attending school—the effects of parent psychopathology on treatment outcome may have been observed.

Our clinical experience suggests that more treatment sessions are required when working with parents displaying anxious or depressive symptoms. Parent psychopathology is likely to moderate outcome when treatment does not provide parents with extra support in acquiring and using behavior management strategies. The situation might be compounded in cases of adolescent school refusal. The adolescent's developmental need for increasing autonomy might overload a mentally ill parent's capacity to adapt his or her parenting style accordingly.

Predictors and Moderators of the Outcome of Indicated Interventions for Truancy

A substantial body of research has examined a host of dispositional and contextual factors associated with or predictive of truant behavior, which in turn has informed the development of truancy interventions. Individual risk factors linked to truancy include demographic variables (e.g., race, age, socioeconomic status), academic variables (e.g., low school engagement, poor academic achievement), and behavioral characteristics (e.g., personality, mental health, learning disabilities, externalizing behaviors) (Corville-Smith, Ryan, Adams, & Dalicandro, 1998; Malcolm, Wilson, Davidson, & Kirk, 2003; Romero & Lee, 2008; Southwell, 2006; Vaughn et al., 2013). Family, school, and other contextual factors have also been implicated as risk factors for truancy. Parents' education and attitudes toward education, parental involvement in their child's school/education, parenting practices, and family conflict are among the many family factors found to be associated with truancy (Corville-Smith et al., 1998; Malcolm et al., 2003; Romero & Lee, 2008). Notable school factors include school culture, environment, and disciplinary practices; quality of teaching; curriculum; poor relationships or interpersonal conflict with teachers; and threats to physical safety such as bullying (Corville-Smith et al., 1998; Malcolm et al., 2003). Community factors such as employment and other opportunities in the community, neighborhood characteristics, levels of social support, community norms, and community violence have also been associated with truancy (Bowen, Bowen, & Ware, 2002; Lyon & Cotler, 2007).

In Maynard, McCrea, and colleagues' (2012) meta-analysis of indicated truancy interventions, moderator analyses were conducted to examine the relationship of several participant variables (race, grade, severity of truancy at pre-test) and intervention variables (program type, focal modality, and whether the intervention was collaborative and multimodal). None of the variables tested was found to moderate effects of interventions; however, due to low statistical power, some moderating effects may not have been detected. Most studies reported in the meta-analysis focused on the direct effects of the intervention. Some examined predictors and moderators of outcomes, with demographic variables being the most frequently examined. Mixed results of the effects of demographic variables were found. Flanagan (2006), Seamans (1996), Jenifer (1995), and Johncox (1994) examined the relationship between demographic variables (e.g., age, gender, race/ethnicity, household classification) and attendance at post-test and found no relationship. Bazemore et al. (2004) found that males were more likely to have improved attendance at 30-day follow-up, and Jenifer (1995) found that gender moderated treatment effects within the intervention group, but these effects did not hold for long-term outcomes. Wright (2000) found that age predicted future truancy, as older youth were more likely to be repeat truants.

In examining pre-test severity of truancy or delinquency on outcomes, Bazemore and colleagues (2004) found that level of delinquency and number of days absent predicted long-term outcomes, with more delinquent youth and youth with more days absent found to be more likely to miss more days of school at post-test. Johncox (1994) also found that less delinquent youth in the treatment group had fewer days absent at post-test. Several other individual and family characteristics have been tested as predictors or moderators. Johncox (1994) found no relationship between impulse control or level of self-concept on intervention outcomes. Trice (1990) found some evidence that locus of control may effect the outcomes of truancy interventions; youth with internal locus of control were more compliant (i.e., not truant or disruptive for 2 weeks) than youth with external locus of control. In examining family characteristics, Seamans (1996) found that family competence and family style did not predict treatment outcome. Johncox (1994) also examined family relationships and found no difference in attendance outcomes between students scoring high and those scoring low on the family relationship scale of a self-image questionnaire.

MEDIATION: EMPIRICAL RESULTS AND THEORETICAL MODELS

Mediators of the Outcome of CBT for School Refusal

Behavioral conceptualizations have a long tradition in the field of school refusal, positing that school attendance is associated with emotional distress and the ensuing avoidance of school is negatively and positively reinforced (Meyer, Hagopian, & Paclawskyj, 1999). As such, increased school attendance is primarily mediated by a reduction in internalizing problems. Treatment strategies (e.g., systematic desensitization; in vivo exposure) are held to reduce anxious arousal by means of counter-conditioning and extinction (Doobay, 2008). The specific mechanisms through which these behavioral strategies work to reduce emotional distress are still a subject of debate; behavioral processes and/or cognitive mediation may be operational (Chu & Harrison, 2007). There is also the question of whether reductions in anxiety primarily facilitate school attendance or whether an increase in school attendance primarily results in reduced anxiety (Valles & Oddy, 1984). In mediation models, school attendance and internalizing problems might best be regarded as separate variables in causal chains, sometimes as a mediating variable and sometimes as an outcome variable, depending on the proposed relationship with the other variables under discussion. In this section we review the only study to examine the mediation of outcome of CBT for school refusal, and we propose several additional mediation models.

Cognitive Factors
The literature contains many anecdotal reports of the negative automatic thoughts of school refusers. A 10-year-old girl, for example, was worried that "something might happen to her while she was away from her parents" (Chorpita, Albano, Heimberg, & Barlow, 1996); a 16-year-old boy was concerned that he would "not have an adequate explanation for the amount of time he missed" (Tolin, 2009); and a 16-year-old girl reported cognitions related to performance ("I'm not prepared enough for the test"), self-evaluation ("I'm worthless"), and evaluation by peers ("others think I'm weird") (Heyne et al., 2014). Some of the unhelpful thinking styles that have been associated with school refusal are pessimism (Place, Hulsmeier, Davis, & Taylor, 2000; Place et al., 2002), overestimation of the likelihood of anxiety-provoking situations occurring at school, underestimation of one's ability to cope with anxiety-provoking situations (Heyne, 2006), and black-and-white thinking about schoolwork (Tolin et al., 2009).

Two studies have systematically investigated cognition in cases of school refusal. Recently, Maric, Heyne, de Heus, van Widenfelt, and Westenberg (2012) found that negative automatic thoughts concerning personal failure and the cognitive error of overgeneralizing both independently predicted school refusal. Earlier, Heyne et al. (1998) assessed school refusers' perceptions of the ability to cope with situations associated with school attendance and found that approximately two-thirds reported low or moderate self-efficacy. The cognitive construct of self-efficacy is of particular relevance to treatment outcome. It is a key target during treatment for school refusal (Heyne & Rollings, 2002; Kearney & Albano, 2007), and it is consistently found to increase following treatment (Heyne et al., 2002; Heyne et al., 2011; King et al., 1998). Based on a cognitive-behavioral perspective of school refusal, which assumes that a young person perceives an aspect of school attendance to be threatening *and also thinks he or she is unable to deal with this situation* (Elliott, 1999, emphasis added), treatment that increases self-efficacy may reduce anxiety and facilitate re-engagement with schooling. If adequate measures have been taken to ensure that the young person's time at school is non-aversive, increasing school attendance will further increase a "sense of mastery" (Chu & Harrison, 2007).

Self-efficacy was examined as a mediator of the effects of CBT on the outcome of treatment with 19 school-refusing adolescents (Maric, Heyne, MacKinnon, van Widenfelt, & Westenberg, 2013).[5] The Dutch Self-Efficacy Questionnaire for School Situations (SEQSS-NL; Heyne et al. 2007) assessed the school refusers' perceptions of their ability to cope with situations associated with school attendance (e.g. "How sure are you that you could handle questions from others about why you've been away from school?"). It was argued that CBT treatment components (e.g., cognitive therapy, role-playing, graded exposure) would promote self-efficacy for facing the challenging situation of attending school, yielding positive treatment outcome. More specifically, increased self-efficacy at post-treatment was expected to mediate increased school attendance, decreased fear of attending school, and decreased anxiety and depression, at post-treatment and at 2-month follow-up. Similarly, increased self-efficacy at follow-up was expected to mediate outcome at follow-up.

Increases in self-efficacy at post-treatment significantly mediated post-treatment increases in school attendance and decreases in fear about attending school. Broader outcomes (i.e., decreases in anxiety and depression) were not mediated by increases in self-efficacy. The fact that increased self-efficacy only had an effect on the two measures most directly associated with school refusal—amount of school attendance and fear associated with attendance—was interpreted as support for specificity in the mechanisms of change during CBT for school refusal. According to Maric et al. (2013), "CBT for school refusal may work predominantly because it helps youth to feel more confident about being at school per se" (p. 558). The authors also proposed that a general measure of self-efficacy (i.e., one not specific to school situations) may have yielded significant mediation effects with respect to the broader outcomes. No mediating effects were observed at 2-month follow-up. According to the authors, self-efficacy might be instrumental in achieving behavior change (i.e., increased school attendance at post-treatment), while other factors might be instrumental in maintaining behavior change at follow-up, such as positive experiences at school. Because Maric and colleagues focused on school-refusing adolescents, the influence of self-efficacy on the outcomes for school-refusing children remains undetermined. In part, receptivity to the cognitive interventions in CBT will vary as a function of cognitive developmental level (Sauter, Heyne, & Westenberg, 2009). Consistent with the notion of moderated mediation, cognitive interventions to enhance self-efficacy may be less effective with children. If this is the case, greater emphasis might be placed on behavioral interventions when working with school-refusing children.

Other types of cognition that may influence school return include overestimation of the likelihood of anxiety-provoking situations occurring at school and black-and-white thinking about school. For these, a general cognitive behavioral perspective can be applied: maladaptive cognition is associated with increased emotional distress (fear, anxiety, sadness), and the ensuing behavioral response (avoiding school) serves to reduce the emotional distress. CBT manuals for school refusal often comprise strategies to reduce maladaptive cognition, and so adaptive changes in thinking (e.g., more realistic expectations, more nuanced interpretations of events and people) could be expected to lead to a reduction in emotional distress and an increase in approach behavior and re-engagement with schooling.

Parent cognition may also play a role in school refusal and its treatment. Anecdotal reports of unhelpful parent cognition include "I shouldn't push" (Mansdorf & Lukens, 1987); "my child is incapable of coping with school attendance" (Coulter, 1995); "something has to change in my child's mind in order for him to be able to attend school" (Anderson et al., 1998); "the school has the answers and there is nothing that I can do" (Heyne, 2006), and "I'll ruin our bond if I tell her she has to go" (Heyne et al., 2014). Parenting self-efficacy has been found to be significantly lower among the parents of school-refusing adolescents relative to the parents of school-attending adolescents (Carless, Melvin, Tonge, & Newman, 2015), and parenting self-efficacy for managing a school attendance problem has been shown to increase following intervention with school-refusing adolescents and their parents (Heyne et al., 2011). Thus, when parent cognition (e.g., negative automatic thoughts, low self-efficacy) serves to maintain school refusal, targeting such cognition in treatment may improve outcomes for the young person. For example, cognitive therapy might be needed to increase parents' willingness to acquire and use important behavior management strategies, rather than parents simply thinking "there is nothing that I can do." Further, positive coping thoughts may help parents remain calm and steadfast while managing non-attendance (Kearney & Roblek, 1998). Coaching parents to think more adaptively can also prevent inadvertent parental modeling of unhelpful cognition for their children.

SOCIAL FACTORS

Earlier in this chapter we discussed the mutually reinforcing association between social anxiety and school refusal. A reduction in social anxiety is thus likely to mediate the relationship between CBT and increased school attendance. With respect to social connection, CBT that helps improve social connection is likely to lead to increased school attendance. In support of this, Alfano, Pina, Beidel, Ammerman, and Crosby (2009) found that decreases in loneliness mediated treatment-related improvements among socially anxious children and adolescents. Because of the inherently social nature of schooling and the increased importance of "fitting in" with the peer group, reduced loneliness may be especially important for school-refusing adolescents. A related factor is friendship quality. Baker and Hudson (2013) found that children and young adolescents (7–13 years) who reported higher friendship quality were more likely to be free of anxiety disorder 6 months following CBT for anxiety. The moderating or mediating role of friendship quality is an important research endeavor in the field of treatment for youth anxiety (Baker & Hudson, 2013), and we contend that it is especially important in studies of treatment for socially anxious school refusers.

Parental Factors

Should parents be involved in the treatment of school refusal? As noted earlier, the randomized trial of Heyne et al. (2002) failed to provide support at follow-up for the added benefit of parental involvement in treatment. However, post hoc analyses suggested that outcome was influenced by the youth's developmental level (Heyne, 1999). The parent-focused treatment reported in Heyne et al. (2002) was not explicitly developmentally sensitive, perhaps explaining the post hoc results reported by Heyne (1999). In the absence of clear empirical support for the (non)involvement of parents in the treatment of school refusal, clinical researchers contend that parental involvement is probably important (e.g., Heyne et al., 2014; Reynolds et al., 2012).

Assuming that parents will be involved in treatment, what role might they play? When the young person's refusal to attend school is conceptualized as avoidance behavior, parents are likely to be instrumental in blocking avoidance. This can take different forms, from being available to support the child when he or she engages in graduated exposures (e.g., Last, 1993) to actively enforcing the young person's attendance at school (e.g., Kearney & Bensaheb, 2006). According to Heyne and Sauter (2013), the question of whether parents employ a supportive role or a steering role will be guided by developmental factors. In the supportive role, parents prompt and reinforce adaptive behaviors while not enforcing their child's school attendance. In cases of adolescent school refusal, parents may first be supportive rather than steering, to account for the adolescent's tendency toward increased autonomy. When adolescents are allowed to "show that they can," they may be more likely to use the skills and knowledge acquired during treatment to increase school attendance. In cases of school refusal in childhood, treatment outcome may be enhanced when parents employ a steering role (Heyne, 1999). From a mediation perspective, parental autonomy-granting in cases of adolescent school refusal mediates the relationship between CBT and treatment outcome. Moreover, moderated mediation will occur when parental autonomy-granting is found to be more effective in cases of adolescent school refusal relative to childhood cases.

A closely related factor is parenting style. Drawing on earlier work, Atkinson, Quarrington, and Cyr (1985) discussed characteristics of parents associated with two types of school refusers. One group consisted of mothers who were demanding and impatient, and the other consisted of passive, subservient mothers and fathers who were unable to set limits. It is not surprising, they argued, that parents in the second group had children who were stubborn and willful at home. Based on clinical experience, Hella and Bernstein (2012) noted that some parents struggled to set limits with their school-refusing child, even when intervention targeted this. They argued for the need to examine parental factors impacting treatment. To our knowledge, no study has examined the role of parenting style and skills in the outcome of treatment for school refusal. Parents' capacity to calmly and assertively issue instructions (e.g., about getting out of bed and getting ready for school) is likely to mediate improvements in school attendance, assuming that developmental factors have been taken into account when determining the role that parents would play in treatment.

FAMILY FACTORS

Studies reporting the proportion of families displaying adaptive or maladaptive functioning suggest that maladaptive functioning is common among one-half to two-thirds of the families of school refusers (Bernstein, Warren, Massie, & Thuras, 1999; Kearney & Silverman, 1995). Recently, Carless et al. (2015) found more problematic functioning among the families of school-refusing adolescents compared with school-attending adolescents and they reported that "the odds of being a school refuser increased by approximately 17% for each additional unit of family dysfunction" (p. 5). To date, just one study has examined the impact of family functioning on the outcome of treatment for school refusal. As noted earlier, a more extreme family type was a marginally significant predictor of youth depression at follow-up (Bernstein et al., 2001).

Kearney and Silverman (1995) drew attention to the diversity in problematic parent-child functioning (i.e., enmeshed, conflictive, detached, isolated, and mixed). Despite this expected diversity, several recurring issues appear in the literature. One issue is enmeshment and, related to this, insufficient independence for school-refusing youth (e.g., Bernstein, Svingen, & Garfinkel, 1990; Hansen, Sanders, Massaro, & Last, 1998; Kearney & Silverman, 1995; Last & Strauss, 1990; Place et al., 2000; Place et al., 2002; Place, Hulsmeier, Brownrigg, & Soulsby, 2005). Bernstein et al. (1999) found increased disengagement among the families of adolescent school refusers, which they interpreted as a possible reaction to earlier enmeshment. Another recurring issue is family conflict, which has been associated with the onset of school refusal (McShane et al., 2001), its maintenance (Kearney & Silverman, 1995), and the consequences of school refusal (Kearney & Bensaheb, 2006; McAnanly, 1986). Valles and Oddy (1984) also observed that there was more conflict in the families of unsuccessfully treated cases of school refusal relative to successfully treated cases.

Clinical researchers argue that a change in family functioning needs to occur in order to effect change in the school refuser's social-emotional adjustment

(Ingul & Nordahl, 2013; Place et al., 2002) and to ensure that there is lasting change (Valles & Oddy, 1984). As such, adaptive family functioning may be regarded as a mediator of treatment outcome. More specifically, emphasis has been placed on altering family interaction patterns (Bernstein et al., 1999; Hansen et al., 1998; Kearney & Silverman, 1995; Place et al., 2000; Valles & Oddy, 1984). For example, Bernstein et al. (1999) argued that adolescent school refusers and parents in disengaged or rigid families need help to become more connected and flexible. Kearney and Silverman (1995) suggested that communication training and problem-solving are important for families characterized by conflict or detachment. These are also important targets when treating youth anxiety (Ginsburg & Schlossberg, 2002) and depression (Restifo & Bogels, 2009). Because adolescent school refusal often involves anxiety, depression, and family conflict, school-refusing adolescents and their parents will likely benefit from enhanced communication and problem-solving.

To the extent that maladaptive family functioning characterizes school refusal cases, we propose that improved family communication and problem-solving will lead to an improvement in school attendance. For the cases involving less severe family dysfunction, communication and problem-solving may lead directly to improved attendance. For example, the parents and young person make decisions about the timing and process for increasing school attendance. For cases involving more severe family dysfunction, the relationship between improved communication and problem-solving, on the one hand, and improved attendance, on the other, may be mediated by other factors such as reduced conflict. The parents and adolescent are empowered to more calmly and confidently discuss the process of increasing attendance. Reduced conflict and tension during such discussions may increase the young person's willingness and ability to follow through with plans for attending school.

Training in communication and problem-solving skills may also benefit families characterized by other forms of maladaptive functioning. In the case of disengagement, effective communication and problem-solving may enhance family members' experience of positive family relationships. In the case of rigidity, training in problem-solving may enhance family members' capacity for developing and employing creative and flexible solutions. In the case of insufficient independence, family discussions based on adaptive communication and problem-solving may foster the young person's capacity for and involvement in decision-making about matters of importance to themselves.

Mediators of the Outcome of Indicated Interventions for Truancy

No truancy intervention studies that we are aware of have employed mediation models. Research related to the causes and correlates of truancy can inform the identification of mediating factors. Another method for identifying potential mediators of indicated truancy intervention outcomes is to examine behavior change strategies underlying truancy interventions. Although many truancy interventions do not explicate an underlying theory or behavior change model, indicated truancy interventions nevertheless are derived from various theories, such as behavioral, cognitive, and social learning theories. Consequently, in examining the underlying constructs of truancy interventions, candidate variables emerge as potential mediators. Some potential mediating variables include student engagement, parenting practices, and neuropsychological and cognitive functioning. For example, truancy is often conceptualized as an indicator of low school engagement; thus some interventions are designed to improve attendance via various strategies to improve engagement of the student in school. Mentoring, peer support, and some group-based interventions are examples of interventions that may work to improve attendance by increasing student engagement. Parenting has been found to mediate intervention effects with other externalizing behaviors (Beauchaine, Webster-Stratton, & Reid, 2005) and is another potential mediating variable through which truancy interventions may increase student attendance. Indeed, several interventions in the Maynard, McCrea, et al. (2012) review employed some form of parent intervention to change parenting skills or parent-child interactions (e.g., Flanagan, 2006; Hess, 1990). Improvement in school attendance could be accounted for by the degree to which parents improve the monitoring and reinforcement of their child's school attendance. Another potential mediator is neuropsychological and cognitive functioning. While most truancy interventions do not target neuropsychological functioning directly, interventions that promote emotion regulation, impulse control, or executive functioning have been found to impact a range of externalizing behaviors and school success (Blair & Diamond, 2008; DeLisi & Vaughn, 2014) and could theoretically act as a mediator of truancy intervention outcomes.

CHALLENGES AND RECOMMENDATIONS FOR MODERATION AND MEDIATION STUDIES

School Refusal

Across studies, a broad range of predictors has been investigated. However, most individual studies investigated few predictors, which were often analyzed independently of each other. Notable exceptions are the studies of Layne et al. (2003), McShane et al. (2004), and Walter et al. (2013), which included numerous predictor variables (7, 12, and 20, respectively) and employed multiple regression analyses. Because these three studies evaluated CBT in the context of multimodal treatment, conclusions about factors influencing the outcome of CBT per se remain limited. Some investigations of predictors focused upon outcome at post-treatment but not at follow-up, and some focused on just one measure of outcome. Studies are required that focus on the outcomes of CBT alone, incorporate multiple predictor variables and multiple outcome measures (attendance as well as emotional distress), evaluate outcome at various time-points (post-treatment and follow-ups), and employ robust statistical procedures.

With respect to the moderation of outcome, our understanding of the benefit of CBT for different groups of school refusers is slowly growing. With respect to the mediation of outcome, we know very little about the components of CBT that make it more effective. To increase our understanding of optimal patient-treatment matching and optimal treatment components, research would ideally account for six key issues.

First, the heterogeneity associated with school refusal calls for studies with large samples, permitting analyses that account for this heterogeneity (e.g., the presence of different anxiety disorders, the presence of depression). An additional strategy to account for heterogeneity is to employ single-subject designs that capture the various mechanisms related to each young person's functioning (Maric et al., 2013).

Second, studies are needed that control for the non-specific aspects of CBT (e.g., therapeutic alliance). Only then can we know whether key mediators (e.g., self-efficacy, social connection) are a result of the cognitive and behavioral interventions included in CBT. Last et al. (1998) reported the only comparison between CBT and a psychological placebo control condition, but treatment group was not taken into account when conducting predictor analyses, and no mediator analyses were conducted.

Third, consistency across studies will benefit later meta-analysis of moderation and mediation studies. School attendance is routinely measured at post-treatment, but it is not consistently employed as an outcome measure at follow-ups. Some studies include measures of fear about school attendance, anxiety, and depression, while others do not. Further, assessment batteries would ideally include measures of cognitive content (e.g., negative and positive automatic thoughts), cognitive process (e.g., cognitive errors), and self-efficacy, to better understand the importance of cognitive change during treatment. Standardized measures of parenting style and family functioning need to be included, and the extent and nature of parental involvement in treatment need to be carefully articulated. Consensus should also be reached regarding the measurement of school refusal severity (Layne et al., 2003). This would aid treatment-matching according to severity and would permit severity-based differentiation between treatment responders and non-responders. There is also considerable variability in CBT manuals for school refusal (see above) stemming from different perspectives on what is essential. Enhanced understanding of the components that make CBT for school refusal more effective should lead to greater consistency across treatment manuals.

Fourth, CBT for school refusal is aimed at the resumption of a normal developmental pathway, as a result of reduced emotional distress and increased school attendance (Heyne & Sauter, 2013). Because te young person's longer-term well-being is of concern, studies need to include follow-ups well beyond the end of treatment. This is underscored in McShane and colleagues' (2004) study, which revealed differences in the prediction of functioning at 3 years after treatment relative to 6 months after treatment.

Fifth, developmental factors (e.g., cognitive development, psychosocial development) need to be measured and accounted for in moderation analyses and perhaps also in mediation analyses. As noted in this chapter, age (as a proxy for developmental level) influences treatment outcome. Specific aspects of development may be related to outcome. For example, a young person's capacity with respect to CBT-relevant cognitive skills will influence the extent to which he or she extracts meaning from and can apply cognitive therapeutic strategies. In this way, capacity will influence the benefit received from treatment, especially if cognitive therapeutic strategies are not delivered in accordance with capacity. It might even be the case that the refinement of cognitive capacities due to engagement in cognitive therapeutic strategies mediates therapeutic gains (Holmbeck et al., 2012).

Sixth, greater attention needs to be paid to school factors. School-based interventions are common in CBT manuals for school refusal, but the benefits of such interventions need to be investigated (Hella & Bernstein, 2012). The influence of school factors has been examined indirectly via attention to the young person's academic and social functioning and directly via attention to school type. Moderation and mediation studies should include other factors, such as the young person's sense of security and belonging at school (Nuttall & Woods, 2013) and emotional and organizational support from teachers (Havik, Bru, & Ertesvåg, 2014).

Other factors receiving scant attention to date may provide additional leads for understanding the effects of CBT. These include the potential moderating and mediating influences of youth's problem-solving (Place et al., 2000) and emotion regulation strategy use (Hughes et al., 2010). A frequently discussed topic requiring more empirical research is when medication should be used together with CBT (Layne et al., 2003).

Truancy

Evidence suggests that there is heterogeneity in the etiology of truancy, in the characteristics of truant youth, and across indicated truancy interventions (Maynard, Salas-Wright, et al., 2012). Thus, there is a myriad of potential predictive, moderating, and mediating variables. Unfortunately, indicated truancy intervention studies rarely examine mediators or moderators of treatment effects; the focus is essentially on main effects of the intervention. A number of challenges present in the truancy intervention research may help explain the lack of tests of moderation and mediation. First, relatively few interventions have demonstrated efficacy or effectiveness in one moderately rigorous trial, and rarely has an intervention been tested in more than one rigorous trial. Before asking which interventions work for whom under what circumstances and by which mechanisms, we must first identify which interventions are effective on the basis of multiple trials using rigorous comparison group designs. Second, indicated truancy intervention research is plagued by low sample sizes and other methodological shortcomings that present challenges to examining moderation and mediation. Statistical tests needed to examine moderation and mediation models require larger samples, especially given the heterogeneity associated with the etiology and characteristics of truant youth. Third, truancy interventions often comprise multiple components that are poorly described. The underlying theories of change are not often explicitly identified, which makes it challenging to identify, measure, and test potential mechanisms of change.

IMPLICATIONS FOR CLINICAL PRACTICE

School Refusal

For many school refusers, but certainly not all, CBT helps reduce emotional distress and increase school attendance. Treatment response is inferior for school-refusing adolescents with SAD relative to those without SAD (Bernstein et al., 2001; Heyne et al., 2011; McShane et al., 2004). Suggestions to improve outcomes for school refusers with SAD have included the following: starting with individual treatment and progressing to group-based treatment (Albano, 1995); adjunctive interventions such as social skills training and pharmacotherapy (Layne et al., 2003); longer and more intensive treatment (Heyne et al., 2011; McShane et al., 2004); targeting social isolation and promoting participation in prosocial activities (Ingul & Nordahl, 2013); and greater flexibility at school (Heyne et al., 2011). Place et al. (2000) argued that there is little likelihood of school refusers ever returning to mainstream schooling if peer functioning cannot be improved. Interventions to improve the quality and probably also the quantity of the youth's social connections are needed. It is unclear whether behavioral interventions (e.g., social skills training, social-related exposures) or cognitive interventions (e.g., cognitive therapy for social anxiety) are most needed. School-based intervention is warranted (e.g., extra monitoring and support, effective buddy systems, temporary reductions in academic demands to compensate for the socially demanding aspect of school). Intervention targeting bullying and teasing is likely to be required at the individual level (e.g., social skills training addressing assertiveness) and the school level (e.g., prevention and response to bullying). There is currently limited support for the benefit of pharmacotherapy for socially avoidant school refusers (Layne et al., 2003).

Another negative prognostic indicator is problem severity. For example, two studies found that lower pre-treatment attendance predicted poorer outcome (Last et al., 1998; Layne et al., 2003). Even though school refusal severity measured by non-attendance appears to be a salient predictor of treatment outcome, it is not clear what the amount of non-attendance tells us about a case. It might be a good indicator of the difficulty a young person has with attending school, but it might be an equally good indicator of a parent's (lack of) effort or competence in getting a child to attend school. In itself, the amount of non-attendance provides no clear direction as to what might be needed in the treatment of severe cases. Another indicator of difficulty attending school might be severity measured by the symptoms associated with school refusal. To date, relationships have been found between pre-treatment mental health problems (Walter et al., 2013), somatic complaints (Bernstein et al., 2001), and comorbid diagnoses (McShane et al., 2004), on the one hand, and measures of treatment outcome on the other. Intervention in more severe cases would target more severe symptoms and the factors cuasing or maintaining them. According to Layne et al. (2003), more severe cases may "require a stronger, more aggressive treatment plan" (p. 323). They noted that this could be in the form of more sessions and/or multimodal treatment.

Additional tentative implications arise from our review of the literature, awaiting further empirical support. Firstly, while we do not yet know whether increased self-efficacy precedes increased school attendance, the results of Maric and colleagues' (2013) mediation study suggest that clinicians should be mindful of building school refusers' self-efficacy. Creating multiple success experiences associated with many achievable exposure-related tasks during the preparation phase (i.e., prior to increasing school attendance) should help. Cognitive interventions may also be used to target low self-efficacy. Secondly, there is a call for greater attention to family functioning in cases of school refusal, coming from the CBT-oriented literature (e.g., Heyne & Sauter, 2013; Kearney & Silverman, 1995) and the broader literature on school refusal (Ingul & Nordahl, 2013; Place et al., 2000; Valles & Oddy, 1984). The lack of empirical support for this assertion rests mostly in the lack of empirical research conducted. Helping parents and youth engage in effective communication and problem-solving is likely to benefit the youth's school attendance as well as the family's overall functioning.

Truancy

The significant and moderate effects of truancy interventions point to the value of intervening with truanting youth (Maynard, McCrea et al., 2012). However, the state of research on truancy intervention outcomes is problematic and lacks the specification and sophistication to adequately inform practice. Relatively few interventions have been rigorously tested, extant outcome studies are fraught with methodological shortcomings, and studies lack attention to moderating and mediating factors. Moreover, when interventions have been examined using more rigorous designs, similar effects have been found across intervention types and modalities, pointing to a lack of evidence to support any one intervention over another (Maynard, McCrea, et al., 2012). While there is a larger body of evidence for school-based interventions than for community- or court-based interventions, the corpus of indicated truancy intervention studies is, overall, quite sparse and not sufficient as a basis for making practice recommendations. Due to the overall lack of evidence that any type of intervention is more effective than others, it seems reasonable at this point for practitioners, schools, and communities to select truancy interventions based on factors that would promote the implementation of any truancy intervention, such as ease of implementation and available resources.

Given the heterogeneity associated with truancy etiology and the characteristics of truant youth, along with what we have learned about factors that influence outcomes of interventions for externalizing behaviors, it is likely that certain types of truant youth will benefit from different types of interventions. Identifying predictors and moderators of intervention outcomes can help us more aptly match youth to appropriate interventions and thus improve the effectiveness and efficiency of interventions. Moreover, it is important to identify treatment non-responders and to develop and test interventions for youth who do not benefit from current practice. In addition, we have yet to thoroughly explicate and then test the mechanisms of truancy interventions. It may be that we are currently providing complex multimodal and expensive interventions unnecessarily, or focusing on the wrong mechanisms to target for change, wasting precious resources and time.

NOTES

1. It is important to bear in mind that multiple risk factors and processes are associated with the development and maintenance of so-called child-motivated school attendance problems, including individual factors (e.g., social difficulties), family factors (e.g., conflict), school factors (e.g., response to learning difficulties), and community factors (e.g., social pressure to achieve academically) (Heyne, 2006; Heyne, King, & Ollendick, 2004).
2. The main results reported in Heyne (1999) were subsequently published in Heyne et al. (2002).
3. Social anxiety disorder was not analyzed as a predictor of treatment outcome.
4. Presumably this is based on unpublished data associated with the study of Last et al. (1998).
5. Maric et al. (2013) analyzed data derived from the treatment completer sample reported in Heyne et al. (2011).

REFERENCES

Albano, A. M. (1995). Treatment of social anxiety in adolescents. *Cognitive and Behavioral Practice, 2*, 271–298.

Alfano, C. A., Pina, A., Beidel, D. C., Ammerman, R. T., & Crosby, L. (2009). Mediators and moderators of outcome in the behavioral treatment of childhood social phobia. *Journal of the American Academy of Child and Adolescent Psychiatry, 48*, 945–953.

American Psychiatric Association. (2013). *Diagnostic and statistical manual of mental disorders* (5th ed.). Arlington, VA: American Psychiatric Publishing.

Anderson, J., King, N., Tonge, B., Rollings, S., Young, D., & Heyne, D. (1998). Cognitive-behavioural intervention for an adolescent school refuser: A comprehensive approach. *Behaviour Change, 15*, 67–73.

Atkinson, L., Quarrington, B., & Cyr, J. J. (1985). School refusal: The heterogeneity of a concept. *American Journal of Orthopsychiatry, 55*, 83–101.

Bahali, K., Tahiroglu, A. Y., Avci, A., & Seydaoglu, G. (2011). Parental psychological symptoms and familial risk factors of children and adolescents who exhibit school refusal. *East Asian Archives of Psychiatry, 21,* 164–169.

Baker, J. R., & Hudson, J. L. (2013). Friendship quality predicts treatment outcome in children with anxiety disorders. *Behaviour Research and Therapy, 51,* 31–36.

Barrett, P. M., & Turner, C. (2000). *FRIENDS for children: Group leader's manual.* Bowen Hills, Australia: Australian Academic Press.

Bazemore, G., Stinchcomb, J. B., & Leip, L. A. (2004). Scared smart or bored straight? Testing deterrence logic in an evaluation of police-led truancy intervention. *Justice Quarterly, 21,* 269–299.

Beauchaine, T. P., Webster-Stratton, C., & Reid, M. J. (2005). Mediators, moderators, and predictors of 1-year outcomes among children treated for early-onset conduct problems: A latent growth curve analysis. *Journal of Consulting and Clinical Psychology, 73,* 371–388.

Beidas, R. S., Crawley, S. A., Mychailyszyn, M. P., Comer, J. S., & Kendall, P. C. (2010), Cognitive-behavioral treatment of anxious youth with comorbid school refusal: Clinical presentation and treatment response. *Psychological Topics, 19,* 255–271.

Bennett, K., Manassis, K., Walter, S. D., Cheung, A., Wilansky-Traynor, P., Diaz-Granados, N., . . . Wood, J. J. (2013). Cognitive behavioral therapy age effects in child and adolescent anxiety: An individual patient data metaanalysis. *Depression and Anxiety, 30,* 829–841.

Berg, I. (1997). School refusal and truancy. *Archives of Disease in Childhood, 76,* 90–91.

Berg, I. (2002). School avoidance, school phobia, and truancy. In M. Lewis (Ed.), *Child and adolescent psychiatry: A comprehensive textbook* (3rd ed., pp. 1260–1266). Sydney: Lippincott Williams & Wilkins.

Berg, I., Butler, A., Franklin, J., Hayes, H., Lucas, C., & Sims, R. (1993). DSM-III-R disorders, social factors and management of school attendance problems in the normal population. *Journal of Child Psychology and Psychiatry, 34,* 1187–1203.

Berg, I., Casswell, G., Goodwin, A., Hullin, R., McGuire, R., & Tagg, G. (1985). Classification of severe school attendance problems. *Psychological Medicine, 15,* 157–165.

Berg, I., Nichols, K., & Pritchard, C. (1969). School phobia: Its classification and relationship to dependency. *Journal of Child Psychology and Psychiatry, 10,* 123–141.

Bernstein, G. A. (1991). Comorbidity and severity of anxiety and depressive disorders in a clinic sample. *Journal of the American Academy of Child and Adolescent Psychiatry, 30,* 43–50.

Bernstein, G. A., Borchardt, C. M., Perwien, A. R., Crosby, R. D., Kushner, M. G., Thuras, P. D., & Last, C. G. (2000). Imipramine plus cognitive-behavioral therapy in the treatment of school refusal. *Journal of the American Academy of Child and Adolescent Psychiatry, 39,* 276–283.

Bernstein, G. A., & Garfinkel, B. D. (1988). Pedigrees, functioning, and psychopathology in families of school phobic children. *American Journal of Psychiatry, 145,* 70–74.

Bernstein, G. A., Hektner, J. M., Borchardt, C. M., & McMillan, M. H. (2001). Treatment of school refusal: One-year follow-up. *Journal of the American Academy of Child and Adolescent Psychiatry, 40,* 206–213.

Bernstein, G. A., Svingen, P. H., & Garfinkel, B. D. (1990). School phobia: Patterns of family functioning. *Journal of the American Academy of Child and Adolescent Psychiatry, 29*, 24–30.

Bernstein, G. A., Warren, S. L., Massie, E. D., & Thuras, P. D. (1999). Family dimensions in anxious-depressed school refusers. *Journal of Anxiety Disorder, 13*, 513–528.

Blair, C., & Diamond, A. (2008). Biological process in prevention and intervention: The promotion of self-regulation as a means of preventing school failure. *Development and Psychopathology, 20*, 899–911.

Blöte, A. W., Miers, A. C., Heyne, D. A., & Westenberg, P. M. (in press). Social anxiety and the school environment of adolescents. In K. Ranta, M. Marttunen, L-J. García-Lopez, and A. M. La Greca (Eds.), *Social anxiety and phobia in adolescents: Development, manifestation and intervention strategies.* Springer.

Bools, C., Foster, J., Brown, I., & Berg, I. (1990). The identification of psychiatric disorders in children who fail to attend school: A cluster analysis of a non-clinical population. *Psychological Medicine, 20*, 171–181.

Bowen, N. K., Bowen, G. L., & Ware, W. B. (2002). Neighborhood social disorganization, families, and the educational behavior of adolescents. *Journal of Adolescent Research, 17*, 468–490.

Breinholst, S., Esbjørn, B. H., Reinholdt-Dunne, M. L., & Stallard, P. (2012). CBT for the treatment of child anxiety disorders: A review of why parental involvement has not enhanced outcomes. *Journal of Anxiety Disorders, 26*, 416–424.

Buitelaar, J. K., Van Andel, H., Duyx, J. H. M., & Van Strien, D. C. (1994). Depressive and anxiety disorders in adolescence: A follow-up study of adolescents with school refusal. *Acta Paedopsychiatrica, 56*, 249–253.

Carless, B., Melvin, G. A., Tonge, B. J., & Newman, L. K. (2015). The role of parental self-efficacy in adolescent school-refusal. *Journal of Family Psychology.* Advance online publication. http://dx.doi.org/10.1037/fam0000050

Chorpita, B. F., Albano, A. M., Heimberg, R. G., & Barlow, D. H. (1996). A systematic replication of the prescriptive treatment of school refusal behavior in a single subject. *Journal of Behavior Therapy and Experimental Psychiatry, 27*, 281–290.

Chu, B. C., & Harrison, T. L. (2007). Disorder-specific effects of CBT for anxious and depressed youth: A meta-analysis of candidate mediators of change. *Clinical Child and Family Psychology Review, 10*, 352–372.

Clarke, G. N., Rohde, P., Lewinsohn, P. M., Hops, H., & Seeley, J. R. (1999). Cognitive-behavioral treatment of adolescent depression: Efficacy of acute group treatment and booster sessions. *Journal of the American Academy of Child and Adolescent Psychiatry, 38*, 272–279.

Corville-Smith, J., Ryan, B. A., Adams, G. R., & Dalicandro, T. (1998). Distinguishing absentee students from regular attenders: The combined influence of personal, family and school factors. *Journal of Youth and Adolescence, 27*, 629–640.

Costello, E. J., Mustillo, S., Erkanli, A., Keeler, G., & Angold, A. (2003). Prevalence and development of psychiatric disorders in childhood and adolescence. *Archives of General Psychiatry, 60*, 837–844.

Contessa, M. A., & Paccione-Dyszlewski, M. R. (1981). An application of a group counseling technique with school-phobic adolescents. *Adolescence, 16*, 901–904.

Coulter, S. (1995). School refusal, parental control and wider systems: Lessons from the management of two cases. *Irish Journal of Psychological Medicine, 12*, 146–149.

Crawley, S. A., Beidas, R. S., Benjamin, C. L., Martin, E., & Kendall, P. C. (2008). Treating socially phobic youth with CBT: Differential outcomes and treatment considerations. *Behavioural and Cognitive Psychotherapy, 36*, 379–389.

DeLisi, M., & Vaughn, M. G. (2014). Foundation for a temperament-based theory of antisocial behavior and criminal justice system involvement. *Journal of Criminal Justice, 42*, 10–25.

Doobay, A. F. (2008). School refusal behavior associated with separation anxiety disorder: A cognitive-behavioral approach to treatment. *Psychology in the Schools, 45*, 261–272.

Durand, V. M., & Crimmins, D. B. (1988). Identifying the variables maintaining self-injurious behavior. *Journal of Autism and Developmental Disorders, 18*, 99–117.

Egger, H. L., Costello, E. J., & Angold, A. (2003). School refusal and psychiatric disorders: A community study. *Journal of the American Academy of Child and Adolescent Psychiatry, 42*, 797–807.

Elliott, J. G. (1999). Practitioner review: School refusal: Issues of conceptualisation, assessment, and treatment. *Journal of Child Psychology and Psychiatry, 40*, 1001–1012.

Flanagan, M. (2006). The effects of a positive behavior support program on the attendance behaviors of students with and without disabilities in a large inner-city public high school. *Dissertation Abstracts International, 67*(07). (UMI No. 3225140).

Ginsburg, G. S., & Schlossberg, M. C. (2002). Family-based treatment of childhood anxiety disorders. *International Review of Psychiatry, 14*, 143–154.

Goodman, R., & Scott, S. (2012). *Child and adolescent psychiatry* (3rd ed.). Chichester, UK: Wiley-Blackwell.

Hansen, C., Sanders, S. L., Massaro, S., & Last, C. G. (1998). Predictors of severity of absenteeism in children with anxiety-based school refusal. *Journal of Clinical Child Psychology, 27*, 246–254.

Havik, T., Bru, E., & Ertesvåg, S. K. (2014). Parental perspectives of the role of school factors in school refusal. *Emotional and Behavioural Difficulties, 19*, 131–153.

Hella, B., & Bernstein, G. A. (2012). Panic disorder and school refusal. *Child and Adolescent Psychiatric Clinics of North America, 21*, 593–606.

Herrick, L. (1992). Effects of an attendance incentive program for chronically absent elementary school students. *Dissertation Abstracts International, 54*, 2010A. (UMI No. 933147).

Hess, A. M. (1990). The effects of contingency contracting and parent training on the truant behavior and classroom performance of students with handicaps. *Dissertation Abstracts International, 51*(5), 1576A. (UMI No. 9030200).

Hess, A. M., Rosenberg, M. S., & Levy, G. K. (1990). Reducing truancy in students with mild handicaps. *Remedial and Special Education, 11*, 14–19.

Heyne, D. (1999). *Evaluation of child therapy and caregiver training in the treatment of school refusal.* Unpublished doctoral dissertation. Monash University, Melbourne, Australia.

Heyne, D. (2006). School refusal. In J. E. Fisher and W. T. O'Donohue (Eds.), *Practitioner's guide to evidence-based psychotherapy* (pp. 599–618). New York: Springer.

Heyne, D., King, N. J., & Ollendick, T. (2004). School refusal. In P. Graham (Ed.), *Cognitive behaviour therapy for children and families* (2nd ed., pp. 320–341). Cambridge: Cambridge University Press.

Heyne, D., King, N., Tonge, B., Rollings, S., Pritchard, M., Young, D., & Myerson, N. (1998). The Self-Efficacy Questionnaire for School Situations: Development and psychometric evaluation. *Behaviour Change, 15*, 31–40.

Heyne, D., King, N. J., Tonge, B., Rollings, S., Young, D., Pritchard, M., & Ollendick, T. H. (2002). Evaluation of child therapy and caregiver training in the treatment of school refusal. *Journal of the American Academy of Child and Adolescent Psychiatry, 41*, 687–695.

Heyne, D., Maric, M., Kaijser, J., Duizer, L., Sijtsma, C., & Van den Leden, S. (2007). *Self-Efficacy Questionnaire for School Situations-Dutch Version*. Unpublished measure. Leiden, The Netherlands: Leiden University.

Heyne, D., & Rollings, S. (2002). *School refusal*. Oxford: Blackwell Scientific Publications.

Heyne, D. A., & Sauter, F. M. (2013). School refusal. In C. A. Essau & T. H. Ollendick (Eds.), *The Wiley-Blackwell handbook of the treatment of childhood and adolescent anxiety* (pp. 471–517). Chichester, UK: John Wiley & Sons.

Heyne, D., Sauter, F. M., Ollendick, T. H., van Widenfelt, B. M., & Westenberg, P. M. (2014). Developmentally sensitive cognitive behavioral therapy for adolescent school refusal: Rationale and illustration. *Clinical Child and Family Psychology Review, 17*, 191–215.

Heyne, D., Sauter, F. M., & Van Hout, R. (2008). *The @school program: Modular cognitive behavior therapy for school refusal in adolescence*. Unpublished treatment manual, Leiden University, Leiden, The Netherlands.

Heyne, D., Sauter, F. M., van Widenfelt, B. M., Vermeiren, R., & Westenberg, P. M. (2011). School refusal and anxiety in adolescence: Non-randomized trial of a developmentally-sensitive cognitive behavioral therapy. *Journal of Anxiety Disorders, 25*, 870–878.

Holmbeck, G. N., Devine, K. A., Wasserman, R., Schellinger, K., & Tuminello, E. (2012). Guides from developmental psychology for therapy with adolescents. In P. C. Kendall (Ed.), *Child and adolescent therapy: Cognitive-behavioral procedures* (pp. 429–470). New York: Guilford Press.

Hughes, E. K., Gullone, E., Dudley, A., & Tonge, B. (2010). A case-control study of emotion regulation and school refusal in children and adolescents. *Journal of Early Adolescence, 30*, 691–706.

Ingul, J. M., & Nordahl, H. M. (2013). Anxiety as a risk factor for school absenteeism: What differentiates anxious school-attenders from non-attenders? *Annals of General Psychiatry, 12*, 25. doi: 10.1186/1744-859X-12-25

Jenifer, S. J. (1995). Effectiveness of high school dropout intervention strategies in reducing absenteeism. *Dissertation Abstracts International, 56*(05), 1601A. (UMI No. 9530554).

Johncox, J. F. (1994). *Intervention effects for treating student nonattenders and their families*. Unpublished MSW clinical research paper, College of St. Catherine & University of St. Thomas, St. Paul, MN.

Kearney, C. A. (2001). *School refusal behavior in youth: A functional approach to assessment and treatment*. Washington, DC: American Psychological Association.

Kearney, C. A. (2002). Identifying the function of school refusal behavior: A revision of the School Refusal Assessment Scale. *Journal of Psychopathology and Behavioral Assessment, 24*, 235–245.

Kearney, C. A. (2003). Bridging the gap among professionals who address youths with school absenteeism: Overview and suggestions for consensus. *Professional Psychology: Research and Practice, 34*, 57–65.

Kearney, C. A. (2006). Confirmatory factor analysis of the School Refusal Assessment Scale—Revised: Child and Parent Versions. *Journal of Psychopathology and Behavioral Assessment, 28*, 139–144.

Kearney, C. A. (2008). An interdisciplinary model of school absenteeism in youth to inform professional practice and public policy. *Educational Psychology Review, 20*, 257–282.

Kearney, C. A., & Albano, A. M. (2004). The functional profiles of school refusal behavior: Diagnostic aspects. *Behavior Modification, 28*, 147–161.

Kearney, C. A., & Albano, A. M. (2007). *When children refuse school: A cognitive-behavioral therapy approach/therapist's guide* (2nd ed.). New York: Oxford University Press.

Kearney, C. A., & Bensaheb, A. (2006). School absenteeism and school refusal behavior: A review and suggestions for school-based health professionals. *Journal of School Health, 76*, 3–7.

Kearney, C. A., & Roblek, T. L. (1998). Parent training in the treatment of school refusal behavior. In J. Briesmeister & C. E. Schaefer (Eds.), *Handbook of parent training: Parents as co-therapists for children's behavior problems* (2nd ed., pp. 225–256). New York: Wiley & Sons.

Kearney, C. A., & Silverman, W. K. (1990). A preliminary analysis of a functional model of assessment and treatment for school refusal behavior. *Behavior Modification, 14*, 340–366.

Kearney, C. A., & Silverman, W. K. (1995). Family environment of youngsters with school refusal behavior: A synopsis with implications for assessment and treatment. *The American Journal of Family Therapy, 23*, 59–72.

Kearney, C. A., & Silverman, W. K. (1999). Functionally based prescriptive and non-prescriptive treatment for children and adolescents with school refusal behavior. *Behavior Therapy, 30*, 673–695.

Kendall, P. C., & Hedtke, K. (2006). *Cognitive-behavioral therapy for anxious children: Therapist manual* (3rd ed.). Ardmore, PA: Workbook Publishing.

King, N. J., Heyne, D., & Ollendick, T. (2005). Cognitive-behavioral treatments for anxiety and phobic disorders in children and adolescents: A review. *Behavioral Disorders, 30*, 241–257.

King, N., Tonge, B., Heyne, D., & Ollendick, T. (2000). Research on the cognitive-behavioral treatment of school refusal: A review and recommendations. *Clinical Psychology Review, 20*, 495–507.

King, N. J., Tonge, B. J., Heyne, D., Pritchard, M., Rollings, S., Young, D., . . . Ollendick, T. H. (1998). Cognitive-behavioral treatment of school-refusing children: A controlled evaluation. *Journal of the American Academy of Child and Adolescent Psychiatry, 37*, 375–403.

King, N., Tonge, B., Heyne, D., Turner, S., Pritchard, M., Young, D., . . . Ollendick, T. H. (2001). Cognitive-behavioral treatment of school-refusing children: Maintenance of improvement at 3- to 5-year follow-up. *Scandinavian Journal of Behavior Therapy, 30*, 85–89.

Last, C. G. (1993). *Therapist treatment manual for NIMH school phobia study: Exposure therapy program.* Unpublished manuscript.

Last, C. G., Francis, G., Hersen, M., Kazdin, A. E., & Strauss, C. C. (1987). Separation anxiety and school phobia: A comparison using DSM-III criteria. *American Journal of Psychiatry, 144,* 653–657.

Last, C. G., Hansen, C., & Franco, N. (1998). Cognitive-behavioral treatment of school phobia. *Journal of the American Academy of Child and Adolescent Psychiatry, 37,* 404–411.

Last, C. G., & Strauss, C. C. (1990). School refusal in anxiety-disordered children and adolescents. *Journal of the American Academy of Child and Adolescent Psychiatry, 29,* 31–35.

Layne, A. E., Bernstein, G. A., Egan, E. A., & Kushner, M. G. (2003). Predictors of treatment response in anxious depressed adolescents with school refusal. *Journal of the American Academy of Child and Adolescent Psychiatry, 42,* 319–326.

Lewinsohn, P. M., Clarke, G. N., Hops, H., & Andrews, J. (1990). Cognitive-behavioral group treatment of depression in adolescents. *Behavior Therapy, 21,* 385–401.

Lyon, A. R., & Cotler, S. (2007). Toward reduced bias and increased utility in the assessment of school refusal behavior: The case for diverse samples and evaluations of context. *Psychology in the Schools, 44,* 551–565.

Malcolm, H., Wilson, V., Davidson, J., & Kirk, S. (2003). *Absence from school: A study of its causes and effects in seven LEAs.* (Department for Education and Skills Research Report RR424). Sherwood Park, UK: National Foundation for Educational Research.

Mansdorf, I. J., & Lukens, E. (1987). Cognitive-behavioral psychotherapy for separation anxious children exhibiting school phobia. *Journal of the American Academy of Child and Adolescent Psychiatry, 26,* 222–225.

Maric, M., Heyne, D. A., de Heus, P., van Widenfelt, B. M., & Westenberg, P. M. (2012). The role of cognition in school refusal: An investigation of automatic thoughts and cognitive errors. *Behavioural and Cognitive Psychotherapy, 40,* 255–269.

Maric, M., Heyne, D. A., MacKinnon, D. P., van Widenfelt, B. M., & Westenberg, P. M. (2013). Cognitive mediation of cognitive-behavioural therapy outcomes for anxiety-based school refusal. *Behavioural and Cognitive Psychotherapy, 41,* 549–564.

Martin, C., Cabrol, S., Bouvard, M. P., Lepine, J. P., & Mouren-Simeoni, M. C. (1999). Anxiety and depressive disorders in fathers and mothers of anxious school-refusing children. *Journal of the American Academy of Child and Adolescent Psychiatry, 38,* 916–922.

Maynard, B. R., McCrea, K. T., Pigott, T. D., & Kelly, M. S. (2012). Indicated truancy interventions: Effects on school attendance among chronic truant students. *Campbell Systematic Reviews, 8*(10). doi: 10.4073/csr.2012.10

Maynard, B. R., McCrea, K. T., Pigott, T. D., & Kelly, M. S. (2013). Indicated truancy interventions for chronic truant students: A Campbell systematic review. *Research on Social Work Practice, 23,* 5–21. doi: 10.1177/1049731512457207

Maynard, B. R., Salas-Wright, C. P., Vaughn, M. G., & Peters, K. E. (2012). Who are truant youth? Examining distinctive profiles of truant youth using latent profile analysis. *Journal of Youth and Adolescence, 41,* 1671–1684.

McAnanly, E. (1986). School phobia: The importance of prompt intervention. *Journal of School Health, 56,* 433–436.

McShane, G., Walter, G., & Rey, J. M. (2001). Characteristics of adolescents with school refusal. *Australian and New Zealand Journal of Psychiatry, 35*, 822–826.

McShane, G., Walter, G., & Rey, J. M. (2004). Functional outcome of adolescents with school refusal. *Clinical Child Psychology and Psychiatry, 9*, 53–60.

Meyer, E. A., Hagopian, L. P., & Paclawskyj, T. R. (1999). A function-based treatment for school refusal behavior using shaping and fading. *Research in Developmental Disabilities, 20*, 401–410.

Nuttall, C., & Woods, K. (2013). Effective intervention for school refusal behavior. *Educational Psychology in Practice, 29*, 347–366.

Okuyama, M., Okada, M., Kuribayashi, M., & Kaneko, S. (1999). Factors responsible for the prolongation of school refusal. *Psychiatry and Clinical Neurosciences, 53*, 461–469.

Pina, A. A., Zerr, A. A., Gonzales, N. A., & Ortiz, C. D. (2009). Psychosocial interventions for school refusal behavior in children and adolescents. *Child Development Perspectives, 3*, 11–20.

Place, M., Hulsmeier, J., Brownrigg, J., & Soulsby, A. (2005). The Family Adaptability and Cohesion Evaluation Scale (FACES): An instrument worthy of rehabilitation? *Psychiatric Bulletin, 29*, 215–218.

Place, M., Hulsmeier, J., Davis, S., & Taylor, E. (2000). School refusal: A changing problem which requires a change of approach? *Clinical Child Psychology and Psychiatry, 5*, 345–355.

Place, M., Hulsmeier, J., Davis, S., & Taylor, E. (2002). The coping mechanisms of children with school refusal. *Journal of Research in Special Educational Needs, 2*, 1–10.

Restifo, K., & Bögels, S. (2009). Family processes in the development of youth depression: Translating the evidence to treatment. *Clinical Psychology Review, 29*, 294–316.

Reynolds, S., Wilson, C., Austin, J., & Hooper, L. (2012). Effects of psychotherapy for anxiety in children and adolescents: A meta-analytic review. *Clinical Psychology Review, 32*, 251–262.

Romero, M., & Lee, Y. S. (2008). *The influence of maternal and family risk on chronic absenteeism in early schooling.* New York: National Center for Children in Poverty, Columbia University.

Sauter, F. M., Heyne, D., & Westenberg, P. M. (2009). Cognitive behavior therapy for anxious adolescents: Developmental influences on treatment design and delivery. *Clinical Child and Family Psychology Review, 12*, 310–335.

Seamans, C. L. (1996). Brief family systems intervention with inner-city truant youths. *Masters Abstracts International, 35*(1), 349. (UMI No. 1381227).

Silverman, W. K., Pina, A. A., & Viswesvaran, C. (2008). Evidence-based psychosocial treatments for phobic and anxiety disorders in children and adolescents. *Journal of Clinical Child and Adolescent Psychology, 37*, 105–130.

Southwell, N. (2006). Truants on truancy—a badness or a valuable indicator of unmet special education needs? *British Journal of Special Education, 33*, 91–97.

TADS (Treatment for Adolescents With Depression Study) Team. (2003). Treatment for Adolescents With Depression Study (TADS): Rationale, design, and methods. *Journal of the American Academy of Child and Adolescent Psychiatry, 42*, 531–542.

Thambirajah, M. S., Grandison, K. J., & De-Hayes, L. (2008). *Understanding school refusal: A handbook for professionals in education, health and social care.* London: Jessica Kingsley Press.

Tichenor, R. M. S. (1991). Making it in middle school: An evaluation of the effects of a guidance program on the school attendance patterns of at-risk sixth-graders. *Dissertation Abstracts International, 52,* 3831A. (UMI No. 9211808).

Tolin, D. F., Whiting, S., Maltby, N., Diefenbach, G. J., Lothstein, M. A., Hardcastle, S., ... Gray, K. (2009). Intensive (daily) behavior therapy for school refusal: A multiple baseline case series. *Cognitive and Behavioral Practice, 16,* 332–344.

Trice, A. D. (1990). Adolescents' locus of control and compliance with contingency contracting and counseling interventions. *Psychological Reports, 67,* 233–234.

Valles, E., & Oddy, M. (1984). The influence of a return to school on the long-term adjustment of school refusers. *Journal of Adolescence, 7,* 35–44.

Vaughn, M. G., Maynard, B. R., Salas-Wright, C. P., Perron, B. E., & Abdon, A. (2013). Prevalence and correlates of truancy in the US: Results from a national sample. *Journal of Adolescence, 36,* 767–776. doi: 10.1016/j.adolescence.2013.03.015

Walter, D., Hautmann, C., Minkus, J., Petermann, M., Lehmkuhl, G., Goertz-Dorten, A., & Doepfner, M. (2013). Predicting outcome of inpatient CBT for adolescents with anxious-depressed school absenteeism. *Clinical Psychology and Psychotherapy, 20,* 206–215.

Walter, D., Hautmann, C., Rizk, S., Petermann, M., Minkus, J., Sinzig, J., ... Doepfner, M. et al. (2010). Short term effects of inpatient cognitive behavioral treatment of adolescents with anxious-depressed school absenteeism: An observational study. *European Child and Adolescent Psychiatry, 19,* 835–844.

Wright, K. J. (2000). A comparison of three truancy treatment programs in Maricopa County, Arizona. *Dissertation Abstracts International, 62,* 2509B. (UMI No. 3016006).

Wu, X., Liu, F., Cai, H., Huang, L., Li, Y., Mo, Z., & Lin, J. (2013). Cognitive behaviour therapy combined fluoxetine treatment superior to cognitive behavior therapy alone for school refusal. *International Journal of Pharmacology, 9,* 197–203.

Moderators and Mediators of Treatments for Youth in Divorced or Separated Families

SHARLENE A. WOLCHIK, NICOLE E. MAHRER,
JENN-YUN TEIN, AND IRWIN N. SANDLER ■

INTRODUCTION

Parental divorce is among the most prevalent stressful adversities that children experience. There is wide variation in the divorce rates. Whereas in 2011, the crude divorce rate (which reflects the number of divorces per 1,000 people including adults and children) in the United States was 3.6, recent rates ranged from 2.0–2.3 in Japan, France, Germany, and the United Kingdom. It is currently estimated that 30%–50% of youth in the United States will experience parental divorce in childhood or adolescence (National Center for Health Statistics, 2008). In Australia and the United Kingdom, it is estimated that about 25% of children will experience parental divorce or will live in a single-parent household by the time they reach 18 years of age (De Vaus, 2004; Bradshaw, 2011).

In this chapter, we first discuss the risks associated with parental divorce and the programs designed to reduce children's mental health problems that have been evaluated in experimental or quasi-experimental trials. We then present a theoretical model of moderation of program effects and discuss the findings on moderators. Next, we discuss theoretical models of mediation of program effects and present findings on mediating mechanisms. We then make recommendations for future research on moderators and mediators of program effects for this group of at-risk youth and discuss the implications of the research findings for clinical practice.

RISKS ASSOCIATED WITH PARENTAL DIVORCE AND VARIABILITY OF OUTCOMES

Risks

There is compelling evidence showing that divorce increases risk for multiple problems in childhood and adolescence. The most comprehensive picture of how youth fare after parental divorce is provided by two meta-analyses that showed more conduct, internalizing, social, and academic problems in youth in divorced versus non-divorced families (Amato, 2001; Amato & Keith, 1991). These differences were consistent across age and gender and were slightly larger in more recent studies. Findings from the Health Survey in England showed that youth from divorced families were 1.8 times more likely than those from non-divorced families to meet criteria for psychological morbidity (McMunn, Nazrooa, Marmota, Borehamb, & Goodman, 2001). Youth in divorced families are also more likely than those in non-divorced families to report elevated levels of substance use (e.g., Paxton, Valois, & Drane, 2007), to drop out of school (McLanahan, 1999), and to experience premarital childbearing (Hetherington, 1999).

For a sizable minority, the effects of parental divorce continue into adulthood. Multiple prospective epidemiologic studies have shown that parental divorce in childhood or adolescence is associated with increases in mental health problems, substance abuse, mental health service use, and psychiatric hospitalization in adulthood. The World Mental Health Survey showed that parental divorce was related to elevated rates of onset of mental health disorders in high-, middle-, and low-income countries (odds ratio range 1.1–1.3), controlling for age, country, and type of disorder (Kessler et al., 2010). Parental divorce is also related to other aspects of functioning in adulthood, including lower educational and occupational attainment (e.g., Biblarz & Gottainer, 2000), more economic problems (e.g., Caspi et al., 1998), poorer marital quality (e.g., Amato, 2000), higher rates of divorce themselves (e.g., Wolfinger, 2000), more health problems (e.g., Maier & Lachman, 2000) and increased mortality risk (Schwartz et al., 1995).

Explaining Variability in Outcomes: Risk and Protective Factors

Although it has been consistently documented that parental divorce is associated with elevations in risk for problems in multiple aspects of functioning, it is important to note that although most youth are highly distressed after parental divorce, most do *not* manifest serious mental health or social adaptation problems after parental divorce (e.g., Amato, 2001). Multiple studies have shown that about 70%–75% of youth from divorced families do *not* experience clinically significant mental health problems. Below, we discuss the risk and protective factors that have been consistently related to children's post-divorce outcomes.

Several environmental and family factors have been shown to predict post-divorce mental health outcomes. A large body of research has shown that interparental conflict is one of the most damaging aspects of divorce (e.g., Kelly, 2012). Researchers have also shown that high levels of other divorce-related stressors, such as changing schools, predict post-divorce mental health problems (e.g., Sandler, Tein, & West, 1994). There is also consistent support for the protective effect of high-quality mother-child and father-child relationships (e.g., Sandler et al., 2012).

Although most research has examined relations between individual factors and children's outcomes, a few researchers have examined the additive and interactive effects of some factors. Several researchers have shown that high-quality parenting mitigates the negative effect of divorce-related stressors on mental health problems (e.g., Wolchik, Wilcox, Tein, & Sandler, 2000). Also, high-quality, responsive parenting by fathers and mothers has been related to lower post-divorce mental health problems, after accounting for the relationship quality with the other parent (King & Sobolewski, 2006).

Several youth factors have been shown to predict post-divorce mental health outcomes. Avoidant coping has been related to higher mental health problems (e.g., Sandler et al., 1994), whereas active coping and coping efficacy have been related to lower problems (e.g., Sandler, Tein, Mehta, Wolchik, & Ayers, 2000). Higher levels of positive illusions (e.g., thinking "someday my parents won't fight anymore" in response to a hypothetical situation in which parents are fighting) were related to lower mental health problems (Mazur, Wolchik, & Sandler, 1992) and mitigated the effects of divorce-related stressors on mental health problems (Mazur, Wolchik, Virdin, Sandler, & West, 1999). Appraisals that events involve high threat (Sheets, Sandler, & West, 1996) and higher levels of negative cognitive errors about divorce stressors (Mazur et al., 1992) were related to higher mental health problems. Also, fear of abandonment predicted higher levels of mental health problems (e.g., Wolchik, Tein, Sandler, & Doyle, 2002), whereas higher levels of self-worth (Sandler, 2001) and higher levels of internal locus of control predicted lower mental health problems (Fogas, Wolchik, Braver, Freedom, & Bay, 1992).

In summary, a large body of research has documented that for a sizable minority of youth, parental divorce is associated with elevated risk for problems in multiple domains of functioning that can last into adulthood. Importantly, researchers have identified potentially modifiable variables that correlate with post-divorce mental health problems in youth or that mitigate the negative relations between divorce-related stressors and mental health problems. Theoretically, if these variables are causally related to post-divorce problems, programs that change them in positive ways should reduce post-divorce problems (Wolchik et al., 1993). This body of research has provided guidance for many of the interventions described below.

Interventions to Reduce or Prevent Children's Post-Divorce Adjustment Problems

There are few rigorous trials of programs for children from divorced families. Although randomized experimental trials provide the strongest tests of such programs, quasi-experimental trials also provide important information about program impact and thus are included in this chapter. The review is organized in terms of the program's focus: on children, on parents, or on both parents and children. The samples in most of the studies included both youth with clinically significant mental health problems and those with subclinical levels of mental health problems at program entry. For example, at pre-test, 42% of Stolberg and Mahler's (1994) sample met diagnosis for a mental disorder and 35% of Wolchik, West, et al.'s (2000) sample scored in the clinical range on internalizing or externalizing behavior problems.

Child-Focused Programs

Although there have been several randomized or quasi-experimental trials of child-focused programs designed to reduce mental health problems, most have been evaluated in a single trial. Positive program effects were found on depression and self-perceptions of scholastic competence and athletic competence in a 6-session, multimodal group counseling program (Crosbie-Burnett & Newcomer,1990), on depression and anxiety in an 8-session program focused on education about divorce, expression of feelings, and problem-solving (Gwynn & Brantley, 1987), and on teacher (but not parent or child) report of behavior problems in a 6-session program focused on identifying feelings, communication skills, and anger management (Bornstein et al., 1988). However, non-significant effects were found in three trials that examined depression, anxiety, school behavior, anxiety, and/or self-esteem: a 10-week program focused on cognitive social role taking and communication skills (Roseby & Deutsch, 1985); a 6-session program focused on coping and feelings about the divorce (Hett & Rose; 1991); and a 6-session program focused on helping children share their feelings and correcting problematic beliefs about divorce (Jupp & Purcell, 1992).

Researchers have conducted multiple evaluations of the Children's Support Group (CSG; Stolberg & Garrison, 1985) and the Children of Divorce Intervention Program (CODIP; Pedro-Carroll & Cowen, 1985). These similar, manualized, 10–12 session, school-based programs focused on providing emotional support and teaching adaptive coping and control beliefs.

In a quasi-experimental trial of the CSG, Stolberg and Garrison (1985) found that children aged 7–13 significantly improved on self-concept at post-test and the 5-month follow-up compared with non-randomized, no-intervention controls. However, program effects on mental health problems were non-significant. A later experimental trial with children aged 8–12 found program effects to reduce internalizing and externalizing problems. Also, the prevalence of clinically significant levels of mental health problems at post-test and 1-year follow-up was lower for youth in the CSG compared with no-intervention controls (Stolberg & Mahler, 1994).

In their experimental trial of the CODIP, Pedro-Carroll and Cowen (1985) found that the program reduced anxiety and learning problems and improved competence at post-test compared to a no-intervention control group. Quasi-experimental trials of this program have shown program effects on competence, shy-anxious behavior, and problem behaviors at post-test (Pedro-Carroll & Alpert-Gillis, 1997; Pedro-Carroll, Alpert-Gillis, & Cowen, 1992) and on anxiety and classroom adjustment problems at a 2-year follow-up compared with non-randomized, no-intervention control groups (Pedro-Carroll, Sutton, & Wyman, 1999).

Parent-Focused Programs

Five programs for parents have been evaluated using experimental or quasi-experimental designs. Three of these targeted residential mothers as change agents, one targeted non-residential fathers, and one targeted both parents.

The 12-session Single Parents' Support Group aimed to facilitate children's adjustment by improving mothers' adjustment through enhancing identity development, social support, and parenting skills. Each group selected the specific topics to be covered in their sessions. In a quasi-experimental trial that involved mothers with 7–13-year-olds, the program's effects on children's mental health problems were non-significant (Stolberg & Garrison, 1985).

Two randomized controlled trials have been conducted on the New Beginnings Program (NBP). This manualized program consists of group sessions (11 in the first trial; 10 in the second trial) and two individual sessions. The program in the first trial was designed to modify the following empirically supported risk and protective factors: mother-child relationship quality; effective discipline; father-child contact; divorce-related stressors, including interparental conflict; and contact with non-parental adults (Wolchik et al., 1993). Based on the lack of positive program effects on father-child contact and non-parental adult support in the first trial, these components were not included in the program tested in the second trial.

The first trial, conducted with mothers of children aged 8–15, found fewer mental health problems at post-test for children whose mothers participated in the NBP compared to those whose mothers were in the wait-list control condition (Wolchik et al., 1993). The second trial was conducted with mothers of 9–12-year-olds. This trial included three conditions: a parenting-focused program for mothers, a dual-component program (parenting-focused program for mothers plus a coping-focused program for children), and a literature control condition, in which mothers and children each received three books about adjusting to divorce. Program effects on externalizing problems were found at post-test and a 6-month follow-up (Wolchik, West, et al., 2000). Also, the proportion of children scoring *below* the clinical cutoff point for internalizing or externalizing problems was significantly higher in the NBP compared to the literature control condition at post-test (82% vs. 72%; Wolchik, West, et al., 2000). The program effects that were moderated will be discussed later in this chapter, in the section on moderation.

Two long-term follow-ups of the sample in the second trial have been conducted. Because comparisons of the parenting-focused program and dual-component program showed only one significant or marginal effect for the 46 outcomes assessed at post-test and short-term follow-ups, these conditions were combined and compared to the literature control condition. The 6-year and 15-year follow-ups occurred when participants were between 15 and 19 years of age and between 24 and 28 years of age, respectively. Significant program effects occurred for 12 of the 15 outcomes assessed in adolescence (Wolchik, Sandler, Weiss, & Winslow, 2007), including reductions in externalizing problems (parent/adolescent report and teacher report), internalizing problems (parent/adolescent report), symptoms of mental disorder, alcohol use, marijuana use, other drug use, polydrug use, and number of sexual partners and improvements in GPA and self-esteem. The NBP also reduced diagnosis of mental disorder in the past year by 37% (14.8% for NBP vs. 23.5% for literature control). Several effects were moderated; these effects will be discussed in the section on moderation. At the 15-year follow-up, young adults in the NBP had a lower incidence of internalizing disorders in the past 9 (7.5% vs. 24.0%) and 15 years (15.5% vs. 34.6) compared to those in the literature control condition. Much of this effect was accounted for by reductions in major depression. The moderated program effects will be discussed in the section on moderation.

The 14-session Parenting Through Change (PTC) program is a manualized program for mothers that targets parenting skills. The experimental trial included mothers with 6–10-year-old sons. The program did *not* have significant direct effects on depressed mood, anxiety, or externalizing problems 12 months after program entry (Forgatch & DeGarmo, 1999). However, 30 months after program entry, program effects occurred for non-compliance (Martinez & Forgatch, 2001), a composite of delinquency, non-compliance, and aggression (DeGarmo, Patterson, & Forgatch, 2004), and a composite of depressed mood, loneliness, and peer rejection (DeGarmo et al., 2004). Program effects occurred on youth report of delinquency 36 months after program entry (DeGarmo & Forgatch, 2005) and on teacher report of delinquency and police arrest records 9 years after participation (Forgatch, Patterson, DeGarmo, & Beldavs, 2009).

The 8-session Dads for Life program (DFL) targets fathers' commitment to parenting, parenting skills, conflict management, and perceived control over divorce events. The randomized controlled trial involved non-residential fathers with 4–12-year-old children. At post-test, mother's report of total behavior problems and father's and mother's report of internalizing problems were reduced for children whose fathers were in the DFL versus those in the literature control condition (Braver, Griffin, & Cookston, 2005).

The Collaborative Divorce Project (CDP) is a comprehensive, court-based program designed for couples with children age 6 or younger (Pruett, Insabella, & Gustafson, 2005). The program consists of seven components (e.g., divorce orientation, psycho-educational parenting classes, mediation-focused therapeutic resolution). Degree of exposure to some components varied based on the couple's needs. Assignment to condition was alternated as families joined the project. At the 9- to 11-month follow-up, children in the CDP had fewer teacher-reported cognitive problems than those in the standard care (community education) control condition.

Combined Child and Residential Mother Programs

Three trials have been conducted on dual-component programs. These programs targeted empirically supported modifiable risk and protective factors that were primarily controlled by children (e.g., coping) and mothers (e.g., effective discipline). The involvement of both mothers and children was expected to yield additive program benefits compared to either child-focused or mother-focused programs alone.

Stolberg and Garrison's (1985) quasi-experimental trial did not find benefits of combining the Children's Support Group (CSG) and Single Parents' Support Group (SPSG). Moreover, program effects for the separate CSG and SPSG groups on children's and mothers' adjustment did *not* occur in the dual-component program. Stolberg and Mahler's (1994) experimental trial that compared the CSG to a condition that included the CSG, four parent workshops, and a workbook for parents designed to help transfer children's gains to the home did not yield additive effects on mental health problems.

Wolchik and her colleagues (2000) compared their parenting program for mothers to a mother-plus-child condition that included the parenting program and a concurrently run program for children. The child program targeted the following empirically supported correlates of children's post-divorce adjustment: coping, negative divorce appraisals, and mother-child relationship quality. At post-test, the dual-component program showed additive effects on threat appraisals and knowledge of adaptive coping but not on mental health problems. Although it is plausible that the effects on these outcomes might require time to affect mental health problems, additive effects did not occur at any of the follow-ups (Wolchik et al., 2000; Wolchik et al., 2002; Wolchik et al., 2007).

Summary

Several rigorously conducted trials have provided support for positive effects of programs to improve post-divorce outcomes in youth. For both child- and residential mother-focused programs, program effects have been found by two or more research groups. Promising effects of programs for non-residential fathers and for couples have also been found. Unexpectedly, dual-component (mother and child) programs did not yield additive effects over single-component programs at post-test or follow-ups. Program effects occurred on a range of outcomes at post-test, including mental health problems, self-concept, competence, and academic and cognitive outcomes. Several evaluations have found program effects at short-term follow-ups that ranged from 6 months to 3 years. For the two programs for residential mothers, the NBP and PTC, follow-ups in subsequent developmental periods of adolescence, young adulthood, or both, have shown long-term effects on a wide range of outcomes. The long-term effects of programs for children, non-residential fathers, or couples have not been assessed.

THEORIES OF MODERATION

Although few researchers have explicitly articulated the theoretical framework underlying their program or its action theory, most of the programs can be considered cognitive behavioral in orientation and teach skills. Thus, variables that are associated with differential skill acquisition and use could theoretically moderate program effects on the targeted outcomes, such that these variables could influence the degree of benefits families derive from the programs. Below, we describe plausible moderators of the effects of prevention programs for divorced families and the mechanisms by which these factors might work. In this section, we draw on the findings in the wider literature on prevention programs and treatments for a wide range of children's problems, as well as the limited research on programs for divorced families.

Several parent characteristics may moderate the effects of programs for divorced families. Psychological distress has been identified as a consistent moderator of program effects, such that parents with higher distress at program entry benefit less than those with lower distress (e.g., Hipke, Wolchik, Sandler, & Braver, 2002; Reyno & McGrath, 2006). Differential benefit may be due to differences in motivation to attend sessions and complete program activities. Level of education may moderate program effects such that parents with less education receive less benefit from program than those with more education due to differences in responsiveness to the classroom-like instruction used in many parenting programs (e.g., Knapp & Deluty, 1989), differences in motivational cognitions that are consistent with most parenting programs, such as internal locus of control (Miller & Prinz, 2003), or differences in obstacles to attendance (e.g., conflicts with work schedules). Ethnicity may moderate program effects such that ethnic minority families benefit less than ethnic majority families because of differences in trust of providers (Keller & McDade, 2000) or the fit between the program skills taught in many programs and cultural values and needs (Zhou, Chen, Cookston, & Wolchik, 2014).

Among child characteristics, strong support has been found for program effects being moderated by the level of children's mental health problems at program entry, with youth who enter programs with greater problems benefiting more than those with fewer problems (e.g., Sandler, Wolchik, Cruden, Mahrer, Ahn & Brown, 2014). This finding may be due to those with fewer problems having less opportunity to improve (Brown & Liao, 1999) or parents of youth with greater problems being more motivated to attend sessions and use the program skills than those whose children have fewer problems (Morawska, Ramadewi, & Sanders, 2014). Gender may moderate program

effects because of differences in levels of problem behaviors, such as externalizing problems and substance use (Lahey et al., 2000), at program entry. Child
temperament might moderate the effects of parent-focused programs because
parents' experience of doing program activities likely differs, depending on
aspects of children's temperament. For example, less improvement might
occur for children with high versus low negative emotionality because of differences in how enjoyable it is for parents to use the program skills with their
children (Dumas, 1984). In addition, age may moderate program effects, such
that older youth may benefit more from child-focused programs than younger
children because they are more able to learn the program skills. Older children may also benefit more from parent-focused programs that emphasize
communication because they are more able to express their thoughts and feelings than younger children (Cedar & Levant, 1990). Alternatively, because
younger children spend more time at home and parents, rather than peers, are
their primary socializing agents (Dodge, 1993), they may benefit more from
parenting-focused programs than adolescents.

Contextual factors could also moderate program effects. For example, families
who experience higher levels of stress may experience greater difficulties attending sessions and/or using program skills because of more pressing concerns
(Lundahl, Risser, & Lovejoy, 2006). The timing of the program may also moderate program effects. Closer to the separation, child-focused concerns may be a
higher priority than they are later in the process of separation, and thus parents
may invest more effort to attend sessions and use the program skills (Winslow,
Bonds, Wolchik, Sandler, & Braver, 2009). Alternatively, because parents may
be overwhelmed with the many changes that occur early in the process of separation, they may be less able to attend sessions or use program skills and thus
benefit less from the program.

Summary

Multiple parent and child characteristics and contextual factors theoretically could moderate the effects of programs for divorced families. In the
larger literature on treatment and prevention programs for youth, it has been
consistently demonstrated that youth with more problems at program entry
benefit more than those with fewer problems and that youth whose mothers
have higher psychological distress benefit less than those whose mothers have
lower distress.

EMPIRICAL RESULTS OF MODERATION

Moderation analyses have been conducted for only one program, the NBP. In
both trials, program effects were moderated by level of children's mental health
problems at program entry, with greater benefits occurring for youth with higher

versus lower mental health problems (Wolchik et al., 1993; Wolchik et al., 2000). Figure 11.1 shows this interactive effect for youth in Wolchik et al.'s (2000) study. At the 6-month follow-up of the second trial, youth with higher externalizing problems at program entry showed greater benefit on externalizing problems than those who entered the program with lower externalizing problems (Wolchik et al., 2000). Also, greater program benefits on externalizing problems occurred at the 6-month follow-up for families in which mothers had lower psychological distress or children had higher self-regulatory skills compared to those with higher psychological distress or lower self-regulatory skills at program entry (Hipke et al., 2002).

At the 6-year follow-up, a broader measure of risk for later problems was tested as a moderator. This index was based on analyses that identified the best pre-test predictors of the 6-year follow-up outcomes of youth in the control group of Wolchik et al.'s (2000) trial. The index, which consisted of the sum of standardized scores on two measures, pre-test externalizing and a composite of environmental stressors, was highly predictive of multiple outcomes in the control group at the 6-year follow-up (Dawson-McClure et al., 2004). Program effects were significantly moderated by risk for 9 of the 15 outcomes tested (Wolchik et al., 2007): symptoms of mental disorder, alcohol use, marijuana use, other drug use, polydrug use, and competence, parent/adolescent reports of internalizing problems, parent/adolescent reports of externalizing problems, and teacher-reported externalizing problems. For each interactive effect, program benefit was significantly greater for those with higher versus lower pre-test risk. Four of the nine interactive effects (i.e., parent/adolescent reports of externalizing problems, teacher-reported externalizing problems, marijuana use, and

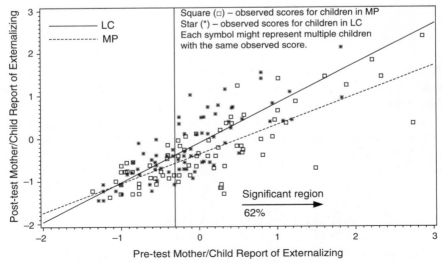

Figure 11.1. Program by baseline effect of the mother program versus literature control condition on post-test externalizing problems.

competence) also showed significant main effects indicating an overall benefit as well as a larger benefit for higher risk participants. Time since divorce moderated program effects on two outcomes at the 6-year follow-up; effects on internalizing problems were greater for youth in families with less recent versus more recent divorces, but effects on diagnosis of mental disorder were greater for those in families with more recent versus less recent divorces.

Although none of the program effects at post-test or 6-month and 6-year follow-ups was moderated by gender, at the 15-year follow-up, the program effects on substance use outcomes were moderated by gender. For males, the NBP reduced the number of substance-related disorders between adolescence and young adulthood and several aspects of substance use, including frequency of polydrug use and other drug use and substance use problems. For females, program participation led to an increase on one of nine measures of substance use: alcohol use in the last month. However, females in both conditions drank between three and five drinks in the past month, an amount not likely to be problematic.

Summary

In both experimental trials of the NBP, greater benefits at post-test were found for youth who entered the program with higher versus lower levels of externalizing problems (Wolchik et al., 1993; Wolchik et al., 2000). Although support for other moderators (i.e., maternal distress, child self-regulation, risk at program entry, gender, and time since divorce) was found at the follow-up assessments, these effects were not consistent across the follow-up assessments or outcomes.

THEORETICAL MODELS OF MEDIATION

As described in earlier chapters, the use of theory in intervention design and evaluation can provide guidance for program development by identifying factors that, if changed, should lead to improvements. Also, it provides a basis for testing the mechanisms by which a program affects outcomes. Because randomization to the experimental and control conditions makes it unlikely that third variables, such as shared genes or parental distress, account for the relation between program-induced change in a risk or protective factor and program-induced change in an outcome, finding that program effects are mediated by experimentally induced change in a risk or protective factor provides considerably stronger evidence of the causal effect of that variable than findings from correlational studies. Further, mediational analyses can identify the core components that need to be preserved in dissemination.

Although many of the programs that worked with children, non-residential fathers, or couples targeted variables that research has shown to be associated with post-divorce outcomes in youth, the developers of these programs have *not*

articulated the theories underlying their interventions. However, the two programs for residential mothers, the NBP and PTC, are based on well-articulated
theoretical models. These theories are described below.

The conceptual model underlying the NBP combined elements of a
person-environment transactional framework and risk and protective factor
model. Transactional models posit that aspects of the social environment affect
the development of problems and competencies, which in turn influence the
social environment and competencies and problems at later developmental stages
(e.g., Cicchetti & Schneider-Rosen, 1986). The risk and protective factor model
posits that the likelihood of mental health problems is affected by exposure to
risk factors and the availability of protective resources. Although not available
when the NBP was developed, Cummings, Davies, and Campbell's (2000) "cascading pathway model," which integrates these two models into a developmental
framework, provides a useful framework for understanding the NBP's long-term
effects. In this model, stressful events, such as divorce, can lead to an unfolding of failures to resolve developmental tasks and thus increase susceptibility for
mental health problems and impairments in competencies. Parenting is viewed
as playing a central role in facilitating children's successful adaptation, and the
skills and resources developed in the resolution of earlier developmental tasks
are seen as important tools for coping with future challenges. Dynamic interactions between children's resources and their competencies are hypothesized
to lead to a positive cascade of adaptive functioning over time. For example,
high-quality mother-child relationships may lead to fewer externalizing problems, which increase the likelihood of positive interactions with others, which
may lead to further reductions in externalizing problems and improvements in
other aspects of functioning.

Based on the research available at the time the NBP was developed, the following potentially modifiable risk and protective factors that had been shown to relate
to children's post-divorce adjustment problems were targeted for change: residential parent-child relationship quality; effective discipline; divorce-related
stressors, including interparental conflict; non-residential parent-child contact;
and non-parental adult support (see Wolchik et al. [1993] for a discussion of the
empirical support for these factors). Because the selected risk factors and protective factors were more under parents' rather than children's control, parents
were selected as change agents. The change strategies were cognitive behavioral
in nature and were based on empirically supported techniques. Because at the
time of the trials, the vast majority of children were in maternal residential living arrangements, only mothers were recruited as participants. The effectiveness
of a father version of the NBP is currently being assessed. Pilot work has shown
that fathers use the program skills effectively with their children and are very
satisfied with the program.

The PTC program (Forgatch & DeGarmo, 1999) was based on social interaction learning and coercion theories. According to social interaction theory,
the effect of negative family contexts on the adjustment of youth is mediated by
parenting practices (Forgatch & DeGarmo, 2002). In this model, divorce puts

parents at risk for poor parenting, which subsequently puts children at risk for negative adjustment outcomes. In coercion theory, children's behavior is seen as directly affected by two aspects of parenting: coercive discipline and effective parenting practices. In some families, coercive transactional patterns develop in which parents model or reinforce their children's negative behaviors through negative reciprocity, escalation, or negative reinforcement. Relatedly, parents may become less warm, less encouraging, and less reinforcing in their interactions with their children (Patterson, Reid, & Dishion, 1992). Numerous studies have linked coercive discipline practices with children's antisocial behavior (e.g., Forgatch & DeGarmo, 1997) and aspects of effective parenting, such as warmth, monitoring, and problem-solving, with children's healthy adjustment (e.g., Dishion, Patterson, & Kavanagh, 1992). The PTC program used empirically supported techniques to change the theoretical mediators of appropriate discipline, monitoring, skill encouragement, problem-solving, and positive involvement.

The PTC investigators used a developmental model with multiple mediators, specifically the Oregon Delinquency Model (Dishion & Patterson, 2006), to understand their program's long-term effects. This model posits that increases in coercive discipline and decreases in effective parenting put children at risk not only for behavior problems but also for association with deviant peers. Such association can lead to subsequent behavior problems, such as engaging in antisocial behaviors with peers and teachers, which may put youth at risk for peer rejection or academic failure and drifting further into a deviant peer group, increasing their risk for deviancy training and other negative outcomes, such as arrest (Dishion, Spracklen, Andrews, & Patterson, 1996).

EMPIRICAL RESULTS OF MEDIATION

Mediational analyses have been conducted for only two of the programs discussed in this chapter, the NBP and PTC. Table 11.1 provides an overview of the mediation results and identifies strengths and weaknesses of the studies. As discussed below, the results of the mediational analyses for both programs provide support for the theories underlying these programs.

In the initial trial of the NBP, the program effect on mental health problems at post-test was mediated by program-induced improvements in mother-child relationship quality (Wolchik et al., 1993). In the second trial, program effects on internalizing problems at post-test were mediated by program-induced improvements in mother-child relationship quality, and program effects on externalizing problems at post-test and the 6-month follow-up were mediated by program-induced improvements in mother-child relationship quality and effective discipline (Tein, Sandler, MacKinnon, & Wolchik, 2004). However, the mediated effects occurred predominantly for families with poorer baseline functioning (i.e., poorer mother-child relationship quality, higher externalizing problems, or both), indicating mediation in the context of moderated program effects (see Muller, Judd, & Yzerbyt, 2005).

Table 11.1. Summary of Mediation Studies With Strengths and Weaknesses

Program/Study	Study Design	Analytic Approach	Strengths and Weaknesses
NBP Wolchik et al. (1993)	70 divorced mothers with children 8–15 years[a] NBP vs. wait-list control[b] Post-test (Mediator [M] and Outcome [O])[c]	Concurrent mediation	Strengths: Multiple reporters Weaknesses: No temporal precedence
NBP Tein et al. (2004)	240 divorced mothers with children 9–12 years NBP vs. Literature control Post-test (M/O) 6 month (O)	Concurrent and sequential mediation	Strengths: Multiple reporters, combined moderation and mediation models Weaknesses: Short-term temporal precedence
NBP Soper et al. (2010)	240 divorced mothers and children 15–19 years NBP vs. Literature control 6-year (M/O)	Concurrent mediation	Strengths: Multiple reporters, combined moderation and mediation models, long-term follow-up Weaknesses: No temporal precedence
NBP McClain et al. (2010)	240 divorced mothers and children 9–12 years -NBP vs. Literature control Post-test (M), 6 month (M), 9 month (M), 6-year (O)	Sequential mediation	Strengths: Temporal precedence, long-term follow-up, multiple reporters, cascading pathways

Study[a]	Sample and follow-up	Study conditions[b]	Assessment points[c]	Mediation	Strengths/Weaknesses
PTC Forgatch & DeGarmo (2002)	238 divorced mothers and sons 6–10 years	PTC vs. Control	12 month (M/O)	Concurrent mediation	*Strengths*: Multiple reporters *Weaknesses*: No temporal precedence
PTC Forgatch & DeGarmo (1999)	238 divorced mothers and sons 6–10 years	PTC vs. Control	12 month (M/O)	Concurrent mediation	*Strengths*: Multiple reporters, latent variables *Weaknesses*: No temporal precedence
PTC Martinez & Forgatch (2001)	238 divorced mothers and sons 6–10 years	PTC vs. Control	change from baseline to 30 months (M) 30 months (O)	Concurrent mediation (with parallel processing growth curve modeling)	*Strengths*: Examined trajectories in mediators and outcomes, multiple reporters, multiple methods *Weaknesses*: Weak temporal precedence
PTC DeGarmo & Forgatch (2005)	238 divorced mothers and sons 6–10 years	PTC vs. Control	12 months (M), 30 months (M), 3 years (O)	Sequential mediation	*Strengths*: Temporal precedence, long-term follow-up Multiple reporters, multiple methods
PTC Forgatch et al. (2009)	238 divorced mothers and sons 6–10 years	PTC vs. Control	12 months (M), 9 years (O)	Sequential mediation (with growth curve modeling)	*Strengths*: Temporal precedence, long-term follow-up, cascading pathways, latent variables, multiple reporters, multiple methods

NOTES: [a] Sample and follow-up, [b] Study conditions, [c] Assessment points of mediator and outcome.

Two studies examined whether the program-induced changes in parenting accounted for the NBP's long-term outcomes. Zhou, Sandler, Millsap, and Wolchik's (2008) analyses showed that program-induced improvement in effective discipline at post-test mediated the program effects on grades at the 6-year follow-up, regardless of risk status. Zhou et al.'s (2008) analyses also showed evidence of mediated moderation. For families with high baseline risk only, improvement in mother-child relationship quality at post-test mediated the 6-year follow-up program effects on symptoms of mental disorder, internalizing problems, and externalizing problems. Also, for those with high baseline risk, improvements in parental monitoring at the 6-year follow-up mediated program effects on alcohol and marijuana use, polydrug use, and other drug use at the 6-year follow-up (Soper, Wolchik, Tein, & Sandler, 2010).

McClain et al. (2010) further linked the short- and longer-term program effects using a sequential mediational model, which posited that program-induced change in parenting would lead to reduced mental health problems in childhood, and that these changes in mental health problems would lead to improved outcomes in adolescence. The analyses revealed a dynamic process of how the program effects in childhood affected outcomes in adolescence and identified different pathways across outcomes. Program-induced improvements in discipline at post-test led to reductions in externalizing problems later in childhood, and program-induced improvements in mother-child relationship quality at post-test led to reductions in internalizing problems later in childhood. As shown in Figure 11.2, reductions in externalizing problems in childhood led to fewer symptoms of mental disorder, less alcohol use, and higher grades in adolescence; reductions in internalizing problems led to fewer symptoms of mental disorder and increased self-esteem in adolescence. The effects of the NBP on internalizing problems and externalizing problems were maintained from childhood to adolescence.

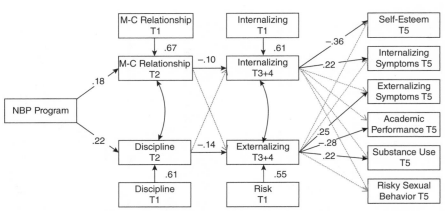

Figure 11.2. Cascading pathway model of the effects of the NBP on adolescent outcomes.
Reproduced from: McClain, D.B., Wolchik, S.A., Winslow, E., Tein, J.-Y., Sandler, I.N., & Millsap, R.E. (2010). Developmental cascade effects of the New Beginnings Program on adolescent adaptation outcomes. *Development and Psychopathology, 22(4),* 771–784, Figure 1, with kind permission from Cambridge University Press.

The results of these analyses are consistent with the NBP's theoretical framework. As hypothesized, program effects on mental health problems at post-test and the 6-month follow-up were mediated by program-induced improvement in two of the risk and protective factors targeted for change: mother-child relationship quality and effective discipline. The analyses also supported a cascading pathway model in which program effects on these putative mediators led to subsequent improvements in mental health problems in childhood, which then affected functioning in multiple domains in adolescence.

Forgatch and her colleagues have conducted mediational analyses of PTC. Program effects on aggression at the 12-month follow-up were mediated by program effects on concurrent measures of effective parenting (i.e., positive parenting and effective discipline) and non-compliance (Forgatch & DeGarmo, 2002). Program effects on teacher-reported externalizing, pro-social behavior, and adaptive functioning at 12 months were mediated by improvements in parenting, assessed concurrently (Forgatch & DeGarmo, 1999). Program effects on non-compliance at 30 months were mediated by change in coercive discipline and positive parenting over the 30 months since baseline (Martinez & Forgatch, 2001). Both mediators showed unique effects, although positive parenting showed stronger effects. The 3-year follow-up effects on teacher-reported delinquency were mediated by changes in effective parenting practices from baseline to 12 months and deviant peer association from baseline to 30 months (DeGarmo & Forgatch, 2005). At the 9-year follow-up, program effects on delinquency and arrests were mediated by change in effective parenting from baseline to 12-month follow-up and reductions in deviant peer associations from 1 to 8 years after the program (Forgatch et al., 2009).

These mediational findings are consistent with the PTC's theoretical framework of coercion theory, which posits that positive and negative parenting affect children's adjustment. The results support independent effects of coercive discipline and positive parenting. Analyses also support a cascading pathway model, showing that program effects on parenting, deviant peer involvement, and delinquency emerged over time.

Summary

Although there are differences in the studies on the NBP and PTC (e.g., measures of parenting, outcomes assessed, time lags), in both programs of research, program-induced improvements in effective parenting mediated program-induced improvements on a wide range of outcomes at post-test and follow-ups. These findings demonstrate that improving post-divorce parenting is a productive approach to prevent a wide range of children's post-divorce problems. These findings also indicate that the program components that focus on effective parenting need to be preserved when these programs are disseminated.

CHALLENGES AND RECOMMENDATIONS FOR FUTURE MODERATION AND MEDIATION ANALYSES

Although consideration of moderators of program effects can provide valuable guidance when developing a program and evaluating its effects, moderators of program effects have been examined for only one program, the NBP. Attention to moderators of the effects of other programs is important to more fully understand the impact of these programs and the populations to which they should be delivered. For example, it is possible that the non-significant program effects that occurred in several evaluations of child-focused programs were due to low levels of mental health problems in the majority of the youth at program entry.

As noted in earlier chapters, consideration of mediators allows the evaluation to move beyond the "black box" question of whether or not the program worked to mechanistic issues that have critical theoretical and practical implications. Mediational analyses have been conducted for only two programs for divorced families, the NBP and PTC. It is important to note that the majority of the studies examining the mediating process of these two programs tested for concurrent mediation (see Table 11.1). The concurrent assessment of mediators and outcomes and their relations is a useful first step for researchers seeking to understand plausible mechanisms of intervention effects. However, to clarify the temporal sequencing of causal processes and rule out bidirectional pathways, it is necessary that the outcomes are assessed at a later time point than the mediators (Kraemer, Stice, Kazdin, Offord, Kupfer, 2001). In the more recent studies examining the long-term effects of the NBP and PTC and the processes that may explain them (e.g., Forgatch et al., 2009; McClain et al., 2010), stronger tests of mediation have been conducted that included both temporal precedence as well as sequential mediation. Such studies not only have shed light on the mechanisms that explain program effects on children's outcomes but also have elucidated cascading pathways that capture the complexity of the process of change over time.

An important direction for future research involves conducting mediational analyses on the effective child-focused, non-residential father-focused and couple-focused programs. The identification of the program components that account for program benefits has important implications for implementing programs in a way that leads to positive outcomes. Also, the results of mediational analyses can be used to revise a program to include only those components that are responsible for program effects, thus reducing the costs of implementation.

Implications for Clinical Practice

This review has several implications for clinicians working with divorced families. There are several relatively brief, empirically supported programs that clinicians could use in their work with divorced families. Programs that worked directly with children and those that involved mothers as change agents have been evaluated by more than one research group and have been shown to have positive short-term effects. Although the long-term effects of child-focused programs have not been assessed, the effects of the programs for mothers have been shown to last up to 15 years after participation. Research on dual-component programs has *not* shown that more components are better. Neither adding a child program to an effective parent program nor adding a parent program to an effective child program augmented benefits. Promising short-term effects have been found for programs for non-residential fathers and divorced couples. However, researchers have not conducted repeated trials or assessed the long-term effects of these programs. The manualized nature of the most well-evaluated programs, the CODIP, CSG, NBP, and PTC, should promote high fidelity of implementation and increase the likelihood of positive program effects in real-world settings.

Findings of moderation and mediation analyses also have implications for clinicians working with divorced families. Findings on moderators could be used to modify a program's format and content to increase benefits for subgroups that did not benefit from the standard program. For example, booster sessions might be used to enhance the maintenance of program effects for mothers who enter the NBP with high psychological distress (Hipke et al., 2002).

The action theory of the programs for which mediation analyses have been conducted, the NBP and PTC, can help translate mediational findings into practice. As discussed in earlier chapters, action theory describes the components of a program that were designed to bring about the observed changes in outcomes. For example, the action theory of the NBP posits that changes in children's outcomes occur through improvements in parent-child relationship quality and effective discipline. The specific skills of Family Fun Time, One-on-One Time, Catch 'em Being Good, and Good Listening Skills are taught to improve parent-child relationship quality, and a step-by-step plan is used to increase effective discipline. When the program skills are well described in a manual and methods are available to teach clinicians to deliver the program effectively, the groundwork is established for using manualized programs in clinical and community settings. Because delivering the NBP and PTC with high quality and fidelity requires considerable clinical skill, intensive programs of training and supervision have been developed to enable clinicians to deliver these programs effectively. The importance of participating in such training is supported by a meta-analysis that found that higher levels of fidelity and quality of implementation of prevention programs were associated with larger effect sizes (Durlak & Dupre, 2008).

REFERENCES

Amato, P. R. (2000). The consequences of divorce for adults and children. *Journal of Marriage and Family, 62,* 1269–1287. doi: 10.1111/j.1741-3737.2000.01269.x

Amato, P. R. (2001). Children of divorce in the 1990s: An update of the Amato and Keith (1991) meta-analysis. *Journal of Family Psychology, 15,* 355–370. doi: 10.103 7%2F0893-3200.15.3.355

Amato, P. R., & Keith, B. (1991). Parental divorce and the well-being of children: A meta-analysis. *Psychological Bulletin, 110,* 26–46. doi: 10.10370033-2909.110.1.26

Biblarz, T. J., & Gottainer, G. (2000). Family structure and children's success: A comparison of widowed and divorced single-mother families. *Journal of Marriage and Family, 62,* 533–548. doi: 10.1111%2Fj.1741-3737.2000.00533.x

Bornstein, M. T., Bornstein, P. H., & Walters, H. A. (1988). Children of divorce: Empirical evaluation of a group-treatment program. *Journal of Clinical Child Psychology, 17,* 248–254. doi: 10.1207/s15374424jccp1703_9

Bradshaw, J. (Ed.). (2011). *The well-being of children in the UK.* Bristol: Policy Press.

Braver, S. L., Griffin, W. A., & Cookston, J. T. (2005). Prevention programs for divorced non-resident fathers. *Family Court Review, 43,* 81–96. doi: 10.1111/j.1744-1617.2005.00009.x

Brown, C. H., & Liao, J. (1999). Principles for designing randomized preventive trials in mental health: An emerging developmental epidemiology paradigm. *American Journal of Community Psychology, 27,* 673–710. doi: 10.1023/a:1022142021441

Caspi, A., Wright, B. R. E., & Moffitt, T. E. (1998). Early failure in the labor market: Childhood and adolescent predictors of unemployment in the transition to adulthood. *American Sociological Review, 63,* 424–451. doi: 10.23072657557

Cedar, B., & Levant, R. F. (1990). A meta-analysis of the effects of parent effectiveness training. *American Journal of Family Therapy, 18,* 373–384. doi: 10.108001926189008250986

Cicchetti, D., & Schneider-Rosen, K. (1986). An organizational approach to childhood depression. In M. Rutter, C. E. Izard, & P. B. Read (Eds.), *Depression in young people: Developmental and clinical perspectives* (pp. 71–134). New York: Guilford Press.

Crosbie-Burnett, M., & Newcomer, L. L. (1990). Group counseling children of divorce. *Journal of Divorce, 13,* 69–78. doi: 10.1300/J279v13n03_06

Cummings, E. M., Davies, P. T., & Campbell, S. B. (2000). New directions in the study of parenting and child development. *Developmental psychopathology and family process: Theory, research, and clinical implications* (pp. 200–250). New York: Guilford Press.

Dawson-McClure, S. R., Sandler, I. N., Wolchik, S. A., & Millsap, R. E. (2004). Risk as a moderator of the effects of prevention programs for children from divorced families: A six-year longitudinal study. *Journal of Abnormal Child Psychology, 32,* 175–190. doi: 0091-0627/04/0400-0175/0

DeGarmo, D. S., & Forgatch, M. S. (2005). Early development of delinquency within divorced families: Evaluating a randomized preventive intervention trial. *Developmental Science, 8,* 229–239. doi: 10.1111/j.1467-7687.2005.00412.x

DeGarmo, D. S., Patterson, G. R., & Forgatch, M. S. (2004). How do outcomes in a specified parent training intervention maintain or wane over time? *Prevention Science, 5,* 73–89. doi: 10.1023/B:PREV.0000023078.30191.e0

De Vaus, D. (2004). *Diversity and change in Australian families: Statistical profiles.* Melbourne: Australian Institute of Family Studies.

Dishion, T. J., & Patterson, G. R. (2006). The development and ecology of antisocial behavior. In D. Cicchetti & D. Cohen (Eds.), *Developmental psychopathology*, Vol. 3: *Risk, disorder, and adaptation* (pp. 503–541). New York: John Wiley & Sons.

Dishion, T. J., Patterson, G. R., & Kavanagh, K. A. (1992). An experimental test of the coercion model: Linking theory, measurement, and intervention. In J. M. R. E. Tremblay (Ed.), *Preventing antisocial behavior: Interventions from birth through adolescence* (pp. 253–282). New York: Guilford Press.

Dishion, T. J., Spracklen, K. M., Andrews, D. W., & Patterson, G. R. (1996). Deviancy training in male adolescent friendships. *Behavior Therapy, 27*, 373–390. doi: 10.1016/S0005-7894(96)80023-2

Dodge, K. A. (1993). The future of research on the treatment of conduct disorder. *Development and Psychopathology, 5*(1–2), 311–319. doi: 10.1017/S0954579400004405

Dumas, J. E. (1984). Child, adult-interactional, and socioeconomic setting events as predictors of parent training outcome. *Education & Treatment of Children, 7*, 351–363.

Durlak, J., & DuPre, E. (2008). Implementation matters: A review of research on the influence of implementation on program outcomes and the factors affecting implementation. *American Journal of Community Psychology, 41*, 327–350.

Fogas, B. S., Wolchik, S. A., Braver, S. L., Freedom, D. S., & Bay, R. C. (1992). Locus of control as a mediator of negative divorce-related events and adjustment problems in children. *American Journal of Orthopsychiatry, 62*, 589–598. doi: 10.1037h0079364

Forgatch, M. S., & DeGarmo, D. (2002). Extending and testing the social interaction learning model with divorce samples. In J. B. Reid, G. R. Patterson, & J. Snyder (Eds.), *Antisocial behavior in children and adolescents: A developmental analysis and model for intervention* (pp. 235–256). Washington, DC: American Psychological Association.

Forgatch, M. S., & DeGarmo, D. S. (1997). Adult problem solving: Contributor to parenting and child outcomes in divorced families. *Social Development, 6*, 237–253. doi: 10.1111/j.1467-9507.1997.tb00104.x

Forgatch, M. S., & DeGarmo, D. S. (1999). Parenting through change: An effective prevention program for single mothers. *Journal of Consulting & Clinical Psychology, 67*, 711–724. doi: 10.1037/0022-006X.67.5.711

Forgatch, M. S., Patterson, G. R., DeGarmo, D. S., & Beldavs, Z. G. (2009). Testing the Oregon delinquency model with 9-year follow-up of the Oregon Divorce Study. *Development and Psychopathology, 21*, 637–660. doi: 10.1017/S0954579409000340

Gwynn, C. A., & Brantley, H. T. (1987). Effects of a divorce group intervention for elementary school children. *Psychology in the Schools, 24*, 161–164. doi: 10.1002/1520-6807

Hetherington, E. M. (1999). Social capital and the development of youth from nondivorced, divorced and remarried families. In B. Laursen & W. A. Collins (Eds.), *Relationships as developmental contexts*, Vol. 30: *The Minnesota symposia on child psychology* (pp. 177–209). Mahwah, NJ: Lawrence Erlbaum.

Hett, G. G., & Rose, C. D. (1991). Counseling children of divorce: A divorce lifeline program. *Canadian Journal of Counseling, 25*(1), 38–49.

Hipke, K. N., Wolchik, S. A., Sandler, I. N., & Braver, S. L. (2002). Predictors of children's intervention-induced resilience in a parenting program for divorced mothers. *Family Relations, 51*, 121–129. doi: 10.1111/j.1741-3729.2002.00121.x

Jupp, J. J., & Purcell, I. P. (1992). A school-based group programme to uncover and change the problematic beliefs of children from divorced families. *School Psychology International*, *13*, 17–29. doi: 10.1177/0143034392131002

Keller, J., & McDade, K. (2000). Attitudes of low-income parents toward seeking help with parenting: Implications for practice. *Child Welfare*, *79*(3), 285–312.

Kelly, J. B. (2012). Risk and protective factors associated with child and adolescent adjustment following separation and divorce: Social science applications. In L. Drozd & K. Khuenle (Eds.), *Parenting plan evaluations: Applied research for the family court*. New York: Oxford University Press.

Kessler, R. C., McLaughlin, K. A., Green, J. G., Gruber, M. J., Sampson, N. A., Zaslavsky, A. M., . . . Williams, D. R. (2010). Childhood adversities and adult psychopathology in the WHO World Mental Health Surveys. *The British Journal of Psychiatry*, *197*, 378–385. doi: 10.1192/bjp.bp.110.080499

King, V., & Sobolewski, J. M. (2006). Nonresident fathers' contributions to adolescent well-being. *Journal of Marriage and Family*, *68*, 537–557. doi: 10.1111/j.1741-3737.2006.00274.x

Knapp, P. A., & Deluty, R. H. (1989). Relative effectiveness of two behavioral parent training programs. *Journal of Clinical Child Psychology*, *18*, 314–322. doi: 10.1207/s15374424jccp1804_4

Kraemer, H. C., Stice, E., Kazdin, A., Offord, D., & Kupfer, D. (2001). How do risk factors work together? Mediators, moderators, and independent, overlapping, and proxy risk factors. *The American Journal of Psychiatry*, *158*, 848–856. doi: 10.1176/appi.ajp.158.6.848

Lahey, B. B., Schwab-Stone, M., Goodman, S. H., Waldman, I. D., Canino, G., Rathouz, P. J., . . . Jensen, P. S. (2000). Age and gender differences in oppositional behavior and conduct problems: A cross-sectional household study of middle childhood and adolescence. *Journal of Abnormal Psychology*, *109*, 488–503. doi: 10.1037/0021-843x.109.3.488

Lundahl, B., Risser, H. J., & Lovejoy, M. C. (2006). A meta-analysis of parent training: Moderators and follow-up effects. *Clinical Psychology Review*, *26*, 86–104. doi: 10.1016/j.cpr.2005.07.004

Maier, E., & Lachman, M. (2000). Consequences of early parental loss and separation for health and well-being in midlife. *International Journal of Behavioral Development*, *24*, 183–189. doi: 10.1080/016502500383304

Martinez, C. R., Jr., & Forgatch, M. S. (2001). Preventing problems with boys' noncompliance: Effects of a parent training intervention for divorcing mothers. *Journal of Consulting and Clinical Psychology*, *69*, 416–428. doi: 10.1037/0022-006x.69.3.416

Mazur, E., Wolchik, S. A., & Sandler, I. N. (1992). Negative cognitive errors and positive illusions for negative divorce events: Predictors of children's psychological adjustment. *Journal of Abnormal Child Psychology*, *20*, 523–542. doi: 10.1007/BF00911238

Mazur, E., Wolchik, S. A., Virdin, L., Sandler, I. N., & West, S. G. (1999). Cognitive moderators of children's adjustment to stressful divorce events: The role of negative cognitive errors and positive illusions. *Child Development*, *70*, 231–245. doi: 10.1111/1467-8624.00017

McClain, D., Wolchik, S. A., Winslow, E. B., Tein, J.-Y., Sandler, I. N., & Millsap, R. E. (2010). Developmental cascade effects of the New Beginnings Program on adolescent adaptation outcomes. *Development and Psychopathology, 22,* 771–784. doi: 10.1017/S0954579410000453

McLanahan, S. (1999). Father absence and the welfare of children. In E. M. Hetherington (Ed.), *Coping with divorce, single parenting, and remarriage* (pp. 117–144). Mahwah, NJ: Lawrence Erlbaum Associates.

McMunn, A. M., Nazroo, J. Y., Marmot, M. G., Boreham, R., & Goodman, R. (2001). Children's emotional and behavioural well-being and the family environment: findings from the Health Survey for England. *Social Science & Medicine, 53,* 423–440. doi: 10.1016/S0277-9536(00)00346-4

Miller, G. E., & Prinz, R. J. (2003). Engagement of families in treatment for childhood conduct problems. *Behavior Therapy, 34,* 517–534. doi: http://dx.doi.org/10.1016/S0005-7894(03)80033-3

Morawska, A., Ramadewi, M. D., & Sanders, M. R. (2014). Using epidemiological survey data to examine factors influencing participation in parent-training programs. *Journal of Early Childhood Research.* 1476718X14536952. doi: 10.1177/1476718X14536952

Muller, D., Judd, C. M., & Yzerbyt, V. Y. (2005). When moderation is mediated and mediation is moderated. *Journal of Personality and Social Psychology, 89,* 852–863. doi: 10.1037/0022-3514.89.6.852

National Center for Health Statistics. (2008). *Marriage and divorce.* http://www.cdc.gov/nchs/fastats/divorce.htm.

Patterson, G. R., Reid, J. B., & Dishion, T. J. (1992). *Antisocial boys: A social interactional approach.* Eugene, OR: Castalia.

Paxton, R., Valois, R., & Drane, J. W. (2007). Is there a relationship between family structure and substance use among public middle school students? *Journal of Child and Family Studies, 16,* 593–605. doi: 10.1007/s10826-006-9109-y

Pedro-Carroll, J., & Alpert-Gillis, L. (1997). Preventive interventions for children of divorce: A developmental model for 5 and 6 year old children. *Journal of Primary Prevention, 18*(1), 5–23. doi: 10.1023/a:1024601421020

Pedro-Carroll, J. L., Alpert-Gillis, L. J., & Cowen, E. L. (1992). An evaluation of the efficacy of a preventive intervention for 4th–6th grade urban children of divorce. *Journal of Primary Prevention, 13,* 115–130. doi: 10.1007/bf01325070

Pedro-Carroll, J. L., & Cowen, E. L. (1985). The Children of Divorce Intervention Program: An investigation of the efficacy of a school-based prevention program. *Journal of Consulting and Clinical Psychology, 53,* 603–611. doi: 10.1037/0022-006x.53.5.603

Pedro-Carroll, J. L., Sutton, S. E., & Wyman, P. A. (1999). A two-year follow-up evaluation of a preventive intervention for young children of divorce. *School Psychology Review, 28,* 467–476.

Pruett, M. K., Insabella, G. M., & Gustafson, K. (2005). The Collaborative Divorce Project: A court-based intervention for separating parents with young children. *Family Court Review, 43*(1), 38–51. doi: 10.1111/j.1744-1617.2005.00006.x

Reyno, S. M., & McGrath, P. J. (2006). Predictors of parent training efficacy for child externalizing behavior problems: A meta-analytic review. *Journal of Child Psychology and Psychiatry, 47,* 99–111. doi: 10.1111/j.1469-7610.2005.01544.x

Roseby, V., & Deutsch, R. (1985). Children of separation and divorce: Effects of a social role-taking group intervention on fourth and fifth graders. *Journal of Clinical Child Psychology, 14,* 55–60. doi: 10.1207/s15374424jccp1401_9

Sandler, I. N. (2001). Quality and ecology of adversity as common mechanisms of risk and resilience. *American Journal of Community Psychology, 29*, 19–61. doi: 10.1023/A:1005237110505

Sandler, I. N., Tein, J.-Y., Mehta, P., Wolchik, S. A., & Ayers, T. S. (2000). Coping efficacy and psychological problems of children of divorce. *Child Development, 71*, 1099–1118. doi: 10.1111/1467-8624.00212

Sandler, I. N., Tein, J.-Y., & West, S. G. (1994). Coping, stress, and the psychological symptoms of children of divorce: A cross-sectional and longitudinal study. *Child Development, 65*, 1744–1763. doi: 10.2307/1131291

Sandler, I. N., Wolchik, S. A., Cruden, G., Mahrer, N., Soyeon, A., Brincks, A., & Brown, C. H. (2014). Overview of meta-analyses of the prevention of mental health, substance use and conduct problems. *Annual Review of Clinical Psychology 10*, 243–273.

Sandler, I. N., Wolchik, S. A., Winslow, E. B., Mahrer, N., Moran, J., & Weinstock, D. (2012). Quality of maternal and parternal parenting following separation and divorce. In K. Kuehnle & L. Drozd (Eds.), *Parenting plan evaluations: Applied research for the family court* (pp. 85–122). New York: Oxford University Press.

Schwartz, J. E., Friedman, H. S., Tucker, J. S., Tomlinson-Keasey, C., Wingard, D. L., & Criqui, M. H. (1995). Sociodemographic and psychosocial factors in childhood as predictors of adult mortality. *American Journal of Public Health, 85*, 1237–1245. doi: 10.2105/ajph.85.9.1237

Sheets, V., Sandler, I. N., & West, S. G. (1996). Appraisals of negative events by preadolescent children of divorce. *Child Development, 67*, 2166–2182. doi: 10.2307/1131616

Soper, A. C., Wolchik, S. A., Tein, J. Y., & Sandler, I. N. (2010). Mediation of a preventive intervention's six-year effects program effects on health risk behaviors. *Psychology of Addictive Behaviors, 24*, 300–310. doi: 10.1037/a0019014

Stolberg, A. L., & Garrison, K. M. (1985). Evaluating a primary prevention program for children of divorce. *American Journal of Community Psychology, 13*, 111–124. doi: 10.1007/bf00905724

Stolberg, A. L., & Mahler, J. (1994). Enhancing treatment gains in a school-based intervention for children of divorce through skill training, parental involvement, and transfer procedures. *Journal of Consulting and Clinical Psychology, 62*, 147–156. doi: 10.1037/0022-006x.62.1.147

Tein, J.-Y., Sandler, I. N., MacKinnon, D. P., & Wolchik, S. A. (2004). How did it work? Who did it work for? Mediation and mediated moderation of a preventive intervention for children of divorce. *Journal of Consulting and Clinical Psychology, 72*, 617–624. doi: 10.1037/0022-006X.72.4.617

United Nations Statistic Division. (2012). *Table 25. Divorces and crude divorces rates by urban/rural residents: 2007–2011.* http://unstats.un.org/unsd/demographic/products/dyb/dyb2011/Table25.pdf.

Winslow, E. B., Bonds, D., Wolchik, S. A., Sandler, I. N., & Braver, S. L. (2009). Predictors of enrollment and retention in a preventive parenting intervention for divorced families. *Journal of Primary Prevention, 30*, 151–172. doi: 10.1007/s10935-009-0170-3

Wolchik, S. A., Sandler, I., Weiss, L., & Winslow, E. B. (2007). New Beginnings: An empirically-based program to help divorced mothers promote resilience in their children. In J. M. Briesmeister & C. E. Schaefer (Eds.), *Handbook of parent training: Helping parents prevent and solve problem behaviors* (pp. 25–62). New York: John Wiley & Sons.

Wolchik, S. A., Tein, J.-Y., Sandler, I. N., & Doyle, K. W. (2002). Fear of abandonment as a mediator of the relations between divorce stressors and mother-child relationship quality and children's adjustment problems. *Journal of Abnormal Child Psychology, 30*, 401–418. doi: 10.1023/A:1015722109114

Wolchik, S. A., West, S. G., Sandler, I. N., Tein, J.-Y., Coatsworth, D., Lengua, L., . . . Griffin, W. A. (2000). An experimental evaluation of theory-based mother and mother-child programs for children of divorce. *Journal of Consulting and Clinical Psychology, 68*, 843–856. doi: 10.1037/0022-006X.68.5.843

Wolchik, S. A., West, S. G., Westover, S., Sandler, I. N., Martin, A., Lustig, J., . . . Fisher, J. (1993). The children of divorce parenting intervention: Outcome evaluation of an empirically based program. *American Journal of Community Psychology, 21*, 293–331. doi: 10.1007/BF00941505

Wolchik, S. A., Wilcox, K. L., Tein, J.-Y., & Sandler, I. N. (2000). Maternal acceptance and consistency of discipline as buffers of divorce stressors on children's psychological adjustment problems. *Journal of Abnormal Child Psychology, 28*, 87–102. doi: 10.1023/A:1005178203702

Wolfinger, N. H. (2000). Beyond the intergenerational transmission of divorce: Do people replicate the patterns of marital instability they grew up with? *Journal of Family Issues, 21*, 1061–1086. doi: 10.1177/019251300021008006

Zhou, Q., Chen, S., Cookston, J. T., & Wolchik, S. A. (2014). Evaluating the cultural fit of the New Beginnings parent program for divorced Asian American mothers: A pilot study. *Asian American Journal of Psychology. Asian American Journal of Psychology, 5*, 126–133.

Zhou, Q., Sandler, I. N., Millsap, R. E., Wolchik, S. A., & Dawson-McClure, S. R. (2008). Mother-child relationship quality and effective discipline as mediators of the 6-year effects of the New Beginnings Program for children from divorced families. *Journal of Consulting and Clinical Psychology, 76*, 579–594. doi: 10.1037/0022-006X.76.4.579

Page numbers ending with a *t* or *f* indicate tables or figures, respectively.